# Quality of Li
# Persons with Di...

## *International Perspectives and Issues*

# David Goode, editor

**Brookline Books**

**Library of Congress Cataloging-in-Publication Data**

Quality of Life for Persons with Disabilities: International Perspectives and Issues / David Goode, editor.
p. cm
Includes bibliographical references and index.
ISBN 0-914797-92-1
1. Mentally handicapped. 2. Quality of Life. 3. Mentally handicapped—Services for. I. Goode, David. 1948-
RC570.2.Q35   1994
362.3'8—dc20

94-12011
CIP

10  9  8  7  6  5  4  3  2  1

If you want to order this book call or send a letter to:
**BROOKLINE BOOKS**
P.O. Box 1046, Cambridge, MA, 02238 Tel (617) 868-0360 Fax (617) 868-1772

*To my family Diane and Peter*
*They taught me more than anyone about what quality of life means.*

# TABLE OF CONTENTS

**Foreword**
**Acknowledgments**
**Editor's Introduction**

## I. QUALITY OF LIFE ISSUES: INTERNATIONAL PERSPECTIVES

# PART II. QUALITY OF LIFE ISSUES: CONTEXTS, CONDITIONS, QUESTIONS, AGES

# Foreword

Since 1959 when I first began to do research in the field of mental retardation, there has been a sea change in how we talk about people with mental retardation and a true paradigm shift in how we think about them. In those days and for some years thereafter, professionals in the field spoke and wrote about "patients," "retarded people," and even "retardates," with a tone of distanced superiority. Whatever terms were used, most professionals thought of persons with mental retardation as people with a cognitive flaw, an all-encompassing intellectual deficit that could be expressed on a linear intelligence quotient scale. The concept of adaptive behavior would come later and even then was so difficult to operationalize that until quite recently, an IQ score remained the de facto index of a person's intelligence and their eligibility for services.

Over time, professionals in the field modified how they referred to people with mental retardation, (even changing the name of the American Association on Mental Deficiency to the American Association on Mental Retardation in 1988), in well-intentioned attempts to acknowledge the worth of these people as human beings and to lessen the discomfort that more pejorative terms might cause them and their families. As important as this humanization of the field is, the realization that intelligence is not a singular or global attribute nor one that is independent of environmental influences is even more significant. In addition to disabusing professionals of the misbegotten idea that a person can be reduced to a numerical score, it emphasizes the interaction between people's various intellectual skills and the many settings in which they live. This new environmental focus on mental retardation, endorsed by the American Association on Mental Retardation in 1992, concentrates not on a person's IQ, but the kinds of supports an individual needs to live a better life.

Three decades ago, there were professionals in the field who were passionately concerned with improving the quality of life that individuals with mental retardation were able to enjoy both within residential institutions and throughout varied community settings, but that concern was not central to the field. Today it is, and that is a mark of the growing maturity and compassion of our field. The intellectual challenges to our thinking posed by the new person-environment interaction and the longitudinal definition of mental retardation raise such profound difficulties for calibrating the levels and intensities of supports that may be optimal, that the entire enterprise, sound though it certainly is in principle, may prove to be unworkable. Be this as it may, the new definition, and the new paradigm it represents, focuses attention squarely on quality of life issues.

I believe that this focus is much to the credit of the field. It should prove to be to the benefit of service providers and their clients. However, attempts to reduce the complex concept of life's quality to specific measures, scales or formulae are hazardous at best, as more than one distinguished contributor to this volume points out with more than a little fervor. One can hope that formulaic reductions of life to simplistic indices will be resisted and that human service providers will continue their efforts to help persons with mental retardation choose among meaningful options on the basis of their own desires and values, not those imposed by agencies.

In this volume, readers will find a kaleidoscope of perspectives on quality of life by 35 authors representing 10 countries. The editor, David A. Goode, has been a leader in the field's drive to help persons with disabilities to have more meaningful lives, and he deserves the thanks of all of us for putting together this most valuable volume. The book addresses and challenges the concept of "quality of life," examines its utility in a variety of contexts and identifies the problems that lie ahead. It should be read, pondered, discussed and acted on by everyone concerned with this field.

*Robert B. Edgerton*
*UCLA, Los Angeles, California*

# Acknowledgments

This book reflects six years of activity around quality of life (QOL) research, which began in 1987 when I became the project coordinator for the Administration on Developmental Disabilities National Quality of Life Project. Since that time I have spoken to literally hundreds of people around the world about quality of life and its relationship to disabilities. I probably have learned something from each of those conversations, especially those with people with disabilities, that helped me to see the importance of this topic and, thus, this book. While I clearly can not acknowledge, or even remember, every one of these persons I do want to thank them all for the lively discussions that precursed this volume.

As described in the editor's introduction, the contributors to this book have been colleagues for several years. The particular chapters in this volume resulted from their exchanges around QOL issues. I want to particularly acknowledge the contributors' role in helping me conceptualize and put together such a broad and inclusive book on this topic.

There have been several individuals who played really decisive roles in the history of this book. One is the anthropologist Robert Edgerton, whose writings on the topic of QOL and discussions with me over the years concerning QOL issues for people with mental retardation were inspirational. Another is Herbert Grossman, a pediatric neurologist whose wisdom about children with mental retardation and their families was similarly inspiring. John Powers and Mariellen Kuehn were instrumental in forging my own views about QOL and how to interpret some of the literature. Ed Roberts, the president of the World Institute on Disability in California, taught me about QOL in the most intimate and profound ways, as have my conversations with Ethan Ellis, the Director of the New Jersey Developmental Disabilities Planning Council. Andy Bacon, Dan Crimmins and Linda Backus at the Westchester Institute of Human Development helped in the initial work that led to several projects described in this book.

I need also to acknowledge the profound influence of the late Burton Blatt who spent three afternoons with me and challenged me to take expertise and examine complex issues such as QOL. In a very real way his encouragement lives in these pages.

Finally I want to thank my friends with disabilities who taught me more about QOL than could ever be written about in book: Christina Robles, Breta Maxey, Bobby Thompson, Robert Smith and Adolph Ulenak. Each of you know what we learned together.

# Editor's Introduction

The idea for this book, that of presenting diverse international perspectives about quality of life (QOL) for people with disabilities, grew out of discussions among several of the contributors in this volume in 1989-90. We had met in 1988 at the International Association for the Scientific Study of Mental Deficiency (now International Association for Scientific Study of Intellectual Disability) in Dublin, Ireland, at which there were several plenary sessions on the topic of QOL. Many of the researchers attending these sessions were struck by how our work and findings about QOL were quite similar in many respects, but also with how they diverged from one another, perhaps we speculated, due to cultural differences, or differences in method.

We discussed the possibility of having an international conference on QOL for people with intellectual disability, but in the end this turned out to be too expensive and difficult to arrange. In 1991, as a way not to let our good intentions die, I proposed this edited volume, a kind of conference proceedings *sans* conference. People reacted well to the idea, and so here before you is the result of our efforts.

There are thirty-five contributors to this collection from ten different countries, making this by far the most extensive collection on the topic of QOL for persons with disabilities published to date. The volume has two parts. In Part I the reader will find ten chapters exploring how quality of life is used in services and research in Denmark, Canada, Australia, Finland, Germany, Hungary, and the United States. In this section of the book the authors were told to provide discussions about how QOL has been employed in their countries, and to have that discussion be as broad or narrow, as exploratory or focused, or as theoretical or concrete as they felt appropiate. Hence in Part I, we find descriptions of projects and their conceptual basis, along with illustrative case and ethnographic material in some cases. Each chapter in this section has its own distinct "sense," style of writing and organization. This has been preserved as much as possible during editing and is seen by the editor as a strength of this volume. In Part II, additional chapters focusing on the use of QOL in such areas as self-advocacy, aging, challenging behavior, severe/profound disability, early intervention, school life, staff training, research, and evaluation, are presented. In these chapters, the authors were asked to consider QOL thematically, and to provide illustrative and conceptual material. The authors in Part II were asked to contain their remarks to relatively few pages; the chapters in Part II are thus somewhat shorter discussions. At the end of Part II a critical essay arguing against the use of QOL in the disabilities field is included.

The purpose of collecting these twenty-one chapters, as interesting and remarkable as many of them are, is not to create the "bible" of QOL, or the authoritative text about QOL, or even the temporarily accepted book of wisdom about QOL. My own interpretation of the current state of affairs in QOL research, policy and program development is that it is much too early in the development of this concept to speak about definitive versions of QOL. As I see it, the development of this concept in the disability field should proceed slowly and carefully. We really *need* to say to ourselves at this time, that this is an exploratory, opening-up period when we should first speak freely and tentatively without worrying about or attempting to resolve differences in perspectives, methods and techniques. That is why and how this book was put together, to expand the debate in the QOL area, not to resolve it. And that is also why, in my own reading of these chapters, this volume is such a rich and varied collection of ideas and approaches. Thinking of the book in this way, as opening up QOL for people with disabilities by collecting in one place such an array of perspectives and kinds of work, it seems to me that it has accomplished its purpose well.

The reader will thus find that the heterogeneity of viewpoints represented in this book does not lend itself to summarization. In the chapters the most basic things, such as the conceptual basis of QOL, or how it should be studied, are points of contention. Diametrically opposed perspectives will be found on almost any proposition. This is not to say there are not trends and consistencies, but rather that, within these pages, there is diversity of opinion on most of these matters.

The one exception to this is with regard to the essentially subjective nature of how individuals experience and construct their own QOL. Leaving the last chapter by Wolfensberger aside, since it is entirely critical of the QOL concept, most contributors agree that QOL needs to be evaluated from the subjective standpoint of the individual. Most believe that the collection of data reflecting how the individual sees his or her QOL occupies an important and critical role in any research, evaluation, policy or programming using this concept. Given this basic agreement, there are then a variety of viewpoints represented about how objective or subjective QOL factors should be included in these activities. And, indeed, the relationship between objective and subjective QOL is one of the principal tensions in many of these chapters. This focus grew out of correspondence and paper exchanges among contributors, and, to some degree, this book reflects the preoccupations of those exchanges.

Finally, this book appears to partially realize the warnings or premonitions of many "inspirational thinkers" in this field with whom I have discussed my interest in QOL over the years. People like Burton Blatt, Sterling Gerrard, George Tarjan, Al Roehrer, Bob Edgerton, Dick Scheerenberger,

Martin Soder, Bengt Nirje and others who commented that QOL was both too complex and too subjective to ever be operationalized scientifically, and that in the end I would be dissatisfied with the concept. To them I say that this book both corroborates and disputes their contention. It lends credence to their proposal that QOL is very complex and highly subjective. But it also shows that QOL has proven to be a useful conceptual framework from within which to consider persons with disabilities and the supports and services we offer to them.

*David Goode, October 1993*

# •Part I•
# Quality of Life Issues:
# International Perspectives

# 1· Co-Write Your Own Life: Quality of Life as Discussed in the Danish Context

by Per Holm, Jesper Holst and Birger Perlt
Social Development Center (SUS)
Copenhagen, Denmark

Seen in historical perspective, the Danish understanding of what is meant by mental abnormality has undergone radical changes in recent decades. Developments that have taken place in Denmark demonstrate that terms such as mentally deficient, mentally subnormal and mentally retarded, etc., are not the expression of an objective or static state of affairs, but rather a temporally limited, social and cultural construction. Predominantly medical treatments have now been replaced by an empathic reaction to the actual situation using socio-cultural concepts (communication, network, fellowship, self-confidence, user democracy, and so on). A central theme in this presentation of research and innovation initiatives reflects these developments for this group of people, offering them a new lifestyle, new challenges and fresh opportunities.

## Innovations Under Way: The Example of Merchants House

The following example of an attempt to provide new living conditions and quality of life for people with mental retardation clearly shows the new approach, in the form of decentralization, removal from institutions, and the placing of the user in the center:

"Købmandsgården" ("Merchant's House") is a commune, in which living quarters, work and instruction form a unified whole in the social and educational services offered to young people with mental retardation. The aim is to create conditions in which people with mental retardation can lead satisfying and meaningful lives in active interaction with other people and the special opportunities offered in the local area.

An old merchant's house in a village was chosen as the base, a process of development was set in motion, and in the course of a short period of time the following initiatives were realized:

- accomodation for people with mental retardation living in the local area;
- job opportunities in the local area; and
- various leisure time activities — both within a subculture reflecting the abilities and limitations of people with

mental retardation, and participation in the socio-cultural community life of the local area.

These developments recognized that contacts with the local community required a more outgoing approach if Merchant's House were not to become a limited, self-sufficient environment, closed in on itself like the usual institutional enclave. It therefore became important to define and initiate a number of activities which could offer people with mental retardation a clearer and more realistic picture of themselves, and at the same time offer opportunities to the other inhabitants of the local area.

To this end, the disused Mission House in the village was bought and fitted out as a music and theatre workshop. In the first place, it was intended to be a meeting and activity center for all persons with mental retardation in the area, a place where they could come together, establish social contacts and build up a subculture on their own terms. At the same time, other people in the area who might be interested could use the facilities of the workshop. In other words, a community center was established along untraditional lines.

In addition, a job team was established to offer employment opportunities to all those in the local area with a marginalized social position — rehabilitees, persons with mental retardation, people on public welfare, and so on. This job team, under the leadership of a professional local craftsman, sells a wide range of services to the local community (gardening, painting fences, building outhouses, structural alterations, and so on). In addition, an ecological greenhouse and garden project has been

started to serve the needs of the community and to sell locally. An arrangement has been made whereby the community will deliver goods for the local co-operative store. Plans are afoot for taking over the local hotel with local residents, who are actively involved as shareholders.

In this way persons with mental retardation become visible and important links in a variety of local networks, and meet local people who are not marginalized or professional workers.

Finally, the evening school activities of Merchant's House links the cultural and productive aspects. The classes are held within the normal framework of remedial teaching, but the teachers are local experts (artists, musicians, craftsmen) who are not "hampered" by an education in social education. The classes are open to all the residents of the area, and in this way the evening school becomes a place where participants can talk about, reflect on and discuss together the varied opportunities and choices of everyday life.

## Innovative Developments in Recent Years

### Current Historical Context

During the 1980's, most of the old central institutions were replaced by decentralized forms of accomodation located in ordinary residential areas in the form of individual accomodation, small communities and mini-institutions with 8-15 residents. In the space of 5 years, more than 20% of all persons with mental retardation were moved into small communities with 4-6 people, aided by personnel provided by local authorities or support centers.

These new forms of accomodation have

called for the development of cultural and recreational activities in the local communities. In spite of the considerable difficulties connected with the integration of people with mental retardation in local communities, much creativity is evident. All over the country, meeting places, coffee shops, cafés, and cultural and activity centers have opened. Independent cultures have developed within which people with mental retardation demonstrate they can manage on their own, without the well-meaning care and intervention of professional workers who "know better."

People with mental retardation thus seem on the point of "taking-off" culturally, in cooperation and dialogue with supportive agencies. New traditions have come to stay: music, theatre festivals, and sports arrangements. Circus tricks, dance and aerobics are among the new activities forming part of a process of innovation which has seen the blossoming of persons with mental retardation who were previously passive and apathetic in the cozy arms of the caring services. The First World Cultural Congress for People with Mental Retardation became a reality in 1987, and is now held annually as a strong statement of the dreams, visions, wishes, demands and creativity of these people.

Efforts to integrate children with disabilities into existing day-care institutions and schools have been given a high priority. There is widespread interest in the use of alternative forms of communication and in the applications of new technology to aid people with disabilities. There is increasing acceptance of the need to help those with communicative disabilities, not only through better training in the use of total communication — in the form of pictograms, Bliss-language, spelling boards, body language, mime, etc. — but even more by focusing on better coordination of the types of communication offered persons with mental retardation by various agencies. Many projects have been started to improve the communicative competence of users and personnel alike because of a better understanding that mental disabilities are partially conditioned by blockages in communication.

There has been criticism of the monotonous and trivial routine work often offered in protected occupational settings. This is being replaced or supplemented with new activities in the form of music, rhythmic movement, drama, theatre, sport, art and other creative processes that play down a product-oriented approach and question the use of paid employment as the measure of identity and self-respect. These innovations create real and coherent forms of cooperation, and stimulate persons with mental retardation to form their own activities and to seek new challenges. As an example, a number of people with mental retardation, with the aid of supporting personnel, have taken over a youth hostel that was threatened with closure. All those involved participate according to their ability in the many work processes involved and have an importance as members of a common project. After two years of work, the group can now boast they are running a hotel and conference center of high repute at a profit.

Both professionally trained support personnel and case workers employed by local authorities who work on behalf of, and with people with mental retardation have shown great interest in becoming better qualified to tackle the new forms of cooperation and dialogue demanded by the user-centered approach. New cooperative working patterns involving different sectors of society also contribute to the creation of greater coherence and unity in the types of service offered to people with mental retardation.

This process of innovation has its roots in changes in administrative practice within the public management of firms, institutions and contacts with citizens. Whereas management by the book within an hierarchic administrative structure was formerly the ideal pattern of public administration, the new style is increasingly based on dialogue, negotiation and the use of research and innovation strategies. Within the last decade, considerable financial resources have been used on research and innovation activities within the social services at the local and regional levels. Such activities can be defined here as a coordinated, goal-oriented and temporally limited series of efforts aimed at finding new ways of carrying out social work, or of improving the framework within which it takes place.

## The Innovation Project: A New Way of Looking at Old Practices

Another factor of importance for the improvement of the quality of life for persons with mental retardation is the Danish tradition relating to the training of *social pedagogue* as support personnel.[1] The course of professional training lasts for 3½ years at the tertiary level and qualifies personnel to use educational, psychological and sociological theories and methods in their work. The last few decades have seen the development of a special way of work-

ing within the training and job situation of the social pedagogue, which has created the relevant methodological basis for research and innovation work, not least in relation to the quality of life of people with mental retardation. It is called project work.

What is special about the planning and implementation of change within the social sector can be expressed in the term *innovation project*, in which research and the process of change have a reciprocal influence on each other. The researcher collects data concerning the processes of change which have been implemented, incorporates them into a broader theoretical framework and participates actively in the evaluation procedures — with the aim of adjusting, developing and consolidating the measures taken at regular intervals.

Change is therefore initiated, or new approaches tried out, not primarily on the basis of written reports or research, but within the framework of the innovation project, which involves all the various groups (persons with mental retardation, social pedagogues, social workers and researchers) in the process of change. This approach seeks to change specified aspects of everyday practice. Participants in an innovation project share to a greater or lesser extent experiences based on the reality of a common life experience. This reality can be perceived in a variety of ways, but the first characteristic of project work is that it is based on the experiences of all the participants. To allow people with mental retardation themselves to join in the debate and share their life experiences with others, innovation projects must therefore provide the necessary support in the form of facilitated communication and the building-up of a sense of security and self-confidence. If we can help our mentally retarded fellow citizens formulate the way they see their situation, we can also help to make it possible that their demands, wishes, dreams and visions can be built into the kind of support services we offer them.

The second important aspect of the project work approach is that the carrying out and evaluation of the process of change should ideally be managed by the participants themselves. Many innovation projects therefore stress such key concepts as free choice, free action and self-determination as ways of understanding the kind of support that will offer persons with mental retardation greater opportunities to master their own lives. An innovation project has therefore to be adjusted regularly, as one set of participants becomes increasingly more able to influence the content and direction of the process of change.

The third and last aspect which especially characterizes the project work approach is the limitation imposed in terms of time and method. An innovation project is problem-oriented in terms of method. This demands a critical attitude to the common reality and the social structures which are to be changed. The core of this problem approach is a combination of critical reflection on aspects of the reality of everyday life, and a wish to change this reality. A well-constructed innovation project must therefore both draw out and incorporate the way people with mental retardation see those aspects of reality which cause all those involved to ask the questions: why do we do what we do, what could we change, and how?

This last question presumes the innovation project is limited in time. If the experiences gained and the desired change are to be properly evaluated, then it is necessary to terminate the project and evaluate both the "product" and the process. Has there in fact been a change for the better? What were the good and bad sides of the process?

Participation in an innovation project demands therefore that everything be seen in what could be called a *relational perspective*, which means:

- that the participants create together a special space-time continuum outside the routine of the daily round;
- that the participants work together in a face-to-face atmosphere of solidarity, marked by equality of worth and a stress on the "we" aspect;
- that social relationships are characterized by a flexible, *ad hoc* structure, allowing for problems and conflicts to be tackled as they arise.

Such an innovation project, based on experience, democratic participation and a problem focused approach, can only be realized within the context of a dialogue between people with mental retardation and support personnel, a dialogue in which at least two sets of people participate with equal weight and worth, with the common desire to change something in the everyday life they share, and which involves changes in the self-knowledge and opportunities for action of all concerned. On the part of people with mental retardation, what we are talking about here is the development of a new consciousness of the self and an improved self-image, because the subject's own view of the world and her desire for change is taken seriously for once. By taking part in the project on an equal footing with the others, the subject develops qualities such as readiness to act, awareness of choice, and an increased sense of mastery — because wishes and visions can be realized in practice (or, if they cannot, one is at least aware of the reason why). On the part of the social pedagogue, participation in an innovation project is in itself a further professional qualification. Experience with the methods used in an innovation project help the social pedagogue to develop a set of tools for analysis and intervention.

Carrying out an innovation project can thus be the key to understand oneself and one's situation in a new way — that is, as an individual who controls his own life within the framework of a dynamic fellowship.

## Normalization

The general developments we have outlined here have also been accompanied by increasing resistance to institutionalized forms of life.

Until the middle of this century, the framework around the daily lives, indeed the whole existence of persons with mental retardation, was symbolized by the walls of the large institutions. Daily life within these walls was based on routine and fixed time schedules not in reference to the needs of persons with mental retardation, but for administrative and institutional logic based on surveillance, control, regularity peace and quiet. In these large institutions the dominant view of people with mental retardation was static. A care and nursing approach dominated the treatment of these patients. It was not a question of personal development or growth, but of treatment, and the protection of both people with mental retardation and of society.

During the 1950's, centralized institu-tions and institutionalized life in general were exposed to increasing criticism, which paved the way for new approaches to the conditions of life and opportunities for people with mental retardation in society. The concept of normalization was intro-duced, turning on a double theoretical axis.

The first axis can best be described with reference to Wolf Wolfensberger's view of normalization, which involves as far as possible the use of means which are cultur-ally typical, in order to create and/or main-tain personal behaviour and characteristics roughly typical of the cultural matrix of the time.

It must be said that this view of normal-ization was at the time both progressive and revolutionary, involving a shift from a care and nursing paradigm towards a develop-mental and learning approach. This change, which did not come about without serious conflicts in the institutions involved, led to the result that doctors and nursing staff were replaced by the social pedagogue "socialpædagog." There arose again a belief that persons with mental retardation were people who could experience development throughout their lives. The emphasis was now laid on programs designed on educa-tional principles, on training and on strat-egies for action. In other words, this devel-opmental approach aimed to make people with mental retardation as "normal" and self-sufficient as possible.

The other axis can be described in terms of the view of normalization put forward by Niels Erik Bank-Mikkelsen, which is not aimed at the normalization of the individ-ual with mental retardation, but rather at the normalization of the social conditions of such people, to ensure that they have the same social rights and opportunities as everyone else. People with mental retardation should be able to lead lives as close to normal as possible. Thus, where Wolfensberger wants to normalize the individual, Mikkelsen wants to normalize social conditions. This latter approach involves a revolt against the long tradition of placing persons with mental retardation in institutions. The aim is normalization, a return to the "ordinary" in the daily lives and opportunities of people with mental retardation. The means are the integration of these people in ordinary residential environments within an ordinary community.

## Training and Moving Out

It is very clear that both these views of normalization have had a considerable influence on the political, educational and administrative measures taken in recent years in relation to persons with mental retardation. Normalization of the conditions of life of people with mental retardation has, in the efforts made at the practical level, been closely linked to the training of these people in self-reliance. In some places, the normalization process has most resembled a process of educational qualification. The first step is to work with plans for educational intervention and training programs within the context of the central institution. Next comes a period in a "moving out" department, where training continues with an eye to the final move out. Not uncommonly, training continues in the newly-established decentralized accomodation.

In practice we have seen a process of development in which, on the one hand, ideas of what constitutes a normal life, including both negative and positive sides,

has set the norm for the arrangement of the external framework for the lives of people with mental retardation. On the other hand, the educational efforts in community accomodation, day centers, schools and kindergartens have been aimed at helping people with mental retardation to function in as ordinary and normal a way as possible. This means that social pedagogues, teachers and other personnel have been able to hold on to the role of the professional expert, who knows what persons with mental retardation need, and upon what it is important to spend time.

As a result of the experience gained through efforts at integration, there has been increasing criticism in the last few years of the accepted normalization theories and of the educational and administrative measures based on them.

A structured life in an institution, which runs to a fixed schedule without opportunities for choices based on one's own wishes and needs regarding the arrangement of everyday life, cannot promote communication and self-mastery. There is a tendency for institutional habits to move out of the centralized institutions along with the residents. Normalization is not just a question of establishing new and smaller living arrangements in those places where normal life is lived. It must also, and perhaps even more, be a question of de-institutionalizing the structure and content of daily life, allowing persons with mental retardation, through the communication of personal wishes, to form their own lives themselves. It is hardly surprising that people who for years have been used to living in close contact with teachers or social pedagogues who always knew the right thing to do, will have difficulty in running their own lives and in making personal choices. Recognition of this fact has led to a greater readiness to listen to suggestions or comments made by individuals with mental handicap. This should lead to a cooperative interplay in everyday life, in which initiatives coming from persons with mental handicap are accorded the same importance as the various plans for educational activities or training programs which have been laid down in advance. The organization of an educational or training environment for children, young people and adults with retardation must leave room for activities and social interplay that arise from the wishes and choices of these users.

The move from centralized institutions to a life on one's own apparently creates other problems. A large number of those who have previously lived in institutions feel lonely and isolated in smaller, local community accomodation. This has raised the question of whether it is right to integrate people with mental retardation formally into local communities without providing them with meeting or activity centers. Such places can take the form of cafés, meeting rooms, or cultural arrangements where persons with mental handicap can be together on their own terms and develop patterns of mutual interaction where they feel that they are both necessary and important to each other.

## The Tyranny of The Normal

In the previous section we adopted a critical attitude to social educational initiatives and plans for action based on one of the normalization themes, namely, the attempt to make persons with mental retardation live as typically as possible in terms of the cultural norms of the time. A similar critical attitude can be applied to administrative measures justified by the idea that people with mental retardation should be able to live a life as close to the normal as possible. It has been our experience that it is precisely what we call "normal" or "ordinary" life that provides the guidelines for the organization of new types of accomodation and new conditions of life for people with mental retardation who are moved out of large institutions.

Yet, problems can arise when that which is statistically "normal" is used as the basis for providing a set of living conditions for a particular group in society. There is a real danger of falling into the naturalistic fallacy. One concludes from a more or less clear idea of what normal life *is*, to what normal life *ought to be* for a particular section of the population. What is normal becomes what is right.

It can be maintained with a certain justification that the life of the average Dane is to a large extent confused, stressful, alienated and isolated. Is this life so "right" that people with mental retardation should have a life based on it?

This question became relevant when the move away from the large institutions began. Planners and social service workers developed and organized life in the new homes largely along the following lines:

- Ordinary people prefer to live in residential estates on the outskirts of towns; persons with mental retardation should also live in such areas. Houses are bought on this basis.
- Ordinary people furnish their homes in various accepted ways with three-piece suites, televisions, bookcases and

easy chairs; the same domestic environment should, therefore, be offered people with mental retardation.

- Ordinary people go to work; persons with mental retardation spend most of the day in special workshops, doing what looks like normal work, but at an abnormally low rate of pay.

This use of normality, or what is generally acceptable, as the norm for the planning of homes and living conditions for the retarded can in practice become a sort of tyranny of the normal, ignoring the wishes, needs and choices of people with mental retardation themselves. Today, therefore, we need a discussion not so much about what is normal, but about quality of life, the good life — a debate about *what* the good life is, *what* determines the quality of life, and about *what* conditions are necessary to enable people to follow their own convictions and shape their own lives.

We need, in other words, to supplement the progressive demands for equality contained in the Danish legislation with other considerations that will break with the tyranny of the normal. Quality of life is more than just living as well (or badly) as everyone else. It is in this context that we have chosen the concept "quality of life" as a motto for the styles of research and action required by the situation in which persons with mental retardation now find themselves.

The communication aspect, *the relationship to others* that is such an important part of the daily lives of persons with mental retardation, seems to be a central factor if one wishes, as we do, to find a new theme to characterize the quality of life of people with mental retardation instead of the nor-malization tendencies of previous decades.

## Quality of Life: The Perspective of Human Relationships

### Previous Attempts to Define Quality of Life

Previous attempts to define the quality of life can, according to Madis Kajandi[2], be reduced to two tendencies:

- *Empirical studies* - where researchers ask either experts or a selection of the population what they understand by this term.
- *Hypothetical studies* - where researchers define the term "objectively", based on psychological or philosophical considerations.

We will here pursue the hypothetical tradition, in the main because research into the quality of human life needs a stipulated objective reference, a critical dimension.

To put it simply, we believe that people's experience of the quality of their own lives depends on their life history and level of awareness in everyday life, their perception of themselves, their expectations and level of aspirations. If one has not developed an objective frame of reference, it is difficult to take a critical attitude to such statements as: "I am happy, because a person like me does not deserve any better", or: "I have a good life because I get three square meals a day and the staff are very kind."

## The Danish Approach to Quality of Life

In previous publications we have developed a theoretical framework, which is not a description of "the good life" as such, but an attempt to outline certain central conditions which could bring the good life to fruition, as a basis for working with the quality of life of persons with mental retardation.[3] In the following we will briefly outline some of the ideas that guided this work.

The good life, or quality of life, is a legitimate goal of the social pedagogue, despite the fact that the concept has suffered from various attempts, of a more or less scientific nature, to define it in quantitative terms. It is almost impossible to imagine social pedagogues who do not justify their professional activity on the grounds that it is an attempt to create opportunities for a better life for those they are working with.

Yet what is a better life, and what are the conditions required for the good life? It is necessary to discuss this question, especially when the cultural values of an earlier age are being challenged. For a long time, the Protestant ethic defined the good life as a life filled with hard work. Today we are experiencing the dissolution of, and an emancipation from this work ethic, a situation which forces us to rethink the problem of the good life as a basic ethical question.

Naturally, the discussion of the concept of quality of life is not without difficulties. There is a risk in defining the quality of life because such a definition may easily lead to the manipulation by officialdom and the caring services of those sections of the population who do not live the "authorized type of good life." In the case of certain marginalized social groups or subcultures, such as people with mental retardation, the procedure becomes nothing less than dangerous, for what new, even mon-

strous and uncontrollable types of treatment might it not lead to? Were not the large centralized institutions of former years designed and built with the aim of improving the quality of life of people with mental retardation?

If despite all this we nevertheless embark along this dubious and dangerous path, it is because when all is said and done — and this is the main message of Siri Næss' argument[4] — all political and educational measures and forms of treatment are based on some vision of the good life and the conviction that it is possible to improve the quality of life. It is therefore important to bring the debate about quality of life, and the good life, into the public forum. It is important, despite the danger of manipulation, that we dare to offer suggestions about the basic conditions of the good life so that we do not act or intervene in the lives of others on the basis of undefined or merely implied ideas of what is good.

Quality of life is not something a person simply has or receives but something the individual actively works to create along with other people, as long as certain basic conditions are fulfilled. Living a "good life" means that one is able to determine the course of one's own life and has the opportunity to create an existence based on one's own dreams, visions, wishes and needs.

This definition has played a central role in the Danish debate about quality of life. The key to an understanding of the conditions and opportunities necessary for the realization of a good life is to be found in interpersonal relationships and in the interaction with other people in daily life. What we have previously attempted to define, therefore, was not "the good life" itself, but rather the conditions necessary for people to be able to create such a life for themselves. What we have stressed in this connection is the type and quality of the social relationships the individual creates and enters into.

According to our way of understanding it, the conditions for quality of life, or the good life, can be discussed in relation to three basic categories:

- *The social network*: one condition for quality of life is that the relationships in this network are marked by involvement, frequency, variation, balance and interaction over a period of time.
- *Mastery:* a second condition is that the individual has mastery of the social relationships he enters into, as this is an important factor in the mastery of one's own life.
- *The self:* the last condition for quality of life is that these relationships lead to a positive experience of the self, and of one's importance to others.

## The Development of Methods to Investigate Quality of Life

The basis of the Danish research model has, therefore, been focused *in theory* on the development of a hermeneutic model based on relationships, and in terms of *method* on the formulation of a new model for social pedagogical innovation. We have not only wanted to describe or measure interpersonal forms of being together or relationships, or the experiences of individuals relating to the quality of life, but have given a high priority to our participation in a process that can contribute to the change or the creation of better conditions for the good life — also for persons with mental retarda-

tion. For this reason we have down-played purely empirical studies in the form of questionnaires, interviews, etc, as well as attempts to formulate objective definitions for quality of life on the basis of psychological or philosophical considerations.

We have participated in the debate about the quality of life in recent years with two major aims in view:

1. to describe the most important preconditions required for social relationships if they are to offer the conditions and opportunities for the development of quality of life for people with mental retardation; and

2. to contribute to the development of methods which can improve the lives of people with mental retardation in terms of self-mastery, influence and democracy — to enable them to be real "co-authors" of their lives.

The development of suitable methods serves two aims which are hard to realise in connection with a traditional scientific approach. One aim is to reveal the way in which people with mental retardation experience themselves and their own world. The other aim is to open the way for providing support and opportunities for development without manipulation. The task of the social pedagogue is to understand what are the *specific* and what are the *universal* aspects of the person one is dealing with. The *specific* aspects are the product of the unique life history of the individual, whereas the *universal* aspects are related to being an individual, that is, a being that acts, reflects and communicates within the context of a specific historical community.

An example may serve to illustrate the double aim of this method of innovation:

A number of people with mental retardation went on a journey with a social pedagogue to visit and revive memories of all the places they have previously lived in. Seeing these places again and talking about their experiences proved to be a good way of opening them up for a better understanding of who they were, and for a development of consciousness which offered new opportunities for mastery and positive action relating to their own lives. In the first place, they (re)discovered their own lives to be far more coherent than they had realized. Secondly they were able to (re)discover the positive and negative contribution made by earlier experiences to their present world. By speaking about their impressions, experiences and remembered situations, in other words, by placing themselves and their own lives in a communicative context, they suddenly became more important in their own eyes. The importance was illuminated by the fact that their eyes were opened to certain connections between society's view of persons with mental retardation and their own view of themselves. This process of re-living and rediscovery within the context of a communicative fellowship leads to the experience and discovery of something new, in which reflection and analysis become important elements. It appears that reflection on one's own life-history in a "natural" setting, as opposed to the therapeutic milieu of an institution, opens the way to a dawning understanding of the reality created by society and of oneself as a social being.

This example also demonstrates some of the techniques which can be used to reveal the view persons with mental retardation have of themselves and the world around them, through observation and discussion, and analysis and discussion.

When choosing methods, it is important to be aware of the effect the choice of methods has on the results of an investigation. There is, for example, little point in sending out questionnaires to people with mental retardation for them to answer themselves. The number and depth of the answers will not provide reliable material and will only give a restricted description of everyday life. Therefore, it is important to be clear about what kind of data and information are to be collected, how it is to be done, what the material is to be used for, and how the conduct of the investigation itself will affect the participants.

Next, there are a number of special factors to be taken into account: does one wish to investigate subjective or objective dimensions of the quality of life? Are quantitative or qualitative methods to be used?

In the first instance, we have chosen to develop ideas and try out methods which will make it possible for persons with mental retardation themselves to describe their own daily lives and their subjective view of their quality of life.

We have mostly worked on ideas for the development of qualitative methods in innovation projects. We have, for example, used ethnographic methods, observation and visits in everyday situations in order to get closer to an objective presentation of the qualities to be found here. These, in turn, will provide the basis for an understanding and evaluation of the way people with mental retardation themselves experience their daily lives.

Finally, we have tried to find methods that can be used in relation to as many people with mental retardation as possible. In many cases, mental retardation is conditioned or amplified by communicative retardation. We have therefore tried to find some methods which can develop the communicative process and at the same time reveal the daily lives of people with mental retardation. This will provide a way to achieve a better insight into the way people with mental retardation experience their lives and the surroundings and situations in which they find themselves.

### Specific Applications of Methods

With this in mind we have worked on the outlines of various models. Our aim is partially to reveal the three aspects of the quality of life, and partially, to establish forms of dialogue between people with mental retardation and support personnel which can lead to increased awareness. We have tried out, and adjusted, a number of these methodological suggestions in connection with several innovation projects.

1. *The self-image of the person with mental retardation.* One method involves letting persons with mental retardation draw themselves in various situations — and then have them comment on the drawings. Self-portraits of this kind are often used in therapy. They can also be an artistic expression of the self-image of the individual.

   Other methods aimed at providing a "portrait" of the person with mental retardation can also be used — video recordings, for example, which the person can see and comment on. A set of photos showing the person from childhood onwards can be used in the same way.

2. *The way in which people with mental retardation experience relationship networks.* Such a network consists of people. One way to come in contact with the way that the person with mental retardation experiences these people is to use pictures of the people involved, and invite comments on them, or, in the case of language deficiency, other kinds of a reaction.

   A network is realized in actual situations, and a way to elicit a dynamic picture of the way the retarded person sees the network is to make a scrapbook showing situations from daily life which the person is then invited to comment on, or react to.

   Both these methods can be used in the case of people with mental retardation who are also physically disabled and relatively immobile: pictures or a scrapbook can of course be brought to them. On the other hand both these methods also involve a degree of selection on the part of the "researcher", in the sense that pictures of people or situations from everyday life have to be chosen. The criteria for deciding which people are important might not be the same for the physically and mentally disabled person as for a mobile, non-disabled person. Another problem can arise if the person with mental retardation does not possess even rudimentary language or is unable to communicate with the help of facilitated communication. How should any given reaction be interpreted? If there is no reaction, should this be put down to the wrong choice of pictures or events, or could the lack of reaction itself be interpreted as a reaction?

   An alternative method to reveal the way

the person with mental retardation sees the relational network is to let the person herself choose a series of pictures from daily life, which, if the person is able to use language, can be the basis for a dialogue about what she finds important in her life. If the person cannot use language, this method can at least reveal what things in daily life engage the interest of the person in question.

3. *Mastery of daily life by persons with mental handicap* . One method we have seen used with good results is to let people with mental retardation comment on video recordings of themselves and their contact with others in ordinary situations. A group of people with mental retardation living together in a little community are shown a video recording of scenes from their daliy lives. Their spontaneous comments on how they view themselves, and those they are living with tackle these familiar and typical situations are recorded as a soundtrack to the video.

Another method, which focuses on the making of choices, is to use a computer game through which the player creates a story. New technological developments can link computer and video together in an "interactive video" situation, in which the mentally retarded person can see himself as a participant in the story being shown on the screen.

The creation of a story through the making of choices can also take place as a collective process, in the form of situational plays in which the spectators, that is, people with mental retardation, offer their reactions and comments, giving the actors

"clues" and guidelines as to how they should develop the next step of the action.

Finally, there are many cases in which the unstructured interview, in the form of a conversation, can also be useful. This method can also be successful in the form of a group interview, in the course of which several mentally retarded persons who live together and know each other can supplement or correct each other's points of view. The group interview has the further advantage that the participants can support each other in terms of the way they formulate or explain themselves, and are less likely to be "'steamrollered" or "paced" by the interviewer.

# Influence and Communication - Two Model Projects

In the following section we offer a more detailed description of two projects that, on the basis of a relational understanding of the quality of life, have tried out methods to improve the amount of influence persons with mental handicap have on their own lives and their opportunities for meaningful contact and communication with the world around them.

## *The 'influence on your own daily life' project*

> *Ole takes a look round the room to see that the coast is clear, goes up behind the leader of the workshop, takes something out of his pocket, looks around again and whispers: "Write down that I want a new case worker and a new home counselor."*

This scene took place at a workshop for eight people with mental retardation and their eight home counselors. When Ole discovered that the home counselor was not annoyed — as he had feared — but instead was willing and ready to listen, he was able to make his position and wishes more precise:

> "The case worker should organize my affairs better, and the home counselor should pay better attention to what I'm saying."

This workshop was one of four sub-projects integrated in a larger project entitled *"The quality of life of persons with mental retardation."* The aim was to develop and try out methods of creating, together with persons with mental retardation, conditions for an improved quality of life and to reveal problem areas which could be the starting point for a process of change.

The idea behind the first workshop was to try out the possibilities offered by a special workshop method, the so-called *future workshop*, and at the same time to gain an insight into the way persons with mental handicap experienced and understood their chances of having an influence on their own lives. A further aim was to cast light on the way social pedagogues viewed the way persons with mental retardation mastered their own daily lives.

The second sub-project involved the use of observation and interviews as methods to reveal possible areas of choice and the use and misuse of time in the daily environment offered people with mental retardation. The material yielded by observation was used to reveal possible areas of choice in this environment, with the aim of making a critical assessment of the extent to which people with mental retardation were

allowed to manage their own lives. In the first place, it was shown how much influence people with mental retardation actually had on where they were at different times of the day, whom they were with, and what they were doing.

Sub-project 3 used photos to reveal the daily lives of individuals and the order of priority of activities. Two methods were used here. A collection of pictures *arranged in advance*, from which the person with mental retardation could choose pictures to talk about "dreams, hopes and utopias", and material *produced by the users themselves*, who were equipped with a Polaroid camera and asked to photograph their own subjects. All these pictures were used to create a scrapbook for each participant, and were also the basis of the ensuing conversation in which the pictures were selected and placed in order of priority. This conversation was video-taped.

Sub-project 4 used video to create biographical portraits of the daily lives of individuals which were later used in self-confrontation sessions. A set of sequences were recorded from the daily lives of persons with mental retardation. These formed the basis of a conversation in the course of which the comments of the participants were also recorded on video. In the first place, this commentary took place in a *free, spontaneous form*, without any leading questions, and then as a *guided* commentary, in answer to questions put by the "investigator."

## The Future Workshop

A variety of workshop methods have come into use in Denmark within the last decade or so, and have been used by educational institutions, decision makers, professional groups and personnel at various institutions to identify and reveal central problem areas.

The *future workshop* is an approach used to release creative capacities in people and helps them to have influence on their own future. By allowing people who share a common situation in daily life to present their wishes and visions of the way they want to live, this method offers them the chance to decide for themselves and run their own lives. The method has a fixed procedure with several stages. It aims to promote an interchange of ideas and show that what at first sight appears to be utopian can be put into practice. The first stage allows the participants to present their criticisms, frustrations and aggressions in relation to a particular topic or situation which has been chosen in advance. This criticism is summarized in a number of broader themes. One or two of these are used in the second stage, in which the imagination is given free rein — why can't we just do this or that instead? The suggestions that arise at this stage are likewise summarized as themes. In the third stage the participants formulate suggestions as to how some of these proposals can be realized in practice. In all three stages, the process is enhanced by writing all statements in a shortened form on posters hung on the wall for all to see, and by the attitude of the leader of the workshop, who makes sure that all negative comments passed on these written statements, or remarks to the effect that some particular suggestion is unworkable, or simply idiotic, are rapidly crushed.

This particular workshop method places persons with mental retardation in a new situation. To express criticism often con-flicts with existing norms, whether the person has been brought up in an institution or at home.

As persons with mental handicap only have a limited capacity for abstract thinking, it is important to create down-to-earth situations and experiences, and to present in a very tangible way. It is important to involve the social pedagogues very directly, so as to engage their support in the realization of the wishes and suggestions put forward. At the moment of writing, two workshops of this kind have been held within the overall project. Eight adults with mental retardation took part in the first one, and again in the second one a month later, when they were joined by their eight home counselors.

The following examples show how the method provokes the expression of dreams and needs, and shows that they can be realized.

It was very important for some of the participants to discuss what it meant to them to be disabled — their own limits and opportunities —. It was decided to arrange an evening when this topic could be discussed. Some of the participants agreed to be responsible for the arrangement, and there was a lively discussion as to whether the social pedagogues should be invited or not.

On the second occasion, each participant was given a large sheet of paper on a table on which they could draw their wishes and utopian visions: dream house, dream sweetheart, dream employment. When the participants had finished a drawing it was hung on the wall as a contribution to the communal social imaginative process. For example, one woman drew her "dream Sunday": a walk to a little lake where the ducks were being fed. Another woman said that she would like to go along too, and they started to arrange a time and place.

Friendship was one of the subjects discussed: what friendship is, what it demands of us, and how to find a friend or a sweetheart. There were a lot of ideas, but the group concluded that a café for people with disabilities would be the best solution, and this of course meant that one would have to approach the politicians.

At one institution, the "dreadful" mornings, with which both staff and users were dissatisfied, were transformed into mornings when everyone got up earlier and began the day with music, a hug and a kiss and a delicious breakfast. In addition, the users were given the responsiblity of getting themselves up. Everyone was equipped with an alarm clock, which freed all concerned from the chore of a communal reveille.

The *future workshops* made visible problem areas of importance for the quality of life of the participants. Attention was focused on a meaningful life: the life of work, a life together with others, the joy of life and the dark side of life, the longing for friendship, love and intimacy, as well as the way people with mental retardation assessed their mastery of their own lives and conditions of life.

It is important that social pedagogues work together with persons with mental retardation to highlight limitations in the influence they have on their own lives, and to find ways of overcoming them. The future workshop can be one such way, but people with mental retardation need professional help. They cannot organize a future workshop themselves, they are dependent on others, and the weakest of them need help to communicate. But it can be

done! The question is how do we face the consequences when persons with mental retardation acquire new knowledge and insights and begin to make demands previously unheard of.

### Project Johannes: An Educational Innovation Project

Johannes is a 16-year-old boy who fell into a river near his home at the age of five. Despite the fact that he had been under the water for 20-30 minutes and his heart had stopped beating, the doctors managed to revive him after a week in a respirator. Johannes had been a normal boy before the accident but was now severely disabled. Spasticity and muscular contractions meant that he had no control over his own body; he spent his time in a wheelchair, and apparently had no way of communicating with the world around him.

Johannes now lives in an institution along with 6-8 other children with disabilities and the personnel who take care of them. He spent the first years of school at a special school, and he now attends an educational center for children with disabilities not far from where he lives.

In 1988, the staff of the institution and the teachers at the special school decided to start a systematic program of educational innovation. The aim was to improve the chidren's opportunities to master their own lives through communication, to create the conditions necessary for an improved quality of life. The project was granted financial support and one of the members of the Danish quality of life research group was attached to the group as a consultant.

The project group consisted of five young people with severe disabilities, the social pedagogue closest to them and their class tutor. Johannes was one of the five children, accompanied by the social pedagogue mainly responsible for him, and by his class tutor.

In brief, the innovation project developed in the following way. The first six months were used to create a common theoretical frame of reference, both in relation to the children, and to such concepts as quality of life, communication and interdisciplinary cooperation. After this, a development program was outlined for each of the children.

In the course of the following six months, five of the development programs were carried out. At the same time the whole project group continued to function as a forum for the collection of information and for the discussion of theoretical questions and supervisory activities in relation to the project. At the end of the project, a report was written collating the experience gained from the project as a whole.

The program of development designed for Johannes was entitled: *When they let you decide something for yourself!* The starting point was the fact that Johannes had no influence on his own life in any way, so much so that those around him had given up hope that he would ever be able to make choices on his own behalf, much less express his wishes and needs. He was unable to control any part of his body intentionally.

However, the social pedagogue and the teacher were reasonably sure that Johannes was able to follow with his eyes things he was interested in. Could this be used to give him even a little influence on his own life? Could a simple method of communication be devised that could be used by support personnel and which would enable Johannes

to respond by expressing agreement or disagreement? The aim, therefore, of the work of educational innovation of which Johannes was a part was to develop a simple means of communicating with him which would convince those around him that Johannes could and would make choices, and in this way have an influence on his own life.

A solution was gradually arrived at consisting of a simple communication tool in the form of a bar with a board at either end and one in the middle. The person who wanted to communicate with Johannes stood directly in front of him so that it was clear which board Johannes's gaze was fixed on. Pictures could be attached to the boards, also a + sign for *yes* and a - sign for *no*. After a short period of use, during which Johannes used the tool to indicate with his eyes what he wanted, it was clear to all that he was actually making choices. He enjoyed being able to make his opinion known, to say what he wanted to eat, whether he was finished on the toilet, whether he wanted to go out for a walk, and so on.

There was no doubt in anyone's mind that this educational innovation project improved Johannes' quality of life. This was not so much because he had learned something new — he had probably been trying to use his eyes to communicate with for a long time — but because the project had linked the roles of the researcher and the social pedagogue and had enabled them, through the use of practical measures, to gain new experience and a better understanding of what the lives of the five children were really like. Amongst other things, we learned that when attempting to create better conditions for people to guide their own lives via communication, the most important thing is not advanced communication technology, or that the children learn pictograms, bliss or other symbols. No, the most important thing is that the children are part of a communicative environment in which their attempts at communication are taken seriously, where there is time to communicate properly, and where choices and the making of choices are a part of everyday life. Johannes' class tutor put this very clearly when he told us that he had discovered that he could go for a walk with Johannes in two ways. Either he could do what had usually done, simply take Johannes out for a walk in the wheelchair. Fresh air is so good for you! Or, alternatively, he could make the walk communicative, by placing himself in front of Johannes with the communication boards at regular intervals and asking him which way he wanted to go: right? left? straight on? In this way, it was Johannes who took the class tutor for a walk.

We also learned that a change of perspective yields fruitful results from time to time. We are accustomed to thinking that it is the retarded child who has problems expressing his wishes and needs; in other words, the child constitutes the problem which has to be solved in terms of education or learning. Yet one could just as easily maintain that it is the child's communication partner, in this case the teacher or social pedagogue, who is unable to understand and interpret the communicative message which the child is in fact sending. The problem to be dealt with therefore is the teacher or the social pedagogue. As Johannes' class tutor put it, it was not Johannes who was stupid.

We learned that it pays to link research and educational practice together in the form of a systematic program of innovation with the aim of creating better conditions for the quality of life.

## Mental Retardation, Quality of Life and Social Pedagogical Practice

The development and testing of methods aimed at revealing or improving the opportunities for people with mental retardation to create quality in their lives in cooperation with other people has also led to a new attitude to mental retardation. It is important to note that in the course of innovation projects social pedagogues frequently begin to ask themselves what mental retardation really means. Or rather: what is there about a person that causes us to label him or her as mentally retarded? There are naturally many answers to this question and they can be classified at various levels. At the first level, answers relate to something tangible — strange appearance, clumsy or violent movements, badly developed language, the inability to read and write. Yet if we then point out that other groups in society share some of the same characteristics — the physically disabled, old people, immigrants, alchoholics, children — we are beginning to shift the answers to a deeper level.

At this level the answers would tend to say that while all the groups named above have some of the characteristics we have referred to, persons with mental retardation possess them all. Mental retardation is the impression made by all these characteristics put together. The whole impression made by these tangible characteristics put together is, however, qualitatively different from the mere sum of the various parts.

This level of answer is interesting because it reveals a unitary approach to describing or defining the concept of *mental retardation* in which the reaction of the perceiver is taken into account.

Mental retardation is thus a special phenomenon arising in the process of interaction between two people: between the expression of the sender, and the impression, the receiver. It is precisely this process of interaction, in which expression and impression blend into each other, that underlines the importance of formulating the framework of a professional ethic that combines elements of normal, close social relationships and the best elements of professional knowledge and practice.

If such a professional ethic is to affect educational practice, it is important to realize that we are not talking about a handbook offering the right attitudes or methods. No one correct solution can ever be found to an educational problem. Social educational practice is determined by the situation, in the sense that the interaction between the social pedagogue and the user can take many different forms and lead to a variety of different results. It is therefore necessary to enter the situation and meet the person with mental retardation on his or her own ground and to continue along this path, following the individuality of the person concerned.

This kind of open approach to situations also involves a meeting between different points of view — the way in which social pedagogues and people with mental retardation view their own individual lives. The application of a professional ethic in this meeting of different points of view requires that the social pedagogue moves:

- from a therapeutic perspective based on strategies of treatment generalized from one type of person or situation to all types of persons and situations to a perspective which turns on real interaction between two people;
- from a perspective focusing on the person with mental retardation's lack of mastery or social competence, to a perspective which places the resources of the user in the center, seeing these as rooted in his or her personal biography;
- from a client or handicap-oriented approach to an understanding of the way in which the relationship itself affects both groups of people involved.

## Notes

[1] Translation Note: The Danish term 'socialpaedagog' has no counterpart in American English but could be translated as "social educationalist". Nor do these persons have an American institutional counterpart. Social pedagogues are something like American 'direct care workers' except that they receive training in special schools and institutions devoted to their education. They are not college educated (and indeed this is seen by some as a critical problem in Denmark), but they are far better trained than their American 'direct care worker' counterparts and often dedicated to their jobs (The Editor).

[2] Madis kajandi: Livskvalitet - En litteraturstudie av livskvalitet som beteendevetenskapligt begrepp samt et förslag til definition. Uppsala 1985.

[3] Per Holm, et al.: Udviklingshæmmedes livskvalitet - livskvalitet for alle. I: Fra forsøg til udvikling. Socialpædagogiske tekster 5. Copenhagen 1989.

Per Holm, et.al.: Det mellemmenneskelige - en udfordring til den professionelle støtte. I: Handicappolitik. Socialpædagogiske Tekster 8. Copenhagen 1991.

[4] Siri Næss: Yrkeskvinde - husmor. Gifte kvinders livskvalitet. INAS report. Oslo 1986.

# 2· The Quality of Life of Adults with Developmental Disabilities in Finland

Leena Matikka, Research Director
The Finnish Association on Mental Retardation

The quality of life (QOL) of people with developmental disabilities has been an object of international research interest for some time. In Finland, the roots of such research can be pinpointed fairly easily, inasmuch as the resources available for it, in this nation of five million, are limited and centralized. In Finnish universities, research in the field takes place disjointedly. The Finnish Association on Mental Retardation maintains the nation's only behavioral science and sociological research unit in the field. The Association acts as a link between service providers and other interested parties. The organization's task is to strengthen methods of care for individuals with developmental disabilities by means of research, training, and the production of instructional materials.

## Why we started with QOL studies?

At the close of the 1980s, the association's research unit sought out new and promising points of departure for research. Until that time, studies had been oriented primarily toward questions of psychology and special education. Such behavioral assessment methods as the AAMD adaptive-behavior scale (Nihira, Foster, Shellhaas & Leland 1975) and the Portage method (Bluma, Shearer, Frohman & Hilliard 1976) had been translated and adapted for use in Finland. Serious consideration had been given to the introduction of Wolfensberger's PASSING method (1983), translations and preliminary investigations had been made. The fact that very few people speak or write Finnish clearly leads to delays, owing first to the slowness of international publication activity, and second, to the cumbersome process of translating foreign-language publications and introducing them into the Finnish system of care for people with developmental disabilities.

The upgrading of services for citizens with developmental disabilities had emphasized the development of rehabilitative and instructional methods. Since 1985, all persons with developmental disabilities in Finland, regardless of developmental level, are obliged to attend school. The development of instructional plans for persons with severe mental retardation had consumed almost all the available resources.

Simultaneously, occupational training and preparatory instruction had been developed. Educational researchers continue to keep themselves busy at the moment with the development of instruction for persons with severe mental retardation after the compulsory-schooling age. Such reforms have been substantial from the international perspective; not so much in terms of pure numbers of students, but rather in that the program affects all of the 28,000 persons with developmental disabilities living in Finland.

As a Nordic country, Finland is among those nations advancing normalization and integration as guiding principles for policy on people with developmental disabilities. Finland is also a welfare state (regardless of the shocks which the welfare state's foundations have absorbed in the current recession). We have retained our very comprehensive public sector, social security and health care systems as an inheritance from the 1970s and 1980s. Beginning at the age of 16, all persons with developmental disabilities receive disability benefits from the Social Insurance Institution. This guarantees them a basic subsistence. In addition, such services as work activity, daytime care, the provision of a residence, guidance services, foster-family care and institutional care are organized. These services are organized regionally: the country is divided into 15 so-called *special-care districts*, in which municipalities and federations of municipalities assume responsibility for services for people with developmental disabilities. As in other parts of the world, large institutions are being dismantled and alternative residential facilities — smaller, more home — like units — are being built. In the field of special services, integrated solutions are being sought in both legislation and practical applications. The revised legislation on state (i.e., national) subsidies, that came into force on January 1, 1993, may increase the proportion of services organized in home municipalities and decrease the number of centralized services, including institutional care, provided by federations of municipalities.

In recent decades, services for persons with developmental disabilities have evolved remarkably. The work has progressed briskly; more services are now available, and many new residential units have been established. In the midst of this good fortune, the time came to ask what all this has meant for citizens with developmental disabilities themselves. In afterthought (as we live through quite a changing era in the economic sense), we can say that everything seemed and felt good in everyone else's opinion, that we were in a position to give the service recipients a turn to speak.

Such an ideological change, in fact, represents a great leap. It has required a simultaneous shift in the climate of social values. The furrowed-browed rationalism of developmental-disability experts has yielded the floor to the feelings and experiential reactions of people with developmental disabilities themselves, to a respect for individuality. We have moved from the modern "experteeism" to the post-modern "equalitarianism."

## What Approach Did We Choose?

An interesting subject. QOL had entered the discussion at the 1988 IASSMD World Congress in Dublin, for example, when David Goode (1988b) and Trevor

Parmenter (1988), among others, presented their approaches. Parmenter presented a model tied primarily to psychological and social-psychological concepts. Goode approached the subject in terms of process, employing sociological concepts. The Finns took a greater interest in Goode's approach, since developmental-disability researchers in Finland wanted to move in a more sociological direction.

Prior Finnish research on well-being lent further support to the sociological approach. Under the direction of Erik Allardt (1976), a broad-based Nordic research project on well-being had been conducted, and interest in lifestyle research was evident in studies carried out by J. P. Roos (1987), Elina Haavio-Mannila (1980), and Matti Kortteinen (1982) on middle-class Finnish life. Qualitative methods of investigation had been introduced into sociological research via research on minority groups — gypsies and alcoholics. (See, for example, Grönfors 1977; Mäkelä, 1990). The time was ripe for research on the QOL of people with developmental disabilities. In ideological terms, we were ready to move on from normalization to QOL; in scientific terms, from well-being research to QOL research.

Thus did the marketing of QOL research in Finland begin. The idea had to be sold; otherwise it would not be funded. Pressures also arose from the desire to involve as many special-care districts as possible. The association attempted to conclude research agreements with service providers so that developments in the field would take place cooperatively. Group discussions with persons with developmental disabilities were initiated.

The partners in these agreements brought their own interests into the sphere of the research. The 15 special-care districts in the country expected results, something visible had to be accomplished quickly. The introduction of an entirely new qualitative research method proved too difficult under the circumstances. Those funding the research could not be assured that results could also be obtained with a qualitative approach, and no research plan emerged to delineate with any clarity what results were to be expected. Consequently, the researchers selected an interview-based study employing traditional methods. At the same time, the research perspective began to dominate more and more in the project's implementation, and the developmental work was postponed until the end of the project.

## Implementation of the Project

Carried out over the years 1989-1992, the project had the following objectives:

1. to depict the QOL of adults with developmental disabilities nationwide, in the country's various regions, and in the individual care units studied,

2. to clarify the contributory factors bearing on the QOL of persons with developmental disabilities,

3. to develop methods for studying the QOL of persons with severe or profound developmental disabilities,

4. to develop methods to help enhance the QOL of individuals with developmental disabilities.

By way of preliminary investigation, group discussions with persons with developmental disabilities were conducted in the spring of 1989.

In order to obtain funding from the special-care districts, a new research plan based on more traditional research methods had to be drafted. All the districts funded the project for the years 1990-1992. The study was the first of its breadth in Finland to be funded by the system for care of people with developmental disabilities.

Owing to the funding structure, individuals from all the special-care districts had to be included in the subject group. The researchers chose to utilize systematic cluster sampling, using a catalogue listing all the residences, sheltered workshops, institutions and other units within the care system. The sample encompassed 98 units and, from these, 822 adults with developmental disabilities (Autio 1992a). The sample was fairly representative of all adults with developmental disabilities who utilize services for people with developmental disabilities. Persons with profound mental retardation and those living in institutions were, however, somewhat underrepresented in the sample.

The researchers chose to use structured interviews as the primary method and an attempt was made to interview everyone included in the sample. With severely and profoundly retarded individuals the interviews did not, however, succeed due to communication difficulties. The interview was completed acceptably with 619 subjects. Some subjects refused to be interviewed or could not be reached.

As a second technique, the researchers chose to post questionnaires to immediate-care providers. All those subjects who could not be interviewed were included in this second group. Answers were received regarding 143 subjects. By this stage, though, a number of subjects had died or moved away.

The QOL of persons with severe and profound mental retardation was also studied using a case-study technique. Of those individuals who could not be interviewed, a group of ten were selected; their day-to-day lives were subsequently analyzed by using videotape observation. An attempt is now being made to prepare biographical studies of these subjects.

The development of methodology in QOL research has reached its present fruition in an era when the individual reigns triumphant. In recent years researchers have thus approached QOL almost exclusively from an individual-centered viewpoint, using each person's resources and subjective experiences as a basis for assessment. The association's project was no exception. Although its sample was developed on the basis of care units, the study included data indicating the QOL of the unit as a whole only with regard to the subject's form of residence. Beyond this, it is possible to conceive of the QOL of the unit only as a sum or average of information from people with developmental disabilities — persons who were living there (see especially, Goode, 1990).

A QOL development program based on the group discussions was planned and tested simultaneously with the research phase.

### Group Discussions

The objectives of the group discussions were (1) to test, in terms of process, i.e., a structured group-discussion method in the delineation of the QOL of persons with developmental disabilities; (2) to depict the QOL of people with developmental disabilities and to define the central factors constituting QOL; and (3) to give persons with developmental disabilities and those closely associated with them experience with group work (Öhman, 1991).

The discussion-group process was based on the model advanced by Goode (1988a). The content of each discussion was analyzed by adapting to the model concepts developed in Nordic research on well-being. Work, residential living and leisure time were the life domains considered. The following schematization of QOL, developed by Siri Naess (1979, 1987), was used in the reporting of results:

1. Activity
   • Commitment
   • Stability
   • Self-fulfillment
   • Freedom
2. Human relations
   • Friendship
   • Couple relationship
   • Parents
3. Self-esteem
   • Self-confidence
   • Self-acceptance
4. A basic mood of happiness
   • Esthetic experiences
   • Security
   • Joy

There were six groups, encompassing a total of 59 participants, of whom 33 were developmentally disabled. The groups assembled in their respective locales eight times. Each session lasted three hours.

Participants with developmental disabilities felt they did not have a right to productive work, and that they had not had adequate opportunities to develop their aptitudes in their working life. Most felt they had been treated fairly as workers, but that no one had been able to value their work contributions as the work of non-retarded persons is valued. In particular, those living in institutions felt their lives to be constricted and their autonomy limited. Although participants with developmental disabilities enjoyed functional relationships with many people, they hoped for more contact with those in their immediate environment. They regarded growing up and leaving their childhood homes as difficult, as sources of conflict. They considered freedom and personal autonomy to be the most important things in life. They also considered security and the possibility to widen one's life-sphere important in both working life and personal relationships (Öhman, 1991, 53-54).

The discussions of one group were also analyzed using the interaction categories developed by Bales (1951) as a framework. These take into account the persons sending and receiving a message as well as the location of the message in the realm of feelings or tasks. The results indicated that positive feelings had played a prominent role in the group's work. The group's members conversed on an egalitarian basis and the developmental disabilities did not adversely affect the understandability of what was said. Participants with developmental disabilities assumed the role of experts in depicting the QOL of persons with developmental disabilities, and in delineating the factors contributing to QOL (Henriksson, 1992).

On the basis of the group discussion results, it was not possible to determine either the boundaries or the center of the problems of QOL research. All life domains seemed important, as did all the themes that the discussions brought to the surface.

### The Interviews

A two-part interview form was developed. The first part consisted of questions on the interviewee's background. These 32 questions, answers for which were sought from relevant documents, encompassed such things as personal data; parents' schooling and occupations, number of siblings, mother tongue, diagnosis, motion, visual, hearing and speech handicaps, verbal expression, literacy; educational level, daytime activity, income, and form of residence. The 188 questions on QOL per se — the second part of the form — were grouped according to the following themes: residential living, working life, subsistence, leisure time, social relations, individual-psychology factors, awareness of disability, and information and access thereto. The intent was to go through the response alternatives conversationally. In the final section of this part, both interviewer and interviewee were asked for their reactions to the interview.

As a basis for drafting the questions, the researchers used prior Nordic research on well-being and QOL (Allardt, 1975; Allardt & Uusitalo 1977; Sauli et al; Fager, 1982; Hjärpe 1984; Kebbon, Nilsson, Sonnander & Hjärpe 1981; Kebbon, Nirje, Hjärpe, Sonnander & Nilsson-Embro 1982; Naess, 1987; Sonnander & Nilsson-Embro 1984), as well as U.S. research (Schalock, 1988; Schalock, Keith, Hoffman & Karan 1989). The thematic headings under which the individual questions were grouped were formulated by combining the QOL sectors proposed by Siri Naess (1987), mentioned earlier, with the grouping proposed by Erik Allardt (1975): having, loving, being. At this stage of the research the concept of QOL was separated from the concept of level of living, as proposed by Allardt (1975, 4):

The interviews were conducted in 1990 and 1991. The interviewers were generally workers in the developmental disability field who had been trained for the purpose. They did not interview subjects from their own units. The 619 interviewees ranged in age from 18 to 69, the average age being 36.9 years (standard deviation 10.9 years). Men made up 51% of the sample. Most of the subjects had either mild retardation (44%) or moderate retardation (39%). Most (92%) neither had been married nor had lived with a common-law domestic partner. Elev-

### Table 2-1. Concept of Quality of Life Proposed by Allardt (1976)

|  | Well-Being | Happiness |
|---|---|---|
| Having | Need-gratification based on material and non-personal resources | Subjective feeling and experiences of the material and external conditions of life |
| Quality of Life | Need-gratification based on relations with nature, society, and other people | Subjective feelings and experiences of relations with nature, society and other people |

en percent had mild motion disabilities, while 6% had severe motion disabilities. Twenty-four percent were illiterate. Forty percent were living in group residences, 30 % with their parents, 14% in their own homes or in service apartments, 7% in institutions and 5% under foster-family care (Autio 1992a).

Thus far, the analysis of the interview material has been reported in fifteen Finnish-language publications. These discuss leisure-time pursuits (Vesala 1992a, 1993), social relations (Öhman 1992), opportunities for sexuality (Autio 1992b), work in the life of persons with developmental disabilities (Autio 1993a), the autonomy of persons with developmental disabilities (Autio 1993b), the formulation of the forms used in the research (Matikka 1993a) and QOL in the country's various regions (Matikka 1993b, 1993c, 1993d, 1993e, 1993f, 1993g). The technical reports present all of the interview responses broken down by gender (Autio 1991, 1992a). QOL as regards residential living has been examined in the context of the material assembled from postal questionnaires answered by immediate-care providers (Vesala, Rehumäki & Saari 1993).

In addition, articles are at present being prepared on the effects of psychological factors on the QOL of people with developmental disabilities (Matikka 1992), awareness of disability among people with developmental disabilities (Matikka 1993h), how adults with developmental disabilities feel about health, stress and alcohol use (Autio 1993c), sources of income of persons with developmental disabilities (Öhman 1993b) and acquiescence in interviews with people with developmental disabilities (Matikka & Vesala 1993).

Interviewees with developmental disabilities were generally satisfied with their lives. The more positive their objective selves — that is, the more positive their assessment of how others perceived them — the happier they were. The greater their self-respect and sense of autonomy, and the more positive their self-image and objective selves, the more positive their assessment of life in general was. They felt more stress if they exhibited less self-respect, if they wanted more autonomy, if they felt that disability affects one's life, and if they were women. Surprisingly, 36% of the interviewees did not consider themselves developmentally disabled (Matikka 1992).

The unmarried men felt able to establish couple relationships more easily than the unmarried women did. The respondents with motion disabilities considered themselves more constricted than others did. Those living in group residences felt freer to establish couple relationships than did those living with their parents. Individuals who had severe retardation considered sexuality and love relationships more important than the more mildly retarded subjects did; however, the former were less likely to have close love relationships, and they also viewed themselves as more constrained in their formation of love relationships (Autio 1992b).

The interviewees had a great variety of leisure-time interests. The more independent subjects generally engaged in such pastimes alone or with friends, while the less independent were more likely to have companions especially for the purpose, generally staff persons or family members. The interests were predominantly such things that could be pursued alone in or around the home. The most common leisure-time pursuit was watching television. Most were satisfied with their pastimes and considered them important (Vesala 1992a).

Ninety-three percent of the interviewees were working. The great majority were employed in sheltered workshops or workshops within institutions. Those who felt they could exert some influence over their work were also more inclined to state that they enjoyed their work. About 50% considered themselves very good workers. Salary was mentioned as the most important aspect of work, even though a pension represented the primary source of income for almost every respondent and the pay for the work was only a small amount of pocket money. However, personal relations at the workplace were considered almost as important (Autio 1992a, 1993a).

Almost all of the subjects had friendships. In spite of large numbers of friends, however, loneliness and a longing for companionship were experienced. The great majority knew their neighbors and talked with them frequently. Relationships with parents and other relatives were considered important, inasmuch as more than half of those who met their parents did so often, and more than a third of those who met other relatives did so often (Öhman 1992).

When the researchers investigated autonomy and the right of choice in type of residence and day-to-day life, it became evident that such factors as speech impairments, female gender, lack of education and lack of independence in residential arrangement correlated with limited autonomy (Autio 1993b).

The subjects felt more stress than Finns do on the average. They used alcohol much less than the rest of the population. Use of alcohol showed a correlation to such fac-

tors as mild developmental disability, young age, urbanness of the place of residence, independent residential arrangement, and feelings of stress (Autio 1993c).

The main source of income was disability benefits, generally FIM 2000-3000 (USD 400-600) per month. In addition to these, those who were working were receiving the pocket money compensation mentioned earlier. The interviewees thought their monthly incomes to be smaller than they were according to the background information. Many did not know how to estimate their monthly incomes at all. Almost all nevertheless, stated that they had enough money (Öhman 1993b).

In order to clarify the connections between QOL and type of residence, the latter was classified, in the case of each interviewee, as supported living, assisted living, supervised living, living with parents or other relatives, or foster-family care. The distinction between supported, supervised and assisted living is in general use in Finland as a means of classifying residential services for people with developmental disabilities. *Supported living* describes persons living alone or in a group. The support person keeps in touch with such persons by telephone and visits them a few times a week at the most. *Supervised living* refers to group residences. The staff helps, guides and plans the residents' activity. The staff is present mornings and/or evenings, but not overnight. In the case of *assisted living*, the group residence has special capabilities for the care of residents who have severe retardation or multiple handicapping conditions. Staff persons are present around the clock.

Type of residence exerted a strong influence on feelings of independence and self-determination as did motion disabilities. Those who were living with their parents were more self-motivated than those in assisted-living residences, but markedly less self-motivated than those in supervised-living formats. Persons living with their parents nevertheless needed about as much assistance as did those in supervised-living residences. Those living with their parents had somewhat more restrictions and somewhat less autonomy than did those in supervised-living residences. People in supported-living residences were clearly more active than the others in performing domestic chores; on the other hand, they were less inclined to pursue social interests outside their homes. Almost all (93%) expressed satisfaction with their residential arrangement. Greater residential independence was correlated with greater general satisfaction. The results corresponded to numerous findings of prior studies (Cattermole et al. 1990), according to which self-determination and opportunities for influence are central factors bearing on the resident's sense of satisfaction (Vesala et al. 1993).

## Inquiries with Immediate Care Providers

An inquiry was planned to gather information on the 143 subjects who could not be interviewed. A questionnaire was sent to relatives and professional workers providing care for those concerned. The questions fell into the same life domains as the interview questions did. An attempt was made to make the questions as similar as possible, in content, to the questions on the interview form (Matikka 1993a). The questionnaire forms were mailed, in two parts, between December 1991 and May 1992.

Ninety-five percent of the questionnaires were answered and returned, (questions left unanswered were generally rare, averaging 5% per questionnaire). Difficulties were relatively more common with questions on the subjects' health, sense of satisfaction, and opportunities for sexuality and access to information. In these cases, questions were left unanswered on 15-54% of the questionnaires. Of those responding, 85% were professional care-providers in the field and 15% were family members (Qvist 1992).

Of the 143 subjects, 48% were men. Persons with severe retardation represented 44% of the group, profound retardation 26%, moderate retardation 14%, and mild retardation 5%. The average age was 35.6 years (standard deviation 11.1 years). Twenty-four percent had mild motion disabilities, 17% severe motion disabilities. Significantly impaired vision afflicted 8%, while 4% were blind. Significantly impaired hearing affected 2%, while 4% were deaf. Twenty-four percent had poor speech comprehension. Speech was unclear in terms of content in 41% of the subjects and unclear in terms of motor facility in 36%. Twenty-seven percent were incapable of speech. Eighty percent were illiterate while 48% had received no education. Twenty-seven percent had attended training schools or other special schools. At the time of the inquiry 36% were living in institutions while 40% had at some time lived in institutions but did no longer (Qvist 1992).

Those living with their parents or under foster-family care were as self-motivated as those living in assisted-living residences, but they had as much autonomy and as few personal restrictions as those living in supervised-living residences. The last-mentioned were the most active in performing domestic chores, pursuing leisure-time interests and visiting the bank, post office, supermarket and health care center (Vesala et al. 1993).

Eighty-three percent took part in daytime activity programs, i.e. sheltered work or other stimulating activity; less than half, however, did so every day. The care providers felt that the central importance of such programs consisted of social interaction and the opportunity for more diversified experiences (Vesala 1992b).

In view of communication difficulties, the maintenance of social relations engendered more problems for this subject group than for the other subjects. About one quarter were not mentioned as having any friends at all. Such things as drinking and eating, travel and outings, and listening to music were listed as producing the greatest pleasure. Displeasure was ascribed to reprimands, bossiness, the imposition of restrictions, homesickness, the longing for company and the lack of attention and interest shown towards people with developmental disabilities and their opinions. The respondents felt that the fostering of variety, stimulation, and activity, along with a reduction in group size and an increase in communication, would improve the subjects' QOL (Qvist 1992, Öhman 1993a).

## Case Studies

The objective of the case studies is to increase understanding of the QOL of persons with severe or profound developmental disabilities. The effort is concentrating on portraying the lives of ten persons on the basis of biographical information, video observation, and interviews with immediate-care providers.

As of this writing, the case studies are not complete. To date, observational material has been collected about the ten persons' lives by means of videotaping. Each person is filmed in his or her normal living environment, for an average of ten hours. The tapes record morning domestic chores, travel to the daytime-activity center, work there, the return home, and bedtime routines. The investigators strove to record the most normal possible daily situations in which the subject occupies the main role. The camera angle was widened as needed in order to take in all those interacting with the subject. The camera persons were six developmental-disability workers who were accustomed to using videos in their work. They received detailed instructions about the videotaping and were trained for the job in a collective training session. It was recommended that the camera persons work in pairs. A set of instructions and a more precise plan were drafted on the basis of preliminary tests.

Video observation involves many problems both in methods and ethics. We considered these, for example at a seminar organized in cooperation with a Danish QOL project. The seminar, which took place in Finland in March, 1992, reached the conclusion that videotaping may violate the depicted person's right to intimacy. For this reason, we felt special attention must be given to how the research results are published. It would be easy to develop the video material into an portrayal of how little satisfaction the needs of persons with severe and profound mental retardation receive, how monotonous their lives are. This must be avoided, since the persons depicted are not themselves able to express an opinion as to whether they want this sort of publicity. It would be more acceptable to create a sort of montage of those moments when the subjects appeared to be enjoying life. It would be tempting to abandon science for art, to begin developing the video material into a movie about the lives of people with severe and profound developmental disabilities.

The analysis of the videotaped material has commenced with an attempt to apply a procedure of the grounded-theory type (see Strauss 1987). The intent is to reduce the material about each person into a condensed picture of his or her mode or style of living. On the basis of these individual portraits, we will look for features common to the whole group. We will then evaluate what QOL means in the lives of these people, and what factors advance or hinder realization of that quality. To facilitate study and further analysis, the researchers will draft, on the basis of the videotapes, a text in which they will relate what they see and hear, adding in their own appraisals of the subject's motives and sentiments. The transformation of the videotapes into a text will facilitate handling with various computer programs. The researchers will, however, have to return to the original video and sound material whenever the need to maintain the proper focus arises.

At this point the approach seems very promising. It is, however, laborious and expensive. To enhance the credibility of the research it would be very helpful to have a number of people go through the material independently and draw their own conclusions. It will be also be important to discuss the events on the videos with those who have daily dealings with the subjects.

Video observation differs substantially from QOL research methods in general use. Although it may be seen as being centered very strongly on the individual, it remains objective in the sense that a consensus can be reached by multiple viewers about what is on the tape. It is also true that video data can be analyzed with a sociological, rather than psychological, perspective. For example, the client-driven, ecological QOL model advanced by Goode (1988a) utilizes the concept of individual behavior outcomes. QOL should be discernible in such behavior. According to Goode (1988a, 4), only a few researchers have attempted to apply measures of QOL as outcome behavior. In his opinion these measures are very much tied to values, and should therefore be developed cooperatively with clients and/or their families or intimates. They should also be subjected to broad general discussion. This video-observation research may further the development of such measures; its real intent, however, is not to quantify the information gathered, but rather to deepen understanding of the lives of persons with severe and profound mental retardation.

According to the interpretations advanced to date, the essential factors in the QOL of such persons will be found in their possibilities for interaction with their environment, the treatment they receive as people, and their opportunities to exert influence over their lives. Since these subjects were originally singled out because they could not be interviewed, the significance of communication is obviously central. The material offers a good opportunity for studying the ways in which the subjects express themselves and make their opinions known, but it also provides a window on the ways in which care professionals interact with these nonspeaking individuals.

It is imperative that the case study process continue from analysis to the next stage development. A project of this sort could also be implemented with the primary purpose being the improvement of the subject group's QOL and the utilization of the research, when needed, as a vehicle for development (cf. Holm, Holst, Knudsen, Balch Olsen & Perlt 1989).

## What Did We Accomplish?

Many enthusiastic individuals with developmental disabilities participated in the initial phase of group discussions. The discussions of QOL were important to them and they would have liked to keep them going. In 1990, the year following the group-discussion phase, the Finnish Association on Mental Retardation organized a study conference at which the groups' participants with developmental disabilities gathered to discuss their subsequent experiences. They felt that the discussion groups had given them new impetus to go forward with their lives, and many had in fact already found better jobs or residential arrangements.

In conjunction with a 1992 study conference, the association organized a QOL seminar for developmentally disabled participants. The seminar attracted over 100 participants. The results of the QOL research were presented, and discussion followed. Autonomy, access to information about various issues, participation in workplace meetings and, above all, the chance to have a love life were viewed as especially important. Many still recalled how important the interview situation had been to them. It was nice when the interviewers asked them about things which they considered important.

Discussion groups have been established in various parts of the country. In 1992, in a special-care district in the province of South Bothnia, an extensive QOL development program was implemented in which the discussion group leaders have now received training and working instructions. QOL developmental work founded on discussion groups is expanding, and more and more persons with developmental disabilities and their immediate-care providers are thus dealing with QOL questions, searching for original solutions designed for their own local needs.

For developmental disability workers, the project furnished an opportunity to explore questions of QOL in both theory and practice. In planning the interview phase the original intent was to have students perform the interviews. Workers in the field showed great enthusiasm for that assignment, however, and the plans changed. For these workers, the interviews were an eye-opening experience. Many recalled having been amazed by the certainty of the opinions which the interviewees held about crucial life issues.

In scientific terms, we strove to increase knowledge about the QOL of Finns with developmental disabilities. Because there really had been no prior research, we can be satisfied with the descriptive information that the research provided. It has also been possible to make comparisons with information gathered on the living conditions of the general Finnish population, and with the findings of prior research on the QOL of persons with developmental disabilities in other countries.

The analysis of the research material is not yet complete. It appears, however, that the interviews conducted with more mildly retarded persons will not bring anything new and earthshaking to light. Rather, these results will confirm those obtained in other countries. The intricate, problematical nature of the QOL concept will complicate the drawing of clear conclusions. To establish its reliability, the research method will require repeated confirmation. We will be obliged to limit both the research sample and the questions.

It will not be possible to make QOL operational in the same way for all persons with developmental disabilities. The life arenas of persons with mild mental retardation who hold jobs and live in supported-living or group residences are more numerous and multifaceted than those of people with severe retardation who have been institutionalized. Even if all people have the same basic logic that can be applied to thinking about their QOL, on the operational level, the same yardsticks, it seems, cannot be applied to both these groups. If an interviewer's questions move to too general a level, they cease to be unequivocally understandable. Concretization requires tieing a question in to the respondent's everyday life. If self-fulfillment for one group of persons means an opportunity for creative work — the pursuit of a trade, for example — while another group sees it as a chance to use finger paints to draw pictures on a piece of white cardboard, are we talking about realization of the same aspect of QOL? And if we are, can we also judge which group's QOL is better when evaluated in this fashion? If we examine autonomy and the control of one's own life from the reference point of these groups' opportunities, it appears that political influence, for example, is important to the more mildly retarded. For more severely retarded individuals, political influence is an absurdity, inasmuch as they have no awareness of what political opportunities are. For such persons, control of one's life can be exemplified by such things as whether one can dress as one chooses, go out when one wants, and so forth. While in both cases we are talking about autonomy, it seems senseless to try to construct any sort of scale of measurement which would lead from the simplest judgments to decisions far more complicated and esoteric.

It seems, rather, that *QOL is very much a question of the individual's resources and his or her relationship with the environment.* If we study people whose personal resources are similar (for example, persons with partial sight, developmental disabilities, and who are incapable of speech), but who live in different environments, we can sense QOL in how those environments allow such individuals to govern their lives and develop on their own terms. If they are able to nurture that self-government, to expand their ability to act in their environments, in their own arenas of activity, we can consider the quality of their lives good (cf. Holzkamp 1983, 1991). But, in the definition of QOL, we thereby shift the emphasis from the individual to the relationship between individual and environment and, increasingly, responsibility shifts to the community.

One basic objective of the project was to have an impact on the professional practices of the system of care for people with developmental disabilities and on Finland's national social policy. We wanted to bring more attention to citizens with developmental disabilities, to open the closed door a bit further and tell those who would listen how people with developmental disabilities live. As the project moved forward we organized numerous informational and training sessions at local levels.

The most visible follow-up measure may be a new project which will investigate the assessment of the productivity and quality of services for people with developmental disabilities. The recession and the simultaneous revision in the legislation on state subsidies have brought with them threatening scenarios, which, if realized, will mean entrusting the services that persons with developmental disabilities need to the service provider who puts in the lowest bid. QOL in itself will not suffice as a criterion of the quality of services: it will be imperative to produce services that are both superior in quality and competitively priced. In evaluating the investments which the health-care system needs, decision-makers in the social-welfare and health-care sectors have already accustomed themselves to the QOL yardsticks which health care economics have introduced (Sintonen & Pekurinen, 1989). By the same token, those providing the services will be forced to develop product descriptions and post prices.

For QOL researchers, the challenge will be to ensure high standards in the quality-assessment of services, *and to see to it that the user's perspective receives adequate respect in this many-sided process.* The interpretation of the opinions which individuals with developmental disabilities express will be the researcher's task — and a weighty one, since the straightforward acceptance of the user's perspective here is fraught with risks. For example, the finding that 93% of all persons with developmental disabilities are satisfied with their residential arrangements invites the conclusion that the arrangements do not need improvement. However, researchers familiar with the subject know that the more miserable the conditions under which people live, the more difficult it is for them to express their hopes, and the more difficult it is to describe what they might be hoping for if those conditions could be improved (Allardt 1976).

# References

Allardt, E. (1975). Dimensions of welfare in a comparative Scandinavian study. Research Group for Comparative Sociology. University of Helsinki. *Research Reports,* No. 9, 1975.

Allardt, E. (1976). *Hyvinvoinnin ulottuvuuksia.* (Dimensions of welfare) Porvoo: WSOY.

Allardt, E. & Uusitalo, H. (1977). Questionnaire and Code Book of the Comparative Scandinavian Welfare Survey in 1972. Research Group for Comparative Sociology. University of Helsinki. *Research Reports,* No. 14, 1977.

Autio, T. (1991). Kehitysvammaisten elämänlaatutietoa. Haastatteluvaiheen tuloksia taulukoina. (The Quality of life of mentally retarded. Interviewing results in tabular form). *Finnish Association on Mental Retardation Publications* 2/1991. Helsinki.

Autio, T. (1992a). The Quality of life of mentally retarded. Interviewing results in tabular form. Quality of life project of the mentally retarded people. *Finnish Association on Mental Retardation Publications* 11/1992. Helsinki.

Autio, T. (1992b). Mahdollisuus seksuaalisuuteen. Kehitysvammaisten näkemyksiä parisuhteesta ja seksuaalisuudesta. (Opportunities for sexuality). *Finnish Association on Mental Retardation Publications* 12/1992. Helsinki.

Autio, T. (1993a). Työ kehitysvammaisten elämässä. (Work in the life of mentally retarded). *Finnish Association on Mental Retardation Publications* 15/1993. Helsinki.

Autio, T. (1993b). Vaikutusmahdollisuudet ja elämänlaatu. Kehitysvammaisten kokemuksia itsemääräämisestä. (Sense of autonomy and quality of life). *Finnish Association on Mental Retardation Publications* 16/1993. Helsinki.

Autio, T. (1993c). Kehitysvammaisten aikuisten kokemuksia terveydestä, stressistä ja alkoholinkäytöstä. (Experiencies about health, stress and alcohol). Finnish Association on mental Retardation. (manuscript)

Bales, R.F. (1951). *Interaction Process Analysis: A Method for the Study of Small Groups.* Cambridge, MA. Addison-Wesley.

Bluma, S., Shearer, M., Frohman, A. & Hilliard, J. (1976). *Portage Guide to Early Education.* Portage, Wisconsin: Cooperative Educational Service Agency.

Cattermole, M., Jahoda, A. & Markova, I. (1990). Quality of life for people with learning difficulties moving to community homes. *Disability, Handicap & Society,* 5 (2), 137-151.

Fager, L. (1982). *"Man får ta lite ansvar" - alternativ till dagcenter.* (Allowance to take the responsibility - alternative of day care center). Projekt Mental Retardation, Psykologavdelningen, Forskningskliniken, Ulleråkers sjukhus, Uppsala.

Goode, D. (1988a). *Discussing Quality of Life: The Process and Findings of the Work Group on Quality of Life for Persons with Disabilities.* New York: Mental Retardation Institute.

Goode, D. (1988b) Quality of life for persons with developmental disabilities: an American perspective. 8th world congress of the International Association for the Scientific Study of Mental Deficiency, Dublin, Ireland.

Goode, D. (1990). Measuring Quality of Life, *AAMR News and Notes* (April). Washington D.C.

Grönfors, M. (1977). *Blood feuding among Finnish gypsies.* Helsinki University.

Haavio-Mannila, E. (1980). *Päivätanssit.* (Daydances).Prvoo: WSOY.

Henriksson, A. (1992). Kehitysvammaiset elämänlaatutyöryhmissä. (People with developmental disabilities in work groups on quality of life). *Finnish Association on Mental Retardation Publications* 11/1992. Helsinki.

Hjärpe, Jan (1984). *Normaliseringens kvalitet. Förutsättningar och utnyttjandegrad inom tre livsområden för utvecklingsstörda: boende, fritid och daglig verksamhet.* (Quality of normalization). Projekt Mental Retradation, Institutionen för psykiatri, Ulleråkers sjuhus, Uppsala.

Holm, P., Holst, J., Knudsen, P., Balch Olsen, S. & Perlt, B. (1989). Udviklingshaemmedes livskvalitet - livskvalitet for alle. (QOL of people with developmental disabilities - QOL for everyone). In Holm, P. and Perlt, B. (eds.) *Fra forsog til udvikling.* Socialpädagogiske tekster 5 (pp. 158-180).

Holzkamp, K. (1983). *Grundlegung der Psychologie.* (The principles of psychology). Frankfurt: Campus Verlag.

Holzkamp, K. (1991). Societal and individual life processes. In Tolman, C.W. and Maiers, W. (eds.) *Critical Psychology. Contributions to an Historical Science of the Subject* (pp 50-64). New York: Cambridge University Press.

Kebbon, L., Nilsson, A.C., Sonnander, K. & Hjärpe, J.(1981). *Normaliseringens kvalitet och gränser. Bakgrund, begreppsanalys och modell.* (Quality and limits of normalization). Projekt Mental Retardation. Uppsala.

Kebbon,L., Nirje, B., Hjärpe, J., Sonnander, K. and Nilsson-Embro, A.-C. (1982). *Six papers IASSMD congress Toronto 1982.* Mental Retardation Projekt, University of Uppsala, Sweden.

Kortteinen, M. (1982). *Lähiö - tutkimus elämäntapojen muutoksesta.* (Suburb - study of lifestyle changes). Helsinki.

Matikka, L.M. (1992). Effects of psychological factors on the quality of life of mentally retarded adults. Paper presented at I.A.S.S.M.D. Congress Brisbane Australia.

Matikka, L.M. (1993a). Elämänlaadun

kysymyksiä. Kehitysvammaisten elämänlaatu -projektin haastattelu- ja kyselylomakkeet.(Questions of QOL).*Mental Handicap Research Unit Reports* 8/1993. Helsinki: Finnish Association on Mental Retardation.

Matikka, L.M. (1993b). Elämänlaatutietoa Uudeltamaalta. (QOL data from Southern Finland.) *Mental Handicap Research Unit Reports* 9/1993. Helsinki: Finnish Association on Mental Retardation.

Matikka, L.M. (1993c). Elämänlaatutietoa Varsinais-Suomesta. (QOL data from South-West Finland region). *Mental Handicap Research Unit Reports* 10/1993. Helsinki: Finnish Association on Mental Retardation.

Matikka, L.M. (1993d). Elämänlaatutietoa Pirkanmaalta. (QOL data from Pirkanmaa region). *Mental Handicap Research Unit Reports* 11/1993. Helsinki: Finnish Association on Mental Retardation.

Matikka, L.M. (1993e). Elämänlaatutietoa Etelä- ja Keski-Pohjanmaalta. (QOL data from Southern and Central Ostrobothnia). *Mental Handicap Research Unit Reports* 12/1993. Helsinki: Finnish Association on Mental Retardation.

Matikka, L.M. (1993f). Elämänlaatutietoa Lapista. (QOL data from Lapland). *Mental Handicap Research Unit Reports* 13/1993. Helsinki: Finnish Association on Mental Retardation.

Matikka, L.M. (1993g). Elämänlaatutietoa Keski-Suomesta. (QOL data from Central Finland). *Mental Handicap Research Unit Reports* 14/1993. Helsinki: Finnish Association on Mental Retardation.

Matikka, L.M. (1993h). Am I mentally retarded? Finnish Association on Mental Retardation. (manuscript).

Mäkelä, K. (ed.) (1990) *Kvalitatiivisen aineiston analyysi ja tulkinta.* (Analysis and interpretation of qualitative data). Helsinki.

Naess, S. (1979). Livskvalitet. Om å ha det godt i byen og på landet. (QOL). *INAS-rapport* 79:2, Oslo.

Naess, S. (1987). *Quality of Life Research. Concepts, Methods, and Applications.* Institute of Applied Social Research, Oslo.

Nihira, K., Foster, R., Shelhaas, M. & Leland, H. (1975). *American Association on Mental Deficiency. Adaptive Behavior Scale 1975-Revision.* Washington, D.C.: AAMD.

Parmenter, T.R., Martin, M., Findlay, S. & Gray, C. (1988). A study of changes in the quality of life of people with severe intellectual and behavoural disabilities following a curriculum-based intervention program. 8th world congress of the International Association for the Scientific Study of Mental Deficiency, Dublin, Ireland.

Quist, A. (1992). Vaikeammin kehitysvammaisten elämänlaatutietoa. Lähihenkilökyselyn tuloksia taulukoina. (Quality of life of more severely mentally retarded). *Mental Handicap Research Unit Reports* 7/1992. Helsinki: Finnish Association on Mental Retardation.

Roos, J.P. (1987). *Suomalainen elämä. Tutkimus tavallisten suomalaisten elämäkerroista.* (Finnish life). Helsinki.

Schalock, R.L. (1988). Quality of Life Questionnaire Data Sheet (1988 Field Test Version).

Schalock, R.L., Keith, K.D., Hoffman, K. & Karan O.C. (1989). Quality of Life: Its maesurement and use. *Mental Retardation,* Vol 27, No. 1, 25-31.

Sintonen, H. & Pekurinen, M. (1989). 15D - askel kohti yleistä terveyteen liittyvän elämänlaadun mittaria. (A generic 15 dimensional measure of health-related quality of life - 15D). *Sosiaalilääketieteellinen Aikakauslehti,* 26, 85-96.

Sonnander, K.& Nilsson-Embro, A.C. (1984). *Utvecklingsstördas livskvalitet.* (QOL of people with developmental disabilities). Projekt Mental Retardation, Institutionen för psykiatri, Ulleråkers sjukhus, Uppsala.

Strauss, A.L. (1987). *Qualitative Analysis for Social Scientists.* New York: Cambridge University Press.

Vesala, H. (1992a). Kehitysvammaisten harrastaminen. (Leisure activities of mentally retarded adults). *Mental Handicap Research Unit Reports* 6/1992. Helsinki: Finnish Association on Mental Retardation.

Vesala, H. (1992b). Vaikeammin kehitysvammaisten päivätoiminta. Lähihenkilökyselyn tuloksia. (Daily activities of the more severely mentally retarded). *Finnish Association on Mental Retardation Publications* 14/1992. Helsinki.

Vesala, H. (1993). Kehitysvammaisten asuminen ja harrastukset Uudellamaalla. (Residential care and leisure activities of people with developmental disabilities living in Southern Finland). *Mental Handicap Research Unit Reports* 15/1993. Helsinki: Finnish Association on Mental Retardation.

Vesala, H., Rehumäki, M. & Saari, T. (1993). Kehitysvammaisten asuminen ja elämänlaatu. (Residential living and QOL of people with developmental disabilities). *Finnish Association on Mental Retardation Publications* 18/1993.

Wolfensberger, W. (1983). *PASSING - Program Analysis of Service Systems' Implementation of Normalization Goals.* Toronto, ON: National Institute on Mental Retardation.

Öhman, A. (1991). Elämänlaatua etsimässä. Ryhmäkeskustelumenetelmän kokeilu. (Searching for the quality of life. An assessment of a group discussion method). *Mental Handicap Research Unit Publications* 57/1991. Helsinki: Finnish Association on Mental Retardation.

Öhman, A. (1992). Ystävät, naapurit ja sukulaiset. Suhteita ja mahdollisuuksia. (Friends, neighbors and relatives). *Finnish Association on Mental Retardation Publications* 13/1992. Helsinki.

Öhman, A. (1993a). Vaikeammin vammaisten sosiaaliset suhteet. (Social relations of people with severe disabilities). *Finnish Association on Mental Retardation Publications* 13/1993. Helsinki.

Öhman, A. (1993b). Kehitysvammaisten taloudellinen toimeentulo. (Sources of income of persons with developmental disabilities).Finnish Association on Mental Retardation. (manuscript).

# 3. A Quality of Life Model: New Challenges Arising from a Six Year Study

Roy I. Brown, Patricia M. Brown, & Max B. Bayer
Rehabilitation Studies, Faculty of Education University of Calgary,
Alberta, Canada

This chapter is a review of a Quality of Life study carried out over a period of six years in Western Canada. Details of the project have been presented in several articles and in two major books (Brown, Bayer and MacFarlane 1989; Brown, Bayer and Brown, 1992). In this chapter we will review briefly the research that was undertaken, this opportunity to look back on the study and to consider some of the issues it raised, along with the implications for research, intervention and education, including the education of professionals.

There seems to be little doubt that the development of Quality of Life as a concept, and the research relating to it, will have a fundamental impact on policies and programs from governmental perspectives and service provision. The issues raised by Quality of Life researchers are broad ranging, affecting both our perception of disability and the concept of service delivery in the context of empowerment and advocacy. The nature of assessment is also affected when it relates to personal perception and the consumer's perspective. During the past 15 years many have argued for a reexamination of the field of disability using concepts of Quality of Life (Goode, 1988; Landesman, 1986; Parmenter, 1988, 1991; Shalock, 1990). As with any new concept, both advantages and disadvantages occur. Therefore, in addition to the positive aspects highlighted in our study, we attempt to discuss some of the concerns which have arisen.

Although our original study was first designed as a retrospective examination of the lifestyles and effectiveness of rehabilitation for people with mild and moderate mental disabilities (Bayer and Brown, 1982), subsequent research was prospective and longitudinal in nature, and developed as its major platform the concept of Quality of Life (Brown, Bayer and MacFarlane, 1989). The project team has been working for twelve years, but this report particularly relates to a six-year study (1982-88) involving an intervention period during the last three years. An important role was played by the initial retrospective study in creating the original questionnaire for assessing quality of life, and in determining the major variables to be examined. One problem associated with any Quality of Life study, which is based on an holistic model as ours was, is the danger that it will be very broadly based and therefore will not study any issue in great depth. It also raises the challenge of developing a wide range of assessment procedures, which may not be entirely desirable in terms of impact on people with developmental disabilities (Goode, 1988). However, tools that measure behavior, in this case individual perception, help to focus scientific and professional attention. They provide in the first instance opportunities to describe perceptions and needs, and eventually programs. Thus, although requiring considerable time, Quality of Life tools will provide major opportunities for direct input and insight from people with disabilities (Brown and Bayer, 1992; Cummins, 1992, Schalock et al., 1990). Such tools must be used carefully.

The six-year follow-up study was divided into two three-year phases. The first phase was concerned with the evaluation of performance and change in the lifestyle of 240 individuals, most of whom were in their late teens or twenties. Following this first phase, the subject group was divided into two: those individuals who wished to partake in a specialized intervention based on the recommendations of phase one, and others who would continue with the original agency-based rehabilitation procedures. We thus had a model that made it possible to compare the performance and perceptions of people over an initial three-year period with the results after a period of specialized intervention. We could also compare individuals who had specialized intervention with those who did not have such intervention. Thus, both longitudinal and cross-sectional aspects of the study were important. Indeed, subsequent analysis showed that it would have been impossible to understand certain aspects of change

unless a longitudinal method had been applied.

The assessments from years one, three and six provided three key points for data analysis. In years 1 and 6 cognitive measures using the Wechsler Adult Intelligence Scale were employed. In years one, three and six, the Quality of Life questionnaire (see Brown and Bayer, 1992) was used along with the Adaptive Functioning Index (Marlett, 1971). The Quality of Life questionnaire had a version for sponsors (generally parents) as well as for clients. Thus direct comparisons could be made using specific sections from which numerical data were obtained. Agency personnel were requested to complete the Value Priorities Scale (Marlett and Hughson, 1978) and a needs analysis was also performed (Brown et al., 1989). During the interventions (phase 2) additional assessments were carried out that specifically related to the choices made by clients. These assessments consisted of interviews, observations, and specifically designed criterion referenced tests (Brown et al., 1992). In addition, questionnaires about intervention were given to both clients and workers, where appropriate in interview format, to assess the perceived effectiveness of the intervention from different perspectives. Both qualitative and quantitative data were obtained and these are described and discussed in detail using graphical and statistical comparisons between intervention and non-intervention groups over the time periods. Years one to three provided comparisons for all subjects in the pre-intervention phase. Data between years three and six provided additional longitudinal comparisons, and detailed the various performances in the intervention phase, resulting in comparisons between intervention and non-intervention subjects.

## Definition and Approach to Quality of Life

For purposes of our study, a needs discrepancy definition of Quality of Life was employed (Brown, Bayer and MacFarlane, 1989). This was derived after examining a wide range of other definitions. Our working definition of Quality of Life, after examining the arguments of Rodgers and Converse (1975) and others, was as follows:

The discrepancy between a person's achieved and unmet needs and desires. This refers to the subjective, or perceived, and objective assessment of an individual's domains. The greater the discrepancy the poorer the Quality of Life. It includes the extent to which an individual increasingly controls aspects of life regardless of original baseline.

In many ways our definition of Quality of Life has its roots in Maslow's system of hierarchy of needs. Challenges and improvements to this definition are discussed later.

A broad description of the areas examined through the Quality of Life model is shown in Figure 1. An holistic model was employed to reflect all aspects or domains of an individual's lifestyle (social, vocational, homeliving and leisure).Socio-political factors and technological expertise were both seen as complex variables, interacting with both learning and opportunity to develop and perform within these domains. The model incorporates, on the one hand, the social ecological approach of Bronfenbrenner (1979) (see adaptation of Mitchell, 1986) the concepts of

Wolfensberger (1983) concerning Social-Role Valorization, and the social perception of handicap as argued by Parmenter (1986).

The Quality of Life questionnaire (Brown & Bayer, 1992) was divided into twelve categories:

• Home living
• Things you do
• Your health
• Your family and friends
• You and your family
• Self-image
• Leisure time
• Employment
• You and the law
• The help you want
• How you feel about life
• Final comments

## Discussion of Approach

Before proceeding further, it is important to define what we initially believed during the first phase of the study to be the key components of a Quality of Life model. Changes as a result of our research, which need to be taken into account within any Quality of Life model are discussed later.

Quality of Life is seen by a number of authors as a subjective concept involving the individual's perspective (Goode, 1988, Parmeter, 1988, Dossa, 1989 and Shalock 1990). It is critical that these aspects are included, particularly when examining any group that is underprivileged, and whose members do not have control of their own lifestyles within the community. This raises a number of challenges. Within our study the majority of individuals had at least rudimentary speech. We also took the pre-

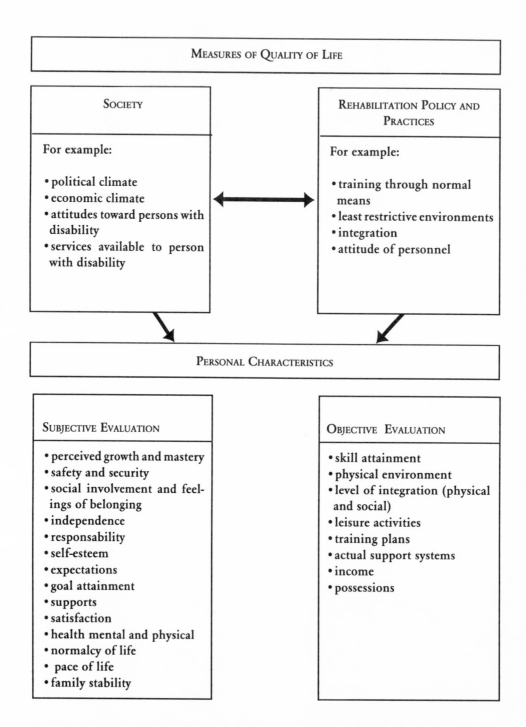

Figure 3-1. Model of Quality of Life. Based on Brown, Bayer & Macfarlane (1989).

caution of having a parental/sponsor version of the questionnaire that could be filled in independently from the consumer. In other words, we allowed for other subjective views about the individuals, although results indicated the importance of regarding the consumer's views as central.

Indeed, we have now decided that exactly the same questionnaire should be given both to the consumers and to their sponsors. Many issues of Quality of Life are very personal. They are frequently not discussed between the consumer who is disabled and the parties who are close to them. Independence in completing a questionnaire is therefore critical. For example, within our study, there were occasions when the consumers made it very clear that they would not be prepared to make certain statements in front of their sponsors. This is a measure of the degree to which they can feel inhibited.

However, many groups of people with disability contain a percentage of individuals who have no speech or very limited language. It is essential that effective future development of Quality of Life involve means of obtaining the non-verbal consumer's view. The reliance on advocates to represent clients who are severely disabled is insufficient. Following our six-year study we have had some experience using observational techniques, and believe that over a wide range of items, non-verbal assessment is indeed a practical alternative. Non-verbal and, in particular, facial responses are now being used by some authors (Autio, 1992) for such assessment, and Goode (1991) also describes techniques for gaining input from persons with severe disabilities.

In many other Quality of Life studies there has been a dilemma over the use of weighting given to objective and subjective measures. In a comprehensive model of Quality of Life, we argue it may be legitimate to include objective measures, and the perceptions of professionals and relatives, including advocates, but the individual consumer's perceptions must remain the crux for decision-making. It is important to examine what people perceive, as against what they actually do or are perceived to do in terms of performance. It is also important to draw a distinction between objective measures of environmental safety and the individual's perceptions of being safe. Both objective and subjective measures were recorded within our study.

It seems logical that there should be a societal view of Quality of Life that reflects community views on standards, requirements and need for change. This is not inconsistent within the ecological model presented by Bronfenbrenner. Such a model is often favored by health groups. Here we argue for the predominance of a personal model of Quality of Life. It is the effective integration of these two views that theoretically can provide a driving force for change. But in such a context how do we deal with individual desire and opportunities for change as well as the wish by others to promote change in the individual? Wishes for change that lead to future needs for many consumers who have mental disabilities are particularly difficult to express. This is also true of those with disabilities such as traumatic brain injury. Indeed, one of the critical issues raised in a Quality of Life model concerns the problems associated with forward planning, or the idea of future organization or life sequence, being piloted or guided by the individual. Thus, Quality of Life raises issues of consciousness, particularly in relation to the lifespan and analysis of drive and opinion by the individual. These aspects have lacked examination and rarely exist in service or training programs. They represent a major area for future development and education.

We discussed why we believe there is sufficient evidence to suggest that individual self-image and its development are irrevocably tied to individual performance and to the likelihood of gaining independence and control of personal lifestyle. Without the development of positive self-image with some concept of one's personal future, we question whether rehabilitation, special education or skills-training is likely to be effective. To date, development of self-concept in these terms has been largely left to chance.

## Major Findings From The Study

The results of the study are detailed in Brown et al., (1989 and 1992). We have provided a summary of the major results as we believe they influence our developing conceptions around the Quality of Life as an area of study:

1.  It is apparent that there still remains in Canada a large number of individuals functioning at above average levels of cognitive performance, with a wide range of effective skills in home and community living, who are still maintained in traditional service agencies. This is a troubling issue, highlighted within a Quality of Life model. Indeed, one valuable feature of such models is that they enable us to view socio-behavioral issues from a fresh perspective.

2.  There is a perception amongst sponsors

that most agency programs do not directly or indirectly meet the emotional needs of the consumers. Indeed, our examination suggests that, of all the areas which receive attention, none is so poorly addressed as the area of emotional development. Elsewhere we have suggested that rehabilitation, as practiced, is the art of keeping people quiet (Brown et al., 1992). An examination of lifestyle within family homes, in residential group homes and within day agencies, suggests that the planning procedures used are generally those which encourage the individual to be as quiet as possible. It is, perhaps, for this reason that those individuals who have shown some assertiveness and aggressive behaviors of a mild nature are more likely to make their way into the community (MacKerracher et al., 1980), while those who show major aggressive problems are likely to be rejected and removed to more congregate and custodial situations (Brown, 1990). Those who "respond appropriately" to professional requests are often likely to remain within their rehabilitation environment. It was also found that the major emotional problems (in terms of the number of persons affected) are not those of aggressive behavior but of anxiety and depression (Brown, 1990). Our study provided evidence of this in a variety of ways. For example, many parents identified emotional needs as an unmet area, and lack of assertiveness was seen as a challenge. Furthermore, most consumers, in most areas in which they were questioned, believed that they had not made progress over the previous year, a finding which suggests widespread poor self-image. As a single issue, this last item is a major indictment of rehabilitation programs It also speaks to how poorly individuals see themselves and their ability to make or not make improvement. As will be seen later, the use of particular types of intervention changed the picture of self-image dramatically. However, it is important to indicate that these changes were found to be more common in females than males, perhaps reflecting important gender differences adversely affecting females.

3.  Quality of Life measures indicated that most agencies still concentrated on vocational programs, whereas needs, as expressed by individuals, lay for the most part in non-vocational areas. It is a fallacy to believe that every adult with disability needs or wishes to have vocational employment. We have argued that, if attention is given to the other areas of need, motivation towards employment may also improve. Individuals who develop new resources are more likely to be successful. It is perhaps remarkable that, when we undertook the initial retrospective study in the seventies, people with developmental disabilities were more readily obtaining employment in the community. During the subsequent six-year study we found that most people remained within a training agency. The data show that less than 4% of the group's time over the first three years of the project was spent in gainful employment. In fact, there is evidence that people who attended day training programs in Canadian rehabilitation agencies during

the eighties were likely to remain in such services. The increase in unemployment in Canada as a whole, the greater degree of disability of people in the agencies now as compared with the seventies (for example see Bayer & Brown, 1982), and a mismatch between programs and individual needs, probably combine to account for the stagnation.

4.  There is evidence that leisure and recreational activities are not encouraged to any major degree in the agencies or homes. The degree to which such activities can provide for a much broader-based lifestyle and can provide opportunities for transfer of skills within normal communities, is misunderstood. Indeed, most of the activities undertaken and encouraged by agencies and parents tend to be spectator-types of recreation. More rigorous activities, and those that involve social and community involvement or self-actualization, tend not to be encouraged. This is alarming in many ways, particularly when we find that amongst our study population there appears to be a decline in the diversity and amount of leisure activities as individuals progress into their thirties. It seems to occur even earlier in persons with Down Syndrome (Brown, 1992). We believe that intervention should make much more use of leisure time resources. Once again a Quality of Life model applied to assessment tends to identify such needs. The importance of longitudinal studies in this area is clearly confirmed because of the relevance to life span changes in Quality of Life.

## Gender differences

Examination of certain data by gender suggests male and female differences within the study were considerable. Primarily, the results suggest that, although there are more males than females born with disabling conditions, proportionally more females with developmental disabilities are likely to be "institutionalized" in the Canadian rehabilitation system. It also appears that males are likely to be given more diverse opportunities for rehabilitation in the community than females. Within our own data, it appeared that females had poorer self-image than males since they frequently believed that they made less progress in a variety of activities than males. Females were also much more restricted and controlled by agency personnel and parents as to the types of activities they could undertake in a variety of domains, including leisure activities. It is of interest that the greatest improvement in self-image was recorded for females who received individualized intervention in the second phase of the study where personal choice predominated. Thus a major finding of this Quality of Life study is the major difference between males and females in terms of the likelihood of being treated as disabled, and of being controlled or protected in terms of the opportunities provided. No doubt these greater restrictions for females are in part related to traditional attitudes towards females within our society. However, it is equally apparent that many females, when given the opportunity, make rapid gains and indeed are capable of rapid rehabilitation.

## Intervention Procedures

The intervention phase of the study employed a number of principles derived from the first phase of the research. In general terms, these principles were as follows:

• The individual with the disability, i.e. the client or consumer, and his or her family should agree to individualized intervention, with the major goals decided upon by the individual client;

• The choice of the client would predominate in terms of activity;

• The client would choose or voluntarily agree to the environments in which to carry out these activities;

• The client would choose or agree to the personnel involved;

• The client would have the right to change choices during the operation of the intervention or to stop any intervention should she or he wish to do so;

• When requested by the client, the intervention would take place within the home environment;

• Staff employed would be highly skilled. Individuals would have professional training in rehabilitation or allied areas, have several years of practice in the field, and accept the criteria outlined above;

• Consulting opportunities would be made available, which both the individual client and frontline personnel could use, if necessary, at various stages during the intervention. The client could accept or reject the recommendations, although the implications of this would be discussed;

• It was estimated from previous work that a major amount of interest would be in social, leisure and emotional areas, and therefore staff selected had to be capable of working in these areas. Staff also had to be in a position to work with parents, and counsel and advise regarding various forms of intervention.

In this model of intervention, frontline personnel became program designers and implementers. As indicated elsewhere, (Brown et al., 1992), the interventions resulted in (a) the need to advocate on the client's behalf in relation to parents who might not like the individual's choices or see their relevance, and (b) the need to deal with situations where agency personnel were not prepared to follow through with the stated interests or choices of the client.

There is no doubt from our study experiences that there were many instances where personnel in agencies did not feel able to support this intervention model. Although the proposed client activities might be commonplace, such as making a meal at an unusual time of the day or undertaking recreation of choice, frontline staff would frequently state that management would object to such initiatives or that they did not fit group routines. Some agencies prevented people having pets or did not provide choice over roommates, or, if they did allow choice, they insisted that the professional team had to agree on these choices before implementation took place. From a Quality of Life perspective, we do not believe this to be legitimate. Choice is the right of the client and, unless it is likely to cause physical harm to the individual or to others, should automatically be accepted. It is not a question for professional staff to debate. Our involvement in the development of intervention programs in three major cities and two other areas in Western

Canada has shown fairly clearly that there have to be major changes in hierarchical and management structures if clients are to have choice and frontline staff are to be the most skilled. One also might argue that frontline staff carrying out this model should therefore be the most highly paid.

We believe these views, which quite clearly arise from the study, are equally appropriate in other areas of health and social service, e.g. those relating to brain injury, aging and disability. It is critical to recognize that Quality of Life provides a window on disability which is at once holistic but also personal. The types of intervention we describe, and the types of systems that were set up, required personalized involvement and the use of natural and community environments. They lessened the major problems of transferring skills from an artificial environment to a community environment. They also provided opportunities for the individual with a disability to be in command in relation to his or her rehabilitation. Thus choice, in this sense, becomes the cornerstone in the development of a Quality of Life model. This led to a revision of the subjective areas of assessment relevant to the client (see Table 3-1). The content is more specific and allows and seeks input involving concerns from the client.

Another implication from the study is that the provision of an "empowering environment" is critical. We are concerned with statements that suggest programs empower people. We believe the study demonstrated that the best that can be done is to provide an empowering environment in which individuals can assert themselves and have opportunities to develop self-image. They may then become empowered. This is very clear when the impact of a choice model on perception and behavior is observed. The individuals seem to improve much more rapidly in terms of their performance in the community. They, in fact, become more critical about social aspects of the environment over which they would like more control. For example, they become less satisfied about where they live. They become less satisfied about relationships and speak to the types of emotional controls they wish to develop. Often this leads to a heightened awareness of needs, and enables individuals to make more use of professional support systems offered. Rather than leading to inappropriate choice or negative behavior, the use of a Quality of Life model promotes increased individualized control, more critical views of the environment, and the desire to improve independence, knowledge, and experience. These assertive characteristics were sometimes seen by agency personnel and by parents as deterioration in behavior rather than improvement. For example, a move to more community involvement by clients in the study was associated with decreased ratings of vocational behavior by agency personnel, whereas other indications of performance improved. We believe this means either personnel had less knowledge of individuals' daily activities and saw the activities and their performance as inappropriate, or gave poorer ratings because individuals were more assertive and were less docile in the raters' presence.

As indicated earlier, the attitudes of staff and parents are often geared towards encouraging people to be quiet and to conform. Effective rehabilitation enables people to challenge, to assert, and to take control of situations. Thus, development

of Quality of Life programming can cause problems or challenges for agencies or parents who wish to control the behavior of their son or daughter, on the grounds of caring for them. In fact, a Quality of Life model may ultimately promote better care, whether this is in the area of wellness (Lawrence et al., 1992) or in the area of greater psychological or social control, because when it is applied it provides opportunities for empowerment. This can be directly the opposite of what many agencies or individuals in society want or are prepared to provide, i.e., they equate care for people who are disabled with protection. A number of years ago, Grant (1971) indicated that many people in rehabilitation select this professional area because they are interested in providing care and support. We believe that one of the first areas of counselling for potential personnel concerns the need for them to recognize that their need to care and to protect may be a major motivating factor in their job selection. However, the best protection occurs when individuals are given opportunities for empowerment, and can come to care for themselves as they wish. Errors will sometimes occur in such an approach, and those errors will often be employed by carers to promote the view that the approach is dangerous and harmful. But learning frequently occurs through error. Of course, it is true that greater freedom can involve greater risk, but in our experience using a Quality of Life model, these negative outcomes did not happen to any of the clients involved.

The type of model we promoted was directed by a specific philosophy and vision. We did not always manage to be consistent with that vision. There were occasions when parents' views seemed much

### Table 3-1. Expansion of Subjective Measures of Quality of Life

Personal Evaluation of:

- Friendship network

- Choice

- Status (adult/child)

- Contribution to others (help, giving)

- Control over environment (eg. house, bedroom noise level)

- Control over activities (eg. employment, leisure, home living)

- Control over privacy

- Emotional needs (eg. companionship, relatedness, love, social-sexual needs, anxiety, worries, future plans

- Control over home activities

- Acceptance (by family, employers, employees, local community)

- Needs and control over change

- Dissatisfaction

more logical, rational and reasonable than the clients' so that we sometimes gave way to such views. In all such cases, the client did poorly in the areas which were chosen. It is important to recognize that the client's choice may not seem reasonable, nor seem to be in an hierarchy of logical, psychological development, but it is what the client wishes to work on, and therefore precedence should be given to such choices. Following the interventions, data concerning individual's performance and self-image and sponsors' perceptions suggested there was a shift whereby perceptions began to approximate one another more closely. The family as a whole begins to agree with and support one another in working on the individual's choices. Thus, the model we propose tends to increase the rewarding and empowering process as it is undertaken. This is essential if one views Quality of Life as both a personal and group construct.

## Professional Education

We are proposing an approach towards intervention that has fundamental implications for philosophy, service and management, including assessment and program delivery. This approach also has implications for the health and long-term functioning of personnel, because the professional role that we have described is a highly personal one. There are few personnel who have had opportunities to function at the frontline level in people's families and local communities, working on individuals' choices. The new approach to programs results in much closer relationships between client and worker. Very often the worker becomes a major advocate for the individual. In the course of the study, friendships with clients developed rather than distant professional-client relationships (Litchy & Johnson, 1992). Friendliness between some front line workers and their clients is nothing new. However, emphasizing such relationships that are less structured, and the use of more personalized settings, raises a number of ethical issues:

• Is it appropriate to develop friendships between client and worker? If so, how and by whom are the boundaries to be defined, if any?
• If "bonding" between client and worker develops, then what happens if the worker has to move on?
• What sorts of relationships are appropriate? In our study there were occasions where individuals met in the home of the worker, where people in the group went out for dinner, and where personal feelings of both worker and the client were discussed .

We believe that such occurrences can be valid within a model aimed at promoting change in self-image and empowerment. The traditional views about professional relationships must therefore, to some degree, be modified. Obviously, the worker is placed in a position where personal integrity must be of the highest order.

Professional rehabilitation workers need intense training in counseling skills and their application (Robertson & Brown, 1992). They must know the client's local community extremely well and feel comfortable working in the community alongside individuals with a handicap. They must also be prepared to discuss issues relating to ethical, social and professional values. There may be occasions when a worker is not prepared to carry out a choice of an individual because it infringes on his or her personal values, but the individual should still be allowed to make the choice. For example, one young woman wanted a worker to introduce her to a male strip club. The female worker accepted her choice but provided reasons for not being prepared to accompany her. It was indicated that other persons might be willing to do this, so that if the individual was still keen to carry out this choice, she was free to do so. These types of dilemmas will arise occasionally, and will require sensitive judgement, and very skilled and experienced workers.

There are occasions when parents or other sponsors disagree with the choice and attempt to insist on their own. For example, one young woman, who had begun to date a young man successfully and appropriately, was suddenly prevented from liaising with him by her parents, who as guardians, wanted her to relate to a "much nicer man" with Down Syndrome. This led to advocacy and counseling with the parents over lunch time by two of the client's rehabilitation team. The parents came to understand they had not acted appropriately. Skills to deal with such situations are not easily acquired and need to be modeled by experienced personnel.

It is critical that projects of a service nature be set up, wherever possible, in collaboration with rehabilitation or allied training programs in universities and colleges so that frontline experience of this type can be obtained. The question is whether college and university personnel are sufficiently well equipped at this time. This again conflicts with the traditional model, for we are arguing that the most highly trained and experienced staff should be at the frontline level.

Such a Quality of Life model does not require the extensive bureaucracies and management systems that are present today. There is also no need for the wide range of buildings and hardware which have been developed. Individual clients can work in collaboration with their professional workers from their own homes. If necessary, a single office in the professional worker's home can prove effective. Most training, counseling discussions, and demonstrations can take place in the individual's own environment. As indicated earlier, the challenges of assertion have been most marked for young females with mental handicap, when a protective atmosphere is replaced by choice and opportunity. As a rule, it is critical that clients have workers of their own gender, who are very much aware of the issues of that gender, and who can provide empathy and role-modeling. The modeling provided in a realistic environment can help resolve a number of issues. For example, instead of attempting to encourage friendship networks through training programs, one provides opportunities for friendships to develop, since people with positive self-image are more likely to take initiative in terms of making relationships.

As we carried out this research, we encountered some agency personnel, parents and others who tried to protect individuals from various social stresses. Bereavement is one example of where it was assumed that the individual did not understand the events taking place, could not conceptualize the issue, and therefore would be upset if he or she became involved in the mourning rituals. In our experience, individuals always knew something serious had happened to a relative or friend and had many questions to ask. Inclusion in the grieving process helped their self-identity, their emotional needs and their recognition as participating members of the family (Webb, 1992).

## Where To From Here?

We have put forward a description of Quality of Life as an encompassing concept of personal development, where choice and opportunities to use natural circumstances and environments predominate. Counseling between partners within families is absolutely critical because the Quality of Life model assumes interaction between individuals. Disability is a feature of environment and relationship, not simply a self-contained attribute of an individual. The social aspects of disability not only relate to the individual who is disabled but to the whole system surrounding and involving that person. There is ample evidence that many areas which make up these social dimensions, such as those concerning self-image, emotional awareness and development, and environmental control, have been omitted from previous rehabilitation models. More specifically, a range of self-promoting leisure and recreative activities have generally been overlooked, and family supports are often lacking throughout the life span.

Using an intervention model based on

Quality of Life, we have observed that individuals with developmental disabilities can make considerably greater progress than in traditional rehabilitation models. The effects in the study were so marked in certain cases that individuals who had been assessed as functioning in the 50-60 I.Q. range, and were perceived as obviously "mentally disabled" were at a later stage no longer seen by members of the community as disabled in any way at all! Development in Quality of Life may not necessarily lead to greater happiness, which seems to be a criterion for Quality of Life in a number of models. Indeed our model, when applied, may lead to a more critical appraisal of needs and environment by the individual concerned. Positive, friendly, peer-type relationships between professional staff, the individual, and the family were found to be critical, but a sound knowledge of programming and the development of appropriate training techniques were also important. The model we describe includes the application of learning and training strategies. The skill of an individual worker to relate to parents and others, to provide counselling, and to deal with issues raised by agencies, was critical.

We remain in two minds about the ability of existing agencies to adapt to this type of model. Our experience has been that, while frontline staff often accept the implications, most agencies do not wish to make the adaptation because it reduces the power and current functions of the existing management system. We did work with agency managers who were willing to cooperate and to change their philosophy and mode of operation in order to pilot and develop the model we proposed. However, generally we argue that new services are

required, where professional staff, working out of their own homes with individuals in their own communities, can develop the types of personal yet professional relationships which enable people to take control of their own lifestyle.

The limits of such a model are not known. It is apparent that many agency staff have not investigated the issues of Quality of Life in the domain of choice. Most of us believe we know what people want and we certainly know what is good for them! Acceptance of a Quality of Life model can help to change such attitudes. This is especially important in working with people who have severe disabilities. We now have experience in using the model in relation to such persons. Choice must be provided even if it is at a tactile or visual level, and even when it contradicts our preconceived perception of what is needed.

The development of Quality of Life models seems to be consistent with the natural unfolding of our knowledge system within the rehabilitation area. We have moved from care of individuals in concrete institutions through sheltered workshops, vocational rehabilitation to group homes, social-education, and, more recently, the inclusion of leisure and recreational skills (Brown and Hughson, 1988). A Quality of Life model consolidates the more positive aspects of these developments and, because of its holistic and personal focus, it also deals with emotional development. One of the implications from the study is that emotional and cognitive issues, when dealt with together, lead to issues of self-awareness and self-image which, in the end, relate to a concept of self — a developing self — over a life span. In other words, individuals appear to develop a strand of consciousness about their past, present and future development. Right now, most people who have developmental disabilities are not encouraged to possess the functional or practical tools that the rest of us usually employ for developing future plans. Calendars, diaries or even photographic records of past events, used to project a sense of self in time, are often lacking. Personal effects in a group home are now recognized as relevant, but they are rarely seen as the artifacts of development and change. It is this aspect of understanding which is so critical to a Quality of Life model. Consciousness, as evidenced in the personal awareness of self and self-direction, appears to be lacking.

There were several individual examples in the study where such issues of consciousness came to the fore. For example, an individual declared that she could not image herself within a situation, and therefore was unaware of her role in the situation. Some time was directed towards these issues, and one of the major developments which seemed to flow from the application of the Quality of Life model was greater integration of emotional and cognitive appraisal. This involved the development of greater self-awareness and conscious pre-planning of events. For most people with developmental disabilities events happen, and they are propelled by the impact of these events into new situations which they have not personally selected or considered. Very few people with developmental disabilities actually initiate, encourage, or control processes so that they may determine the options and outcomes. The challenge which is set by any Quality of Life model is the demand for a wide range of new types of exploration and study.

## Research Implications

One of the interesting findings from this particular study arose from the fact that individuals who became involved in the interventions did so by choice. Some individuals wished to be involved in intervention for whom we did not have the resources, but there was also a larger number of individuals who did not wish to be involved or whose parents or sponsors were unwilling to give consent for participation. As we look back at the records of individuals over the six years of the study, it is apparent that those who wished to become involved in intervention were already beginning to make some movements in the directions we have described under the term 'Quality of Life.' The importance of longitudinal studies became apparent. Without such information we would not have recognized that some of our subjects were already improving, and that their improvement may have been related to their own and their sponsors' motivation for intervention. Conversely, for many of our subjects or their sponsors who were not yet ready to make this first step, lack of improvement appeared to lead to lack of selection. Our evidence points to even greater changes in behavior as a result of intervention. There appear to be links between the way people perceive an individual, and how that individual perceives himself or herself, and the extent to which that individual will be given an opportunity to take part in innovation and learning. We therefore come back to our earlier statement — rehabilitation has generally been designed to keep people quiet. If sponsors believe that clients cannot make progress, they appear unlikely to support client involvement in a new program. It is critical that challenge and opportunity are available for all people with disabilities. Advocacy for this is needed when individuals themselves do not make demands, and when many workers and sponsors only believe the individuals must conform and learn specific skills if they are to progress. The individual consumer has to become assertive about his or her own life, and it is those whose family or workers believe the individual can change who are more likely to make the first steps towards rehabilitation. One of the critical issues in the field of rehabilitation is to convince families, friends and rehabilitation workers that change is indeed possible. Indeed, we cannot predict the extent of change that can occur for, if opportunity comes within the command of the individual, a new energy apparently enters the equation.

Although many of the results we have recounted are of a qualitative nature, quantitative data are also reported. There were those in our study team (Lichty and Johnson, 1992) who particularly believed that qualitative results should be considered as a priority within research paradigms, and that much of the quantitative findings underestimate or do not measure the actual changes which take place. In the study, we made both types of measures and advocate

their use within a Quality of Life model. If we accept the notion that Quality of Life is an individualized concept and an account of personal journeys made by individuals, discourse analysis and narrative become important attributes of the paradigms within the model. We are not advocating for a change to a totally new research paradigm, but for a blend of methodologies, including the use of qualitative analysis. We also believe that the data in the study show quite clearly that it is not easy to predict the amount of change that individuals are likely to make. We know that judgments made by individuals about their Quality of Life, including judgments of performance, self-image, change and control processes, are highly relevant to an understanding of the rehabilitation processes. We believe tools in this area should be developed, and that these tools should be used in the development of programs of the individual's choice. It is extremely important, not just to ask people casually what they want to do, but to explore their needs and goals in a systematic way with the individual in control of the dialogue; verbally or nonverbally. This is a far cry from imposing a formal curriculum or training in specific skills, although these may play a role once a program has been planned to address the individual's choice.

## References

Autio, Tiina. (1992). *The Quality of Life of Mentally Retarded. Interviewing Results in Tabular Form.* The Finnish Association on Mental Retardation Research and Experimentation Unit. Helsinki.

Bayer, M.B. & Brown, R.I. (1982). *Benefits and Costs of Rehabilitation at the Vocational and Rehabilitation Research Institute.* Vols. I & II. Report for Health & Welfare Canada. Ottawa.

Bronfenbrenner, U. (1979). *The Ecology of Human Development.* Cambridge, MA: Harvard University Press.

Brown, R.I. (1990). Quality of Life for People

with Hearing Dififculties: The Challenge for Behaviorial and Emotional Disturbance. *International Review of Psychiatry 2*, 21-30.

Brown, R.I. and Bayer, M.B. (1992). *Rehabilitation Questionnaire and Manual: A Personal Guide to the Individual's Quality of Life*. Toronto, ON: Captus University Publications.

Brown, R.I., Bayer, M.B. and MacFarlane, C.M. (1989). *Rehabilitation Programs: Performance and Quality of Life of Adults with Developmental Handicaps*. Toronto: Lugus.

Brown, R.I., Bayer, M.B. and Brown, P.M. (1992). *Empowerment and Developmental Handicaps: Choices and Quality of Life*. Toronto, ON: Captus University Publications.

Brown, R.I., Mills, J., Lawrence, P. and Estay, I. (1992). *Challenges and Practical Approaches for Adults with Down Syndrome*. Paper presented to the I.A.S.S.M.D. Conference, Brisbane, Australia.

Cummins, Robert A. (1992). *Comprehensive Quality of Life Scale - Intellectual Disability. ComQol-ID)*. Manual Third Edition. Psychology Research Centre, Deakin University, Toorak, Australia.

Dossa, Parin A. (1989). Quality of Life: Individualism or Holism? *A Critical Review of the Literature*. International Journal of Rehabilitation Research. 12(2), 121-136.

Goode, D.A. (1988). *Discussing Quality of Life: The Process and Findings of the Work Group on Quality of Life for Persons with Disabilities*. Mental Retardation Institute, A University Affiliated Program, Westchester County Medical Center in Affiliation with New York Medical College, Valhalla, New York.

Goode, D.A. (1991). *How Is It Possible for Children with Deaf-Blindness and No Formal Language and Adults Who See, Hear and Speak to Understand One Another?: On the Social Organization of Communicating Indexical Bodily Expressions in the World of Daily Life*. International Association for the Education of the Deaf-Blind. Orebro: Sweden.

Grant, W.B. (1971). *Some Management Problems of Providing Work for the Mentally Disordered*

*with Particular Reference to Mental Handicap*. Unpublished M.Sc. thesis, University of Manchester.

Landesman, S. (1986). Quality of Life and Personal Satisfaction: Definition and Personal Satisfaction. *Journal of Mental Retardation* 24, 141-143.

Lawrence, P.M., Brown, R.I., Mills, J., and Estay, I. (1992). *Adults with Down Syndrome: Together we can do it*. Toronto, On: Captus Press and Calgary, AB: Canadian National Down Syndrome Association.

Litchy, J. & Johnson, P. (1992). *Client Intervention: Another Team's Experience*. In R.I. Brown, M.B. Bayer & P.M. Brown, *Choices and Quality of Life*. Toronto, On: Captus University Publications, London: Chapman & Hall.

MacKerracher, D.W., Brown, R.I., Marlett, N., and Zwirner, W.W. (1980). *A Study of the Utility of Assessment and Prediction Procedures in the Selection of handicapped Persons for Industrial and Social Rehabiitation Programs*. Final Report for Health and Welfare Canada (Grant No. 566-34-8), Vocational and Rehabilitation Research Institute, Calgary, Canada.

Marlett, N.J. (1971; revised 1976). *Adaptive Functioning Index*. Vocational and Rehabilitation Research Institute: Calgary.

Marlett, N.J. and Hughson, E. A. (1978). *Rehabilitation Programmes Manual*. Vocational and Rehabilitation Research Institute: Calgary.

Mitchell, D.R. (1986). A Developmental Systems Approach to Planning and Evaluating Services for Persons with Handicaps. In R.I. Brown, *Management and Administration of Rehabilitation Programs*. London: Croom Helm.

Parmenter, T.R. (1988). An Analysis of the Dimensions of Quality of Life for People with Physical Disabilities. In R.I. Brown, *Quality of Life for Handicapped People*. London: Croom Helm.

Parmenter, T.R., Briggs, L. and Sullivan, R. (1989). *Quality of Life: Intellectual Disabilities and Community Living*. Evaluation Journal of Australia 3(1) 12-27.

Robertson, S. and Brown, R.I. (1992). *Rehabilitation Counselling: Approaches in the Field of Disability. A Series in Rehabilitation Education, Volume 5*. London: Chapman and Hall.

Rodgers, W.L., and Converse, P.E. (1975). *Measurement of the Perceived Quality of Life. Social Indicators Research 2*, 127-152.

Schalock, R.L. (1990) *Attempts to Conceptualize and Measure Quality of Life*. In R.L. Schalock (ed.), *Quality of Life: Perspectives and Issues* (pp. 141-148). American Association on Mental Retardation:. Washington, DC.

Schalock, R.L., Keith, K.D. & Hoffman, K. (1990). *1990 Quality of Life Questionnaire: Standardization Manual*. Hastings, NE: Mid-Nebraska Mental Retardation Services.

Webb, S.B. (1991). *Disability Counselling: Grieving the Loss*. In S.E. Robertson and R.I. Brown (eds), *Rehabilitation Counselling: Approaches in the Field of Disability*. London: Chapman & Hall.

Wolfensberger, W. (1983). Social Role Valorization: A Proposed New Term for the Principle of Normalization. *Mental Retardation 21*(6), 234-239.

# 4. Being, Belonging, Becoming: An Approach to the Quality of Life of Persons with Developmental Disabilities

Gary Woodill, School of Early Childhood Education, Ryerson Polytechnical Institute; Rebecca Renwick, Department of Rehabilitation Medicine, University of Toronto; Ivan Brown, Center for Health Promotion University of Toronto; Dennis Raphael, Department of Behavioural Science, University of Toronto.

In *From Asylum to Welfare* Simmons (1982) documents what he refers to as a "century of failure" in the treatment and care of persons with developmental disabilities in the Canadian province of Ontario. This history is, of course, similar to that of many other jurisdictions in North America and can be seen to have moved through phases dominated by the "asylum model," the "educational model," the "custodial model" and the "deinstitutionalization model" (Simmons, 1982). The deinstitutionalization phase is still in progress, and has given rise to such issues as normalization, community living and quality of life for persons with a developmental disability.

The normalization movement in human services in Ontario, which began in the early 1970s, in part a result of the influence of Wolf Wolfensberger who was working in Toronto at that time (Wolfensberger, 1972), resulted in a number of profound changes in the treatment and public perception of persons with disabilities. First, as a result of lobbying by parents' groups, in particular the Ontario Association for the Mentally Retarded (now the Ontario Association for Community Liv-

ing), a policy change made funding for deinstitutionalization available from the Ontario government. At the same time, the school system moved toward some form of integration of children with disabilities with their non-disabled peers.

As well, a conscious effort was made to change the language used to refer to persons with a disability. The changes in language in Ontario have resulted in most former associations for the "mentally retarded" now calling themselves "associations for community living." The National Institute on Mental Retardation in Toronto is now known as the G.A. Roeher Institute. "Mental retardation" is now refered to in the Ontario literature as "developmental disability," in contrast to the American literature in which "mental retardation" is still an accepted term, and where "developmental disabilities" refer to a broader range of conditions than the term "mental retardation." Part of the motivation for the change of language was to change thinking about developmental disability from being seen primarily seen in a deficit-oriented, sympathy producing way, to a view which respected persons with a developmental disability as having worthwhile lives to live and contributions to make to others.

The initial phase of the deinstitutionalization movement was to remove persons with developmental disabilities from the large custodial institutions to smaller group homes and individual apartments. While this shift has proceeded quite smoothly in Ontario, it has not been without its problems. In particular, there has been resistance to the placing of group homes in specific neighbourhoods, and there have been criticisms of the "dumping" of residents of institutions into the community without proper support systems or preparation. This has, in part, led to the current focus on the "quality of life" of persons with a developmental disability living in the community.

In 1991, the Ontario Ministry of Community and Social Services funded a group of researchers based at the Centre for Health Promotion at the University of Toronto to conceptualize and design an approach to measurement as the first phase of a province-wide study of the quality of life of persons with developmental disabilities. (For a full report of Phase I of this project, see Rootman et al., 1992). This initiative followed recommendations from the report *Challenges and Opportunities: Community Living For People with Developmental Handicaps* (Ontario Ministry of Community and Social Services, 1987) which outlined the Ontario government's policy direction regarding services for persons with developmental disabilities.

Based on that report, the Ontario government's long-term goal has been to enhance the lives of persons with developmental disabilities by phasing out institutional placements and by establishing a comprehensive community service-delivery system. In 1987, the Ministry of Community and Social Services of the Ontario government made a commitment, in its Multi-Year Plan, to promote an environment in which persons with developmental disabilities can live, and receive required support, in their home communities. The plan is a framework designed to implement, over a 25-year period, the goals and objectives outlined in *Challenges and Opportunities*. In order to obtain the information necessary to evaluate the results of the Multi-Year Plan, the ministry called for proposals for a quality of life research project that would develop a methodology for measuring the quality of life of persons with developmental disabilities in Ontario.

## The Approach Taken Toward the Concept of Quality of Life

One of the challenges for Phase 1 of the Quality of Life Project was to develop an approach for conceptualizing and measuring the quality of life of *all* persons with developmental disabilities. This population is one that encompasses a large range of physical, cognitive and ability levels, from people who do not use formal communication systems and are highly dependent on others for care, to people who live and work independently and do not receive any direct professional services from others.

The approach reported here addresses this challenge by conceptualizing and measuring quality of life around the principle that people are much more alike than they are different. Human characteristics that are common to all people serve as the foundation for quality of life, while individual differences are seen as the various —

and often unique — ways that individuals have of expressing these common characteristics according to their own personalities and their own environments. Therefore our approach to measuring quality of life is intended to be appropriate for all people, not only for people at various levels of developmental disability, but also for those with or without other kinds of disabilities; that is, it is a *generic* approach to quality of life.

But this also means that those characteristics that are common *only* to subgroups of people, such as seniors with developmental disabilities, people who live and work independently, or people with severe disabilities who require direct care from others, may not be specifically addressed. For such subgroups, methods of assessment that address common characteristics of these particular subgroups in more detail (e.g. Brown, 1988; McCreary, Oullette-Kuntz, Minnes & Stanton, 1988) might be useful companions to the approach for assessing quality of life described in this chapter.

## Designing a Quality of Life Study

Developing a conceptual framework and instruments for measuring quality of life under contract for a provincial government has a set of constraints and influences which might not be present in studies carried out in other contexts.

First, any proposed system of measurement had to fit within legal frameworks such as Human Rights Codes for both Canada and Ontario. In Ontario, the Human Rights Code protects people from several sources of discrimination, including discrimination based on physical or mental handicap. Canada's Charter of Rights, proclaimed in 1982, provides Canadian citizens a variety of personal and civil rights that extend to all people. Such rights draw attention to issues regarding equality among groups of people and to issues regarding inclusion of disadvantaged groups of people, such as persons with developmental disabilities.

Second, the research team recognized that their work could be used to evaluate the functioning of the service system available to persons with developmental disabilities in Ontario, and that the results of any assessment of this population would influence future social policies concerning this group. In particular, we realized that with the trend towards budget constraints and fiscal responsibility, quality of life measures could be used as outcome measures to see whether the services being provided are resulting in positive or negative changes in people's lives.

Third, the team was aware of the need to be cognizant of the *multicultural* nature of the Ontario population in designing quality of life measures. In particular, there was a need to show acceptance of linguistic and cultural diversity, as this has been expressed in the policies of the Canadian, the Ontario, and many municipal governments. Such policies reflect a general cultural value that divergence from the norm not only is acceptable, but also contributes to the general well-being and quality of the culture. This value of respect for individual differences extends, to a considerable degree, to persons with developmental disabilities who, by definition, diverge from the norm.

Finally, the team needed to design their assessment of quality of life in the Canadian context, especially given the fact that most of the recent literature on this topic is American or European. For example, over the past several decades in all regions of Canada, there has been political and social commitment to providing a *social safety network* for all citizens in a universal way. This commitment works to influence a general view that all people, including those with developmental disabilities, deserve to have minimum standards for such things as health care, education, and social services.

### Basic Assumptions

In order to go beyond an approach based on the simple creation of lists of characteristics of 'a good life,' the research team used a process of consultation, discussion, and conceptual analysis to uncover their basic assumptions in developing an approach to measuring the quality of life of persons with developmental disabilities. The results of this process most certainly reflect the culture and collective historical background of the investigators, and the constraints of developing a concept of quality of life for a specific funder as outlined above. However, it was considered that by analyzing the background assumptions to their approach, the research team would able to formulate its own principles for developing a fresh look at the concept of quality of life.

As the researchers analyzed the concept of quality of life, two very basic but important questions emerged. These were: *what is life?* and, *what is quality of life?* Our answers to these questions are rooted in the pluralistic culture of the province of Ontario, as well as in the collective academic training and experiences of the investigators. The backgrounds of the members of the re-

search team included education, rehabilitation, family medicine, social work, psychology and health promotion.

Like many others in the field, the team began with the assumption that *the concept of quality of life, if it was not to be an exclusionary term, must apply to all human beings, whether they are disabled or non-disabled.* Persons with developmental disabilities were not viewed as a distinct grouping with a separate set of criteria for what constituted a good quality of life. Second, although we would inevitably look at various aspects of a person's life, we made the assumption that *one must take a holistic approach to conceptualizing and measuring quality of life* to avoid making judgements on just one dimension of a person's life. Rather, a multidimensional approach, which looked at as many interrelated aspects of the person's life as possible, was considered more appropriate. Third, we made the assumption that *quality of life must incorporate the notion of maximizing the personal control each person has over his/her own life, while keeping in mind the limits on freedom imposed by the principle 'danger to self and others', and by the rights of other people.* Although it is useful to gather data from others, the team took the approach that the perspective of persons with developmental disabilities themselves should be emphasized when measuring and studying quality of life. Fourth, the team supported *the principle of normalization* (Wolfensberger, 1972) for all human beings, including the notion of "social role valorization" (Wolfensberger, 1983) for those persons who have been traditionally stigmatized in our society.

Finally, the team was cognizant of the current trend towards self-advocacy by persons with disabilities, as exemplified by the philosophy of the Independent Living movement (DeJong, 1979; Carpenter, 1991), and the development of such organizations as People First, which represents the movement for self-advocacy among persons with a developmental disability in North America. People First began in the mid-1970s in the United States and spread to Canada in the early 1980s. By 1985 there were 60 to 70 local self-advocacy groups for persons with developmental disabilities in Canada, most of which were in Ontario (Worrell, 1985). The principles of the People First groups are similar to those of the Independent Living movement: "Independence is what self-advocacy is all about - people speaking out for themsleves" (Worrell, 1985, p. 39). In this sense, self-advocacy goes beyond the principle of normalization.

The basic principles of the Independent Living movement are *choice, flexibility, and control* for disabled consumers in their own lives. These principles were included in the approach described in this chapter to measuring the quality of life of persons with a developmental disability. In particular, the team wanted an approach that would allow unique perspectives on life goals to be respected rather than have a standardized view of quality of life against which everyone is measured. As well, the team tried to devise an approach allowing the perspective of persons with developmental disabilites to be heard, concerning the quality of their own lives, rather than an approach that mainly relied on outside observers. While there is a role for significant others to provide information about a person's quality of life, the views, needs and wishes of each person with a developmental disability must be given priority in any assessment of that person's quality of life (Goode, 1990).

## Being, Belonging, and Becoming

The model of quality of life used by the team was a synthesis of several sources, but can be described as an existential-humanistic approach. This approach "involves centering upon the *existing* person and emphasizes the human being as...*emerging, becoming*" (May, 1969, p. 11). "We *are* our choices," says May, "within the limits of our given world" (p.13). As well, existenialist-humanistic psychology is about *being* and *non-being*. May adds, "...*without* some concepts of "being and "non-being" we cannot even understand our most commonly used psychological mechanisms" (p. 15-16).

At the most fundamental level, to speak about a human life implies the existence of a person in a "lived body" (Leder, 1990). A detailed description of the phenomenology of embodiment, especially when that body has been labelled "disabled," was beyond the scope of this project. (For a discussion of this area see, for example, Merleau-Ponty, 1968 and Zaner, 1981.) It is important to remember, however, that human life is lived within a particular body, a body that is a communicative medium for both the person and for others (O'Neill, 1989). Yet, our existence is not merely physical. Besides a particular body, individuals develop psychological structures that we sometimes refer to as "identity," "self," or "personality." It is this *person* that is in the world. Moreover, this person is generally in the world with others; we are all "persons in relation" (MacMurray, 1957). Finally, as we develop from childhood to adulthood, the world becomes "funded with meaning" (Becker, 1971). Becker describes four levels of meaning that individuals may construct for themselves:

1.  The first, most intimate, basic level, is what we could call the Personal one. It is level of what one is oneself, her "true" self, her special gift or talent, what she feels herself to be deep down inside, the person she talks to when she is alone, the secret heroine of her inner scenario.

2.  The second or next highest level we could call the Social. It represents the most immediate extension of oneself to a select few intimate others: one's spouse, her friends, her relatives, perhaps even her pets.

3.  The third and next higher level we could call the Secular. It consists of symbols of allegiance at a greater personal distance and often higher in power and more compelling: the corporation, the party, the nation, science, history, humanity.

4.  The fourth and highest level of power and meaning we would call the Sacred. It is the invisible and unknown level of power, the insides of nature, the source of creation, God. (Becker, 1971, p. 186)

We have referred, in our conceptual framework, to some of these aspects of human life (physical, psychological, and spiritual) as BEING.

However, Being is always experienced in a particular context, a certain time, place and culture. This social specificness of being a person is of critical analytic importance.

Most individuals grow up learning a particular set of cultural, personal, and linguistic experiences. These experiences become part of individuals, part of their unconscious framework for reacting to the world. Important to this experience of context is living with others, often in a group of other human beings which is commonly labelled "family." From those who interact closely with them, individuals learn their idioms, behaviours, and limits. Part of being a fully functioning, healthy human is to be accepted and rooted in a community, an aspect of life referred to here as BELONGING.

Life is not simply a script in which persons play prescribed roles. Most individuals also have some room to make decisions about their lives. In Canadian society, at least, there is an ethic of giving control to adults in such matters as choosing a mate, where to live, what kind of work to do, and what type of education to acquire. Individuals do have pasts and roots, but it is also possible to change direction, to forge a new path. The things people choose to do in their lives make them who they are, and who they will become. This unfolding aspect of life is referred to here as BECOMING.

There is a certain healthy tension between BELONGING and BECOMING in most people's lives. In *The Duality of Human Existence*, Bakan (1964) refers to these two directions as "community" vs. "achievement." The French sociologist, Pierre Bourdieu (1977) names these concepts "habitus" and "project," while Sullivan (1984) translates habitus as "socialization" and project as "transformation." Dewey (1958) uses the terms "undergoing" and "doing" to describe these two aspects of life, and the necessary balance between them.

But as Sullivan (1984) points out, the

aspects of life associated with what have been referred to here as BELONGING and BECOMING can be experienced as alienating or exclusionary. Individuals can be raised in particular places that stigmatize and reject their human status. Similarly, any individual's life can be controlled by others. At the core of this issue is an individual's power and relations with others. Persons with developmental disabilities often lack any degree of privacy, because things are often done for them, because they may be the subject of intensive "programming," or simply because other people often see them as "different."

There is a need for consensual validation through meaningful relationships within a human community for a person to maintain an identity. The "emergent properties of relationships" (Duck and Lea, 1983) include similarity, where a person identifies with someone else; intimacy, where a person comes close to someone else through close contact; and public identity, where a person is seen in a relationship with others. People with developmental disabilities often lack these steps in developing relationships. For persons with developmental disabilities, there is often a psychological distance from non-disabled people over which they have little control. This overabundance of "being-for-others" (Sartre, 1965), the result of the control of the body by institutional forces and by the lack of privacy caused by being different, can be manifested in a weak sense of self or a loss of identity. The phenomenology of being an object regarded negatively by others can have a strong influence on the self-image of the developing child with a disability (Goffman, 1963).

The power of others to create a sense of alienation from oneself is captured by Zaner in the following quote:

> Realizing that I have been "looked at" by the Other, I realize (become to) myself as a *thing*....The otherness of my own body thus suffuses its sense of intimacy; what is intimately mine is yet a heaviness, a mass having its own weight and seemingly alien nature. With impaired, maimed, or mortally ill persons; it seems that the latter sense becomes pronounced, almost as if the life of the person were dissipating, dissolving in the very "look" and peculiar stillness of glance, gesture and body attitudes....Other-than-me, my body or even one of its members seems somehow to lose its intimacy, and with that my sense of caring for it. (Zaner, 1981, p. 56.)

Thus, persons with disabilities are in danger of being doubly alienated from the world. Not only is it difficult for them to develop a sense of personal empowerment, but also, because they are often under the control of professionals or their parents throughout most of their lives, individuals with developmental disabilities often do not interact fully with the surrounding culture of every-day life. Using the field of medicine and criminology as examples, Foucault (1979, 1980) refers to the growth of professional control over the lives of identified groups as "bio-technico-power:"

> Bio-power is the increasing ordering in all realms under the guise of improving the welfare of the individual and the population. To the genealogist this order reveals itself to be a strategy, with no

one directing it and everyone increasingly emeshed in it whose only end is the increase of power and order itself...[Foucault] shows us how our culture attempts to normalize individuals through increasingly rationalized means, by turning them into meaningful subjects and docile objects. (Dreyfus and Rabinow, 1982, pp. xxii-xxiii).

In the case of persons with a disability, bio-power has been felt in many ways. Historically, developmentally-disabled persons have been confined in institutions, subjected to involuntary sterilization, drugs and electric shock, restricted from marriage and voting through legislation, and denied access to normal schooling. All have been many times the object of the "medical gaze" (Foucault, 1973) and examination by other professionals. A person with a disability often lacks any degree of privacy, because things are done for him or her, because he or she may be the subject of intensive "programming," or simply because in public people continually stare (Diamond, 1981). A developing sense of personal power is critical for the development of a healthy self-concept (Becker, 1964), and to acting with intentionality (Shotter, 1974).

For these reasons, the research team took the perspective that the conceptualization and measurement of quality of life must emphasize the *empowerment* of people with developmental disabilities, and not serve as a vehicle to increase the power and control of others over the lives of persons with disabilities. Empowerment is not a state which one reaches, but is "a process of change" whereby the persons who are empowered gain real control over their own lives (Lord, 1991).

The empahsis on empowerment and individual control meant that this project was *not* about what has been referred to in the literature as *quality assurance*. The quality of individual people's lives does not *necessarily* reflect the quality of resources that are available, the quality of the care that is given, or the quality of the services that are provided. These things obviously influence how good one's life is, but they cannot, by themselves, *make* a person have a "good life." They can provide opportunities, but even the best resources, care and services do not always result in people considering their lives to have improved.

## Need for a Multidimensional Approach

Bredo and Feinberg (1982) outline three main branches in social science research: positivistic approaches, interpretative approaches, and critical approaches. These approaches differ with respect to the relationship between the "knower" and the "known." Positivistic research, such as behavioristic or statistical approaches to research, "assumes a strict subject-object dichotomy in which the knower is uninvolved with the known" (Bredo and Feinberg, 1982, p.5). An interpretative approach, such as phenomenology, hermeneutics, or narrative analysis "views knower and known as being much more closely involved with one another" (Bredo and Feinberg, 1982, p.6). With this approach one's expectations are used as a "sounding board" to interpret the phenomena under study. With critical theories "the knowledge generated is a part of a process of mutual growth or evolution on the part of both parties. The researcher is inevitably an agent of change or a reinforcer of the status quo" (Bredo and Feinberg, 1982, p.6).

Each of these three approaches to knowledge has a particular "human interest" (Habermas, 1982). For positivistic research this interest may be *explanation, control or prediction*, for interpretative approaches the goal is *understanding*, while for critical inquiry the purpose is *emancipation*. While the research team members intended that their approach would be emancipatory, they also recognized that any approach could be used as an instrument of power over others — what David Goode (1991) has referred to as a potential "tyranny of quality of life."

Traditional positivistic psychometric approaches to measurement are based on several assumptions (Argyris, Putnam, and Smith, 1987): (a) agreement that reality exists "out there" and can be measured by observers using a common yardstick; (b) the measures developed and applied have equal meaning and appropriateness for most subjects; (c) the responses elicited from the subjects of inquiry are accurate and truthful; (d) the commonalities among the subjects are more important than the differences; and (e) the focus of inquiry has been well delineated before carrying out of the actual study.

It was apparent to the research team that a study of the quality of life of persons with developmental disabilities would not fit with the above assumptions. The assumption that quality of life of individuals exists solely "out there," independent of the environmental context ran counter to the conceptual framework that was developed. Rather, quality of life was seen as an outcome of unique interactions between each individual and his or her environment.

Second, it was strongly felt that the uniqueness of persons with developmental disabilities, their specific interests, strengths and limitations, and their highly-individualized life situations required recognition. What was needed was to develop measures which could be adaptable and sensitive to these highly individualized life situations. Third, the limited research on quality of life of persons with developmental disabilities suggested problems with reliability of responses when relying *solely* upon traditional objective measures such as self-report or standardized interview protocols (Heal and Sigelman, 1990). Fourth, the measures needed to be able to capture the diversity among individuals' lives as well as the commonalities. Finally, although it was considered that the important dimensions of the lives of persons with developmental disabilities had been outlined, the investigators felt a responsibility to allow the communication of unique, unexpected aspects of individuals' lives.

Naturalistic observation methods used in qualitative research (Lincoln and Guba, 1985) deal with many of the concerns outlined above. These approaches allow for the identification and documentation of the unique life circumstances of individuals. The use of open-ended descriptive approaches focuses primarily upon the processes of the topic of interest — quality of life of persons with developmental disabilities — and allows for the uniqueness of individuals to emerge. Importantly, open-ended approaches allow for the communication of life's successes and trials; this is an important part of the present approach to defining and measuring quality of life of persons with developmental disabilities.

The naturalistic approach has shortcomings as well. These occur primarily in communicating generalizable findings from a sample to a population and the testing of specific hypotheses developed from policy, theory, or practical concerns.

The approach that was developed for this project balances the need for objective communicable data with a desire for developing a means of communicating the unique life circumstances of persons with developmental disabilities, and the strengths and weaknesses of both approaches. The measures are an attempt to consider individual differences in perception of importance as applied to various components of the person's immediate and social environments. The investigators also recognized that perceptions of a person's quality of life could differ between reporters (parents vs. the individual vs. the support worker vs. the observer). These differences would not be seen as reflecting "measurement error" as much as divergence in valid perceptions among individuals.

Based upon the acceptance of multiple sources of data, multiple types of data, and the various components of quality of life, the data to be collected would be communicated in the forms of complex profiles for each individual. These data could also be aggregated upward for population estimation and determination of trends and hypothesis testing.

## Defining quality of life

*Quality of life* is a term used in various ways for various purposes, although its meanings are roughly associated with "the good life." In spite of quality of life being an elusive concept (Taylor & Bogdan, 1990), it is a term that has become widely known and is being used in many fields (e.g. health promotion, rehabilitation, psychology, medicine) and in many countries.

A review of the literature indicates many measures of quality of life have been developed but few definitions and detailed conceptualizations of this idea have been offered. Furthermore, developers of quality of life instruments frequently do not state whether their measures have a particular conceptual foundation. This is the case for quality of life measures designed with reference to the general population as well as for quality of life of persons with developmental disabilities. Landesman (1986) recognized the problems this presented for meaningfully assessing the quality of life of persons with developmental disabilities and called for answers to several relevant questions, including the following:

(a) What does quality of life mean? What ideas does this concept encompass? (b) How can the concepts of quality of life and personal life satisfaction be operationally defined? (d) What sets of environmental variables are most likely to enhance the quality of life for different types of individuals at different times in their lives? (Landesman, 1986, p. 142.)

A number of authors, taking different approaches, have attempted to address these questions by defining and/or conceptualizing quality of life for persons with developmental disabilities (for example, see Shalock, 1990). However, these approaches often do not emphasize the relative significance to the person of various aspects of his or her life, nor the degree of choice a person has in each of these areas. The new definition and conceptualization of quality of life presented in this chapter do emphasize these important dimensions of quality of life as well as the holistic nature of persons, and the uniqueness of quality of life as experienced by each individual. Thus, this new approach provides a substantive basis for the measurement of quality of life for individuals with developmental disabilities.

The research team developed a new definition of quality of life as follows: *Quality of Life is the degree to which the person enjoys the important possibilities of his or her life.* The term 'possibilities' refers to the constraints and opportunities within a person's life. In real life situations with persons with developmental disabilities, this definition can be simplified to — *How good is your life for you?* This simplified version was developed in consultation with developmentally disabled consumers and was found, through pilot testing, to be an effective method of conveying the essence of the concept of quality of life.

The definition refers to "possibilities," of which there are two types — those which are determined and those which are created. Determined possibilities are not under a person's direct control (e.g., a person's gender, race, and inherited physical disorders, historical time of birth, etc.). Created possibilities are those over which the person has some degree of control. This includes the decisions and choices a person makes (e.g., choosing friends, deciding to take a holiday in a particular destination). As well, determined and created possibilities interact with one another. For instance, a person may be born into a middle class family (determined possibility) but the choices he or she makes about educational programs and jobs (created possibilities) may result in a lower-level socioeconomic status.

Many possibilities occur at any given point in a person's life. However, a person can deal with only some of these possibilities at any particular time. Of these possibilities that a person can deal with, some will take on importance or meaning for him or her. These important possibilities are the ones that have significance for the person and his or her quality of life.

Quality of life needs to be a flexible and dynamic construct in that the conditions of life and their relative importance differ from one person to another. No two individuals have the same life possibilities by chance, heredity, and endowment nor do they create the same possibilities through the choices and decisions that they make in their lives. As well, neither an individual's environments nor his or her constellation of attitudes, values, beliefs, and interests remain static over time. Thus, it is likely that new life possibilities will arise for the individual and some older ones will recede. Furthermore, the basis on which the individual evaluates both the importance or meaning of these possibilities and the degree of enjoyment associated with his or her various life possibilities is likely to change over time (Velche, 1991).

## Defining the Components of Quality of Life

After developing the philosophical assumptions of the approach and the definition of quality of life, the research team then developed the conceptual framework for measuring quality of life. The components of Being, Belonging and Becoming were each divided into three subcomponents, giving nine distinct areas for assessment. The major components and subcomponents were defined for the purpose of measurement as follows:

1. *Being.* The Being component of quality of life is concerned with the most basic personal aspects of "who one is" as an individual. It refers to parts of the self that are essential to all functioning human beings. For the puposes of assessing quality of life, the team divided Being into three subcomponents: physical, psychological, and spiritual being.

2. *Physical Being.* This subcomponent incorporates the individual's physical person and well-being. It includes physical aspects of health, nutrition, exercise, personal hygiene and grooming, clothing, and overall physical appearance.

3. *Psychological Being.* This subcomponent encompasses the person's psychological well-being. It includes the person's psychological health and adjustment, that is, cognitions, feelings, and evaluations concerning the self (e.g., self-esteem, self-concept, and view of his/her own sexuality), and sense of control over him/herself.

4. *Spiritual Being.* This subcomponent embodies the individual's own personal values, personal standards to live by, and spiritual beliefs. Spiritual beliefs may or may not be religious in nature (i.e., characteristic of a formally organized religion).

5. *Belonging.* This component refers to how well the person fits and is accepted in the social, physical, and resource-related aspects of his or her various environments. Accordingly, the Belonging aspect of quality of life consists of three subcomponents: physical, social, and community belonging.

6. *Physical Belonging.* This subcomponent incorporates the links which the person has with his/her physical environments (i.e., home, neighbourhood, school, workplace and larger community). Personal safety and having a private, physical space of one's own are also included here.

7. *Social Belonging.* This subcomponent encompasses the bonds which the person has with his/her social environments. This includes the sense of belonging with and acceptance by his/her intimate other, family, friends, co-workers, others in his/her neighbourhood and community as well as members of his/her cultural (or sub-cultural) or ethnic group.

8. *Community Belonging.* This subcomponent embodies the connections which the person has with various resources typically available to members of his/her community and society. This includes availability of information about and access to sources of adequate income, employment, educational and recreational programs, health and social services, as well as community events and activities.

9. *Becoming.* This component is concerned with the purposeful activities the individual does in order to achieve his/her own goals, hopes, and aspirations (i.e., both immediate and long-term). Included here are the leisure activities

that the individual engages in as a means of "re-creating" himself/herself. The Becoming aspect of quality of life was divided into the following subcomponents: practical, leisure, and personal growth activities.

10. *Practical Activities.* This subcomponent encompasses practical, purposeful activities in a variety of areas. It includes domestic chores, paid work, going to school, volunteer activities, other activities that are directed towards helping others, and seeking out services helpful to the individual (e.g., health or social services).

11. *Leisure Activities.* This subcomponent embodies leisure-time activities that do not necessarily have an obvious instrumental (practical) value. These activities serve to promote relaxation, stress reduction, and "re-creation" of the person's sense of balance between work and play in his/her life. Included here are activities of relatively short duration (e.g., a game of ping pong, a stroll through a neighbourhood park, or a social visit with friends) or the cluster of activities of longer duration usually associated with taking a vacation.

12. *Personal Growth Activities.* This subcomponent includes activities that foster the development of the individual's own knowledge and skills. A person usually engages in these activities in order to learn new information or a new skill, to enhance an existing skill, explore new things, or to solve a problem. Both formal and informal educational and learning activities are relevant here.

## Methods of Data Collection

After the conceptual framework described above had been developed, the research team then created a set of procedures for assessing a person's quality of life, based on the three identified components of living — *Being, Belonging, and Becoming.* The investigators faced the task of designing a measurement approach which would capture the richness and complexity of quality of life of persons with developmental disabilities. Yet, the practical objectives of the project had to be met, such as providing generalizable inferences concerning the quality of life of persons with developmental disabilities and providing a means of testing specific hypotheses concerning influences upon quality of life.

The measurement approach met three important and immediate goals. The first was to provide indicators of the personal characteristics, social environments, and immediate communities of persons with developmental disabilities. These indicators would describe the quality of life of populations of persons with developmental disabilities. That is, the Ministry of Community and Social Services required measures which could be used to evaluate its Multi-Year Plan, the provision of services throughout the province by both government and agencies, and the efficacy of its efforts to improve the quality of life of recipients of Ministry support. The second goal was to develop measures that could be used by agencies and service providers to monitor, evaluate, and improve the services provided to clients. In reality, these agencies frequently provide the most immediate source of resources to persons with developmental disabilities. The third, and perhaps most important, goal was to define measures that could provide the basis for describing the unique life situations of individual persons with developmental disabilities. With respect to this last goal, the measures had to provide a vehicle for capturing, communicating, and documenting the struggles, successes, and disappointments experienced on an ongoing basis by individuals with developmental disabilities. In principle, we tried to develop measures that would allow persons to communicate the essence of their lives.

The principal technique developed by the research team to profile the quality of life of an individual with a developmental disability is a rating scheme for data gathered concerning each of the subcomponents of Being, Belonging, and Becoming. The rating scheme provides, for each subcomponent, three *main* judgments of quality of life: *very acceptable, acceptable,* and *problematic.* There will also be two additional ratings which will draw attention to extraordinary cases: *model* and *unacceptable.* Thus, the following profile could be obtained for the Being themes for an individual based upon their self-report:

Being:  Physical        -   acceptable
        Psychological -   very acceptable
        Spiritual       -   problematic

## Sources of Information

The profiles of ratings are obtained through data from a variety of persons familiar with the individual whose quality of life is being assessed. For any one individual these sources include: (a) the individual, (b) at least one close caregiver or family member, and (c) observations of an interviewer specifically trained to use the devel-

oped measures with persons with a developmental disability. Information may also come from such sources as professional caregivers and agency personnel, parents, friends, roommates, neighbours and others. The specific sources of collection need to be determined by the life situation of each individual. The data collector is also a source of information concerning the person's quality of life. Review of consumer records can also be considered, if full informed consent is given both by the person in question and by the family or agency where the records are kept. *However, it should be noted that in the event of conflict among the various accounts of a person's life, primacy is given to the self-reports, especially when assessment data could be the basis of making life changes for an individual.*

In the next phase of the study, information will be collected using three main sources of data: Self-Report Measures, Report-By-Others Measures, and Observer Measures (see Table 4-1). The specific methods, for the Self-Report Measures, are interview, diary, checklist, and observation; for the Report-By-Others Measures, also interview, diary, checklist, and observation; and for the Observer Measures, checklists for both environmental and personal characteristics. Except for the environmental checklist, these measures allow for ratings based on each of the nine subcomponents — three aspects each of Being, Belonging, and Becoming—contained in the conceptual framework of quality of life.

The organizing theme of these methods is the collection of data that reflects how important each subcomponent of quality of life is to the individual (Importance), and how satisfied each person is with each subcomponent (Enjoyment). Also collect-

### Table 4-1. Types of measures used to gather data for assessing QOL

| Type of measure | Measured by | Format | Product |
| --- | --- | --- | --- |
| 1. Self-report measures | Interviewee, but administered by interviewer. | Interview Diary Checklist Observation | • quality of life sub-scores and composite quality of life score. <br> • Anecdotal data. |
| 2. Report-by others measures | Other person who knows interviewee well (e.g. family member; service worker) | Interview Diary Checklist Observation | • quality of life sub-scores and composite quality of life score. <br> • Anecdotal data. |
| 3. Observer measures | Outside observer with some access to interviewee or service provider of family member. | Checklist Description | • quality of life sub-scores and composite quality of life score. <br> • Anecdotal data. |

ed are aspects of the extent of control that the person has over each subcomponent of quality of life (Control), as well as the possibilities for enhancement or change in these areas (Potential Opportunities).

Data collection requires on-site visits of at least one day duration (but perhaps longer) for each individual. During this time the data collector observes and notes the occurrences and situations related to the individual under assessment. The observations are noted through a modified ethnographic approach and used in the assessment of the quality of life ratings.

The people responsible for collecting these data should have experience working with persons with developmental disabilities. These persons may be seconded from agencies and trained in the various data collection procedures. Eventually, these instruments may be used by trained service providers, parents, and peers of those with developmental disabilities.

## Adaptations for Persons Who Use Nonverbal Communication Systems

Persons with developmental disabilities have communication skills that vary widely. Most express their own ideas verbally, but others communicate in alternative ways. Those who communicate by using formal but nonverbal systems, such as Blissymbolics or technical devices, may be interviewed in that system of communication. For people with marginal formal communication skills, interviewers may supplement techniques used for people who do not use formal communication systems. For example, people who do not use formal communication systems express their pleasure and displeasure in informal ways (Goode, 1982).

Nonverbal methods that are used to indicate their feelings of pleasure and displeasure should be observed and recorded for each person. A close family member or caregiver might suggest some of these ways. It is particularly important, when assessing the quality of life of people without formal communication systems, to pay close attention to how *frequently* things that they enjoy and dislike occur in their lives. Observation and participant observation techniques are most useful for the "interviewer" to make quality of life judgements about people who do not communicate using formal systems.

## Conclusions

A sense of being, having a connection with others, and developing to one's own potential are important to all humans. The approach described in this chapter provides a conceptual framework for the measurement of quality of life which emphasizes the view that a person has about his or her own life, while, at the same time, acknowledging the value of supplementary information from the perspectives of trained observers and other people who know the person well. It also recognizes the importance of people's sense of control in various areas of their lives, and emphasizes that the quality of life of people with developmental disabilities, and that of other people consists of the same essential elements. It does not assume that disability, by itself, is necessarily a reason for increased or decreased quality of life, and provides a method for measuring quality of life of people with developmental disabilities that recognizes the individuality of each person.

Persons with developmental disabilities should not have to earn the privilege of belonging with others; rather, opportunities to be part of the community should be readily available. The extent to which individuals participate in their family, neighbourhood, and other aspects of community life, including vocational, leisure and recreational opportunities, is relevant to quality of life. The conceptual framework and the instrument package which follow from it emphasize this connection with others and the community.

As well, a person becomes an individual partly through the choices he or she makes. Physical, social or mental disadvantages do not rule out the possibility of maximizing one's potential. The quality of life framework developed in this project addresses the choices one makes in the process of defining what the important elements are in becoming one's self. But a person also becomes an individual through responding to conditions and opportunities that arise in his or her environment. Thus, the approach to quality of life presented here takes into account the potential opportunities that are perceived to occur in people's lives and that are essential for making responsible choices. This is not an attempt to categorize, classify or compare one individual with others. Rather, it is an attempt to understand the circumstances as well as the perceptions of individuals about the way they experience their being, belonging and becoming.

## Notes

For further information, contact Dr. Gary Woodill, School of Early Childhood Education, Ryerson Polytechnical Institute, 350 Victoria St., Toronto, Ontario, Canada M5B 2K3

# References

Argyris, C., Putnam, R. and Smith, D. (1987). *Action science*. San Francisco: Jossey Bass.

Bakan, D. (1964). *The duality of human existence: Isolation and communion in western man.* Boston: Beacon.

Becker, E. (1964). *Revolution in psychiatry*. New York: The Free Press.

Becker, E. (1971). *The birth and death of meaning,* 2nd ed. New York: The Free Press.

Bourdieu, P. (1977) *Outline of a Theory of Practice.* London: Cambridge University Press.

Bredo, E. and Feinberg, W. (Eds.) (1982) *Knowledge and Values in Social and Educational research.* Philadelphia: Temple Univ. Press.

Brown, R. (1988). *Quality of life for handicapped people.* London: Croom Helm.

Carpenter, S. (1991) The Canadian model of independent living centres: trends and issues. *Rehabilitation Digest, 22,* 3-7

DeJong, G. (1979) Independent Living: From social movement to analytic paradigm. *Archives of Physical Medicine and Rehabilitation,* 60(10), 435-446.

Dewey, J. (1958) *Experience and Nature.* (first published 1925). New York: Dover Books.

Diamond, S. (1981). Growing up with parents of a handicapped child: a handicapped person's perspective. In J. Paul (Ed.), *Understanding and Working with Parents of Children with Special Needs.* New York: Holt, Rinehart and Winston.

Dreyfus, H. and Rabinow, P. (1982). *Michel Foucault: Beyond Structuralism and Hermeneutics.* Chicago: University of Chicago Press.

Duck, S. and Lea, M. (1983). Breakdown of relationahips as a threat to personal identity. In G.M. Breakwell (Ed.), *Threatened Identities.* London: Wiley.

Foucault, M. (1973). *The Birth of the Clinic: An Archaeology of Medical Perception.* New York: Vintage House.

Foucault, M. (1979). *Discipline and Punish: The Birth of the Prison.* New York: Vintage.

Foucault, M. *Power/Knowledge* New York: Pantheon

Goffman, E. (1963) *Stigma.* Englewood Cliffs, N.J.: Prentice-Hall.

Goode, D. (1982) Socially produced identities, intimacy, and the problem of competence among the retarded. In L. Barton and S. Tomlinson (Eds.) *Special Education and Social Interests.* London: Croom Helm.

Goode, D. (1990). Thinking about and discussing quality of life. In R. Schalock (Ed.), *Quality of life: Perspectives and issues.* Washington, D.C.: American Association on Mental Retardation.

Goode, D. (1991) Personal communication.

Habermas, Jurgen. (1982) *Knowledge and Human Interests.*

Heal, L. and Sigelman, C. (1990). Methodological issues in measuring the quality of life of individuals with mental retardation. In R. Schalock (Ed.), *Quality of life: Perspectives and issues.* Washington D.C.: American Association on Mental Retardation.

Landesman, S. (1986). Quality of life and personal satisfaction: Definition and measurement issues. *Mental Retardation, 24,* 141-143.

Leder, D. (1990). *The absent body.* Chicago: University of Chicago Press.

Lincoln, Y. and Guba, E. (1985). *Naturalistic inquiry.* Newbury Park, CA: Sage.

Lord, John. (1991) *Lives in Transition: the process of personal empowerment.* Kitchener, Ontario: Centre for Research and Education.

MacMurray, J. (1957) *The self as agent.* London: Faber and Faber.

May, Rollo. (1969) The emergence of existential psychology. In Rollo May (Ed.) *Existential Psychology.* New York: Random House.

McCreary, B., Oullette-Kuntz, H., Minnes, P. and Stanton, B. (1988). *QUOLIS.* Manuscript, Queen's University, Kingston, ON.

Merleau-Ponty, J. (1968). *The visible and the invisible.* Evanston, IL: Northwestern University Press.

O'Neill, John (1989). *The communicative body.* Evanston, IL.: Northwestern University Press.

Ontario Ministry of Community and Social Services (1987). *Challenges and opportunities: Community living for people with developmental handicaps.* Toronto: Queen's Printer for Ontario.

Rootman, I., Raphael, D., Shewchuk, D., Renwick, R., Friefeld, S., Garber, M., Talbot, Y. and Woodill, G. (1992) *Development of an approach and an instrument package to measure the quality of life of persons with developmental disabilities.* Toronto: Centre for Health Promotion.

Sartre, J. *Being and Nothingness.* Secaucus, N.J.: Citadel Press, 1965.

Schalock, R. (1990). *Quality of life: Perspectives and issues.* Washington, D.C.: American Association on Mental Retardation.

Shotter, J. The development of personal powers. In M. Richards (Ed.), *The Integration of a Child into a Social World.* London: Cambridge University Press, 1974, pp.215-244.

Simmons, H. (1982). *From Asylum to Welfare.* Toronto: NIMR.

Sullivan, E. (1984). *A critical psychology: Interpretation of the personal world.* New York: Plenum.

Taylor, S. and Bogdan, R. (1990). Quality of life and the individual perspective. In R. Schalock (Ed.), *Quality of life: Perspectives and issues.* Washington, DC: American Association on Mental Retardation.

Velche, D. (1991) Personal communication.

Wolfensberger, W. (1983). Social role valorization: A proposed new term for the principle of normalization. *Mental Retardation,* 21,234-239.

Wolfensberger, W. (1972). *The principle of normalization in human services.* Toronto: National Institute on Mental Retardation.

Worrell, B. (1985) People First: a perspective. *Canadian Journal on Mental Retardation,* 35(3), 37-42.

Zaner, R. (1981). *The context of self: A phenomenological inquiry using medicine as a clue.* Athens, OH: Ohio University Press.

# 5• The View from Australia: Australian legislation, service delivery and quality of life

by Trevor R. Parmenter, Macquarie University, Sydney, Australia
Robert Cummins, Deakin University, Melbourne, Australia,
Anthony J. Shaddock, University of Canberra, Canberra, Australia,
Roger Stancliffe, Macquarie University, Sydney, Australia

This chapter will present an historical development of Australian services for people with disabilities in the context of disability legislation that has supported the funding of services and provided guidelines for their delivery. It will provide a review of research that has examined the effects various government policies have had upon program outcomes for people with disabilities, especially ways in which these policies have affected the quality of their lives.

The philosophies and principles that have driven the evaluation of Australian disability programs have not been dissimilar to those of many other Western countries. While there have been quite strenuous attempts to demonstrate that changes in service delivery have led to significant improvements in the quality of life of people with disabilities, it will be shown that many of the advances have been more apparent than real. Despite what appear to be honest attempts to give people with disabilities more control and say in the way they conduct their lives, there is in Australia a superficial grasp of what quality of life really means. Perhaps in our efforts to provide better program outcomes for people with disabilities we have overlooked an injunction provided by Knoll (1990, p.235) who suggested that "the definition of program standards and quality is a process that transcends empiricism. This process ultimately appeals to the fundamental values of society."

The vast Australian continent (77 million square kilometres) is populated by approximately 17m people — nearly 65 per cent of whom live in the capital cities of the six states and two territories. The majority of the population live in two coastal regions, the largest along the south eastern seaboard and the smaller along the south western coast. Almost three quarters of the Australian land mass is relatively uninhabited.

Australia has a federal system of government with the six individual states and two territories having their own legislatures; a situation somewhat similar to Canada and the United States. However, the Australian parliamentary structures are based upon the British Westminster system.

Despite its relative geographical isolation, Australia has been significantly influenced by the philosophical and legislative developments in the field of disability services experienced in older and more populous western countries. Consequently, similar patterns of service delivery and community attitudes towards people with disabilities have emerged in Australia's relatively short history of white settlement spanning two hundred years.

Typically, the presence of a disability was viewed as a tragedy and something to be avoided. Not surprisingly, the person with the disability was identified primarily as being synonymous with the impairment. Hence the person with the disability incorporated the negative connotations that were ascribed to the condition evidenced by the derogative terms such as "the retarded", "the epileptic", "the cerebral palsied", etc.

With the emergence of welfare systems by the federal and state governments, the needs of people with disabilities and their families were recognized through the provision of invalid pensions, rehabilitation programs, nursing homes and, for those more severely disabled, institutional care.

It is noteworthy that the Australian Federal Government enacted legislation in 1910 to provide the first invalid pension scheme for people with disabilities. The Social Services Act of 1947-77 broadened the range of pensions, benefits and allowances and led to the establishment of the Commonwealth Rehabilitation Service. This Service essentially provided a medically oriented rehabilitation program to people with physical or sensory impairments in a number of large hospital-like centers situated in the capital cities of the various states.

The role nongovernment agencies could play in the provision of services was recognized by the provision in 1967 of Federal Government funds that subsidized the establishment of educational, residential, vocational and day activity programs.

There was little, if any, recognition that the people with the disability had the right to comment upon the types of services provided or, indeed, the impact the services were having upon their lives.

The combination of the welfare and charity models saw a rapid increase in congregate residential and vocational programs throughout Australia in the post World War II period; especially in the 1960s and 1970s. Nongovernment agencies were subsidized by the Federal Government on a $4 for $1 basis for capital expenses and between 50 and 100 per cent for salary costs. The introduction of the Handicapped Persons Welfare Assistance Act in 1974 extended the subsidies to activity therapy centers for people unable to be placed in sheltered workshops.

Despite one of the stated goals of sheltered employment being preparation for open employment, only a miniscule number of disabled workers ever transferred to regular community-based jobs. Prior to the 1980s there was little contemplation of community-based residential programs for people who were in the several large state conducted "mental hospitals," which catered for people with severe intellectual disability or psychiatric illness.

However, during the 1970s Australia was being influenced by a number of social and philosophical forces, including the world-wide emergence of the independent living movement for people with a physical disability and the growing acceptance of the normalization principle for people with intellectual disabilities as enunciated by Nirje (1969) and Wolfensberger (1980). The election of a reformist Federal Government in 1972 provided a change in the essentially conservative climate that had permeated the welfare services in Australia. A clear example of the reformist role the national government was to increasingly play in disability policy was in the area of special education where the Federal Government endorsed its commitment to the integration of children with disabilities into the mainstream educational systems by the provision of significant funds for teacher training, research, and the assumption by the government school system of nongovernment schools for children with severe disabilities. The proclamation of 1981 as the International Year of Disabled Persons provided a further impetus for governments, consumers and service providers to re-examine their attitudes towards the way services were being provided to people with disabilities.

Don Grimes, the Federal Minister for Community Services, in 1983, sponsored three initiatives that were to have a profound effect upon disability service delivery in Australia. The first was the funding of an Australian chapter of Disabled Peoples' International, the second the establishment of the Disability Advisory Council of Australia that consisted of people with disabilities or their advocates, and the third was the setting up of the Handicapped Programs Review.

The latter has been acclaimed as a landmark development in the Australian disability scene. The review which involved a nationwide consultation with people with disabilities, their families and service providers, culminated in the publication of *New Directions. Report of the Handicapped Programs Review* (Grimes, 1985) and the

enactment of the *Disability Services Act* (1986) that replaced earlier disability legislation.

The focus of the review and the subsequent Act was the promulgation of seven positive consumer outcomes as a basis for program development for people with disabilities. The key outcomes were:

- A place to live
- Paid employment
- Competence and self-reliance
- Community participation
- Security
- Choice
- Positive image

Grimes (1985, p. 13) summarised the focus of the review as follows:

The Commonwealth Government should set and promote philosophical directions to create an atmosphere and environment which will ensure equality of access and opportunity for all Australians, free from unnecessary restrictions on the individual.

People who have disabilities share the same rights as all other people. The recognition of equal rights of people with disabilities will be assisted by the provision of programs which are based on the needs of disabled consumers.

Not surprisingly, the Handicapped Programs Review has shown the paramount concerns of people with disabilities to be the achievement of particular goals such as choice, security and independence in their daily lives and the extent to which government provisions can facilitate the realisation of these goals.

It is clear that government activity should be focused to a greater extent on the consumer. The principle of positive consumer outcomes should be the basis of program development for people with disabilities. Such a principle will enable the development of a system which concentrates on the consumer. The particular consumer outcomes which are felt to be desirable will vary according to societal values at any given time and on the type of service being considered. Shaddock (1990) has conceptualized the consumer outcomes advocated by the *Review* within a model of quality of life that incorporates the relationship among philosophy, goals, services and outcomes along the lines of the work of Schalock (1987) (see Fig. 5-1).

These initiatives of the Federal Government in the 1980s were paralleled by similar developments in several of the Australian states and territories, either by way of major government reports and/or legislation. The developments at the state level were primarily concerned with residential accommodation for people with severe intellectual or psychiatric disabilities and resulted in a commitment to community-based living arrangements for numbers of these people, although large institutions for people with disabilities still exist throughout Australia.

*The Disability Services Act* (1986) basically took the initiative for the planning and execution of disability services away from the service providers and attempted to shift them to consumer groups although, as will be pointed out later, the shift was essentially from the service sector to the bureaucratic machinery of government. Incorporated into the Act were seven principles and fourteen objectives that were to become the basic yardstick against which programs and services would be measured (see Appendix 1). In a

statement to the Australian Senate in 1986 Senator Grimes commented:

The Principles recognise that people with disabilities are individuals who have an inherent right to respect for their human worth and dignity, and, irrespective of the origin, nature, type and degree of disability have the same fundamental rights as do other members of society. This applies to the realisation of individual potential; to involvement in decision-making in matters affecting their lives; to the pursuit of grievances and rights; and to services which offer the least restrictive alternative in the achievement of these ends.

The Objectives relate more directly to service delivery and cover aspects such as a focus on consumer benefits, integration of services into regular service structure where possible, and a community-based focus for specialist services where these are required.

Adoption of the Principles and Objectives will have some very practical consequences for service delivery. They will demand new standards of accountability by service providers to their disabled clients. They will require a new emphasis on the rights of privacy and confidentiality. They will herald a drawing to close of an era in which regrettably it has been possible for single organisations, in some cases without any accountability, to control the entire life of a person with a disability.

The legislation supported the following categories of service:

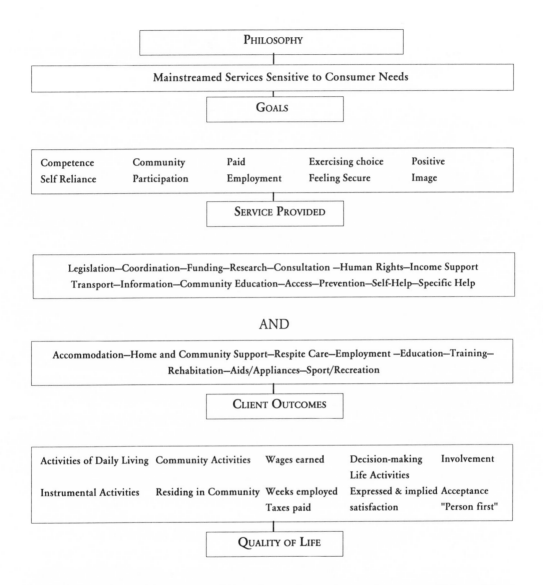

Figure 5-1. Relationships among philosophy, goals, services and outcomes (Adapted from Schalock, 1987, and Handicapped Persons' Review, 1985)

- Accommodation support;
- Respite care
- Supported employment
- Competitive employment, training and placement
- Independent living training

- Advocacy and information
- Recreation; and,
- Services for people with a print disability

Embodied in the Act was a timetable for existing service provisions to transit to the approved service types. The acceptance of the Act and its implementation for changes in the outcomes of programs was not without its difficulties. Opposition came in part from families who resisted the notions of community-based living and working programs and from service providers, especially sheltered workshop managers, who complained that there were insufficient funds being provided to enable them to establish community-based employment programs.

The Federal Government countered this resistance by sponsoring new vocational programs that emphasised community rather than sheltered environments. In spite of a very energetic program to extend these new services, they currently serve only a very small proportion of the disabled population. One of the contributing factors for this slow expansion, suggests Morath (1992), is that change has been bureaucratically driven rather than being a cooperative effort led by the service sector.

Two more recent initiatives have been the introduction of the Disability Reform Package and the Commonwealth/State Disability Agreement. The key components of the former, that came into operation late in 1991, include a replacement of the Invalid Pension by a Disability Support Pension and a cooperation between three Federal G overnments: Social Security; Employment, Education and Training; and Health, Housing, and Community Services, to provide a more integrated and streamlined service to people with disabilities. The major thrust of the Disability Reform Package is to enable more people with disabilities to enter or re-enter the workforce, with a specific emphasis upon younger disabled people.

The Commonwealth/State Disability Agreement is a joint agreement between the Federal, State and Territory Governments to streamline the delivery of disability services nationally. The key ingredient of the agreement is the assumption of the responsibility for funding vocational programs by the Federal Government and accommodation services by the respective State and Territory Governments. Before the Federal Government provides additional funding to the States and Territories, each has been required to enact complementary legislation to the *Disability Services Act* (1986), especially embracing the Principles and Objectives. The stated goal of the Agreement is to rationalize the delivery of services to people with disabilities and to enable these people and their families to be more involved in making decisions about how services work.

It is interesting that Senator Grimes, the architect of the *Disability Services Act* (1986), in reviewing the progress that Australia has made since its implementation, recently commented that there were two concerns about the processes that had ensued. These were concern about *rigidity* and concern about *over-caution*. He noted that,

> The Principles and Objectives that were set out in the Disability Services legislation in 1986 are as clear and as sensible as can be found in most places. But I must remind those involved...that they are but standards and guidelines to help us in the development of programs to assist people to fulfil their developments in society. They can never be immutable. (Grimes, 1992, p.5)

Grimes, who has recently returned to Australia having been the Ambassador to

The Netherlands, has recognized the negative side of the bureaucratically driven changes in disability services and the "political correctness" movement which has polarized the conservative and reformist streams of thinking.

In respect to the second concern of over-caution, Grimes has identified the excessive caution "which overtakes politicians and policy makers, and the bureaucratic process, for fear that they will be criticized when something fails" (Grimes, 1992, p6). Here Australia faces a critical problem. As one of the major driving forces for change and reform has been government and its bureaucracy, the issues have become highly politicized. Enterprising initiatives by individuals and individual organizations have been seen by some as attempts by governments to foster favored programs to the detriment of traditional service types.

To some extent there has been a reluctance by government agencies, both state and federal, to sponsor research programs that might examine the processes and outcomes of a variety of disability services. Driven by economic rationalist policies, governments have tended to employ economic and business consultancy firms for research programs. Grimes (1992) also noted this trend in his comment that,

> consultants are used to delay the implementation of programs when the real reasons are budgetary or even political....I have the greatest respect for accountants, economists and management specialists in their place but, if they are left alone to produce solutions to problems, they have an unfortunate tendency to forget they are dealing with

individuals and not just numbers or beans. (p.7)

There has been an economic emphasis in research especially evident in the vocational area, to the detriment of research that is both process and outcome oriented. Outcome research that has examined both the subjective and objective dimensions of quality of life has not been high on government agendas.

Nevertheless, there have been some enterprising pieces of research in Australia that have addressed the specific effects that programs have had upon the quality of the lives of people with disabilities. These encompass areas such as choice and decision-making; personal competence and self-reliance; and community participation. Following the model developed in Figure 5-1, each of these will be described and commented upon in the context of the emergence of disability policy in Australia.

## Choice

Having the right and the opportunity to make choices is expressed or implied in most conceptualizations of quality of life. These rights also feature in the Disability Services Act (1986) which emphasizes choice and participation in decision-making. The principles and objectives of the Act state that, like other members of Australian society, people with disabilities have the rights to "participate in decisions which affect their lives" (principle 5), to "the least restriction of their rights and opportunities" (principle 6) and to "pursuit of any grievance" (principle 7). Objectives 11 and 13 focus on the provision of advocacy support, where necessary, to assist with decision-making and participation in the planning and operation of services. This emphasis on self-determination has been paralleled by the growth of the self-advocacy movement in Australia in recent years. Advocacy is an approved service type under this Act and a number of self-advocacy groups, funded under the Disability Services Act, are in operation throughout Australia.

The legislation contains admirable statements of rights. However, Australian research into choice and decision-making has not always indicated that these rights are available in practice to people with an intellectual disability. In retrospect, one of the weaknesses of the Disability Services Act was the lack of enforcement mechanisms when consumers felt that their rights had been infringed. Unlike the United States, Australia does not have a system of constitutional rights and freedoms enforceable at law.

What has the Australian research told us about choice and decision-making by people with an intellectual disability?

### Choice in Institutional, Segregated and Community Settings

Kent (1990) found that staff ratings of residents' opportunities for decision-making were positively related to residents' self-expressed satisfaction with their life, thereby underlining the importance of choice in relation to satisfaction and subjective quality of life. She found that staff ratings of resident decision-making indicated that institutional residents were allowed to make decisions about fewer matters than those who lived in community group homes or at a farm-based residence (regarded as being between the institution and the community). Barlow and Kirby (1991) compared the residential satisfaction of adults with mild

intellectual disability living in an institution with former residents of the same institution now living unsupported in the community. Almost half of the institutional group lived in houses on the grounds of the institution and the institution was said to have "relatively few restrictions." Barlow and Kirby found few differences in satisfaction between the institutional and community groups, but community residents were significantly more satisfied with their *autonomy* than institution dwellers. In responding to a question about the best feature of their accommodation, almost twice as many community residents (47%) as the institutional group (26%) nominated "the freedom." Jiranek and Kirby (1990) reported somewhat similar findings concerning employment. They found that workers with an intellectual disability in open employment reported greater satisfaction with their freedom to make decisions at work than was the case for those who worked in a sheltered workshop. In another work-based study, Shaddock, Zilber, Guggenheimer, Dowse, Bennett and Browne (in press) observed differences in the number of choices made in different settings. Consumers in "community access" programs made significantly more choices than those in sheltered workshops and small businesses. Taken together, these findings suggest that choice and personal autonomy may be more available in integrated and community-based settings in Australia.

### Availability of Choice

There is a considerable variability in findings about choices available to people with an intellectual disability in community accommodation. This variation may relate to a number of variables including staff's perception of the consumer's intellectual ability, the gender of consumers and the actual freedom available in different settings. For example, a significant association has been found between staff's perception of the consumer's level of intellectual functioning and number of choices, with people considered to be more intellectually able being given, or making, more choices (Shaddock, Bennett, Dowse, Guggenheimer, Stancliffe, Zilber, 1992). Although no gender differences in relation to choice-making in residences were found in the above study, Shaddock, Zilber et al. (in press) found a significant association between gender and choice-making in work settings, with males making more choices than females.

Different settings appear to offer varying levels of freedom. For example, Shaddock, Bennett et al. (1992) surveyed decision-making by adults with intellectual disability in private homes, group homes, hostels and institutions. Carers were asked to observe and record who made day-to-day decisions during the week and on weekends. Although carers recorded that consumers made more decisions on the weekend about when to get up, whether to take a shower, when to come home, etc., it was evident that people were denied the opportunity to make their basic decisions in all settings. Similarly, Parmenter, Briggs and Sullivan (1991) reported low levels of choice availability amongst younger (11-21 years), recently deinstitutionalized individuals with low moderate or severe intellectual disability living in group homes. The majority of these consumers had little or no say about routine daily events such as meals, the clothes they wore, the television programs they watched, spending money, participating in group activities and telephoning

family and friends. On average across these six items 16 per cent of consumers had "a lot" of say and another 15 per cent had "some" say.

In contrast to these findings, Stancliffe (1993), using an almost identical assessment instrument (taken from Kishi, Teelucksingh, Zollers, Park-Lee & Meyer, 1988), reported much higher levels of choice for adults living in group homes or semi-independently in supported apartments. In each of the six routine decision-making areas listed above, Stancliffe's subjects almost all (an average of 87% across items) reported that they could make the choice whenever they wanted. A further 11 %, on average, said they could make these decisions sometimes. Independent staff ratings of these consumers on the same items yielded similar results. Another study, using a different assessment procedure, was conducted by Jenkinson, Copeland, Drivas, Scoon and Yap (in press), who looked at choices available to 20 adults with mild or moderate intellectual disability who lived in community group homes. They asked about specific aspects of seven major life areas, as well as family and advocate involvement in decision-making. Because of the somewhat different assessment procedure, Jenkinson et al.'s results are not as readily comparable with those reported above. Jenkinson et al. found an average of 55 per cent of consumers said they made the decisions (34% according to staff ratings).

Markedly different levels of everyday choice appear to have been available to the various groups studied above. Overall, the variability in findings suggests that community living by no means guarantees the availability of even quite mundane choices about one's daily life.

In Stancliffe's research, the areas in which people had less choice were those involving more major life decisions such as who to live with and what work to do. Similarly, when 140 choices observed in the Shaddock, Zilber et al. study were analyzed according to critical dimensions of choice, it was found that nearly all related to concrete here and now options and had minor life impact. Jenkinson et al. reported quite similar findings and, according to staff reports, the majority of consumers did not make their own decisions about their living situation and living companions (none were perceived to make this choice), choice of workplace and work done (18% made this choice) and choice of doctor (24%). It appears that people with an intellectual disability have differing degrees of access to different types of choices. These data provide support for the notion that such individuals are less likely to have the opportunity to make certain major life decisions independently.

One shortcoming of the Australian research on the availability of choice has been a lack of comparison data with the choices available to non-disabled Australians in similar circumstances. It seems self-evident that Parmenter et al.'s and Shaddock, Zilber et al.'s subjects had considerably less choice than the norm, but no data are available to determine whether the greater freedom of choice available to the adults living semi-independently studied by Stancliffe (1992, 1993) was within ordinary expectations. Stancliffe (1992) noted that many of his subjects who lived in apartments reported having limited choice about matters such as having pets, because their lease precluded it or they needed to seek their landlord's permission. This situation

was no different for non-disabled tenants in their building and it seemed as if their freedom to have a pet was no more restricted than their neighbors.

### Choice and Service Provision

In Australia, the predominant model of community living service is the group home, with full or part-time staffing. The limitations on choice imposed by this form of group living were explored in participant observation studies by Stancliffe (1991) and Bennett, Shaddock and Guggenheimer (1992). Both studies found that a range of individual preferences regarding meals, household routines, leisure, etc., could not be met because of the needs of other residents or of the group as a whole. Interpersonal conflict arose partly because moving into a group home brings with it the necessity of living with the others who already reside there, even if they are not the people with whom one would otherwise have chosen to live. Staff are faced with the difficult task of responding to the choices of more assertive individuals and encouraging choice-making by less assertive people in the home. Parmenter et al. (1991) reported that community excursions undertaken by group home residents were usually supervised *group* activities. This suggests that there was little room to indulge or develop individual preferences. Stancliffe (1992, 1993) found that there were a number of areas where residents of supported apartments had more choice than their counterparts in group homes.

Bennett et al. (1992) drew attention to issues associated with choice and "duty of care" in group homes. It is expected that staff will look after the health and welfare of consumers in group homes and promote choice. However, consumers may be unaware of the consequences of their choices so trial and error learning could be dangerous. There are no clear guidelines for carers about when it is legitimate to stand back, allowing the person to learn from consequences, and when they should intervene to protect the person (and themselves). It appears that the lack of clear directions for staff on the extent of their responsibilities in relation to consumer's choices and their consequences helps to maintain overly conservative practices in Australia. Perhaps the dominance of the fully staffed group home as the principal option available for community living should be re-examined, if true choice is to be available and individual preferences are to be pursued.

### Individual Service Plans

One of the main formal mechanisms for participation by consumers in decisions about the services they receive is through direct involvement in the individual planning process. Several authors have described procedures for the evaluation of such plans (Hudson & Cummins, 1991; Shaddock & Bramston, 1991).

Australian research evidence reveals a mixed level of compliance with the individual planning process and a low level of consumer participation. Some organizations are struggling to come to terms with developing individual plans and the gap between legislation and implementation has been apparent wherever such plans have been evaluated. Stancliffe (1988) reviewed an entire service system made up of 20 group homes and 86 residents. He reported that only 33 per cent of the residents had any written program at all, with a mere 10 per cent having a genuine individual plan

which dealt with their life, needs and preferences as a whole. For the majority of residents in this study, there was no formal individual planning process in which they could participate to make choices about goals. Contrary findings were reported by Shaddock and Bramston (1991), who found that 50 of 52 (96%) randomly selected government-run residences had individual plans for the consumers. However, only 26 per cent of the individual plans they reviewed referred to the previous plan, suggesting that individual planning may have been a very recently introduced practice in these houses. Shaddock and Bramston noted that, while an average of 6.2 people were in attendance at an Individual Program Plan meeting, the person most important in the process, the client about whom the plan was being formulated, was present at only 53 per cent of the individual planning meetings. The presence of a relative or advocate to assist the consumer was even less frequent. Even when individual planning is under way, it seems that the most basic form of consumer participation (physical presence at the meeting) is often absent.

If the consumer is present at the individual planning meeting, what degree of participation and control does he or she experience? Stancliffe (1992) asked staff and residents of community living services about individual plans. Staff responses indicated that only 13 per cent of consumers did not have an individual plan, whereas about half of the consumers stated that they did not know anything about their plan or did no have one. This suggests a low level of awareness by consumers of their individual plan. In the light of Shaddock and Bramston's findings, it could well indicate a lack of consumer involvement in the individual planning processes. Amongst the consumers in Stancliffe's study who were aware of their plan, over two thirds felt that they had limited or no say about the individual plan goals. They mostly saw staff and family members as the ones who decided about these goals.

Some people with an intellectual disability are dubious of the individual planning process itself and its impact on their lives. Shaddock, Guggenheimer, Bennett and Bugel (in preparation) found that many self-advocates thought that such plans were ineffective ways of giving choice and that they were "unnatural," because only people with disabilities have them. Others were more positive, but stressed the importance of collaborative and sensitive implementation, and the need for the plan to target the *individual's* opinions, needs and best interests. Although the individual planning process is meant to involve and empower consumers, these research findings suggest that it may have little effect on the person's quality of life.

### Self-Reported Choice versus Third Party Report

Quantitative research requires that technical factors such as reliability and validity be addressed. One issue which has occupied the attention of some Australian researchers has been the relative merits of self-report and third party informants in providing information about choice and quality of life. Burnett (1989) compared responses to the *Residential Satisfaction Inventory* from staff and people with moderate or mild intellectual disability who lived in community residential units or hostels and found a correlation of .11. Interpretation of this very low level of agreement was confounded by substantial problems of acquiescence

(the instrument has a yes/no response format) and unreliability for the consumer responses. Kent (1990) reported very poor inter-rater agreement between residential staff members in response to questions about responsibility, autonomy and choice available to clients. She suggested that *"staff are not as reliable a source of information as the residents themselves"* (Kent, 1990, p.230).

Parmenter et al., (1991) reported discrepancies between staff statements that most residents are involved in decision-making and the results of assessment of choices available to residents. Jenkinson et al. (in press) reported a marked divergence of opinion between residents and staff in relation to three items — choice of living companions, choice of workplace and work performed, and choice of activities in one's free time. Substantially more residents reported that they had a choice about the first two of these matters. Resident autonomy on these items was indicated by a "yes" response, but Jenkinson et al. did not include any specific safeguards against acquiescence, so the interpretation of these resident-staff differences is open to question. Stancliffe (1993) identified and eliminated all acquiescent responses by administering oppositely worded versions of the Kishi et al., (1988) checklist. As already noted, Stancliffe's subjects had very high levels of choice on many items. A "ceiling effect" may have been partly responsible for the fairly high level of consumer-staff agreement on many items (average agreement was 77% for the six items mentioned earlier). There was a significant difference between consumer self-ratings and staff ratings of these consumers on two items — choosing whom to live with and choosing what job to have or what work to do (average agreement 41%). Consumers rated themselves as having a greater degree of choice than did staff.

It seems that consumers and staff often differ in their perception of the availability of choice in certain areas. This reinforces the fundamentally *subjective* nature of individual perceptions of choice and the importance of obtaining information about choice *directly from the person* whenever possible. If the person does not feel that he/she has a choice, then it is reasonable to assert that no choice is really available regardless of opinions to the contrary.

These findings have obvious implications for further research on choice. The validity of third party data is questionable, and where self report is possible, it should be used. Also, more work is needed on the development of ways of gaining valid and reliable information from consumers, particularly those with severe intellectual disability and communication impairment. For example, Shaddock, Dowse, Zilber and Bennett (1992) are currently researching a "communication profile" designed to help carers and staff who may not know a person well to promote the expression of choices.

### Summary and Conclusions on Choice

Significant Australian research attention has only recently been given to the topic of choice and people with an intellectual disability. The importance of choice as a component of quality of life is widely agreed upon, but the high levels of choice and autonomy heralded by recent legislation such as the *Disability Services Act* (1986) appear not to have become widely accessible. Whilst greater choice is available in integrated and community settings, living in the community by no means guarantees

a high level of choice. Research has shown the availability of choice to be quite variable in community accommodation and in work settings, with disturbingly low levels being reported in some cases. Data about the degree of choice available to non-disabled Australians would be helpful in interpreting such research findings more fully. There is evidence to suggest that people with an intellectual disability are less likely to have a free choice about certain major life decisions, including major decisions about service delivery. Although group homes are the predominant form of community living service in Australia, significant difficulties were perceived in providing real choice and catering to individual preferences in such settings. Individual planning processes are by no means universal in Australia. Research indicates that there is limited involvement by consumers in their own individual planning meetings, with an even lower level of choice about one's individual plan goals. Australian research suggests that a distinction should be drawn between self-reports of choice versus third party reports. In conclusion, although Australian legislation has given prominence to the values of choice, autonomy and involvement for Australian citizens with an intellectual disability, there is an alarming gap between policy and practice.

### Personal Competence and Self-Reliance

Competence and self-reliance are amongst the key "positive consumer outcomes" which have been a focus of recent Australian legislation, such as the *Disability Services Act*, 1986. Major deinstitutionalization initiatives have taken place in a number of Australian states. Australian research has examined the effects of these initiatives on aspects of the quality of life of the people with intellectual disabilities, including changes in competence and self-reliance resulting from the move to the community.

### Deinstitutionalization

The most extensive study of deinstitutionalization in Australia has been conducted by Cummins et al., (Cummins & Dunt, 1990; Cummins, Polzin & Theobald, 1990a; 1990b; Dunt & Cummins, 1990). This series of reports describe the relocation of about 100 adolescents from St. Nicholas hospital in Melbourne, Victoria, to small group homes and charts their progress over a four year period.

St. Nicholas Hospital was the epitome of Dickensian institutional architecture. Located in the inner-city, it comprised four wards with high ceilings and bare walls. The accommodation offered no privacy, primitive ablution facilities, and a need for daytime artificial lighting due to small windows. All meals were cooked in a central kitchen and the elevators were old and unreliable. This facility housed some of the most disabled children and adolescents in the state of Victoria.

Well before the institution's closure, a study was commissioned to record the progress of clients and staff as they moved into their new homes. Two baseline measures were made on a wide variety of variables before the move, and then at 1.0, 1.4 and 4.1 years following relocation.

Despite a history of similar research in North America, this study has special significance due to the extreme level of client disability. All had been diagnosed as being severely/profoundly intellectually disabled, almost all had additional multiple disabilities and were nonverbal. Because of this, the move was undertaken with some trepidation in fear that it might increase mortality and have no long-term benefits.

In fact, none of these fears was supported by follow-up data. Briefly stated, there was no increase in mortality and life-quality was substantially improved. Life-routines became more normalized, living conditions were vastly improved, interaction with parents and the community increased, and life-skill development was substantial.

Of all the results to come from this study, the latter are of most interest. At the time of leaving the hospital the clients had a mean age of 16 years. The Progress Assessment Chart (Gunzberg, 1973) was used to determine their level of life-skill development at each of the intervals previously described. What was expected, on the basis of previous literature was, at best, a short-burst of development following relocation, after which the rate of development would decrease or even revert to institutional levels. In fact, the data showed an initial burst of development, as predicted, but this was followed by sustained skill acquisition. Over the period 1.4 to 4.1 years following relocation, six of the nine skill domains showed a significant level of development. Moreover a retrospective analysis of the overall skills acquisition rate indicated a total gain of 1.6 developmental years over that which would have been expected had these clients remained in the hospital.

An additional point of interest was the reaction to parents to the move. Consistent with previous North American studies, the families reported some initial concern with the idea that their son or daughter was to be relocated (Cummins & Dunt, 1990). However, this was also tempered by a generally positive view of how their child would cope in their new group home environment. Ellis (1984) administered a questionnaire to 67 parents of the total 101 children. She found that they generally held positive expectations of their relative's ability to adapt to the new environment; 57 per cent felt that their son or daughter would easily adapt to the new physical environment, 50 per cent to new staff, and 70 per cent to the smaller group structure. Following the move these positive expectations were confirmed for most families. Cummins and Dunt (1990) reported that 18 months after the move many of the families initial concerns had dissipated; a trend which was even more marked after 4 years (Cummins, 1993).

### Support for families

Deinstitutionalization and the closure of institutions has, as one consequence, an increased pressure on families to keep their disabled son or daughter at home. Moreover, there is no doubt that severe deficiencies in personal competence act as a stressor within the family environment. This is particularly the case when combined with overt behavior problems. Kupinski, Mackenzie, Meredith, and Stoller (1973) reported that the most common reason parents sought the institutionalization of their child was behavior problems and the consequential disruption to family life.

So, in order to ameliorate this burden, families have been surveyed in an attempt to establish the kinds of service support most useful to them. As an example, Baxter (1989) studied the kinds of needs expressed by parents caring for children with a moderate/severe level of disability in Victoria. She found that foremost amongst these was the need to receive appropriate information about, and direct help with the child. This was so irrespective of social status, it was somewhat disconcerting to find, therefore, that a majority of parents of moderately/severely disabled teenagers had never received direct support from agencies (Baxter, 1986), even though such services were available. One reason for this may have been a simple lack of knowledge about such services. In a Queensland survey of parents and clients, Brown and Ringma (1989) found that 60 per cent had experienced difficulty in obtaining information on services. Moreover, the information had generally been acquired in haphazard ways, with few people realising they could seek relevant information from government departments.

### Issues of Maladaptive Behavior

A detracting influence on personal competence and self-reliance is maladaptive behaviour. Tonge and Einfeld (1991) have confirmed that the incidence of serious emotional and behavioural disorders among children and adolescents with an intellectual disability is two to three times the rate of non-disabled children.

Various forms of treatment have been proposed to eliminate such behaviours. For example, King, Ollendick, Gullone, Cummins, and Josephs (1990) have concluded that maladaptive fears and phobias in such children can be successfully treated by exposure-based interventions and, in Victoria, Behavioral Intervention Support Teams currently provide behavioral training for parents and clients in the home environment with considerable success. A similar program was initiated in the state of New South Wales (Parmenter, Gray & Martin, 1990).

A more serious issue is raised by people involved in crime, either as the perpetrator or the victim. In the case of the former, some conflicting reports are available with Hayes (1991) reporting that 12-13 per cent of the NSW prisoner population have an intellectual disability, while Jones and Coombes (1990) claimed an incidence of 1.2 per cent in Western Australia. The difference may, in part, reflect different committal procedures. Jones and Coombes claim that 'up to one third' of charges made in Western Australia against people with intellectual disabilities are withdrawn because the people are clients of the Authority for Intellectually Handicapped Persons.

These two reports are also notable for their differences in the reported incidence of violent crime. Jones and Coombes (1990) reported that 47 per cent of the prisoner population considered either to have an intellectual disability or to be "boderline" were serving a sentence for a violent crime against a person and, of these, 78 per cent were sexual offenders. Overall, 37 per cent of prisoners who could be classified as intellectually disabled or borderline were serving terms for sexual offences; about three times the incidence of the rest of the prisoner population (13%). Hayes (1991), on the other hand, concluded that in New South Wales there was no evidence that people with intellectual disabilities were over-represented in the sex offender population.

There are several reasons to suspect that the Jones and Coombes (1990) data are inflated. In the first place their sample size was small; only 6 people diagnosed as having an intellectual disability and 13 people designated "borderline". Secondly, their definition of the 'borderline classification was very loose. Finally, the differen-

tial committal procedures referred to above may well have resulted in the selective retention of those people charged with more serious crimes.

These data do not provide compelling evidence that people with intellectual disabilities are more likely to commit sex-related offences. They are, however, certainly more likely to be the victims of crime. Carmody (1991) detailed figures from the Sexual Assault Service (NSW) which record that in the first six months of operation in 1989, of the 855 referred adults, 6.4 per cent were intellectually disabled. In support of this high incidence she cited the Office of the Public Advocate (1988) which concluded that sexual offences and sexual assault are the most frequently recorded crimes against this population. This issue is especially important as feelings of security and safety have been shown to be a key factor in the quality of life of this population (Halpern, Nave, Close, & Nelson, 1986).

These concerns are highly relevant to the issue of sex education. As Carmody (1991) noted, a lack of sex education and opportunities to develop a sexual identity results in confusion and uncertainty about what is acceptable behaviour from other people. This, coupled with the persistent experience of powerlessness in the face of authority, may allow these people to be unaware that they have been the victim of a crime, or that they are entitled to seek police assistance.

### Summary and Conclusions on Personal Competence and Self-Reliance

Efforts to enhance personal competence and self-reliance have focused especially upon deinstitutionalization and community-based training. The former has resulted in a substantially improved life quality for those people who have returned to the community. This has been found to apply particularly for people with a severe/profound level of disability in terms of their skill development, normalizaton of routines and personal interaction. Community-based support and training, on the other hand, is undergoing a phase of rapid development where much of the focus is related to issues of maladaptive behavior. Of particular concern in the area of community living are people who are the victims of sex-related crime or exploitation; a situation which is certainly related to the overall inadequacy of sex education programs in this country for people with intellectual disabilities.

## Community Participation

The extent to which people participate in community-based activities is a component of quality of life (see Figure 5-1) and another of the "positive consumer outcomes" targeted by the *Disability Services Act 1986*. Australian research has provided insight into the forces influencing levels of community participation in areas such as community living, education, health care and employment.

### *Opportunity for Community Participation*

One force which operates on many people with intellectual disabilities is the attitude held toward their community participation by parents or care-givers. These attitudes tend to be conservative. For example, Ellis (1984) asked the parents of St. Nicholas Hospital children how they antic-ipated the level of community acceptance of their children once they had moved to a group home. While the overall level of anticipation was generally positive, 21 % expected that the neighbours would have trouble accepting the group home, while a further 33 % anticipated no more than partial acceptance.

More recently, Grbich and Sykes (1990) interviewed Victorian parents of children aged 13-18 years with a severe level of intellectual disability. While most parents (83%) agreed in principle with the ideals of normalization, in practice they were concerned that the lack of community service resources might have unfortunate consequences for their offspring. Moreover, when asked to nominate the expected future living placement for their children, a relatively high proportion nominated an institution (8% for males; 21% for females), with the other options being family care (35% M; 44% F), group home (53% M; 28% F), and independent living (4% M; 7% F). In terms of their perceived future work environment, the majority nominated a segregated setting (60% M; 83% F).

There is, however, some evidence for changing parental attitudes towards higher levels of community participation. Foreman and Neilands (1991), in a survey of retrospective data, found that whereas only 8 per cent of parents whose children were born in the 1970s regarded a regular class as the ideal placement for their child, for the parents of children born in the 1980s this had risen to 21 per cent.

Another critical factor affecting community participation is care-giver and professional attitudes. In a survey of New South Wales group homes, Parmenter et al. (1991) found that the majority of staff

(65%) were definitely positive in their views of people with disabilities living in the community. However, some concerns were also expressed and 23 per cent felt that the residents were gaining few benefits from community living. This attitude was related to the low level of community interaction achieved by some of the residents and their continued high levels of dependency.

A Victorian survey of staff in Special Development Schools for children with a severe/profound level of disability produced similarly cautious attitudes concerning the value of integration for their students (Grbich & Sykes, 1990). These staff viewed social benefits as the only positive feature of integration, an attitude probably influenced by poor support services and inadequate teacher education.

Other professional groups hold more substantial conservative attitudes. Beran (1990) conducted a survey amongst medical staff involved in the area of developmental disabilities and concluded that they felt devalued, were experiencing declining morale, and that their authority was being undermined by the nursing staff. The author also expressed dismay that 'patients' were being integrated into environments in which they could not cope and that there was "an evolving ineptitude in dealing with this sector of health delivery for which no one appeared to show much concern" (p.277).

In terms of community understanding about intellectual disability, surveys conducted during the 1980s have generally indicated a high level of knowledge concerning the characteristics of this disorder (Ellis, 1984; Foreman & Andrews, 1988). Unfortunately, however, community attitudes are characterized by the same stereo-types as are found in other Western cultures. Gething (1990), for example, has reported the general perception of people with disabilities to be that they are less well adjusted and less capable in terms of personal characteristics which have no necessary link with their actual disability.

The level of community concern with deinstitutionalization, however, seems to be low, with little overt opposition to the establishment of group homes. Foreman and Andrews (1988) conducted a survey using retrospective data on neighbor attitudes after at least one year of group home occupancy. They reported before vs. after attitudes to have changed towards positive (41% to 93%) and away from negative (17% to 2%).

An important aspect of enhanced community participation should be consumer consultation on the nature of support services required. Unfortunately, however, the extent of client consultation has been found to be low. In their Queensland survey of parents and clients, Brown and Ringma (1989) found that they had generally not been consulted by the service delivery agencies, and had not participated in making decisions regarding the agency. However, a persistent finding in this area is that parents and clients usually regard such lack of consultation as appropriate. Brown and Ringma (1989) reported that consumers expressed a personal reluctance and a sense of inadequacy regarding such participation. In many ways this finding is not surprising given the substantial and sustained power-differential which dominates the parent/client-professional interaction. However, it is highly undesirable if the aim of understanding consumer needs is to be achieved.

### Employment

Of all areas of community participation, none is so coveted as paid employment. Not only do people with disabilities prefer open employment (Parmenter, 1988), but those who actually gain open employment seem to evidence a higher level of job satisfaction to those in sheltered employment (Jiranek & Kirby, 1990). Compared with people who are unemployed, however, both employment groups provide evidence of enhanced psychological well-being.

Despite this, the manner of integrating and supporting people in open industry is a poorly researched area. One recent study has reported on the success of an "enclave model" at the Australian Mint (Warth, 1990). In this situation a small group of workers worked as a unit within the industry, with payment linked to productivity. It will be interesting to see whether this model survives, with its overtones of sheltered employment in a community setting.

The preponderance of research in vocational areas has been driven by economic imperatives, rather than a conscious effort to determine the effects the various competitive and supported employment programs are having upon the person's life quality. Undoubtedly, there are good economic reasons for having people with disabilities as part of the paid workforce. For instance, Jeltes (1991) found that there were substantial financial benefits for people with an intellectual disability who are in a supported employment program as well as for the taxpayer. In a sample of 38 job placements over a four-year period it was found that for every public dollar spent a consumer earned 84 cents compared to 21 cents for persons employed in sheltered workshops. Two comprehensive economic analyses of one of Australia's leading supported employment services, *Jobsupport*, have revealed that over time supporting people with significant intellectual disabilities in the open workforce compares favorably in both cost and employment outcomes with other models of support, especially with payments of a pension alone (Tuckerman, Morgan, Smith & Delahunt, 1992). Jeltes (1991), and Clear and Mank (1990) have highlighted the need of many people in supported or competitive employment programs for support, particularly in the area of social integration, as well as job skills training. Parmenter (1992b) suggested that one of the major reasons for the slow growth of innovative employment programs worldwide was the lack of adequately trained personnel to implement comprehensive training programs that addressed both the vocational and personal needs of people with disabilities. The push for economic and social independence of people with disabilities espoused by government legislation presents somewhat of a paradox when viewed from a social welfare perspective.

This situation is especially evident for people with severe and multiple disabilities, for whom significant periods of employment may not be feasible or may not be their preferred option. In a survey of post school options for people with disabilities, Parmenter and Knox (1989) found the group most underserved in the provision of day options was this population, a situation that still obtains in 1993.

In an attempt to address the wider social and personal issues of community-based employment, some promising insights are being revealed in studies that are utilizing a qualitative methodology. In a study of the social networks and support mechanisms for people with mild intellectual disability in competitive employment, Knox and Parmenter (1993) found that the major sources of social support came from the person's family and/or from social organizations catering for people with disabilities. Support obtained in the workplace generally did not extend beyond it, nor was it integrated with the wider support networks. This in-depth study of nine people suggested that a more detailed analysis needs to be made of the social support construct. In particular, the roles that friendship networks play need to be examined, as it appears that community-based employment is not providing the same opportunities for friendship development as it does for people without disabilities.

A similar study of ten people with a severe intellectual disability employed in a supported work program operating as a small business, which also employed non-disabled workers, showed that most of the observed interactions between the ten targeted employees and others were initiated by the work supervisors and most were work related (Ford, Parmenter & Koop 1992). Nevertheless thirty-two percent of the interactions were between the ten targeted employees and other disabled employees. Overall the targeted employees were, for the most part, passive interactors in that they initiated far fewer interactions than they received. Not surprisingly, the majority of interactions were work-related but during periods of arrival, departure and break times the incidences of teasing and joking between supported employees and their non-disabled co-workers significantly increased. The results of this study highlight the need for a closer examination of the processes of relationship building between workers in community-based employment programs.

## Actual Levels of Community Participation

In Australian institutions, as the world over, the extent of client participation in community activities is very low, even when measured against contact with their own families. In Victoria, Krupinski et al. (1973) reported on family contact with people in institutions. They reported that of those with parents still living, only about half were visited at the institution, and less than half had been home during the past twelve months. Moreover, 53 per cent had no visitors other than parents and 51 per cent had not left the institution at all during the preceding year. More recently, Suttie and Ashman (1989) have also reported very limited levels of community contact in people with a mild/moderate level of disability living either in institutions or large group homes. They found that less than 30 per cent participated in general community leisure activities on a regular basis, about two-thirds never received visits from family members, and none reported friendships outside their residential setting.

Cummins et al. (1990) found even lower levels of community participation among the ex-St. Nicholas residents. While a substantial increase in the proportion of clients who engaged in community activities was recorded following deinstitutionalization, from 13 % — 33 % in absolute terms the degree of participation remained low. After four years living in the community the average resident engaged in two community-based activities per week. This includes such activities as going for walks and shopping. Their level of social contact also remained low, at about once per two months for relatives, and three times per month for friends. It was hypothesized that these low levels reflect a legacy of the almost total community isolation while in the hospital. The severity of their disability is also likely to have been a contributing factor.

In terms of the kinds of leisure activities engaged in by people living in the community, Barlow and Kirby (1991) found them to be quite similar to the general population. Of the top ten leisure pursuits, six were in the top ten of the general community.

### Community Involvement and Life Quality

While it is very clear that the objective life quality of people has improved following their return to the community, the data on subjective well-being are scarce and ambiguous. Barlow and Kirby (1991) compared two groups of people with mild intellectual disability employed full-time in a sheltered work environment, one group was living in an institution and the other in the community. Comparisons revealed essentially the same level of life satisfaction, self-esteem, and locus of control between the two groups. The only significant difference was that those in the institution were more satisfied with their social life, and those in the community with their autonomy.

More recently, Cummins (1992a) has developed the Comprehensive Quality of Life Scale (ComQol) which measures both objective and subjective life quality across life "domains" of material things, health, productivity, intimacy, place in community, safety, and emotional well-being. For non-disabled adults the scale is self-administered. However, for people with an intellectual disability it is more difficult to administer since the subjective scales require quite a high level of cognitive functioning in order to be completed validly. They require the conceptualization of the abstract terms "importance" and "satisfaction" and the ability to rate these onto a Likert scale.

Therefore the version for people with intellectual disabilities (ComQol-ID) incorporates a pre-testing protocol to determine whether the person being tested can validly use the scales. This involves a three-step process.

- Arranging wooden blocks in order of large to small
- Matching the blocks to a 'ladder' scale of size on paper
- Using an Importance Scale with objects known to be important to the persons being tested

If the person is able to succeed with this pre-testing, then they can use a version of ComQol that adjusts the complexity of the Likert scale to match the person's level of competence. At a minimal level of usage this involves a binary choice for each item.

The ComQol-ID Scale has recently been tested on 60 clients and their carers; the clients responded for themselves and the carers provided additional third-party responses for their clients (Cummins, 1992b). In summary, the clients' subjective responses indicated a life quality within the normal range. However, major discrepancies were found between the individual carer-estimations of client life quality and the estimations obtained directly from the clients. These results emphasise the danger of replying on third-party estimations of subjective QOL.

### Summary and conclusions on community particpation

Opportunities for Community participation appear to be governed substantially by the attitudes of families, service providers, and members of the general community. In general, such attitudes have been found to be mainly positive, with the level of acceptance increasing over time. Such attitudes can also tend to be conservative, especially relating to such issues as integrating children with severe to profound levels of disability into regular schools, and in relation to providing effective medical care to group homes. There is an increased level of community participation among people who were previously institutionalized, albeit at quite a low level of absolute terms. Moreover, employment confers a heightened state of well-being among these people just as it does for members of the broader community. However, a closer analysis needs to be made of the broader dimensions of working in the community, especially a study of support networks. The development of the Comprehensive Quality of Life Scale has enabled people with an intellectual disability to rate the importance of items according to their perceived importance.

## The Future

There is little doubt that the last decade has witnessed a major revolution in the way services are provided for people with disabilities in Australia. One of the major catalysts in the paradigm shift has obviously been the federal government's leadership in enacting its 1986 legislation that will possibly be judged as Australia's most significant contribution to disability services in this century.

Despite the great promise held by rhetorical statements such as those contained in the Principles and Objectives of the *Disability Services Act* (1986), research detailed in this chapter reveals that much has yet to be realized in people with disabilities achieving those aspects of life quality that are very personal and subjective. Many would argue that while structural changes to a person's lifestyle are necessary prerequisites for the achievement of a desired quality of life, they are not alone sufficient. Thus it is not the environments alone that should be emphasised, but the way in which people interact within those environments, and in so doing develop a self-identity with which they are comfortable and from which they derive satisfaction.

Therefore, while we have established a better infrastructure upon which to base our disability services, with emphasis upon community-based living and working, much remains to be accomplished before the essential elements of desired quality of life can be achieved. A significant impediment to the realisation of this goal lies in the ever present danger that we may, in Burton Blatt's (1979) term "bureaucratize" the very values on which services rest.

The roles that governments play in shaping social policies need to be critically examined. In Australia, at present, there is an uneasy relationship between government, disability advocacy groups and major service organizations. Much of the debate centers naturally upon financial resources and mechanisms to implement and monitor services. As this review has revealed, too little of the debate has focused upon those outcomes that include the extent to which people with disabilities feel satisfied with their lives in areas such as choice and decision-making, personal competence and self-reliance, community participation, friendships, and the feeling of being a part of a secure, interdependent and supportive community. The research undertaken to date has overly concentrated upon comparisons between the institutional and noninstitutional lifestyles of people with disabilities. There is a need to examine their quality of life relative to non-disabled Australians.

Quality of life is, to a significant extent, in the eye of the beholder. Its fundamental-ly subjective nature means that individual perceptions of what constitutes quality of life are an essential feature of research in this area. However, collaboration with people with disabilities in setting the quality of life research agenda has been noticeably absent in Australia. This represents an important challenge for future Australian research. One important step in this direction has been the inclusion within Cummins' *ComQol ID* instrument of a method whereby the respondent can weight the different aspects of quality of life according to their perceived importance to him or her.

## References

Barlow, J., & Kirby, N. (1991). Residential satisfaction of persons with an intellectual disability living in an institution or in the community. *Australia and New Zealand Journal of Developmental Disabilities, 17,* 7-23.

Baxter, C. (1986). Intellectual disability: Parental perceptions and stigma as stress. Unpublished doctoral thesis, Monash University

Baxter, C. (1989). Parental access to assistance from services: Social status and age-related differences. *Australia and New Zealand Journal of Developmental Disabilities, 15,* 15-25.

Bennett, M., Shaddock, A., & Guggenheimer, S. (1992). The complexities of providing choice in a community group home for people with severe intellectual disabilities. Paper presented at the 9th World Congress of the International Association for the Scientific Study of Mental Deficiency, Broadbeach, Queensland.

Beran, R.G. (1990). Doctors' perspectives regarding the changes in the delivery of health care to people with developmental disabilities. *Australia and New Zealand Journal of Developmental Disabilities, 16,* 275-80.

Blatt, B. (1979). *In and out of mental retardation. Essays on educability, disability, and human policy.* Baltimore, MD: University Park Press.

Brown, C., & Ringma, C. (1989). Consumer perspectives on disability services in Queensland: The long road to new directions. *Australia and New Zealand Journal of Developmental Disabilities, 15,* 41-48.

Burnett, P. (1989). Assessing satisfaction in people with an intellectual disability: Living in community-based residential facilities. *Australian Disability Review, 1,* 14-19.

Carmody, M. (1991). Invisible victims: Sexual assault of people with an intellectual disability. *Australia and New Zealand Journal of Developmental Disabilities, 17,* 229-236.

Clear, M.E., & Mank, D.M. (1990). Supported and competitive employment outcomes and sources of support for individuals with disabilities in integrated jobs in New South Wales. *Australia and New Zealand Journal of Developmental Disabilities, 16,* 245-257.

Cubbage, M., & Burdon, R. (1991). A practical look at work crews. *Australian Disablity Review, 1,* 10-18.

Cummins, R.A. (1991). The Comprehensive Quality of Life Scale-Intellectual Disability: An instrument under development. *Australia and New Zealand Journal of Developmental Disabilities, 17,* 259-264.

Cummins, R.A. (1992). *The Comprehensive Quality of Life Scale: Intellectual Disability.* Third edition. Melbourne: Psychology Research Centre, Deakin University.

Cummins, R.A. (1993). In the community: An evaluation of the Community Living Support Service. Melbourne: Community Services Victoria (in press).

Cummins, R.A., & Dunt, D. (1990). The deinstitutionalization of St. Nicholas Hospital: II. Lifestyle, community contact and family attitudes. *Australia and New Zealand Journal of Developmental Disabilities, 16,* 19-32.

Cummins, R.A., Polzin, U., & Theobold, T. (1990a). The deinstitutionalization of St. Nicholas Hospital: III. Four-year follow-up of life-skill development. *Australia and New Zealand Journal of Developmental Disabilities, 16,* 209-232.

Cummins, R.A., Polzin, U., & Theobold, T. 1990(b). The deinstitutionalization of St. Nicholas Hospital: IV. A four-year follow-up of resident routines and activities. *Australia and New Zealand Journal of Developmental Disabilities, 16,* 305-321.

Disablity Services Act 1986, No. 129 of 1986.

Dunt, D., & Cummins, R.A. (1990). The deinstitutionalization of St. Nicholas Hospital: I. Adaptive behavior and physical health. *Australia and New Zealand Journal of Developmental Disabilities, 16,* 5-18.

Ellis, T. (1984). *Attitudes towards the deinstitutionalization of intellectually handicapped residents of St. Nicholas hospital.* Melbourne: Unpublished Masters Thesis, Swinburne Institute of Technology.

Ford, J., Parmenter, T.R., & Koop, A.J. (1992). A qualitative study of social interactions in supported employment settings. Paper presented to 9th World Congress of the International Association for the Scientific Study

of Mental Deficiency. Broadbeach, Queensland.

Foreman, P.J., & Andrews, G. (1988). Community reaction to group homes for persons with disabilities. *Australian Society for the Study of Intellectual Disability Newsletter, 8,* (3), 28.

Foreman, P.J., & Neilands, J. (1991). Parental perceptions of services to children with intellectual disabilities. *Australia and New Zealand Journal of Developmental Disabilities, 17,* 249-258.

Gething, L. (1990). Interaction with disabled persons scale. *Australian Disability Review, 1,* 21-23.

Gething, L. (1991). A report on administration of the interaction with disabled persons scale to subscribers of the Australian Disability Review. *Australian Disability Review, 4-91,* 20-30.

Grbich, C., & Sykes, S. (1990). A study of persons with severe disabilities: Gender, the home environment, schooling and outcomes. *Australia and New Zealand Journal of Developmental Disabilities, 16,* 259-73.

Grimes, D. (1985). *New directions. Report of the Handicapped Programs review.* Canberra: Australian Government Publishing Service.

Grimes, D. (1992). The Disability Services Act - lessons for the future. *Australian Disability Review, 1,* 1-13.

Gunzburg, H.C. (1974). *Progress Assessment Chart of Social and Personal Development Manual* (4th Edition) Warwickshire, England: Sefa Ltd.

Halpern, A.S., Nave, G., Close, D., & Nelson, D.J. (1986). An empirical analysis of dimensions of community adjustment for adults with mental retardation. *Australia and New Zealand Journal of Developmental Disabilities, 12,* 147-157.

Handicapped Persons Assistance Welfare Act of 1974.

Hayes, S. (1991). Sex offenders. *Australia and New Zealand Journal of Developmental Disabilities, 17,* 221-227.

Hudson, A., & Cummins, R.A. (1991). General

service plans: An evaluation of their content within two service delivery systems. *Australia and New Zealand Journal of Developmental Disabilities,* 17, 401-412.

Jeltes, G. (1991). An analysis of financial and employment outcomes for people with an intellectual disability provided in a supported community based employment service. *Australian Disablity Review,* 1, 29-34.

Jenkinson, J., Copeland, C., Drivas, V., Scoon, H., & Hap, M.L. (in press) Decision making by community residents with an intellectual disability. *Australia and New Zealand Journal of Developmental Disabilities.*

Jiranek, D., & Kirby, N. (1990). The job satisfaction and/or psychological well being of young adults with an intellectual disability and non-disabled young adults in either sheltered employment, competitive employment or unemployment. *Australia and New Zealand Journal of Developmental Disabilities,* 16, 133-148.

Jones, G.P., & Coombes, K. (1990). *The prevalence of intellectual deficit among the Western Australian Prisoner population.* Perth: The Western Australian Department of corrective Services.

Kent, P. (1990). Measuring quality of life: Developing a questionnaire to measure satisfaction with lifestyle of people with an intellectual disability. Unpublished thesis. University of Adelaide, Adelaide.

King, N.J., Ollendick, T.H., Gullone, E., Cummins, R.A., & Josephs, A. (1990). Fears and phobias in children and adolescents with intellectual disabilities: Assessment and intervention strategies. *Australia and New Zealand Journal of Developmental Disabilities,* 16, 97-108.

Kishi, G., Teelucksingh, B., Zollers, N., Park-Lee S., & Meyer, L. (1988). Daily decision-making in community residences: *A social comparison of adults with and without mental retardation. American Journal on Mental Retardation,* 92, 430-435.

Knoll, J.A. (1990). Defining quality in residential services. In V.J. Bradley & H.A. Bersani (Eds) *Quality assurance for individuals with developmental disabilities. It's everybody's business.* Baltimore, M.D.: Paul H. Brookes.

Knox, M., & Parmenter, T.R. (1993). Social networks and support mechanisms for people with mild intellectual disability in competitive employment. *International Journal of Rehabilitation Research,* 16.

Krupsinski, J., Mackenzie, A., Meredith, E., & Stoller, A. (1973). *A follow-up of mentally retarded young adults. Special Publications. (3).* Melbourne: Mental Health Authority of Victoria.

Morath, P. (1992). Upgrading employment services for people with disabilities: Policy implications for the Australian Government. Unpublished PhD thesis. Macquarie University.

Nirje, B. (1969). The normalization principle and its human management implications. In R. Kugel and W. Wolfensberger (Eds) *Changing patterns in residential services for the mentally retarded.* Washington: President's Committee on Mental retardation.

Office of the Public Advocate (1988). Cited in M.Carmody (1991) Invisible victims: Sexual assault of 22 people with an intellectual disability. *Australia and New Zealand Journal of Developmental Disabilities,* 17, 229-236.

Parmenter, T.R. (1988a). The development of a quality of life model as an outcome measure of rehabilitation programs for people with developmental disabilities. Paper presented to Ninth Annual Conference of Young Adult Institute, Employment, Integration and Community Competence: The keys to quality of life and community coalescence. New York.

Parmenter, T.R. (1988b). An analysis of the dimensions of quality of life for people with physical disabilities. In R. Brown (Ed.) *Quality of life for handicapped people.* London: Croom Helm.

Parmenter, T.R. (1992a). Quality of life for people with developmental disabilities. In N.W. Bray (Ed) *International Review of Re-*

*search in Mental Retardation, Vol. 18*, New York: Academic Press.

Parmenter, T.R. (1992b). An international perspective of vocational options for people with an intellectual disability: The promise and the reality. Keynote paper presented to the 9th World Congress of the International Association for the Scientific Study of Mental Deficiency. Broadbeach, Queensland.

Parmenter, T.R., & Knox, M. (1989). *A study of the range and variety of postschool options for people with disabilities.* Sydney: Macquarie University.

Parmenter, T.R., Gray, C., & Martin, M. (1990). The evaluation of the Training Resource Unit: A unit for the management of severe challenging behaviours in young people with severe intellectual disabilities. *Journal of Special Education, 12*, 5-16.

Parmenter, T.R., Briggs, L., & Sullivan, R. (1991). Quality of life: Intellectual disabilities and community living. *Evaluation Journal of Australasia, 3*, 212-25.

Schalock, R. (1987). Disabled people and the 21st Century. In E. Bartnik, G.M. Lewis, & P.A. O'Connor (Eds) *Technology, resources and consumer outcomes.* Perth: P.E. Publications

Shaddock, A.J. (1990). Research and policy in services for people with severe intellectual disability in Australia. *Australia and New Zealand Journal of Developmental Disabilities, 16*, 195-206.

Shaddock, A.J., Bennett, M., Dowse, L., Guggenheimer, S., Stancliff, R., & Zilber, D. (1992). Choice-making: The challenge of linking policy, research and practice. Symposium presented at the 9th World Congress of Association for the Scientific Study of Mental Deficiency, Broadbeach, Queensland.

Shaddock, A.J., & Bramston, P. (1991). Individual service plans: The policy-practice gap. *Australia and New Zealand Journal of Developmental Disabilities, 17*, 73-80.

Shaddock, A.J., Dowse, L., Zilber, D., & Bennett, M. (1992). Individual recommendations for increasing expression of choices: A survey of those who know the person well. Unpublished manuscript, Faculty of Education, University of Canberra.

Shaddock, A.J., Guggenheimer, S., Benett, M., & Bugel, E. What are the views and priorities of self-advocates on the issue of ways of promoting choice and decision-making by people with a severe intellectual disability? (in preparation).

Shaddock, A.J., Zilber, D., Guggenheimer, S., Dowse, L., Bennett, M., & Browne, F. (in press) Opportunities for choice in day programs for adults with severe intellectual disabilities. *Australasian Journal of Special Education.*

Social Services Act 1947-77.

Stancliffe, R.J. (1988). Community living program for persons with disabilities. Unpublished report: Sydney.

Stancliffe, R.J. (1991). Choice-making by adults in supported community accommodation: Hobson's choice? *Interaction, 5*, 23-33.

Stancliffe, R.J. (1992). Everyday choice making and community living. Paper presented at the 9th World Congress, International Association for the Scientific Study of Mental Deficiency, Gold Coast, Queensland, August 5-9.

Stancliffe, R.J. (1993). Assessing opportunities for choice making: A comparison of self-report and staff reports. Unpublished paper. Macquarie University, Sydney.

Suttie, J.N., & Ashman, A.F. (1989). An acceptable living standard and quality of life: Fact or fiction for aging persons with an intellectual disability. Paper presented to 25th Annual Conference of the Australian Society for the Study of Intellectual Disability.

Tonge, B., & Enfield, S. (1991). Intellectual disability and psychopathology in Australian children. *Australia and New Zealand Journal of Developmental Disabilities, 17*, 155-167.

Tuckerman, P., Morgan, J., Smith, B., & Delahunt, R (1992). The relative costs of supported employment: Job support six years on. *Australian Disablity Review, 4-92,* 49-60.

Tunstin, R.D., & Bond, M.J. (1991). Assessing the ability to give informed consent to medical and dental procedures. *Australia and New Zealand Journal of Developmental Disabilities, 17,* 35-47.

Warth, S. (1990). Supported employment: Re-port of a successful enclave model. *Australia and New Zealand Journal of Developmental Disabilities, 16,* 57-63.

Wolfensberger, W. (1980). The definition of normalization: Update, problems, disagree-ments and misunderstandings. In R.J. Flynn & K.E. Nitsh (Eds) *Normalization, social integration and community services.* Baltimore: University Park Press.

# Appendix 1·
# Disability Services Act (1986): Principles and Objectives

## Principles

1. People with disabilities are individuals who have the inherent right to respect for their human worth and dignity.
2. People with disabilities, whatever the ori-gin, nature, type and degree of disability, have the same basic human rights as other members of Australian society.
3. People with disabilities have the same rights as other members of Australian society to realise their individual capacities for physi-cal, social, emotional and intellectual de-velopment.
4. People with disabilities have the same rights as other members of Australian society to services which will support their attaining a reasonable quality of life.
5. People with disabilities have the same rights as other members of Australian society to participate in the decisions which affect their lives.
6. People with disabilities receiving services have the same right as other members of Australian society to receive those services in a manner which results in the least restric-tion of their rights and opportunities.
7. People with disabilities have the same right of pursuit of any grievance in relation to services as have other members of Austra-lian society.

## Objectives

1. Services should have as their focus the achievement of positive outcomes for people with disabilities, such as increased indepen-dence, employment opportunities and in-tegration into the community.
2. Services should contribute to ensuring that the conditions of the every-day life of people with disabilities are the same as, or as close as possible to, norms and patterns which are valued in the general commu-nity.
3. Services should be provided as part of local co-ordinated service systems and be inte-grated with services generally available to members of the community, wherever pos-sible.
4. Services should be tailored to meet the individual needs and goals of the people with disabilities receiving those services.
5. Programs and services should be designed and administered so as to meet the needs of people with disabilities who experience a

double disadvantage as a result of their sex, ethnic origin, or Aboriginality.

6. Programs and services should be designed and administered so as to promote recognition of the competence of, and enhance the image of, people with disabilities.

7. Programs and services should be designed and administered so as to promote the participation of people with disabilities in the life of the local community through maximum physical and social integration in that community.

8. Programs and services should be designed and administered so as to ensure that no single organisation providing services should exercise control over all or most aspects of the life of an individual with disabilities.

9. Organisations providing services, whether those services are provided specifically to people with disabilities or generally to members of the community, should be accountable to those people with disabilities who use their services, the advocates of such people, the Commonwealth and the community generally for the provision of information from which the quality of their services can be judged.

10. Programs and services should be designed and administered so as to provide opportunities for people with disabilities to reach goals and enjoy lifestyles which are valued by the community generally and are appropriate to their chronological age.

11. Services should be designed and administered so as to ensure that people with disabilities have access to advocacy support where necessary to ensure adequate participation in decision-making about the services they receive.

12. Programs and services should be designed and administered so as to ensure that appropriate avenues exist for people with disabilities to raise and have resolved any grievances about services.

13. Services should be designed and administered so as to provide people with disabilities with, and encourage them to make use of, avenues for participating in the planning and operation of services which they receive and the Commonwealth and organisations should provide opportunities for consultation in relation to major policy and program changes.

14. Programs and services should be designed and administered so as to respect the rights of people with disabilities to privacy and confidentiality.

# 6• Quality of Life for Mentally Retarded People in Germany: An Overview of Theory and Practice

Iris Beck, Ph.D., University of Oldenburg, and
Andreas Konig, Ph.D, International Labour Organization
United Nations, Geneva, Switzerland

Quite recently, a German court ordered a travel agency to pay back a certain percentage of the price of a package tour to Turkey a family had undertaken for their summer vacation. The family had complained of not being able to fully enjoy their hotel due to the fact that they had to take their meals together with a group of men and women with mental retardation. *Whose Quality of Life is at Stake Here ?*

This article can not give a comprehensive answer to this question. Nor can it provide a complete review of the empirical conditions of quaity of life for persons with disabilities in Germany. The article is divided into two parts. The first part reviews the policies and life conditions pertaining to people with mental retardation in Germany. After introducing the target group as it is defined in Germany, the reader will be introduced to the social policy and the system of social security for people with mental retardation in Germany. These shape, to a large extent, their living environments. This is followed by a rough description of these various environments.

In part two, the concept of quality of life for people with disabilities, as seen in Germany, will be elaborated and the first research efforts and their results summarized. A final discussion is provided to help the reader grasp the scope of further developments necessary to counteract incidents as the one mentioned above. Such incidents occur in a climate of increasing xenophobia that questions the right of people with mental retardation and other disabilities to enjoy a life full of quality and equal opportunity.

## An Overview of Policies and Services for People with Mental Retardation in Germany

### Definition of the Population

The Committee on Terminology and Classification of the AAMR, a generally acknowledged body in the USA, fulfills the function of making authoritative statements regarding definition, classification and terminology of mental retardation.

A comparable body does not exist in Germany. It is therefore not surprising that there is no unified approach for understanding and defining mental retardation.

A broad definition was formulated in

1973 by the German Council of Education, a group of independent experts, who critically reviewed the (West) German education system at that time. This definition is as follows:

> A person is described as mentally retarded if, due to an organic-genetic or other impairment, his/her overall mental development and learning capacity is retarded to the extent that he/she likely will be in need of life-long social and educational support. The cognitive disability is often accompanied by those of the language, social, emotional and motoric development.

The main difference with the AAMR definition lies with the specification of causing factors as well as the emphasis of a *relative* stability of the condition. However, these differences do not automatically lead to the conclusion that we have different populations under the same label. Nevertheless, as will be demonstrated further on, there exists a considerable variation in the understanding of mental retardation in the USA and Germany.

Let us look at prevalance rates first.

While in the U.S., 3% of the population are labelled as being "mentally retarded", the same estimate for Germany is between 0.5 and 0.6 %. These estimates, which rely on quotations from the still dominating special (and segregated) services such as early intervention, special kindergarten, special school, sheltered workshops, special residences and institutions, contain also a certain number of persons who are completely misplaced in psychiatric hospitals or nursing homes.

The lack of exact data on mental retardation in Germany can be explained by the general resistance to register any kind of disability. This is due to the misuse of disability registers in Nazi Germany, which in the end were instrumental as a mechanism of selection in the implementation of "Euthanasia", the killing of thousands of mentally retarded and mentally ill persons.

The big difference in the prevalance rate of two the States, which are more similar than different in their overall socio-economic structure, leads to the hypothesis that two different populations are apparently labeled by the same terminology.

In psychometric terms Bach, one of the "founding fathers" of mental retardation research in Germany, speaks in his standard

## Table 6-1. Classification of "mental retardation"

| USA | | GERMANY | |
|---|---|---|---|
| IQ 70-55/50 | mild retarded | IQ 80/75 | Lernbehinderung |
| IQ 55/50-40/35 | moderate retarded | 60/55 | (learning disabilities) |
| IQ 40/35-25/20 | severe retarded | IQ 60/55 | geistige Behinderung |
| IQ 25/20 or less | profund retarded | and (mental ) less retardation | |

publication "Handbuch der Sonder-pädagogik" (Handbook of Special Education, 1979), of a tentative orientation at an IQ of 55/60 as the upper level of mental retardation, a limit which is generally accepted in Germany. It has to be emphasized, however, that the IQ is not a major argument in discussing mental retardation and its definition in Germany.

Nevertheless, a comparison of populations in the context of this publication is best possible by utilizing psychometric categories. This produces the following picture:

The juxtapositioning of the data shows that under the psychometric approach the population labelled "moderately, severely and profoundly retarded" in the USA is more or less equivalent to the population that is labelled as "geistig behindert" (that is, mentally retarded) in Germany. A reference to the psychometric data reconfirms this statement. The rate of 0.4% given in the USA for the part of the population with an IQ of less than 50 can roughly be related to the 0.5-0.6% quoted in Germany for the population with an IQ of 60/55 and less.

Consequently, *all statements in this article refer to a population that is labelled in the USA as "moderately, severely or profoundly disabled."*

## Social Policy and the System of Social Security for People with Mental Retardation in Germany

"Whereas social policy is a matter of decades, the people affected by it think in terms of years, even months."
—Christian von Ferber 1989, p. 265

### Guiding Principles of the German System of Social Security

Social policy is a sphere of political actions and decisions made on the grounds of shared values in order to influence society and societal living conditions. As much as social policy is an effective cause for social change, issues, goals and programs of social policy are influenced by historical and social forces. The life-situations of people with mental retardation are being influenced directly by social policy, and the quality of social services relate directly to the quality of their lives. The concept of quality of life, therefore, should be regarded within the context of social policy, of societal attitudes and ideologies, and of the social services' philosophy of service-providing.

The beginning of German social policy and the welfare state was closely connected with the negative consequences of early industrialization. The prevailing models of organization of work led to social conflicts, to problems of distribution and to poor living conditions for workers and their families. The introduction of the statutory social insurance funds in Germany in 1881, aimed at covering the so-called 'standard-risks' of life-situations that arose from the organization of work in modern societies: unemployment, illness, (work-)accidents and retirement. Problematic life-situations that do not emerge from one of these risks were covered by the statutory system of public assistance or, since 1961, by the system of social aid according to the Federal Social Aid Bill. The so-called standard-risks of all gainfully employed persons and their families, and with them the majority of the German population, are comparatively well covered by the statutory social insurance system.

The system of public assistance mainly covers risks of life-situations of persons employed by or serving for the State and can be compared with the social insurance system. A main idea regarding the life-situation of the population in Germany is the differentiation made between the population with disabilities and normal life-problems: while problems of working people are seen as *socially caused-collective problems of life* all other risks are being treated as *individual problems*, which are *not* (mainly) caused socially and therefore *not* covered by the collective system of social insurance. Persons not able to work, e.g., because of a disability, are dependent on this separate system of social aid.

Most of the services and benefits fixed by federal laws are not being provided by public services. Services are done by legal bodies of social services, for example, a body of the statutory health insurance funds, that provide the services in the name of the Government, but which are self-responsible, as defined by what is called the "principle of subsidiarity and self-responsibility." This means, that the self-organized activity of society takes precedence over the public activity. In the field of Social Aid, the principle of subsidiarity defines public assistance as having precedence over self-help-activities. The principle of self-responsibility of society is most consequential: Social Aid according to the Federal Social Aid Bill, is the 'last net' of the welfare-state, (covering only life-problems) *if all other resources of support (self-help-ability, also by family members) are exhausted.* Social Aid aims at enabling persons to help themselves, and refers primarily to financial aid (subsistence aid, provided by the legal bodies of social aid) and to social services (aid for special life-situations). Because of the principle of subsidiarity, social services according to the Federal Social Aid Bill are being provided by non-governmental welfare organizations, the so-called "free bodies of the welfare work." The precedence of free bodies of welfare work before public activity is laid down in the Federal Social Aid Bill; they have the right to provide services, according to existing laws, on the basis of their ideological principles. Social services and support according to this law are almost exclusively carried out by free bodies of welfare work, while in the field of services and benefits according to the Federal Social Insurance Law and the Federal Public Assistance Law numerous — in the field of education almost exclusively — public services and institutions are being offered.

All in all, the German structured system of social security defines: a) the population (employed or former employed resp. family members who not employed), b) the bodies of services and benefits (legal - free; pension insurance, health insurance, unemployment insurance etc.) c) the services and benefits (financial aid, social service, goods that are further differentiated by the kind of service, e. g., medical aid, vocational aid etc.). A main problem of this system is the differentiation, parceling, and dissipation of the field of assistance for disabled people, and the consequences are problems of planning, controlling, directing, coordination and cooperation in the field of services.

By including all working people and their families in the social insurance system and by extending the services for special life situations to nearly all life-problems not covered by social insurance, social policy today affects directly individual life-situations and life-chances of the whole population, including people with disabilities. The welfare state can, by means of active social policy-making, promote the quality of life of the population by supporting the equality of chance and eliminating disparities. The economizing of social policy, on the other hand, may limit the interest in quality of life in favor of economic interests. The future trends of social policy are decisive to the interest that society takes in the quality of life of people with mental retardation.

### Free Welfare Work in Germany

In Germany, the non-profit-organizations in the field of social services form an alliance of six associations, the so-called top organizations of welfare work. These six top organizations cooperate with the legal bodies of social services and the ministries of social affairs in the federal states: Arbeiterwohlfahrt Bundesverband e. V. (Federal Association of Workers' Welfare), Diakonisches Werk der EKD (Welfare Work of the Protestant Churches), Deutscher Caritasverband e.V. (Welfare Work of the Catholic Church), Deutscher Paritätischer Wohlfahrtsverband (Parity Welfare Association), Deutsches Rotes Kreuz (German Red Cross) and Zentralwohlfahrtsstelle der Juden in Deutschland e. V. (Central Welfare Work of Jews). As of January, 1990, these six organizations ran 68,446 social services with 2,624,923 places (beds) and 751,126 staff (old federal states, former West Germany). They are present in all fields of social or health services and in the field of vocational and advanced training for social and care professions. In the field of assistance for people with mental retar-

dation, they maintain 345 full-time institutions (defined as consisting of more than 40 places or slots), 290 residential centres (up to 40 places), 87 semi-independent living units, 248 special kindergartens, 42 day activity centers for children, 205 special schools, 453 workshops, 20 day activity centers for grown up people as well as peadiatric services, early intervention centers, ambulatory services, counselling services etc.

*There is no homogenous classification and categorization of services and institutions in Germany, and no statistical report on the exact number, the type and the providers of all social services exists.* The proportional rate of services maintained by the free welfare work compared with the number of publicly or privately run services can only be estimated and must be determined for every type of service. Most local or regional social services are members of one of the six organizations; commercial or private organizations are of minor importance in Germany. These organizations' strong position, embodied in the Federal Social Aid Bill and in the "Grundgesetz" (German equivalent of a constitution), is unparalleled in Europe, and the field of assistance for disabled people in Germany is substantially influenced by their actions and policies.

The securing of quality standards and criteria, therefore, is a struggle between competing models and programs: the models of the welfare organizations, based on their philosophy, the models, programs and legal principles of the State, and the perspectives and needs of the people concerned. Those "who have the chance of engaging on their behalf strong professional or administrative interests" (von Ferber, 1989, 273) may be able to receive the kind of support they need for their life-situation with a disability. Other groups, like people with mental retardation, need support in order to make claims for their interests and to secure quality as a function of their own needs and their own prspectives about quality of life.

### Policy and Services for People with Mental Retardation

The education and training of people with mental retardation is subject to changing historical conditions. Political, social and economic developments are determinants of this process of change. For a long time (and still today), parents and charitable organizations cared for the education of people with mental retardation. During the 19th century, institutions were founded in Germany like in many other countries, based on humanitarian, Christian, pedagogical, but also medical approaches. The public "Hilfsschulen" (assistance schools), increasingly established at the end of the nineteenth century, served to educate children with learning disabilities, but also with mental retardation. Humanitarian, Christian and pedagogical efforts in institutions and in schools led to a theoretically and practically based care and education of people with mental retardation. At the beginning of the twentieth century, a countermovement took roots from eugenic, economic and utilitaristic thinking, which led to the separation of mentally retarded people from the "Hilfsschulen" and finally to the cruel "euthanasia-actions" of Nazi Germany. The societal conflict between solidarity and the performance principle, a conflict concerning all societal minority groups, was decided after World War II against the democratic support of people

with mental retardation. A more widespread interest in understanding the history of the extermination of disabled people in Nazi Germany (practically a whole generation of people with a mental retardation were destroyed in this period) came into being in the 1970s and 80s. The analysis and discussion of these crimes and of this part of history is a task and a duty in practice and science in Germany.

In view of a near complete breakdown of service structures and as a consequence of very poor living conditions for people with mental retardation after World War II, parents began to organize themselves, inspired by international parents movements. The Federal Association Lebenshilfe for people with mental retardation was founded, an organization committed to the principle of normalization, community integration and to the concept of quality of life. The 1960s were a time of reform: "more quality of life and equality of opportunities", the slogan of the Social Democratic Party, was also the program for improving the rehabilitation system, the rights and living conditions of disabled people in the 1960s and 1970s. Public schools for children with mental retardation were set up. The training of teachers and special educationalists was established at the universities and community integrated services and workshops were founded. While this phase was mainly characterized by a quantitative growth of services and by the establishment of a local or regional service-structure, a new orientation was realized during the 1970s: disabled people themselves and their family members made claims for self-determination, independent living and integration. The professional system, criticized for bureaucratic, hierarchic and isolating service provision, slowly changed its philosophy, and integrated community, needs-oriented services were and still are realized step by step. The new "Betreuungsrecht" (Law of Care), set in force 1st of January 1992, inspired by the philosophy of advocacy and self-determination rather than by the philosophy of guardianship, has led to an improvement in the legal position of people with mental retardation.

The basic principle "social integration by way of normalizing the assistance given" demands that the quality of life of people with mental retardation be equivalent to that of the general population, and should include an orientation on objective standards and on subjective needs and perspectives. The second Report of the Federal Government on the Situation of the Disabled and the Development of the Rehabilitation of 1989 (*Bundesminister Für Arbeit Und Sozialordnung* 1989) explicitly contains the principle of integration, normalization, individualized and needs-oriented program planning and the "Finalprinzip" as the programmatic goals of the government. The "Finalprinzip" is an important principle for service provision. It means that assistance and services should not be given according to the cause of impairment (e. g., work accident), but according to the (medical, vocational, social etc.)[1] consequences of the impairment for coping with everyday life. A mandatory schedule of treatment requirements, combined with a state guarantee of payment for these services, takes precedence over all other considerations as to which particular social service body is to be debited (cf. von Ferber 1989, 269).

Yet the realization of this principle and the principles of normalization and inte-gration runs into obstacles: "disability" as an individual situation of neediness and as a societal problem of minorities goes beyond the structured system of social security with *its* differentiation of the population. Depending on membership to the gainfully employed population, people with disabilities receive their services and benefits from the social insurance fund or from the social aid fund. So the "Finalprinzip" is broken by the principle of causality: people with disabilities not gainfully employed receive numerous (not all) rehabilitative services according to the Federal Social Aid Bill. The German rehabilitation services include medical, vocational, pedagogical and social assistance. (re-)Habilitation services are provided by the different service-bodies of the social insurance system and the social aid system. Thus, the different fields of habilitation services are split and belong to different parts of the legislation. Although numerous improvements could have been realized during the last thirty years, "disability" is still legally defined in terms of an impairment, mainly of earning capacity, and not in terms of the social consequences of impairments and disabilities; the structured system of social security itself is not being questioned by the government.

In general, people with mental retardation in Germany are not gainfully employed in the "normal" labor market and thus depend on the system of social aid. An important part of assistance and support has to be provided by parents and families. In spite of a well-developed system of professional services and institutions, *the informal social networks of families with relatives with mental retardation are still more burdened with continuing support than the social net-*

*works of other families.* The professional services and support are mainly organized by free bodies of the welfare work making the families dependent on these charitable organizations. Therefore, neither the families nor the people with mental retardation themselves can decide on and determine the type of service-provider and the quality of assistance they want.

The (re-)habilitation system represents itself, by following the structured system of social security, as a split, differentiated and complicated system to many people with mental retardation and their families. The "chaos in the system of rehabilitation" (Depner et al., 1980) is additionally increased by the multitude of laws, of service-bodies, and occupational groups. Planning and financing of (re-)habilitation services is generally not based on local responsibilities and therefore local and regional needs, but at the level of the 16 federal states. The problems of quality securing and developing may be characterized with the words of Christian von Ferber (1989, 273):

1.  Professional and administrative interests tend to outweigh those of the people concerned. The needs of the disabled people are not sufficiently taken into consideration, and

2.  a communal infrastructure is missing. Continuity of help for the individual disabled person demands a locally secured responsibility for the maintenance of service quality.

In our view, to improve the quality of life of people with mental retardation and to create a consumer role for them, people with mental retardation have to be inte-

grated into the collective system of social insurance and should be able to choose freely their service-provider according to the quality of services offered. Given the social problems in Germany in the course of the reunification and the trends and tendencies in western industrial states, in general, to cut their expenditures for social policy on the grounds of economic problems, it is reasonable not to expect a financial improvement in the quality of life for people with mental retardation. Moreover, the public climate against minorities seems to be changing from one of tolerance to one of prejudices and intolerance. For the future, it will be of decisive importance to work against tendencies of individualization of social and societal problems and against utilitaristic orientations. Instead increased efficiency of the services systems' use of resources is required to improve the quality of life of people with mental retardation.

## Specific Programs and Services

### *Prevention and Early Intervention*

Every year in Germany, around 50,000 children are born with disabilities or disorders which could result in a disability later in life. Under the country's statutory health insurance schemes, which cover practically the whole population, all children up to the age of four are entitled to eight free medical check-ups.

There are around 80 socio-pediatric institutions in operation which follow-up on the first diagnosis of a pediatrician, offering specialized diagnostic and therapeutical services backed by psycho-social care facilities. These are often run by private, non-profit organizations. At approximately 450 socio-medical units set up to help children with mental retardation and their families, parents receive advice from educational specialists, psychologists, social workers, physiotherapists, speech therapists and medical or paramedical staff.

These centers often also provide specialized kindergarten facilities. They offer highly individualized programs, however, in a strictly segregated environment that often proves to be negative for the child's social learning. Therefore, more and more, parents request the integration of their child with mental retardation in a regular kindergarten. Currently, the existing number of places in kindergarten and preschool are limited. This does not facilitate the integration of a child with mental retardation, who is often rejected strictly on the "lack of places" argument.

### School

Schooling for the child with mental retardation is still predominantly provided in a segregated, self-contained setting, which is part of a highly specialized, but very much segregated special education system (special schools for children with mental retardation, learning disabilities, behavior disabilities, blindness, visual impairment, deafness, hearing impairment, physical disabilities).

Schools for children with mental retardation offer — with a few differences in the 16 German States — an individualized curriculum in an adapted learning environment. Classes are small (8-10 students) and no child, independently of the severity of the disability, can be rejected. Very often, children with severe and profound mental retardation find themselves in special classes inside the segregated school for students with mental retardation.

More and more parents and academics have become dissatisfied with the segregated school approach and fervently request the integration of students with mental retardation in the mainstream school system. So far, only a few pilot integration classes have been approved by the various state school authorities. Results have been encouraging on the primary level and the extension of the pilot classes into the secondary school system is foreseen. It is not probable, however, that a full-fledged integration policy will replace the segregated self-contained schools in the near future.

### Residential Services

The majority of mentally-retarded people, particularly children and youth, live within their family. The provision of a school program for each child irrespective of the severity of the retardation has certainly helped to strengthen the families' abilities to keep their child at home.

However, in recent years, more severely and profoundly retarded children are referred to residential centers. This is due primarily to parents not knowing how to simultaenously meet the double challenge of adequately supporting their child and meeting the increased pressures from a highly competitive, non-supportive environment. Particularly, single-parent households (mostly women) feel the lack of respite care services and individualized support.

Residential centers and institutions for people with mental retardation, mostly administered by private organizations associated either with the protestant or the catholic church, cater for about 40,000 adults with mental retardation. Most of these institutions, with between 200 and 1,500 places, can be found in rural areas and, in spite of important improvements in recent years regarding their program and physical structure, tend to keep their "clients" in isolation from the mainstream of society.

A significant problem is the approximately 10,000 men and women with mental retardation who are placed in psychiatric institutions. These run under a medical paradigm and were, until recently, not prepared to adapt themselves to the educational and rehabilitative needs of persons with mental retardation. Various states are currently revising this status, de-institutionalizing those clients who do not show a medico-psychiatric need and creating appropriate environments for those who need special attention also from a mental health perspective.

Approximately 18,000 persons live today in "community residences for mentally retarded people", many of which have a size of 40 to 60 places. The "Lebenshilfe" responsible for about 60% of this kind of residential service recommends to limit new community residences to only 24 places with groups of 6 to 8 people each. Still this number would certainly be more than that which is accepted in the United States as defining a good "group home."

Small community residences in family size apartments (3-5 places), apartments for couples or individual residences are limited in number. This can be explained, in part, by the lack of adequate support services and funding problems. It is widely agreed that more individualized residential services will have to be created to put into practice the generally accepted principle of normalizing the lives of men and women with mental retardation. The current problems of the German housing market (high demand and low construction lead to a sharp

increase in prices for houses and apartments) make the realization of this goal very doubtful.

### Vocational Training and Employment

German social policy puts a lot of importance on integrating men and women with disabilities into the workforce.

All employers with a workforce of more than 16 are obliged to set aside six percent of their jobs for employees with disabilities. For every vacancy not filled with these funds, the employer has to pay a levy of DM 200 (approx. US$ 145) per month into a fund managed by the federal and state governments. This fund is used for either providing special workplace aids and assistance to adapt existing jobs to the needs of disabled people or to build and equip special workshops. Of course, not all employers, neither public nor private, meet their obligation. Vocational training for disabled people is mostly given in specialized vocational training centers, which lead to state-recognized qualifications. In the framework of the dual system of vocational training (practical in a company – theoretical in a school), these specialized training centers do offer both components to their trainees and provide special support in relation to development of training material, therapies and daily living skills. These specialized training centers are residential and trainees live and learn there for a period of up to three years. Graduates usually meet the strict requirements of the German labor market upon completion of their courses after having passed the state-recognized exams. But, *very often do not have the social skills necessary to compete on the open labor market as they lived and learned in a segregated as well as protected environment.*

People with mental retardation are seen only rarely in these facilities. With rare exceptions, they all attend a sheltered workshop, there are currently about 600 in the unified country. Their 120,000 places are mainly taken by mentally retarded people, but also people with a severe physical and with psychosocial disability can be found in this kind of environment.

In terms of facilities, safety and operation, a workshop must meet certain requirements set by federal law. Every workshop must offer at least 120 places; it must be managed efficiently and staffed by the required number of specialists (foreworkers from industry who have gone through a special preparatory course on the shop-floor, social workers on the program management, economists on the business management). The typical workshop fulfills easy and low-paid piece-work for industry, some have their own production units (toys, printing, book-binding) or have embarked into the service sector (agricultural production, gardening).

A person first entering a workshop undergoes an orientation and training phase. Upon completion, the workshop management, in cooperation with the local employment exchange, reviews the individual's opportunity for transferring to the open labor market. This change, however, is extremly rare. Usually a person with mental retardation transfers from the sheltered workshop's training department into the workshop's production unit.

The costs of introductory and work training measures are usually borne by the Federal Labor Office. The costs for the work operations of these certified sheltered workshops are paid by regional welfare assistance agencies. People working in sheltered workshops do not have the legal status of an employee, and therefore do not work under a contract, they don't have the opportunity to participate in collective bargaining and are not unionized. Their salaries, not much more than an honorarium, are DM 220 in average (US$145) per month. However, they are fully covered by health and pension insurance. Provision of adequate insurance can be seen as a major advance, however, the lack of any alternative to the sheltered workshop system constrains most people with mental retardation in Germany. Supported employment programs have not been implemented as they do not seem to fit into the administrative structure of the regional welfare assistance agencies.

### Lifelong Learning

In recent years, an increasing number of initiatives have been found, particularly, in larger cities. They offer structured courses and programs for mentally-retarded adults either to strengthen skills learned at school, to initiate new learning or just to offer a more diversified leisure time. Most of these initiatives suffer from a constant lack of funds. Cooperation with mainstream adult education programs run by local authorities, offer some financial support and some possibilities for integration at the same time. A national association has been founded recently, to defend the right of life-long learning for mentally-retarded people.

## The Concept of Quality of Life: A New Perspective in Practice and Research

### Present Tendencies and Trends in Theory and Practice

In theory and practice, new orientations have emerged in the education of people with mental retardation in Germany. Some of these may be summarized as following:

- developmental model of mental retardation instead of a deficit-oriented model,
- a multidimensional concept of disability, mainly focusing on the social consequences of impairments and disabilities,
- a growing significance of ecological approaches, interactionist theoretical approaches in social science, with an emphasis on the individual and his/her environment, e.g. the growing meaning of the concept of social networks/social support as a theoretical framework and as a perspective for practical interventions,
- growing meaning of values, goals and ethical questions in theory and practice,
- a change of the organizational structures of the services: from institutional to community, from hierarchical to teamwork-oriented, from centralized to regionalized structures,
- the growing importance of integrative living and learning and of theoretical and practical conceptualization of integrative models,
- the promotion of the participation and self-determination of people with mental retardation in all questions concerning their lives.

All in all, these developments have a common focus–the processes of exchange between individuals and their environment; they strengthen the participation of the people concerned, help to regard quality of life as consisting of objective and subjective indicators, and assist in studying the effects of social services on the quality of life of people with mental retardation.

Social integration can be achieved by normalizing the assistance given. In the German understanding of the principle: such integration is based on equality and means the *normalization of the assistance given to give assistance to a life, similar to that of non-disabled people, and is subjectively perceived as a satisfying life with an individual lifestyle.* Assistance given should be oriented on everyday living conditions, not on the goals and needs of services. Therefore, the system of services should be organized, decentralized and needs-oriented.

The concept of quality of life, however, must be theoretically conceptualized and empirically concretized in order to effect changes. Goals and values may be influenced by implicit normative orientations, which are in contrast or not similar to explicitly declared programs. The reference to concepts like "needs" or "everyday life" may be an official service policy, but a bureaucratic and formal organization of services may lead to a dominance of the professional system and service goals instead of an orientation toward consumers' needs. The normative meanings and orientations and the empirical meaning of "quality of life" therefore need to be discussed between consumers, practitioners and scientists:

In German educational sciences, discussions about the quality of life of people with mental retardation are mainly influenced by medical issues related to the right of living for so-called "profoundly disabled people." The developments in the field of genetic technology and prenatal diagnos-

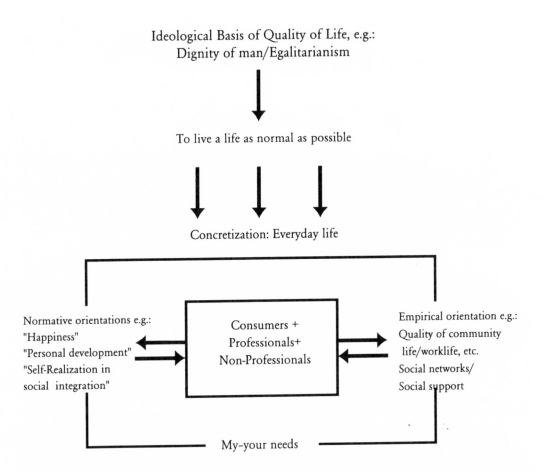

Figure 6-1. (cf.THIMM 1986.)

tics may have negative effects on societal attitudes towards people with disabilities. The societal rejection of illness and impairments and an utilitaristic philosophy lead to judgments of the quality of life of people with disabilities in terms such as 'harm', 'misfortune' etc. Also, as a result of the widespread discussions on the utilaristic concepts promulgated by Singer, the necessity of ethical discourses in the German special education and rehabilitation sciences, e. g., with biologists, genetic researchers, physicians, has been recognized. This seems to be a pre-condition for defending the right of people with disabilities to experience a quality of life that is based on their own conception of life. Individual quality of life is, above all, a subjective experience, and people with mental retardation often are treated as objects, not as subjects. Discussions of ethical problems and of the relevance of societal attitudes and discourses on quality of life should be part of the training of teachers and social workers, and of other occupational groups in the field of (re-)habilitation. The realization of quality of life as a service policy must include a consumer-orientation in the services' philosophy and a theoretically and empirically conceptualized framework that maximizes consumer-oriented planning, developing, measuring and evaluating of quality of life.

Services that do not ensure the participation, independence and self-determination of people with disabilities, including people with a mental retardation, will ultimately be rejected by consumers. Without a changed awareness within the professional system, be it the scientific system or the practical system of habilitation services, such a new orientation will hardly be realized.

## Research Initiatives Involving Quality of Life

The first application of the concept of quality of life in the context of mental retardation per se in Germany was put forward by Thimm (1978), inspired by the research of Zapf (1975) on the quality of life in West Germany. Zapf's definition of quality of life as 'subjective satisfaction in accordance with objective living standards' was developed with regard to the macrostructural study of a population's quality of life. The research interest concentrated on the correlation between objective living conditions and subjective well-being. The operationalization of important life domains of a society was developed according to a typology of basic needs; the way to fulfill these needs and the satisfaction of the population with the fulfillment represents the living standard of a society. Thimm (1978) regarded this concept as a chance to operationalize the goals of integration efforts in a multi-dimensional and complex way, to study the life-situation of people

with disabilities compared to that of non-disabled people, and to get more knowledge on factors contributing to the quality of life of people with disabilities. A comparative study of the life-situation of people with mental retardation in West Germany and in Denmark, Thimm et al., (1985) studied the realization of normal living conditions. The study made evident that the social security for people with mental retardation and their families, their legal position, the structure of the services, the life-situation of the families and the attitudes of staff and managers are important criteria for (objective) quality of life.

## A First Example: Research on Quality of Life of People with Mental Retardation Living in Institutions

Due to the lack of any other suitable instrument encompassing the German socio-cultural environment, König and his co-researchers utilized PASSING 1986-1988 in assessing the living conditions of seven institutions for mentally retarded people in (West-)Germany. These seven institutions differed considerably in their size (57 - 1332 residents, average 553 residents) and their age (18 - 90 years, average approx. 65 years).

This instrument, developed by Wolfensberger and Thomas (1983) and sometimes criticized as lacking the reliability, validity and objectivity of a viable empirical instrument, offers an interactionistic approach towards evaluating social services and focuses on the following categories:

- relevance
- intensity
- integrativeness

- felicity
- physical setting of service
- service-structured groupings & relationships among people
- service-structured activities & other uses of time
- miscellaneous other service language, symbols & images

Although the results of this research are far from representative, (random selection only and very limited number of institutions covered), they are interesting to the extent that they point out deficits and problems that seem to be typical when talking about the quality of life of many people with mental retardation in Germany.

After assessing 83 residential units in the seven institutions participating, critical deficits were noted, particularly, in the following items:

- Promotion of client autonomy and rights.
- Promotion of client socio-sexual identity.
- Competency-related intra-service client grouping-size.
- Individualizing features of setting.
- Internal setting appearance congruity with culturally valued analogue.

Regarding promotion of residents' autonomy and rights, a considerable number of operations were assessed, many of which appear to have been withdrawn from the residents' control without any justification. For example, time for leaving the place or receiving visitors was limited, the use of money was controlled, time for getting up and/or going for sleep as well as for meals were given and controlled and residents were made to participate in religious services. In addition to these procedures of everyday life that maintain strict control over the individual, the system of centralized services limited the residents' autonomy. The existence of a central kitchen, a central dry-cleaner, a central ordering department for furniture and household goods, sometimes also a central depot for the purchase and distribution of clothes, limits individuality and restricts the residents' potential for growth. Unable to shop, to cook, to wash one's self stabilizes or sometimes even creates dependency instead of strengthening autonomy.

Concerning the support of residents with sexual problems, difficulties could be found in all institutions. Very often professionals working in the residential units with residents whose heterosexual or homosexual relations were noted, would repudiate the issue, and display helplessness and fear. Instead of finding support, residents were often left alone with their needs as well as their problems. Usually, staff clearly expressed their uneasiness and lack of orientation regarding this situation. It cannot be of any surprise, that co-ed residences were rather an exception.

The sizes of the assessed residential units did not often meet the desirable standard for the optimal living and learning environment. In some of the institutions, the average size of the residential unit was between 15 and 16 residents. Even in the two institutions with the smallest units, the average was between 9 and 10. Some units of the participating institutions had more than 25 residents (mostly in multi-bed-rooms), small residential units with three or four residents existed, but they were the exception.

Concerning the individualizing features of setting, two of the seven institutions were notable in that their residents live in single rooms. This was the case in the two relatively new institutions. The other five, built about ninety years ago, provided double and multi-bedrooms, in spite of many renovation measures that continue to take place. However, the provision of single or double rooms alone is certainly not sufficient for using the full individualization potential of a physical design of a residential unit. Too often, the drabness of the furniture, of the floor, wallpaper, curtains, lamps, towels, sheets etc. creates uniformity. There has been a distinct lack of innovation in the use of these items; wall decorations such as posters, pictures, flowers etc., create individual and unique living environments.

There was a negative finding regarding the issue of the required similarity of a residential unit with the structure of the private residence. This analogy could be found only in 29 of the 83 residential units. Far reaching divergences in some units were, for example, multi-bedrooms, dining halls, corridors with a length of 25 yards and more, bathrooms with ten sinks and more. Also, some units had to serve as corridor for reaching another, some had to share their kitchen or their bathroom/ toilet with others, some even included rooms which served other purposes than those of the proper residents (e.g. pharmacy, guestroom, time-out room for the entire institution).

Another negative factor for five of the seven assessed institutions was their isolation in rural areas, poorly served by public transport. This factor limited the potential for integration, as natural learning environments (such as shopping in the supermarket, going to the movies etc.) were un- or underutilized. At the same time, existing segregation was reinforced.

Here are some of the strengths that have been identified during the PASSING assessment:

The interaction of residents and staff in the residential units were of particularly good quality. Often, they were characterized by respect, sensitivity and spontaneity. Of overwhelming importance for the quality of life of the individuals concerned was the intensity of staff-residents relations in some units with persons with a profound retardation.

Also, individual rehabilitation plans had been developed for most residents, thus supporting a reasonable and responsible structure of daily activities.

Returning to the seven categories mentioned above, we can summarize that particular weaknesses in the overall picture of the seven institutions assessed occur in the categories *relevance, integrativeness, and physical setting of services.* It has to be noted, that there were, however, considerable differences between the seven institutions as well as among the units of each institution.

In relation to our criterion of quality of life, the negative result regarding "relevance" seems to be of particular importance. It means that a significant part of the residents live in an non-adequate environment that does not relate to their needs.

Comparing this study with other writings in Germany today, it is clear that a step towards improving their quality of life for pesons with disabilities would mean offering them more decentralized and individualized living environments in the communities. This would certainly not guarantee women and men with a mental retardation an automatically high quality of life and full personal satisfaction; isolation and segregation are also possible while living in the city; sadness and depression are still possible when living with friends. But, the opportunities generally given in a non-institutionalized setting seem to make it easier to provide people with mental retardation with experiences and opportunities that are seen, in the US as well as in Germany, as very much related to high quality of life.

### A Look into the Future

While social indicators concretize collective objective living conditions empirically, they hardly give a view of the subjective, individual quality of life and they hardly allow a view of the effects of services on the individual quality of life. A basic requirement of individual quality of life experience is the participation in structures of interaction and communication. Integration in a sociological sense means nothing less than the uniting individuals to a group, a community, and a society. The integration of people with mental retardation in different social systems throws an illuminating light on their previous isolation to their participation in communication and interaction, and on the values and norms that determine interaction and communication in social systems.

Integration may be regarded as a processional, dynamic process of role-taking and needs-realization that should be studied thoroughly: the integration in societal systems (political, economical, educational, etc.) should be distinguished from the integration in informal social networks in everyday life (social and personal integration). Physical and functional (access to and use of resources) integration are prerequisites for processes of exchange and needs fulfillment between individual and environment. Furthermore, these processes should be regarded differently for various life settings and life periods: different life settings contribute to satisfying different needs, preferences of needs change in different periods of life. Nevertheless, the connection between life-settings should also be regarded; quality of worklife influences the quality of family life. Transitions between life-settings and life-periods may mean a fracture in the process of integration with the goal of improving the quality of life, especially if no coordinated assistance is given for coping with transitions and with special needs in different life-periods and settings.

Integration by normalizing the assistance given should be conceived as a means and/or an end in order to satisfy needs and realize goals (aspects of quality of life). Quality of life is the framework for and the outcome of all efforts, while integration is rather a (neutral) process than a goal per se. The relevance of integrative and normalizing processes is based on their contribution to improvements for the individual quality of life; underlying values and norms of these processes and of the idea of a "good life" should be made explicit. Every discussion of quality of life should therefore refer to different life-settings, life-periods, aspects of integration as prerequisites of needs-realization and to values and norms:

Quality of life consists of objective living conditions, and social and subjective factors (satisfaction, well-being). Research on the correlation between subjective and objective determinants of quality of life has clearly shown that individual well-being is influenced by the quality of living condi-

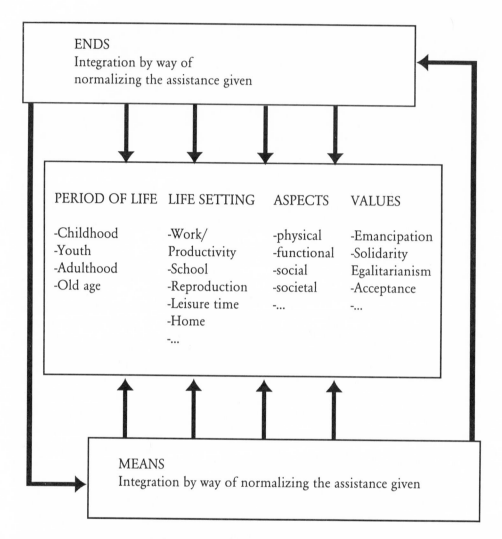

Figure 6-2. A View of QOL Factors (cf. SHILLER 1987 and BECK 1992).

tions like income, housing etc. But such research has also demonstrated that needs like self-realization, affiliation and appreciation are more important for individual well-being (cf. e. g. Badura et al. 1987; Campbell et al. 1976; Glatzer & Zapf 1984; Schiller 1987; Thimm, Schiller & Beck, 1987). Furthermore, it is the self-evaluation of quality of life which is decisive for the experience of individual well-being; needs-realization must be subjectively perceived positively in order to contribute to well-being. The ability to articulate needs, to choose the way of needs-realization and fulfillment, is dependant on the availability of *external resources* of support (like good living conditions, a high service quality, but also meaningful social support and social relationships) and on *internal resources* (self-image, competence etc.).

While objective living-conditions are a product of societal welfare, the 'producers' of subjective welfare (affiliation, appreciation) are found within social relationships and in social networks. Thus, individual quality of life can best be analyzed by studying micro-structural social relationships and processes of interaction and communication within the concept of social networks/social support. Such an analysis always should include the individual assessment of social relationships and resources of support, as perceived by the people concerned. Social services and their staff are always part of the networks of people with disabilities and can be regarded as external resources of support. An important question for the study of quality of life is, in what ways can informal and professional resources of support complement each other most effectively to improve the subjective well-being of people with mental retardation? Social services are the seam for the transmission of service quality into quality of life; the development of service quality in a way that services contribute to everyday coping and to the experience of meaningful social relationships is a current challenge for the professional system.

In Germany, the first theoretically-based application of the concept of social networks/social support within the context of coping with disabilities can be found in Schiller (1987) and Thimm, Schiller & Beck (1987). These studies focused upon: a) coping with everyday life and the consequences of impairments; and, b) structural and functional aspects of social networks/social support (availability of, adequacy of and satisfaction with resources of support and the social integration of people with blindness and physical disabilities. People

with mental retardation, however, depend more than other groups on professional support, and an analysis of social networks/social support of people with mental retardation must take their special needs and the important role of social services and their organization into consideration.

Because of its missing tradition of evaluating services, Germany is still at the beginning of studying the effects of social services on the individual quality of life of people with mental retardation. However, the interest in Germany in quality of life development, measurement and assessment is growing, and the free bodies of welfare work have begun to take an interest in systematic approaches to quality of life-oriented service planning and evaluating. The Federal Association Lebenshilfe organized the first congress in quality of life-oriented development and measurement for residential services (Bundesvereinigung Lebenshilfe, 1992). The "Quality Evaluation Guidelines as a Means of Renewal and Revitalization of Services by Voluntary Associations" of the International League of Societies for Persons with Mental Disability (ILSMH, 1988) is an important document in discussions of QOL. The German Society for Heilpädagogik assigns a key function to the quality of life concept by strengthening the participation of people with mental retardation in planning, developing and evaluating services. Moreover, the society expresses interest in the development of quality of life-oriented evaluation instruments, as well as in methods and procedures for participative definition, planning and evaluating of quality of life and for coordination and cooperation between services (DHG, 1991). It will be of decisive importance to prevent misuse of evaluation instruments simply as means of improving the cost-effectiveness or of control. The use of instruments therefore should be embedded in and be part of a quality-of-life-oriented framework for services.

Quality of life is a 'complex' concept, concerning societal living conditions, service organization, communities and the individual level. Every dimension should be analyzed with regard to factors and determinants contributing to or impeding quality of life (cf. Goode, 1988a-d). But no analysis of factors will give a complete view on quality of life without including factors developed and assessed by the people with mental retardation and their families themselves. More and more complex research designs or evaluation and assessment procedures may allow a more complex view of possible factors of quality of life, but human action and processes of interaction and communication are more complex and subjective than empirical research is able to represent. Quality of life is mainly a subjective concept. It ultimately will place limits upon the professional and scientific 'delusion of practicability', the 'pedagogics of effecting' by shifting the structures and processes of legitimation, decision and control to the consumers. Also, it will realize a common, equally entitled arrangement of existence (cf. Kobi, 1988) between consumers and professionals, and between people with disabilities and those without.

Beginning with the powerful position of the top organizations of welfare work in Germany, and the differentiated, heterogenous and split structure of services, it will be necessary to begin with open discussions on the definition, on standards and criteria for quality of life in theory and practice, to develop procedures for coordination and cooperation between services and procedures for the participation of people with mental retardation and their families on planning and controling of service quality. Priority tasks in order to conceptualize and realize the concept of quality of life in Germany include:

- Multidimensional operationalization of needs and resources and of structural and functional aspects of social services, with regard to different life-settings and life periods.
- Research designs for assessing the subjective perspectives and needs of people with mental retardation and their families.
- Study of the well-being, satisfaction and social integration of people with mental retardation.
- The conceptualization of frameworks for the definition, development and assessment of quality of life, development of quality of life-oriented evaluation instruments and assessment proceedures.
- Participation of people with mental retardation in proceedures of decision and assessment and improving their representation of interests, development of quality of life-oriented concepts for counseling social service organizations.
- Development of procedures and methods for better coordination and cooperation in order to overcome the differentiation and splitting of the service system.

These developments are both challenges and opportunities to persons with mental retardation and those who provide services to them in Germany. In the future, we believe that quality of life will occupy an increasingly central role in policy and services to this population.

## References

Andrews, F.M. (Hg.) (1986). *Research on the quality of life.* Ann Arbor: Michigan.

Bach, H. (Hg.) (1979). *Pädagogik der Geistigbehinderten. Handbuch der Sonderpädagogik, Band. 5.* Berlin.

Badura, B. et al. (1987). *Leben mit dem Herzinfarkt. Eine sozial-epidemio-logische Studie.* Berlin.

Beck, I. (1990). Normalisierung und Lebensqualität: Zielperspektiven und Beurteilungsfragen. In: *Bundesvereinigung Lebenshilfe Für Geistig Behinderte E.V.* (Hg.), 1992: 11-36.

___(1992). Neuorientierung in der Organisation pädagogisch-sozialer Dienstleistungen für behinderte Menschen: Ziel-perspektiven und Bewertungsfragen. Carl von Ossietzky-Universität Oldenburg.

___& Thimm, W. (Hg.) (1989). *Integration Heute and Mergen.* (Integration Measures of Today and Tomorrow.) Düsseldorf.

Bleidick, U. (Hg.) (1985). Theorie der Behindertenpädagogik. *Handbuch der Sonderpädagogik,* Band 1. Berlin.

___(1988). Betrifft Integration: behinderte Schüler in allgemeinen Schulen. *Konzepte der Integration: Darstellung und Ideologiekritik.* Berlin.

Bott, E. (1957). *Family and social network.* London.

Bundesarbeits Gemeinschaft der Freien Wohlfahrtspflege (Hg.) (1990). Gesamtstatistik der Einrichtungen der freien Wohlfahrtspflege. Bonn

Bundesminister Für Arbeit Und Sozialordnung. (1989). Behinderte und Rehabilitation. Zweiter Bericht der Bundesregierung über die Lage der Behinderten und die Entwicklung der Rehabilitation. Bonn

Bundesvereinigung Lebenshilfe Für Geistig Behinderte e.V. (Hg.) (1986). Normalisierung - eine Chance für Menschen mit geistiger Behinderung. Groâe Schriftenreihe der Bundesvereinigung Lebenshilfe für geistig behinderte Menschen e.V., Band 14. Marburg.

___(1992). Qualitätsbeurteilung und entwicklung von Wohneinrichtungen für Menschen mit geistiger Behinderung. Bericht über eine Fachtagung. Marburg.

Campbell, A., Converse, P.E. & Rodgers, W.L. (1976). *The quality of American life: Perceptions, evaluations, and satisfactions.* New York.

Cohen, S. & Syme, L. (1985). *Social support and health.* New York.

Depner, R, Linden, H. & Menzel, E. (1983). *Chaos im System der Behindertenhilfe.* Weinheim.

Deutsche Heilpädagogische Gesellschaft e.V. (1991). Satzung und Positionen der Deutschen Heilpäda-gogischen Gesellschaft. Düsseldorf.

Deutscher Bildungsrat. (1973). Empfehlungen der Bildungskommission: Zur pädagogischen Förderung behinderter und von Behinderung bedrohter Kinder und Jugendlicher. Bonn.

von Ferber, Ch. (1983). Soziale Netzwerke: ein neuer Name für eine alte Sache? - *Geistige Behinderung (4):* 250-258.

___(1989). Future-oriented policies for disabled people. In: Beck, I. & Thimm, W. (Hg.): 265-280.

Glatzer, W. & Zapf, W. (Hg.) (1984). *Lebensqualität in der Bundesrepublik. Objektive Lebensbedingungen und subjektives Wohlbefinden.* Darmstadt.

Goode, D.(1988a). *Quality of life for persons with disabilities. A review and synthesis of the literature.* Valhalla/New York.

___(1988b). *Discussing quality of life: The process and findings of the work group on quality of life for persons with disabilities.* Valhalla/New York.

____(1988c). The proceedings of the National Conference on Quality of Life for Persons with Disabilities. Valhalla/New York.

____(1988d). Principles and recommendations from the quality of life project. Valhalla/New York.

Gromann-Richter, P. (Hg.) (1991). *Was heisst hier Auflösung? Die Schliessung der Klinik Blankenburg.* Bonn.

International League of Societies for People with Mental Disability. (1988). Quality evaluation guidelines as a means of renewal and revitalization of services by voluntary associations. Bruxelles.

Jakobs, H., Koenig, A. & Theunissen, G. (Hg) (1987). *Lebensräume Lebensperspektiven. Erwachsene mit geistiger Behinderung in der Bundes-republik Deutschland.* Frankfurt/M.

Keupp, H. & Roehrle, B. (Hg). (1987). *Soziale Netzwerke.* Frankfurt/M.

Klee, E. (1983). *"Euthanasie" im NS-Staat. Die "Vernichtung lebensunwerten Lebens".* Frankfurt/M.

Klee, E. (Hg.) (1986). *Dokumente zur "Euthanasie".* Frankfurt/M.

Kobi, E.E. (1988). *Heilpädagogische Daseinsgestaltung.* Luzern.

Koenig, A. (1986). *Normalisierung und Bürgerrechte - Geistig behinderte Erwachsene in den USA.* Frankfurt/M.

____(1991). Ist Qualität messbar? Qualitätserfassung von Einrichtungen für Menschen mit geistiger Behinderung nach dem PASS-ING Verfahren von Wolfensberger. *Geistige Behinderung (3)*: 240-249

Luhmann, N. & Schorr, K. E. (Hg.) (1982a). *Zwischen Technologie und Selbstreferenz. Fragen an die Pädagogik.* Frankfurt/M.

Maslow, A.H. (1970). *Motivation and personality.* New York.

von Nell-Breuning, O. (1976). Das Subsidiaritätsprinzip. *Theorie und Praxis der sozialen Dienste 27(1)*: 6-17.

Olk, Th. & Otto, H.-U. (Hg.) (1985). Der Wohlfahrtsstaat in der Wende. Umrisse einer künftigen Sozialarbeit. Weinheim, München.

Organization for Economic Co-operation and Development. (1973). List of social concerns common to most OECD countries. Paris.

Röhrle, B. & Stark, W. (1985). *Soziale Netzwerke und Stützsysteme.* Tübingen.

Schalock, R. L. (1990a). *Quality of life: Perspectives and issues.* Washington, D.C.: American Association on Mental Retardation.

____& Jensen, C.M. (1986). Assessing the goodness-of-fit between persons and their environments. *Journal of the Association for Persons with Severe Disabilities 11(2)*: 103-109.

____et al. (1989). Quality of life: Its measurement and use. *Mental Retardation 27(1)*: 25-31.

Schiller, B. (1987). *Soziale Netzwerke behinderter Menschen. Das Konzept sozia-ler Hilfe- und Schutzfaktoren im son-derpädagogischen Kontext.* Frankfurt/M.

Schmidt-Ohlemann, M. & Harms, J. (Hg.) (1990). *Soziale Netzwerke und Regionalisierung, Perspektiven für Behinderte.* Frankfurt/M.

Sozialgesetze, (1984). *Textausgabe mit einer Einführung von Prof. Dr. P. Krause.* Darmstadt.

Sozialhilferecht. (1991). *Textausgabe.* Darmstadt.

Speck, O. (1988). *System Heilpädagogik. Eine ökologisch reflexive Grundlegung.* München, Basel.

____& Martin, K.-R. (Hg.) (1990). Sonderpädagogik und Sozialpädagogik. *Handbuch der Sonderpädagogik, Band 10.* Berlin.

Thimm, W. (1978). Behinderungsbegriff und Lebensqualität. Ansätze zu einer Vermittlung zwischen sonderpädagogischer Theorie und Praxis. In: *Brennpunkt Sonderschule*: 24-30.

____(1986). Normalisierung und alltägliche Lebensbedingungen. In: *Bundesvereinigung Lebenshilfe Für Geistig Behinderte e.V. (Hg.), 100-114.*

____(Hg.) (1989). Ethische Aspekte der Hilfen für Behinderte. Groâe Schriftenreihe der Bundesvereinigung Lebenshilfe für geistig Behinderte e.V. Band 19, Marburg.

Thimm, W. (1991) Integration, oder: ein Versuch,

etwas Diffuses auf den Begriff zu bringen. Gedanken zur Integrationsproblematik bei Personen mit Sehbehinderungen. *Sonderpädagogik 21*(1): 4-11.

___Schiller, B. & Beck, I. (1987). *Soziale Netzwerke behinderter Menschen. Bericht an die Deutsche Forschungsgemeinschaft.* Carl von Ossietzky Universität Oldenburg.

___von Ferber, Ch., Schiller, B. & Wedekind, R. (1985). Ein Leben so normal wie möglich führen... Zum Normalisierungskonzept in der Bundesrepublik Deutschland und in Dänemark. *Groâe Schriftenreihe der Bundesvereinigung Lebenshilfe für geistig Behinderte e.V.* Band 11, Marburg.

Thoits, P. (1982). Conceptual, methodological, and theoretical problems in studying social support as a buffer against life stress. *Journal of Health and Social Behavior 23:* 145-159.

VDS - Fachverband für Behindertenpädagogik (Hg.), (1989). *Dokumentation: Human-genetik, Behinderung, Euthanasie.* Anmerkungen zu einer aktuellen DiskussionE. Lingen.

Windisch, M. et al. (1991). Wohnformen und soziale Netzwerke von Erwachsenen mit geistiger und psychischer Behinderung. *Neue Praxis* (2): 138-150.

Wolfensberger, W. & Thomas, S. (1983). *Passing-Manual.* Toronto.

Zapf, W. (Hg.) (1975). Soziale Indikatoren. In: Schiller, B. & Beck, I., (1987). *Soziale Netzwerke behinderter Menschen. Bericht an die Deutsche Forschungs-gemeinschaft.*

# 7· Quality of Life and Unemployment: An Empirical Study About the Effects of Unemployment on People with Disabilities in Hungary

Csaba Banfalvy
Bascai Training College, Budapest, Hungary

As it is widely demonstrated in the literature, work is an organic element of quality of life. In the modern society work and employment are so closely related that the spectre of unemployment causes great distress for those without a job (see eg., Allen, 1986, Jahoda, 1982, Warr, 1987).

Employment is fundamental for a healthy way of life, not only for the normal people but for people with disabilities as well.[1] While employment is the main source of income, it can also provide a valuable source of information. It creates the framework of social contacts, it determines a persons time schedule and it is also a basis of social status. Unemployed persons can suffer a great deal of financial, social and psychological difficulties.

In short, we believe employment to be a basic necessity for people in the modern society and one of the main determinants of Quality of Life.

However, at least in Hungary, when it comes to people with disabilities, we tend to neglect the importance of work, believing, for some reason, that employment isn't as necessary for persons with disabilities as it is for the non-disabled individuals. There-fore, when people with disabilities are un-employed, references are made to their alternative source of income (eg. welfare programs for the unemployed or help from the family). In Hungary, it goes as far as discounting persons with disabilities living on welfare as part of the labor force. And, to make matters worse, they are not consid-ered as unemployed either (see: Banfalvy, 1989, 1991). One can forget that unemploy-ment is not exclusively a financial diffi-culty, but a very complex social and psycho-logical challenge as well.

Our empirical research, conducted in 1991 and 1992 in Hungary, focused on the adjustment problems and perceived quality of life of the unemployed in general. We also collected data about the state of health and the possible disabilities of those in the sample.

## Description of the Research

In our research, promoted by the Hun-garian Academy of Sciences, we used writ-ten questionnaires obtained from 5840 people. At a later time, we conducted about one hundred taped interviews with unemployed people, public administration experts in unemployment offices and company managers. We also conducted a content analysis of four local and national newspapers writing about unemployment or the situation of the unemployed.

In the spring of 1991, we conducted interviews of about 1200 unemployed and 1340 employed people. In the spring of 1992, interviews of some 2400 unemployed and 900 employed persons were collected. In 1991, our information came from 14 pre-selected settlements in the country and in 1992, from 24 pre-selected cities and villages in Hungary. The settlements represent seven different types of labor market regions (labor market segments); the modern, rapidly developing capital of the country, the tourist-oriented western parts of Hungary, the traditional heavy metal industry regions of the north-east, and the underdeveloped small agricultural villages of the countryside.

Our research is representative for age and sex, but city dwellers and those qualified educationally higher than average are slightly overrepresented compared to the population as a whole, or compared to the officially registered unemployed population.

In the following pages we use the findings of our research to demonstrate some of the problems connected with quality of life, unemployment, employment and the situation of persons with disabilities in Hungary. We also raise some theoretical questions concerning the meaning of unemployment in the case of individuals with disabilities.

## Socio-Demographic Characteristics of the Survey Sample

There were 169 people among the unemployed in the sample who indicated they have some kind of disability(4.7%). Of this total 105 of them were men and 64 were women. There were only 69 disabled persons among the employed or self-employed (the economically active). This means that the rate of those disabled was 4.1 % among those employed or self-employed; 61 % of the disabled were unemployed. In effect we may conclude that the rate of unemploy-

### Table 7-1. Marital Status of the unemployed and the economically active

| Marital Status | Unemployed | | Active | |
|---|---|---|---|---|
| | Disabled | Non-disabled | Disabled | Non-disabled |
| Married or live in couple | 47.6 | 57.6 | 71.0 | 71.1 |
| Single | 38.1 | 30.5 | 21.7 | 19.5 |
| Divorced or separated | 12.5 | 10.5 | 05.8 | 06.8 |
| Widowed | 01.8 | 01.4 | 01.4 | 02.1 |
| TOTAL | 100.0 | 100.0 | 100.0 | 100.0 |

## Table 7-2. Level of Education of the Unemployed and the Economically Active

| Educational Level | Unemployed | | Active | |
|---|---|---|---|---|
| | Disabled | Non-disabled | Disabled | Non-disabled |
| Max.primary school | 30.8 | 30.8 | 27.5 | 19.1 |
| Secondary vocational | 40.9 | 39.2 | 40.5 | 49 |
| Secondary grammar | 18.3 | 12.3 | 14.5 | 16.4 |
| Higher education | 10.1 | 7.7 | 17.4 | 15.5 |
| TOTAL | 100.0 | 100.0 | 100.0 | 100.0 |

ment was higher among persons with disabilities than among non-disabled people, and that within the disabled group the majority were unemployed.

Marital status it is not only a fundamental determinant of the quality of life, but it is important from an economic standpoint. The adult living alone is more sensitive to economic losses derived from unemployment than two or more adults with families.

People with disabilities live more frequently outside of the traditional family relations and live alone more often, compared to the normal population. This has very serious financial consequences for those unemployed as there is not a helping hand nearby who could ease the economic difficulties and can assist during the emotionally, difficult unemployment period.

When we compare the two groups of disabled persons, we find those who are unemployed live alone far more frequently than the economically active persons with disabilities.

If we take into account that living alone is the economically, socially and psychologically most disadvantageous situation for the unemployed, then we can summarize our findings thusly: Persons in the employed category with and without disabilities are in a better position than the nondisabled unemployed. The unemployed group of disabled persons have the worst position of all.

Still, because a person has a disability, it does not mean that the person is in a more disadvantageous position in the labor market than those who have no disability whatsoever. Some people with disabilities are in a better position than some of the non-disabled. Socio-economic and medical-pedagogical factors affect one's fate in a complex, combined way as does the level of educational qualification.

Here again, we have to make our investigation in two different directions, according to employment status and disabilities. People with disabilities are over represented in the less and the most educated groups among the employed, and are either much less or more educated than the non-dis-

**Table 7-3. Distribution of the unemployed according to the way they became unemployed**

|  | Disabled | Non-disabled |
|---|---|---|
| could not find a job after school | 09.7 | 07.7 |
| company bankruptcy | 14.2 | 16.7 |
| lay off | 37.4 | 44.7 |
| fired for inappropriate behavior | 01.9 | 01.7 |
| resign | 15.5 | 15.2 |
| other ways | 21.3 | 14.0 |
| TOTAL | 100.0 | 100.0 |

abled employees. Those people with disabilities who are highly educated were, in most cases, not disabled at birth but became so during their adult life as a consequence of accident or age. Those disabled at birth were, as a rule, less educated than the normal population. Very few have a higher education degree. Most reach only the secondary school level.

We can not say, however, that persons with disabilities per se are less educated than the normal population. Level of education itself can not be a reason why persons with disabilities are over represented among the unemployed. The disability, itself, is related to the overall likelihood of being without a job. Among the unemployed people with disabilities we observe higher levels of education than among the nondisabled unemployed.

To conclude, a disability has an influential and disadvantageous role on employment possibilities. In many cases its influence is indirect, working through factors like marital status or schooling. The situation of people with disabilities can only be understood, therefore, as a result of a complex set of socio-demographic determinants.

## How People Became Unemployed

Most of the unemployed people lost their jobs because of company bankruptcy, through redundancies, or could not find employment after school.

Two examples demonstrate the effect of a disability: more people with disabilities found it difficult to get a job after school and more of them became unemployed because of illness (included in the category: 'other' in the table). Still, it is not obvious that by virtue of being disabled, people would more easily lose their jobs than nondisabled persons (for instance persons with disabilities are less likely to be unemployed through layoffs).

The majority of the unemployed who were interviewed were generally satisfied with their previous job.

The only aspect in which both groups were unsatisfied is with their salary in their previous job. People with disabilities were less satisfied with their bosses at the previous workplace than the other unemployed. For the most part, the majority of both groups were satisfied with the previous job and became unemployed against their will.

While less than 3% of the normal unemployed will not seek employment in the future, the proportion of those leaving the labor market is almost 6% among persons with disabilities. This fact raises a very important question.

People with disabilities are often accused of being unambitious and therefore do not seek employment. Moreover, they prefer to live on welfare, to which they are entitled even if they do not have, or have never had, employment. It is true that many persons with disabilities really prefer to stay on welfare or living with their family's assistance instead of searching for some job. The explanation for that, however, is not that they are lazier than the normal population, but that — at least in Hungary

— they are not socialized for the harsh life in the larger society.

In the Hungarian educational system, there are separate schools for persons with disabilities and only the mildly mentally disabled (debilis) have some chance for integration into the normal society during their studies. More importantly, disabled children, in many cases, are also separated and are distinct from the everyday life of their families because the schools for persons with disabilities are centralized. Most of the children remain in boarding schools where they seldom meet anybody except their teachers and the pupils of the same disability category they belong to.

This separation has its negative impact on the quality of life of persons with disabilities more generally and for their employment possibilities. Paradoxically, often it is the person with disabilities who chooses non-employment, thereby forefeiting all the positive benefits employment could mean for their quality of life.

## Table 7-4. Satisfaction with Previous Job

|                     | Disabled | Non-disabled |
|---------------------|----------|--------------|
| salary/wage         | 27.3     | 27.1         |
| position            | 62.0     | 65.3         |
| the work he/she did | 64.1     | 68.0         |
| working time        | 64.8     | 62.0         |
| atmosphere          | 65.5     | 66.4         |
| collegues           | 73.8     | 74.7         |
| the bosses          | 49.0     | 56.3         |
| TOTAL               | 100.0    | 100.0        |

They often feel more familiar with the segregated and isolated life of the disabled community where there is a feeling of belonging. They find it more than daunting to enter the more or less unknown territories of normal social life. Living on welfare can become a safer option than risking failure and humiliation at a workplace.

The separate school system results not only in the intended exit of persons with disabilities from the labor market but fuels negative prejudices against persons with disabilities in normal society and especially, at job sites. Because normal people know very little about persons with disabilities, fears such as that persons with disabilities can be dangerous either to him\herself or to the work mates at the workplace are widespread. The result is twofold. Some employers do not employ anyone who is disabled, others, who have always had people with disabilities among their labor force, hesitate to fire anybody who has a disability. Often the employed person with a disability is kept on the job because the employer is not only satisfied with their work performance, but is also fully aware that the unemployed disabled person has a very small chance of finding another job. It is difficult for persons with disabilities to find employment.

## How People Spend Their Time While Unemployed

The difficulties mentioned are more prevalent in the case of the unemployed in Eastern Europe because unemployment is a very new phenomenon. People have not had the time or the opportunity to learn what unemployment means and how they can defend themselves from its negative consequences. Unemployment in Eastern Europe is a much bigger social, psychological and economic challenge than the simple unemployment data indicate.

Thus when we investigate how unemployed people try to adjust to the changed situation of their lives, we must take into consideration that people in the ex-communist countries have no experience of being unemployed. In effect, this means, adjusting to a new unemployment routine, finding out what social assistance they are eligible for, searching for a seemingly elusive job, trying to use their time which used to be occupied by work constructively, and finally, replacing or rebuilding an alternative arena of social contacts which would have once been fulfilled by the workplace. Unfortunately, it does not end there: people also find it very difficult to rebuild their self-esteem, especially when relatives, neighbors and the wider public is unsupportive and at times almost condemning.

It might be supposed that this adjustment process rings less true in the case of the disabled. The status of "disabled living on welfare" offers them an escape from the humiliating social label of being unemployed. But this should only be a supposition, for, in spite of all this, unemployed people with disabilities suffer from being without a job. They, perhaps, suffer more from unemployment than the non-disabled unemployed because employment may provide them with more satisfaction than the non-disabled.

Unemployed people, in general, seem to have a less organized and systematic life, more greyish and meaningless, at least compared to those who are employed.

One of the possible advantages of being unemployed is that people can decide rela-

**Table 7-5. The Percentage of Those Agreeing with the Statements Below**

|                                                     | Unemployed |      | Active |      |
| --------------------------------------------------- | ---------- | ---- | ------ | ---- |
|                                                     | D          | ND   | D      | ND   |
| I meet a broad range of people in my everyday life  | 40.4       | 39.4 | 64.4   | 62.2 |
| Things I have to do keep me busy most of the day    | 52.4       | 57.4 | 95.5   | 85.1 |
| Much of the day I have to do things at regular times | 57.8      | 63.2 | 92.4   | 86.0 |
| I make a positive contribution to society at large  | 23.3       | 28.4 | 75.8   | 72.0 |
| Society in general respects people like me          | 24.8       | 25.3 | 47.0   | 46.7 |

D: Disabled ND: Non-disabled

tively freely how to spend their time. We found that many of the unemployed used a great proportion of their time for doing different types of informal work. What is surprising is that those respondents who self-identified as being disabled do as much work during unemployment as those who are not disabled.

The main area of economic activity is the household but occasionally people work in the market economy too. Fifty-six % of persons with disabilities and 59% of the normal unemployed do relatively more housework during the period of unemployment than they used to do before losing their jobs. This indicates that people try to substitute work done in the non-formalized sectors of the economy for the work performed while employed.

The non-formalized and non-institutionalized (second economy) work relegates people to a "second society," which exists on the margins of social life. Those unemployed in the long run, disabled or not, have to adjust themselves to the new rules of the second society. Unfortunately, more and more unemployed persons with disabilities are being forced outside the main stream of social life. Invariably, a status of marginality creates a backlash in the normal society against persons with disabilities, compounding the problems of unemployment. This process — unemployment and marginalisation — would appear to have definite negative implications for the quality of life for persons, and in Hungary, in this present economic climate, it is a problem we are trying to combat.

## Notes

[1] In this paper the word "normal" always means *non-handicapped* and is meant in a purely descriptive way.

[2] The questions used in this table are from the study of Heywood, F. & Miles, I. The experience of unemployment and the sexual division of labor, in D. Fryer & P. Ullah (Eds.), (1987). The authors used these questions in their research to measure social contact, activity, collective purpose, status and time structure self evaluation by people in their sample.

## References

Allen, S., et al. (1986). *The Experience of Unemployment*. British Sociological Association, London.

Ashton, D.N. (1986). *Unemployment under Capitalism. The Sociology of British and American Labour Markets*. London: Harvester Press.

Banfalvy, Csaba. (1991). *A munkanelkuliseg es tarsadalmihatasai*. (Unemployment and its Social Consequences) Budapest.

Banfalvy, Csaba. (1989). Fogyatekosok a munkaeropiacon.(Handicapped People on the labour Market) *Szocialis Munka, (4)*.

Belyo, Pal. (1984). Szolgaltatasok: Kereslet es kinalat. (Services: Demand and Supply) *Gazdasag, (2)*.

Bokor, Agnes. (1987). *Szegenyseg a mai Magyarorszagon*. (Poverty in Hungary Today) Magveto, Budapest.

Brenner, S. et al. (1988). Unemployment and Health in Sweden: Public Issues and Private Troubles. *Journal of Social Issues, (4)*.

Cantor, D., and Land, K.C. (1985). Unemployment and Crime Rates in the Post-World War II United States: a Theoretical and Empirical Analysis. *American Sociological Review (50)*, pp. 317-332.

Fineman, S. (1987). *Unemployment, Personal and Social Consequences*. Tavistock Publications.

Forrester, K., and Ward, K. (1991). *Unemployment, Education and Training*. Sacramento, California: Caddo Gap Press.

Fryer, D., and Ullah, P. (1987). *Unemployed People: Social and Psychological Perspectives*. Open University Press.

Gershuny, J. (1978). *After Industrial Society? The Emerging Self-Service Economy*. London-Basingstoke: MacMillan.

Iversen, L., and Sabroe, S. (1988). Psychological Well-Being Among Unemployed and Employed People After a Company Close-down: A Longitudinal Study. *Journal of Social Issues, (4)*.

Jahoda, M. (1982). *Employment and Unemployment, a Social-psychological Analysis*. Cambridge: Cambridge University Press.

Kessler, R.C., Turner, J.B., and House, J.S. Effects of Unemployment on Health in a Community Survey: Main, Modifying and Mediating Effects. *Journal of Social Issues, 1988, (4)*.

Kornai, Janos. (1986). *Contradictions and dilemma*. Cambridge: MIT Press.

*Labour Market Policies for the 1990s*. OECD, Paris. 1990.

Lindbeck, A., and Snower, D.B. (1988). Long-term Unemployment and Macroeconomic Policy. *American Economic Review, (78)*, pp. 38-43.

Munkaeropiaci Informaciok. (Labour Market Informations) Budapest, Orszagos Munkaeropiaci Kozpont.

Norris, G.M. (1987). Unemployment, Sub-employment and Personal Characteristics: Job separation and work histories:the alternative approach. *The Sociological Review, (5)*.

Stern, J. (1983). The Relationship between Unemployment, Morbidity and Mortality in Britain. *Population Studies, (37)*, pp. 61-74.

Thornberry, T.P., and Christenson, R.L. (1984). Unemployment and Criminal Involvement: an Investigation of Reciprocal Causal Structures. *American Sociological Review, (49)*, pp. 398-411.

Warr, P. (1987). *Work, Employment and Mental Health*. Oxford, England: Clarendon Press.

# 8• Quality of Life of People with Disabilities in Hungary After Leaving School ·

Viktor Gollesz,
Budapest Training College for
Teachers of Handicapped Children

In Hungary, compulsory education begins for people with disabilities as early as 6-years-old and continues until age sixteen. This is the same compulsory education requirement that exists for non-disabled children.

Thus, the optimal case is that a child with disabilities will stay in school until the age of 16, although this may not be the case for those who are considered unfit for school education. On the other hand, if a sixteen-year-old person should fail to graduate but show a capability for subsequent development and schooling, then his or her education may be prolonged to age eighteen; by which time it is expected that he or she would have graduated. This educational arrangement has implications for the social care services that succeed special education, which must be focused upon a broad range of concerns related to young people with disabilities aged fourteen through eighteen.

The coordination of services for young people with disabilities who have passed school age is integrated into a ministry responsible for adult social care and protection. The Social Rehabilitation Center is involved in the social and vocational rehabilitation of young people, who were disabled from birth or infancy. The Ministry of Public Health is responsible for the Social Rehabilitation Center. The Center, as well as other institutions under its control, are supported by the national budget, and their existence is assured by the state.

At the Social Rehabilitation Center, a team of special educators and psychologists provide vocational and related assessments upon which subsequent rehabilitation efforts are based. This same group is engaged in scientific research and conducts experiments related to the rehabilitation problems of persons with disabilities.

Currently, there are fourteen institutions and eight sheltered workshops, all rehabilitation-oriented, which are controlled by the Social Rehabilitation Center. These institutions are responsible for the care of eighteen hundred young persons with mental, visual, hearing and/or motor disabilities. In addition, two hundred and forty young people are working in sheltered workshops and, in order to learn a profession, two hundred and fifty young persons attend special workshops at three training centers offering skilled vocational training.

## Overview of Services to Disability Groups

The following reviews the main forms of social care for persons with disabilities by considering the various categories of disabilities.

### People with Visual Disabilities

People with visual disabilities show great variation in concerns and vocational choice. Young people with visual disabilities are admitted each year to institutions, (there are enough placements to allow this), for further study or training. They are given vocational training within a skilled worker's training center for persons without disabilities, but in a special classroom where they learn professions such as broom or brush making, basket weaving, book binding, re-upholstery, or medicinal massage.

In addition to vocational training, people with visual disabilities have the opportunity to continue their secondary school, grammar school or even college or university studies in normal classes with non-disabled persons. The institutions under the Center's control provide hostel accommodation with full board for people with blindness who are attending continuing education or vocational training. Moreover, tutors and resident masters assist them with their studies.

Other options for vocational development available to young people with visual disabilities, who because of age or other reasons can not continue with their education but who are otherwise trainable, are courses provided by the Alliance of the Blind and People of Impaired Vision. Through such courses they may be trained

as telephone operators, or to work in any part of the operations of broom or brush making. Vocational placement is assured by the Alliance.

Finally, however, there is a ubiquitous problem with the training and vocational placement of persons with visual and mental disabilities. For a population whose productive work can only be carried out under continuous guidance and control and at reduced time and work loads, there is a profound lack of appropriate supports and services.

For those young people with only visual disabilities who are successful in their vocational lives, the elimination of antiquated traditions of education and training often found in institutions is very important. They would prefer to see forms of rehabilitation that emphasize preparation for an independent life, with an emphasis on extra-institutional involvements.

### People With Motor Disabilities

People with motor disabilities may be admitted to two types of institutions in order to obtain training or employment. There are special classes located within the skilled worker's vocational training centers where girls with motor disabilities may receive training in dressmaking, or boys, in mechanical instrument making. These young persons live in hostels attached to the training centers. The training centers assure all the facilities necessary for their training. There are environmental adaptations such as railings, and adjustable chairs in workshops. The vocational training is for the most part similar to that of young persons without disabilities, however, it differs in that it is carried out by trained nursing staff. The staff at the Social Rehabilitation Center provide technical support in problems related to special education and rehabilitation. Young people with motor disabilities are admitted to these training programs at the suggestion of the Social Rehabilitation Center and if they meet the ability tests set by the training center. A certain number of boys with motor disability may attend vocational training in watchmaking, though these lack hostel arrangments.

In addition to these services, there are social homes with a training orientation operating under the Center's control. In such homes the care, vocational formation, and employment of young men and women with motor disabilities is carried out. Grammar and secondary school classes are provided, and classes for short hand and typing are given. Those young persons who live in these homes may also attend the worker's training centers and pursue careers and trades (for example, fancy leather goods making, men's tailoring, radio engineering).

These homes may also provide services to persons with motor disability who are beyond the age limit of compulsory education but who may not have finished primary school, for example, because of extended illness. In such homes they may complete their education with the help of a special educator and a tutor.

If a young person with a motor disability is judged unfit for professional training or continued training they may attend special occupation workshops where they earn money and are taught a form of work which, hopefully, could later provide them with a satisfactory feeling of working, allow them to contribute to their costs of living, or even earn their own living.

Once again, there are problems with the care of young persons with multiple disabilities, especially because we do not have experience in providing appropriate programs and supports for this population. Nor do we have good solutions to the problems related to their aftercare and with the overall conceptualization of their rehabilitation process.

### Persons with Mental Retardation

The care of young persons with mental retardation is realized in two types of institutions. Institutions for social occupation accept persons with mental retardation who are unable to live independently and earn their own living, and whose family is unable to cope with their care at home. Such persons may be, in all other ways, successfully occupied in the community and their readiness for work developed. In these institutions there are available occupations in fields such as: agriculture, gardening, animal breeding, and industrial workshops. In the industrial workshops, special departments of the the production process, items such as car washing brushes, carbon brushes, and gluing paper bags are produced. In some institutions professional circles are operating; the girls' needle work circle already produces great work. These institutions' educational and occupational results have advanced considerably over the past several years.

Since 1967, we have had a network of sheltered workshops. In the past five years particularly, we have seen the standard of work as well as the number of workers in sheltered workshops increase dramatically. Two types of sheltered workshops have been developed: the family background type and the workers' hostel background type. In the family background sheltered workshop the persons work in isolated workshops. They come to the workshop from their family circle and it is their family who provides for their life should they be unable to earn their own cost of living. In these workshops there are reduced work requirements, and the young persons working there get paid according to their achieved work. They work under constant work and educational guidance. Their work is limited to making of artificial flowers, packing, and assembling mechanical parts. The majority of young people with mental retardation in such workshops have moderate mental retardation without serious behavioral or personality problems.

Those young persons with mental retardation who have already attended an institution for social occupation may attend the sheltered workshops with a workers' hostel background. They live in workers' hostels and work together with non-disabled workers. The work requirements and wages are comparable to non-disabled workers, although, while working, those with mental disabilities are under the direct control and guidance of a special foreman. After work they return to the hostel maintained by the enterprise for whom they work. There a social worker looks after them while they are residents of the hostel. A special attendant is there to help them with financial matters e.g., managing their money. The use of free time, entertainment and general quality of life is supervised by the special educator. Entry into these sheltered workshops depends on the clinical and vocational assessments performed by the Social Rehabilitation Center's staff.

Currently, we are concerned with the expansion of the sheltered workshop net-

work and with the use of research to help evaluate new work areas.

### People with Hearing Disabilities

The occupational rehabilitation of young people with hearing disabilities is solved through special schools for skilled worker's vocational formation, provided by the National Association of the Deaf and of People Hard of Hearing. Their continued education is organized by this Association and carried out partly in special classes, and partly in classes with students without disabilities.

The Association, similar to that of the Association for the Blind and Persons of Impaired Vision, is organized around the idea of safeguarding interests. The adult person with deafness rarely requires admittance to an institution and generally they work among the non-disabled workforce. It is the Association that gives them assistance necessary for their employment, helps solve problems related to the workplace and also organizes cultural and sport activities.

## Quality of Life and People with Disabilities In Hungary

In Hungary today, we approach the care of persons with disabilities after school as a task involving multiple systems and disciplines. Multidisciplinary knowledge coupled with a high level of training, a strong humanistic attitude and skill in social politics is required to successfully provide vocational and educational programs for these persons. This is why, at the Budapest Training College for Teachers of Handicapped Children, we have started four new classes in these areas. It will be the task of experts graduating from these classes both to increase the level of vocational and social services provided in the area of adult protective services, and to organize rehabilitation and care in later stages of the life cycle. We thus recognize the central role played by well trained professionals in promoting the quality of life of young adults with disabilities.

This essay has been only an overview of the vocational and related services provided to various disability groups after school age, and it should be noted that recently there have been tremendous strides in the quality of educational and vocational life experienced by persons with disabilities in Hungary.

# 9. The National Quality of Life for Persons with Disabilities Project: A Quality of Life Agenda for the United States[1]

David A. Goode
City University of New York

The ideas leading to the National Quality of Life for Persons with Disabilities Project conducted in 1987-88 in the United States were the result of many changes in the field of human services for the past decade: deinstitutionalization, normalization, educational mainstreaming, self-advocacy and inclusion. Some of these changes resulted in the field beginning to ask questions about issues related to "quality." In interaction with persons with disabilities, with their parents and with persons who worked with them, there began to be clearly evidenced an increasing concern with quality of services and supports, and what quality meant. This concern was, in my own experience, international in nature. One of the forms it took was in the research literature on quality of life (QOL) of persons with disabilities. There are now several books and a plethora of articles on this topic, and several countries have conducted national QOL projects. Some four years after the end of the National QOL Project in the United States, QOL has become one of the most researched topics in the field today.[2] There are many QOL research and citizen projects all over the world, some of which are represented in this volume.

The National Quality of Life Project in the U.S. was supported by the Administration on Developmental Disabilities (A.D.D.) and was the first of its type; a premature but courageous attempt to wrestle with the definition of QOL and explore the potential of this term to the field of disabilities. Its conception was the result of the thinking of several persons, working within a rapidly changing "post-normalization" service system. The actual phrase "The National QOL Project" was first voiced in the back of a taxi cab in London, when the then Commissioner of A.D.D. was finally convinced that the agency needed to conduct another strong project to parallel that of the "Employment Initiative". It was this Employment Initiative that had earned her national, and now international, recognition (she was accepting an award from a well known international foundation in disabilities). And it was the Employment Initiative that had been successful in beginning job placements and new forms of employment supports for thousands of persons with developmental disabilities.

Our discussion with her after her award ceremony and later in the cab posed another kind of concern. Recognizing the importance of work and employment, we asked her, "Within what overall policy context do you provide supports for people with disabilities? How can you provide sevices that fit with what people with disabilities want? How and what do they think about their lives? What does living a quality of life mean to them?". We had agreed that these ideas were of interest to the Administration in Washington.

We agreed also on a mechanism through which these questions might be addressed. The Mental Retardation Institute would conduct a National QOL Project that would involve significant input from persons with disabilities and their families, and would examine the potential of the concept of QOL for the disabilities field. The Commissioner also wanted the QOL Project to produce at least a framework for the measurement of QOL because the government had an interest in evaluating the QOL impact of the dollars allocated to persons with disabilities.

The agreement forged in the cab actually covered what was done by the QOL Project to a large degree. Of course it was several years and two Commissioners later that the project was finished, but it did progress remarkably like that first agreement intended!

## The Process

Exactly what the QOL Project did and how is described in several technical publications (Goode, 1988 a,b,c,d) and a book chapter (Goode, 1990a). While this writing will briefly summarize some of the approach and process of the project, it will concentrate more upon its results, and specifically the "QOL Agenda" that was produced for A.D.D. The agenda, or overall program to be used to develop the concept of QOL for people with disabilities remains as valid today as when it was formulated in 1988, and could prove still useful as an outline for the development of the QOL concept in the United States and other countries.

A general aspect of the conduct of the QOL Project was that the expertise and opinions of persons with disabilities were of central concern and almost all important decisions were made with their significant input. Three major phases to the project were identified as part of the 'method' to investigate QOL: 1) finding out what we already knew about QOL; 2) using what we knew to help structure the input of persons with disabilities when they discussed their own QOL; and 3) holding a conference at the end to help summarize and emphasize what we had learned about QOL.

A decision made early on, with the input of friends with disabilities, A.D.D., and the professionals involved in the project, was that the approach taken to QOL would be generic and not particular to the lives of persons with disabilities. The idea of looking at the research on QOL generally, and formulating an approach to QOL that was consistent with research, was also a decision made early in the QOL Project. It was thought that the framework identified in the research literature might be useful in structuring the discussions of groups of people with disabilities reflecting on their QOL. It was reasoned that discussions of QOL should not "give away" what might have been found out already about QOL.

The project thus began with a review of QOL literature (Goode, 1988b). This review of the literature was done with a particular perspective: to identify critical factors and relationships that have been found to be of concern when individuals examine their QOL. That is, the way in which QOL was looked at was from the point of view of the individual. In addition, social relationships were stressed, thus leading to an individual, social ecological model of QOL presented in Figure 9-1 below.

This research model is "true" in some sense to a main body of findings in the QOL research literature, a literature that is over fifty years old, but it is far from being free of contradiction.[3] The circles in the model are "subjective" factors, while the squares "objective" ones, thus capturing the dual character of QOL. The complexity of the model represents with some accuracy the potential complexity of QOL for any individual. This model can be used to generate hypotheses and thinking about QOL. But the model is far too complex to be used in structuring discussions about QOL. Thus the model was simplified, and

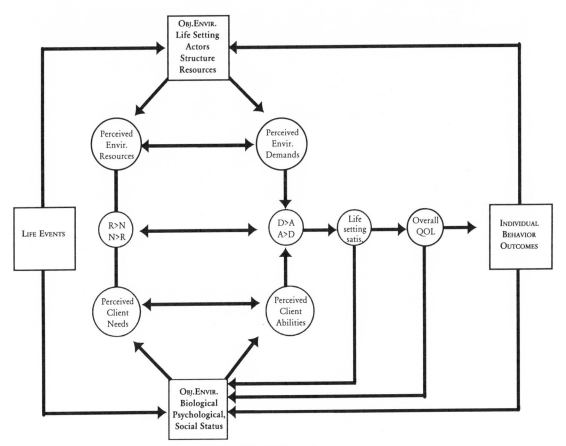

Figure 9-1. A Client-Driven, Ecological, QOL Model.

four basic factors related to QOL were employed for purposes of structuring QOL discussions: the individual's needs, the expectations that these needs are subject to in his/her society, the resources required by the person to meet his/her needs in a socially acceptable fashion, and the environmental issues related to meeting needs/expectations. This model, that was used to structure discussions about QOL is presented in Figure 9-2.

The center of this model is the desired QOL behavior outcome. These factors were then employed to structure discussions about QOL.

The best way to understand how this model works is through illustration. I will use a real one. One group discussed what QOL meant to adults with developmental disabilities when they are working in an integrated work site with non-disabled workers as coworkers. They concluded, among other things, that persons with disabilities had a need for friendships in these settings (factor 1 of the model). They then discussed the kinds of expectations (factor 2 of the model) these needs set up in others e.g., if you want to make a friend, what are the things that people will want to see from you? This is a basic problem for all of us in our daily lives: how to resolve our needs with the social expectations that such needs bring forth. If one could agree on exactly what one needed to do to achieve a better QOL, then it becomes possible to talk about the resources one needed (factor 4), and how others or the environment might help or hinder you (factor 5). Thus if you want friends at work, you will need to know certain things, and be able to do certain things that are usually the expected things that friends do. What are those things? What do you need to do them? How can the environment or others enhance the attempt?

This is the way the QOL literature was

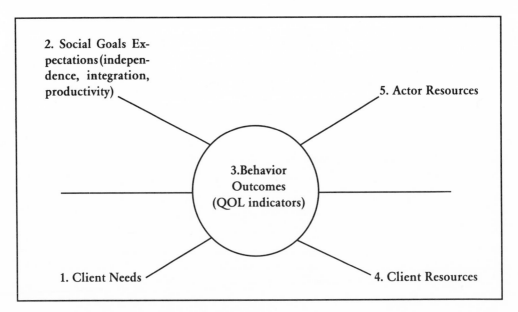

Figure 9-2. Quality of Life Discussion Framework

used to structure QOL discussions involving persons with disabilities, professionals, parents and others. Approximately 45 people, about one third of whom had a disability, assembled in a retreat setting to discuss QOL. These were divided into five small discussion groups They were instructed by facilitators to discuss QOL in a structured way using the model we had suggested, and also to discuss quality of life in an age graded and setting-specific way. Thus, each group discussed QOL for a specific age group (infants, school age children, young adults, adult, aged) and for a specific setting (own apartment, in a hospital, at the church, etc.).

The decisions to use age groups and setting-specificity were consistent with the research literature on QOL. QOL varies in some critical dimensions with age. The school age child and the working parent have, to some degree and quality, different needs and expectations to which they are subject. Equally important, QOL is not the same within different institutional spheres. One does not look to the family, the school, the 'guys and girls' you hang with at the mall, or the church for the same kinds of needs and relationships. This is why the discussion of quality of life required all groups to be very specific and concrete about what they meant. They had to specify the age group, setting, particular others who were in the setting, the needs that were seen to be important to the setting, the expectations to which those needs were subject, the desired resolution between the need and the expectation, and the personal and environmental resources that were required. The matrix provided in Table 9-1 displays the kinds of information required from each group in their discussion.

This matrix is actually a graphic reinterpretation of Figure 9-1. Groups were asked to fill these matrices out for several settings in their assigned age group.

The actual course of the next days had not been well predicted. There were many serious discussions. Groups had professionals, parents and persons with disabilities in them, and this led to a certain amount of 'perspectival conflict.' The groups were very animated and commited to their discussions, many working an incredible number of hours over the course of the retreat. There were several reactions to and revolts against the model we proposed. It was interesting and remarkable, although, that all groups eventually returned to the model or some recognizably transformed version of it.[4]

## Findings of the Quality of Life Project

One of the most interesting set of findings of the QOL project are the reports of these discussion groups (Goode, 1988c). Individually and assembled, they are the most detailed and comprehensive discussion of QOL for persons with disability ever attempted. While they cannot be presented or described in this current writing, the reader is invited to request them in their original publication. Because of the seriousness with which groups took to their task, the completed matrices and modified matrices were tremendously detailed representations of what a QOL meant for a mentally retarded child living for three months in a hospital, or for a person with mental retardation to be working in a regular job site with non-retarded workers. One is struck by the fact that despite some

## Table 9-1. Needs/Goals Matrix

| Age Group: | | Settings: | Other primary actors: | |
|---|---|---|---|---|
| Need (1) | Need Salience | Social Goals & Expectations (2) | | |
| | | Independence (Decision-Making) | Integration (Participation) | Participation (Responsability) |
| Love | H__M__L | * | | |
| Acceptance | H__M__L | | | |
| Sexuality | H__M__L | | | |
| Friendship | H__M__L | | | |
| Personal Growth | H__M__L | | | |
| Health | H__M__L | | | |
| Possessions | H__M__L | | | |
| Financial Security | H__M__L | | | |
| Stable Environment | H__M__L | | | |
| Recreation/ Leisure | H__M__L | | | |
| Culture/Faith | H__M__L | | | |

*Boxes when filled in refer to element 3 of the QOL discussion framework desired behavior outcomes.

serious disagreements in nearly all groups, each group was able to arrive at some consensus about QOL for a specific age group in a particular context; all groups submitted at least several completed matrices. That this kind of consensus was achievable, was itself remarkable, and convinced many of those involved that QOL had real potential as a policy concept in the field. Table 9-2 presents a completed matrix appear below by way of example, to illustrate the richness and detail of the QOL discussions.

This chart illustrates the adult group discussing employment in an integrated work site. The need of feeling "accepted" is pursued in some detail in Table 9-2. The matrix shows that QOL discussions can be very concrete, complex and useful in program development for persons with disabilities. The fact that many persons agreed about issues related to QOL showed us that

## Table 9-2. Completed Needs/Goals Matrix

| Age Group: Adult | | Settings: Integrated Work Setting | Other primary actors: Supervisor, Co-workeres | |
|---|---|---|---|---|
| | | Social Goals & Expectations (2) | | |
| Need (1) | Need Salience | Independence (Decision-Making) | Integration (Participation) | Participation (Responsability) |
| Love | H__M__L* | | | |
| Acceptance | H_*_M__L | choose a work enviroment in which you will be able to relate favorably to others | optional work environments & opportunity to accept or reject | recognize your supervisor's position & authority; accept cultural & behavioral differences among co-workers |
| Sexuality | H__M__L* | | | |
| Friendship | H__M_*_L | choose people to be friendly with and relate to | access to informal groups during breaks and lunch | initiate inter-relationships & talk or socialize with other people |
| Personal Growth | H_*_M__L | choose to work in an enviroment that gives opportunities for advancement | available options to move ahead | finish options for training: seek out & develop knowledge & skills to move up the ladder |
| Health | H_*_M__L | choose a safe environment to work within | seek out safe working conditions; sit with non-smokers | maintain your own health, safe working conditions; report unsafe working conditions |
| Possessions | H__M_*_L | be able to choose your own environment; work space | opportunity to provide & receive feedback regarding supplies, equipment & work space | accept the parameters of the organization & maintain equipment & supplies |
| Financial Security | H_*_M__L | choose job with wages & benefits you need to do what you want to do | opportunity for jobs with optimum wage scales & benefits & the potential for increases | seek jobs that give wage and benefits |
| Stable Enviroment | H_*_M__L | choose a job with long-term prospects | assess the jobs | be an efficient, productive worker |
| Recreation/ Leisure | H__M__L* | | | |
| Culture/Faith | H__M__L* | | | |

*H=high; M=medium; L=low.

QOL can be defined consensually. It also showed us that such discussions can provide strong indicators of the kinds of supports and services necessary to help people with disability achieve better QOL. The process also indicated that with proper facilitation persons with cognitive disabilities can meaningfully participate in complex discussions such as those described above.[5]

There was the 'only apparent complexity' of our QOL discussions that should also be noted. In one sense, when you got down to the details of the discussions a lot of what we find in the matrices filled out by the group is simple, common sense. It seems obvious after having said it. A person will have a better QOL if he or she has friends at work. To meet friends at work the person needs to know $x$ or $y$, and the others around him or her might need to know $a$ or $b$ about that person. We were somewhat taken aback at first that all this complicated research and structured input of persons with disability had led to somewhat commonsensical ideas about QOL. But we came to appreciate this as a strength of our approach in that it produced ideas and actions consistent with what persons involved knew to be the case. The power of the QOL framework was that it got what everyone knew to be the case out in the open and then held them accountable to it. There was a kind of paradox in the way QOL was appreciated in the project— as potentially incredibly complex, while at the same time very simple. The best 'QOL is simple' quote comes from Ed Roberts who said,

> "In one way QOL is simple. What we want to know is, 'Are people [with disabilities] out there doing it the way

they want to? If not, why not, and what can we do to help?"

## The National QOL Conference

Another set of results of the QOL Project was the National Quality of Life Conference and its proceedings. In this gathering, 150 persons, about one third of whom were disabled, listened to presentations by persons with disabilities discussing their QOL, and participated in workshops such as research, policy, programming, evaluations, family support, etc., to help formulate recommendations about what should be done in QOL in these areas. This was the final phase of our project that was intended to summarize what we had learned about QOL and formulate recommendations to the federal government about how to proceed in the QOL arena. A proceedings of that conference is available (Goode, 1988d).

## The QOL Agenda: The Principles and Recommendations of The National QOL Project

In order to best disseminate the essence of what the National QOL Project had learned about QOL it was decided that a summary document describing the essential principles and recommendations of the QOL Project be written. The remainder of this chapter is adapted from that technical report (Goode, 1988a).

A small work group of persons with disabilities and professionals was assembled with this task in mind. The document was approached from the standpoint of trying to summarize the Project's essential perspective and implications of this perspective for the field of disabilities. In drafting the document all previous project materials were considered by the group. After synthesizing the recommendations of this group, a draft of the project's principles and recommendations were circulated to about 300 persons who had been involved in the project. Many of these wrote back with comments and criticism that were generally incorporated into the final draft. Thus, the *Principles and Recommendations* document represents the consensus of a considerable number of persons with disabilities, family members and professionals about what to do with QOL in the field of disabilities in the United States at that time.

In the preparation of this document it was decided that a core set of values and principles needed to be articulated. This was partly because there has been an increasing emphasis in the field of disabilities on using explicit value systems in services, and in making agency actions accountable to these values. It was also done because participants in the project saw that there were two levels of axioms involved in the work of the project. One was an acceptance of certain human values that are beyond demonstration in any scientific sense, and another an acceptance of certain basic principles that flowed from these basic values, our QOL discussions and the research literature.

We used the form of a Prologue to introduce the value axioms. The Prologue was the result of discussions with Edward Roberts and others from the World Institute on Disabilities. It reflected the kinds of comments we had heard from people with disabilities throughout the Project. The following is the text of the Prologue to that report.

*"QOL is something that all persons understand and relate to in similar way and is basically a simple thing. This makes QOL a powerful social policy concept and orientation to delivery of supports and services. A QOL orientation to supporting persons with disabilities is based upon these values. It organizes the provision of supports and services to make these values realities in the lives of persons with disabilities. Because QOL as it was used in this project was only partially based upon the findings of empirical research, it was important to include a preamble explicitly stating some of the value assumptions associated with this approach to QOL.*

*An approach to the term Quality of Life (QOL) for persons with disabilities consistent with usage in the Quality of Life Project is one that emphasizes the whole individual, not just his or her disability. Looking at individuals from a QOL perspective focuses on the strengths and abilities of persons with disabilities. It also acknowledges that people with disabilities are essentially similar to other people in society, but with certain functional limitations. Most persons with disabilities have expectations and dreams, and like others want to control decisions concerning their lives as much as possible. Most persons with disabilities want to have friends, to be able to choose to be involved in the social relationships that make up their community, to feel valued and to be economically and/or socially productive, to be able to choose to participate as citizens in government, to have the choice to take risks that are necessary to achieve goals meaningful to them, to have the choice to be a romantic or sexual person, and so on. In short, most persons with disabilities want for themselves the same choices others in the society want. QOL is a concept that gives primacy to the individual's point of view. It can and should account for the experiences of persons with severe cognitive, emotional or physical disabilities and reflect the very different ways such persons may see the world and set goals within it. QOL is a concept based primarily upon a cognizance of and respect for the viewpoints and perspectives of persons with all types and degrees of disabilities."*

Based upon these values and what we had learned collectively about QOL, nine QOL principles were formulated. These appear in boldface and italics in the body of the QOL Agenda that appears below. The principles are grouped, along with associated specific recommendations, into three content areas: defining and conceptualizing QOL, measuring and assessing QOL, and impacting the system/enhancing QOL. In addition, within each content area, recommendations are divided into those primarily of concern to individuals with disabilities, those primarily of interest to professionals, and more general ones.

## Defining and Conceptualizing QOL

### Principles

*QOL for persons with disabilities is made up of the same factors and relationships that have been shown to be of import to persons without disabilities.*

*QOL is experienced when a person's basic needs are met and when he or she has the opportunity to pursue and achieve goals in major life settings.*
*The meaning of QOL in major life settings*

*can be consensually validated by a wide array of persons representing the viewpoints of persons with disabilities, their families, professionals, service providers, advocates, and others.*

*The QOL of an individual is intrinsically related to the QOL of other persons in his or her environment.*

*QOL of a person reflects the cultural heritage of the person and of those who surround him or her.*[6]

### Recommendations for persons with disabilities

1.  In order to assure that the definition of QOL employed in social policy is consistent with the way persons with disabilities and their families think about QOL, *additional input from consumers is required.*

    Several individuals and the work group recommended that additional input from consumers about QOL definition and issues was an important next step. The group suggested open discussions, Delphi method, focus groups, and in-depth interviews as methods to get such input. Currently projects in New York and California are collecting additional data from consumers and their families utilizing these approaches. Additional states should consider implementing similar projects.

2.  Because of the social nature of QOL, *it is critical to develop supports and services that are based on an understanding of the relationship between QOL family supports, independent living, personal attendant care, and staff quality*

of work life (for example quality of work life in community residences).

For a person with a disability to experience a good QOL he must be in settings where others also experience a good QOL. The most important dimension in determining QOL is the relationship between the individual with disabilities and those who regularly and directly interact with him/her in the setting. There is a direct link between quality of family life and quality of work life and the QOL of individuals with disabilities. Family supports, quality of work life programs and staff development, and approaches to integration that are sensitive to these relationships and consistent with QOL principles should be supported.

3. *Ethical studies evaluating the use of QOL in decisions* regarding persons with disabilities across the life cycle *need to be undertaken.*

QOL is used differently in different parts of the human service system. For example, in neonates in intensive care units, equations that factor out QOL components are used to come to decisions about the use of medical resources in specific cases. This use of QOL is substantively different from the way it was used in this project. There is considerable danger to the use of QOL in the human service field, particularly when it is not associated with an explicit and accountable values system. These moral risks need to be understood as part of any comprehensive effort to develop this concept for the human services field. The various ethical contexts in which QOL is used should be studied critically and from a clearly articulated value base.

### Provider/Professional Recommendations

4. *The entire concept of service provision has to be* redefined around individual needs.

As has been recognized for some time now, there is a tendency to define services in terms of what is available rather than the needs of individuals. Supports and services should be based upon the individual's needs to the maximum degree possible. Programs and supports should be selected by the individual to the degree possible. Programs and service models that successfully do this need to be identified and information about them disseminated.

5. In addition to considering QOL in the direct supports and services given to consumers, *providers need to develop a* quality of work life orientation towards service delivery *staff.*

A direct implication of Recommendation #2 is that providers of services need to develop an explicit orientation to staff development that would include enhancement of quality of work life (QOWL) for their staff. This would importantly include advocating for higher salary levels, provision of resources and supports that would enhance awareness, knowledge and skills, development of employee-administration committees, providing staff with control of work-related decisions, developing options for career growth and development, etc. There is activity of this type occurring all over the nation but it needs to be consolidated and examined carefully. Exemplary programs should be identified and information about them disseminated.

6. *The concept of provider should be expanded to include unpaid persons such as community members, volunteers and relatives.*

The organization of supports should be thought more broadly to include not only the professional providers but also peer and other volunteers, community members and organizations, families and friends. There are many models of supports being currently developed that include these elements (peer counseling, Joshua Tree and circle groups, direct stipend family support services, community-based planning, etc).

7. *Providers need training in a QOL, value-based orientation to service delivery.*

Providers of services do not always design practices on a an explicit value-base. There are training models for management by values that should be evaluated and the best of these should be replicated throughout the service system generally. Training would need to be on-going and supported through existing agency training resources. See Recommendation #23.

### General Recommendations

8. *QOL policy, assessments, and programs need to reflect* cultural differences and promote cultural identity.
Being able to participate in activities that promote cultural identity is an important way for many persons with and without disabilities to enhance their QOL.
Supporting organizations and opportunities that allow for persons with disabilities to do this is a crucial to QOL for these persons. Model programs need identification, dissemination and replication.

9. A.D.D. needs to guide the impact of QOL development on persons with disabilities, providers and professionals, and the system. See Recommendations #29 and 37 (below).

## Measuring and Assessing QOL

### Principles
*The development of measurement and assessment procedures that are based upon the concept of QOL is important in the development of resources and supports for persons with disabilities and their families.*

*QOL is a construct best assessed through primary consideration of subjective factors as determined by individuals with disabilities and their families, as well as through a consideration of social factors as determined through social validation.*

### Recommendations For People With Disabilities
10. *A methodical approach to developing person-centered instruments and procedures to determine individual QOL needs to be undertaken.*

While there is a tremendous amount of activity in this area it is thus far fragmented. The various models for QOL planning (though not always called that) need to be reviewed. A relatively small group of researchers, clinicians, self-advocates and others should be supported to develop a process and instrumentation for a client-centered and driven model of individual program planning. This group should have sufficient support to achieve this goal (perhaps three years continous funding) as well as others related to QOL assessment and evaluation (see Recommendation #13). A system that can accomodate persons with profound mental retardation or significant communication disorders needs to be a central consideration for this group.

11. *Planning of supports and services for individuals needs to be linked to QOL outcomes for these persons* (Individual QOL Enhancement Planning).

An important aspect of designing the QOL assessment system described under recommendation #10 is the development of an evaluation process and instrumentation that links QOL planning with outcomes for individuals.
Such an evaluation process should involve the person with the disability *to the maximum degree possible*. The group working on assessing QOL should also have as a goal the development of an evaluation process that is outcome oriented.

12. Flexible quality of family life self-assessments need to be designed and linked to family supports.

Paralleling Recommendations #10 &

11 a similar process is needed that allows families to self-assess quality of family life, links these self assessments to supports, and evaluates impact of supports on quality of family life. The family needs to choose how and one what terms evaluation should proceed. Process and instrumentation could be developed through the same mechanism described in #10.

## Professional/Provider Recommendations

13. *Program evaluations that are QOL-oriented, have high-consumer participation and that are useful to providers need to be designed.*

Another set of QOL evaluation processes need to be designed to determine a program's effectiveness in enhancing QOL for its clients. The evaluation of a program in terms of its ability to enhance QOL for its overall client population should be based upon the assessment of QOL for individual clients in that program.
Because of the relatedness of recommendations # 10, 11, 12 & 13 (and #15) and the desirability of methodological consistency in these instruments and procedures, it is suggested that one set of persons be responsible for working on these assessment/evaluation procedures. Some institutional structures to support such activities are described in Recommendation #29.

14. *Professionals and providers need training in how to employ client/family self-assessments of QOL and support individuals and families in these activities.*

It should be understood that the production of QOL assessments and evaluations needs to be accompanied by training for managment, staff and professionals in a values-based, QOL-oriented way of thinking about providing services and support (see Recommendation #7).
This should include training in how to support individuals and families in QOL assessment and evaluation of service impact. Such training should be part of the development of the protocols described in recommendations #10, 11, 12, 13 and 15.

15. *A system to measure quality of work life in organizations serving persons with disabilities needs to be designed and linked to staff development.*

See Recommendations #2 and 13. Quality of work life assessment and enhancement is a critical component of any system designed to enhance the QOL of persons with disabilities who live in residential service settings.
Staff should have a program of staff development, career opportunities, perks and rewards for good performance, power in job-related decisions and should be held accountable in terms of their contribution to programmatic and individual QOL enhancement efforts.
Quality of work life assessment will only make sense in an organization with a strong management and staff development orientation.

16. *Managers in service agencies need to be trained in a management by values orientation.*

Related to Recommendation #7. There is a general need for management training in our field, and for attracting more competent administrators and managers. Especially important in human services is the sensitivity of management to values underpinning service philosophies and policies. Training in values that enhance QOL in human service management needs to be supported. There are some good beginnings in this area and these should be disseminated more widely. More progressive management styles should be fostered.

### General Recommendations

17. A.D.D. should develop a *structured agenda to support QOL assessment, evaluation, research and policy activities for persons with disabilities.*

The fact that there are several related agendas that need to be coordinated in order to guide the impact of QOL policy on the field suggests that some mechanism exist through which a structured agenda could be produced in these areas. There are several ways this could be achieved. Through an Institute mechanism, as suggested in Recommendation #29, or through a program project grant from the government, or through other structures. This kind of coordination is, however, strongly suggested in the future development of this concept.

## Impacting the System and Enhancing Quality of Life

### Principles

*QOL enhancement consists of activities that*

*are consistent with a value structure that emphasizes the strengths and capabilities of persons with disabilities and their families.*

*The concept of QOL is important to examine as the basis for social policy in our country generally, as well as for its specific application to social policy for persons with disabilities.*

### Recommendations For Persons With Disabilities

18. *Building upon the strengths and abilities of persons with disabilities and their families in order to allow them to control their own lives to the maximum degree possible is a primary way to enhance their QOL.*

It was generally felt by many project participants that one of the primary issues in QOL was the control of persons with disabilities and their families over their own lives. Support of training, programs, planning, policy and other efforts that build upon this value and recognize these capabilities and strengths is a general recommendation of the QOL Project.

19. *In order to build upon strengths and abilities it is necessary to train families and individuals in the rights and responsibilities of decision-making, and to support them in the decision-making process.*

A critical avenue to allow persons with disabilities to assume control of their lives in a meaningful way is to provide them with the necessary information and supports for informed decision-making. Family decision-making should be supported in medical, developmen-

tal and educational settings. This means actively engaging the family in decision-making and supporting them during the process. Similarly individuals with disabilities must be provided information and supports that allow them to participate in a decision-making process to the degree that they are capable. Decision-making curricula exist and there are service settings that employ procedures such as those described. These should be examined, evaluated and disseminated. If no satisfactory curricula exist, they should be developed.

20. *The training activities of self-advocacy groups that have as their mission empowering consumers and their families should be supported.*

Consumer and self-advocacy groups conduct two types of training: training consumers in advocacy skills (such as by People First or the Partners in Policy project) and dissemination activities that have a values, policy or public education orientation. Part of QOL for persons with disabilities is the society's time and interest to listen to what they have to say. Opportunities for persons with disabilities to sensitize others to those aspects of the physical and social environment that enhance their QOL and are important should be supported.

Occasions when persons with disabilities can come together and network around key policy and service issues are also necessary.

21. *Persons with developmental disabilities*

*should be recruited into the system in positions of authority.*

Because the experience of disability is best understood by people with disabilities, they should 'run their own show' to the degree that this is possible. This includes helping to run the service and regulatory system in significant ways. Persons with disabilities who have the appropriate skills and abilities should be recruited into the system. This will allow them to take control of their own lives to an even greater degree, as well as influence the development of policy, programs and training in ways that are consistent with the experience of disability.[7]

### Professional/Provider Recommendations

22. Professionals and providers need to be trained in a *values-based orientation to services that emphasizes client and family strengths and capacities.*

Paralleling Recommendation #7, all levels of persons involved in helping persons with disabilities and their families need to be trained in a values orientation in providing services and supports. Training should not be done one time only but must be on-going. One needs a constant awareness of value issues in decision making related to provision of services; those involved face such decisions every day and need a community of support to help make correct decisions. It is important to identify training programs that are value-based and that can be used with direct-care and professional staff.

These training programs should be evaluated and those that are succesful should be disseminated and replicated. It is also important to incorporate regular meetings around value issues in the management plan for organizations. It may be worth considering the creation of a task force or special committee on values in human services for persons with developmental disabilities whose mandate would be to guide the development of management by value training and training in a value orientation to direct care and professional staff.

23. *Direct care staff require training that will allow them to support persons with disabilities and their families to enhance their QOL.*

This is a very important recommendation. Currently most training for direct care staff does not include information and skills that are specifically related to enhancing QOL for consumers. Persons with severe physical disabilities or mental retardation often have problems in meeting people and having friendships. They have trouble getting and keeping jobs, or finding community groups to join, in getting out of the house, and so on. These are the things that they find most important and should occupy an important place in training direct care staff to enhance QOL for persons with disabilities. The general idea is that training curricula need to be developed that are consistent with enhancing QOL as it is perceived by persons with disabilities.

24. *Funding and regulatory strategies need to be found that allow providers to be innovative*

*and rewarded for success. Current policies do not facilitate innovation.*

Many involved in the QOL Project felt that the current systems of regulation, evaluation and funding do not allow service providers to be innovative in their attempts. Providers are not generally rewarded for success at habilitation or integration. (Conversely, it was also noted that many poor quality providers are not held account able for not doing a good job) (see Recommendation # 36). The problem of lack of incentives for good performance and innovation is recognized in many states. Strategies that have been identified to deal with this problem and that have been successful should be identified and disseminated. A document such as Strategies for Innovation and Success that describes and integrates these attempts would be appropriate.

25. The provider community can enhance QOL of persons with disabilities by *developing peer counseling programs* that match persons with disabilities who enjoy productive, independent and integrated lives with individuals who are less so.

Of particular merit in enhancing the lives of persons with disabilities are programs that utilize the experience and capabilities of other disabled persons as peer counselors and/or friends. Peers who are disabled and that have successfully dealt with some of the problems that persons with disabilities face can be strong role models to those who may not yet have dealt with issues. Peers with

disabilities have a better understanding of the position of other persons with disabilities and of the dynamics involved in many of the problems that persons with disabilities face. There are many examples of peer counseling programs that are claimed to be highly effective. Effective peer counseling/friends programs should be replicated nationally.

26. Rather than adopting the notion of an ever more 'normal' continuum of vocational and residential services, *providers should aim at achieving a relatively stable, self-selected life style for consumers.*
The notion of a continuum of services, graded from restrictive to unrestrictive or less normal to more normal, and through which all persons need to progress should be reconceptualized. As a continuum functions in some systems they constitute an endless series of hurdles for clients. Just as soon as persons with disabilities are successful in mastering one environment, they are told that they now have to move on to a more normal environment. Rather than looking at it this way, it should be the decision of the person with disabilities about how he or she wants to live that should be the goal of residential services. There should be residential options from which a person may choose rather than a system through which he or she must progress.

### *General Recommendations*
27. *QOL is sufficiently generic to serve as the basis for a general national social policy, and as the basis for a national social policy for persons with disabilities. There is a need for such a policy.*

The conclusion that QOL should be used as a social policy concept for all citizens was reached by many individuals involved in the QOL Project. It is generic and this is it's strength as a social policy concept. At the same time it has a clear pertinence to persons with disabilities and should be developed with their concerns at its center. Thus there is a need to focus policy activities on an interagency level to consider how quality of life might serve as the basis for social policy generally in our society, and to develop specific quality of life policy in the field of developmental disabilities.

28. *All future activities related to QOL for persons with disabilities needs to be strongly coordinated with major disability groups.*

A general feeling of those active in the QOL Project was that even stronger coordination of QOL development activities needs to exist with consumer organizations.While QOL is a generic concept to which everyone relates, QOL for persons with disabilities and their families is what is of primary importance to the disability community. For QOL to reach its potential as a social policy concept it must be developed so that it reflects the input of persons with disabilities, and it must be oriented to by the disability community. One way to ensure that this would be the case is by creating a National Task Force on the Enhancement of Quality of Life for Persons with Disabilities and Their Families. Such a group could be composed primarily of representatives from self-advocacy and consumer groups and

would both monitor and suggest activities related to QOL enhancement for this population.

29. Because of the complexity and scope of activities required to advance the investigation of QOL and utilization of QOL in the disabilities field, a coordinating entity such as *a National Institute on QOL for Persons with Disabilities (or a Research and Training Center)* should be established.

An important result of the QOL Project is the conclusion that QOL is sufficiently dynamic and generic to act as a fundamental concept in the field of disabilities. A long term strategy to the development of QOL needs to be formulated and an overarching structure needs to be constructed as a way to focus and coordinate activities. There are several ways to think about how this might be done: a Research & Training Center on Quality of Life; an Institute on QOL funded by A.D.D.; an Institute funded by multiple federal agencies; and an Institute funded from different kinds of funding streams (federal, private, state). The purpose of creating such a structure would be to carry out activities in QOL program development, research and training, and dissemination, and coordinate activities of professionals, consumers and others active in this area. Because there is no individual QOL assessment instrument, (or individual QOL program development procedures), or QOL program evaluation methods, the development of instruments that are consistent with what we know about QOL must be a primary focus of a QOL Institute or Research & Training Center.

30. *QOL must be marketed to all parts of the disability system* including: Protection &Advocacy systems, Developmental Disability Planning Councils, University Affiliated Programs, Independent Living Centers, Research & Training Centers, consumer groups, self-advocacy organizations and professional groups.

While QOL is clearly an issue of growing interest to many in the disability field both nationally and internationally, its importance and value is not known to most persons in the field. The concept needs to be explained to all segments of the system. These groups need to know what role they can play in helping to promote QOL as a social policy in the disabilities field. Targeted publications aimed at achieving this for these audiences need to be produced and disseminated.

31. *Public education combatting old stereotypes about disabilities and emphasizing integration and QOL need to be undertaken.*

Part of the promotion of QOL should include public education activities aimed at debunking stereotypes of persons with disabilities and their families. One way to do this is by promoting public education done by persons with disabilities themselves. Public service announcements and other public media presentations conveying information about the strengths of persons with disabilities and their viewpoints about achieving a good QOL for themselves should be undertaken.

32. Activities that facilitate participation of persons with disabilities and their families in policy formation, community and other forms of planning, and in networking around QOL issues should be supported.

Related to Recommendation #18, this recommendation highlights the importance of creating a community of interest around QOL by *supporting community-based, and other levels of, planning and networking around QOL issues. The inclusion of persons with disabilities and their families into these kinds of efforts is a primary way to enhance their QOL.* The projects currently being run in New York and California will begin networking in each state around QOL issues. Other states should consider running similar workgroups about QOL issues.

33. One important way to strengthen community participation and integration of persons with disabilities is by *enhancing their participation in community secondary associations* such as Boy Scouts, Girl Scouts, Boys Clubs, Ys, etc.

Activity with community groups and associations is a primary avenue for some persons to enhance their QOL and should be available equally to persons with disabilities and their families. Secondary associations that currently operate successful mainstreaming programs for children and adults with disabilities should be identified and described. Training and technical assistance that allow for successful inclusion of persons with disabilities needs to be made available more generally to the generic community organizations.

34. The *building of informal, unpaid networks of supporters* (circle building) and person-centered teams of paid and unpaid supporters is another important way to enhance community participation of persons with disabilities.

Related to Recommendation #6. Particularly interesting new approaches to support systems exist that involve volunteers and other paid and unpaid providers. These are named Joshua Tree groups, circles and person-centered teams. These new approaches should be evaluated carefully and those that are successful in enhancing QOL for those involved should be disseminated and replicated.

35. An immediate way to impact on the evaluation of programs is to *incorporate QOL in national accreditation processes such as ACDD, JCAHO, and CARF.*[8]

The development of QOL evaluation and program planning protocols and instruments will take some time. In the meanwhile one immediate way to impact service delivery with a QOL orientation would be to consider including QOL standards in national accreditation processes. This could be done by first providing each of these accreditation groups with training in a QOL orientation. Each of the organizations could then institute activities that would institute such an orientation in their

accreditation process. Accreditation is one important way to effect system change to enhance QOL.

36. *The system needs to have "guts"* — reward good programs and eliminate bad ones. Presently too many programs of poor quality are tolerated and supported.

Related to Recommendation #24. For a variety of reasons, the current system both allows poor programs to continue providing services even though unsuccessful and fails to reward programs that are. The issues involved with the closing of poor programs are sometimes complex but must be faced. Likewise figuring out how to reward programs for good performance may also be difficult but must be done. States that have instituted quality assurance and enhancement mechanisms that do both of these things need to be reviewed and disseminated. New programs and solutions that will allow for the system to have 'guts' need to be formulated.

37. An important way for A.D.D. to assure that program development, training and research is consistent with QOL enhancement is to utilize QOL principles as the basis for their Request For Proposal process (RFP).[9]

One important way to systematically ensure that programs and training supported by A.D.D. serves to potentially enhance QOL is to utilize the QOL principles in this document as the value-base for decisions about competitive applications in the RFP process. This suggests that in addition to the criteria suggested in the specific announcement for competition, applications will be judged in terms of their consistency with QOL principles. There should be a special announcement of these principles in the Federal Register and they should appear thereafter with regularity as part of the announcement for RFPs.

## Discussion

Taken in aggregate these thirty seven conceptually ordered recommendations contain, if not a coherent program, at least a collection of relevant concerns about QOL as it might be utilized in the field of disabilities. When one considers the five years of developments in the field of QOL and disabilities since the writing of this QOL Agenda, many of the suggestions and principles are as true today as they were then. There has been slow progress in many areas, but at least it has been progress. It is to the credit of all involved that they were able to come up with ideas and recommendations that in many ways anticipated the future.

The unusually astute or particularly motivated readers may be asking themselves, 'what about the QOL framework for measuring QOL that the A.D.D. Commissioner asked for?' No such product was delivered by the project, although in our report to A.D.D. we did point out that an evaluation specialist could transform the QOL matrices into an evaluation process and structure. The leadership of that project chose not to deliver such an evaluation package, convinced in 1988 that it was a premature move. We had only just begun to seriously listen to people with disabilities'

views about QOL [(It is argued by some we still only listen to those views we want to hear and have no "freedom for the thought we hate" (to paraphrase Oliver Wendall Holmes)]. The idea of constructing a scale based upon the initial exploration of even several hundred people did not appear to be methodologically proper nor a politically liberating move for persons with disabilities.[10]

In a short editorial (Goode, 1990b), I commented upon the state of QOL measurement and made recommendations for a person-centered, individually tailored way to define and measure a person's QOL. I argued that such a radical subjective measurement process is the only one that is true to the nature of the phenomenon, and the only one that might not serve to further victimize and dominate persons with disabilities. A QOL measurement system in which the individual's perspective about QOL is the dominant perspective and force in the system, where he or she controls the content and its weighting, has yet to be devised. This is not to say that many QOL scales have been and are still under development. That is basically what happened to the measurement system asked for by the A.D.D. Commissioner.

While the international applicability of all of the principles and recommendations in the QOL Agenda is clearly limited, it was thought that other governments and groups of citizens with disabilities in other countries would have benefited from exposure to the above agenda. One thing the National QOL Project experience suggests is that *other countries should well consider the production of a similar QOL agenda. The significant involvement of persons with disabilities in such a process can be an important political step forward in many countries.* This is because QOL for persons with disabilities is part of a global movement in the field of disabilities, one which is seeing the self-conscious, political emergence of this minority group. In America, Canada, Australia, Denmark, Finland, Hungary and elsewhere, people with significant disabilities are finally beginning to gain control over the affairs that effect their everyday lives and to achieve a better QOL. It is being recognized that they have the same rights as nondisabled persons to do this. We, the researchers and professionals involved in the field, need to understand their lives and how they perceive them better in order to help persons with disabilities better them. The above agenda suggests some ways that the United States government might facilitate in this attempt.

## Notes

[1]Funding provided for this project was provided from the Administraion on Developmental Disabilities through a special projects grant to the Mental Retardation Institute University Affiliated Program in Valhalla, New York (OHDS #03DD0156/04). All technical materials related to this project are available from the QOL Project Coordinator, David A. Goode/ PSA Department/ College of Staten Island/ 715 Ocean Terrace, H-5/ Staten Island, New York 10301.
[2]This was very much in recent evidence in the 1992 program for the International Association for the Scientific Study of Mental Deficiency, with over 30 presentations submitted dealing with QOL.
[3]No pretense is made about the reading of the literature being objective. It is, based upon the reactions of several research scientists familiar with QOL and QOWL literature, a very credible review of many of the findings that have been advanced.
[4]While there are many definitions and approaches to QOL nationally and internationally, I have had the opportunity to present this particular model many times to a variety of audiences and cultures. It seems to be intuitive and somewhat easy to grasp, rarely meeting with serious objections from the audience. The fact that QOL is seen as the product of the person consciously acting in a situation that confronts his own needs with that of the society is particularly appealing to persons with disabilities, many of whom see themselves this way already. It should be noted that this model was not influenced at all by notions of political correctness. This QOL model of the individual actively involved in resolving conflict/cooperation with his society is equally applicable to people without disability.
[5]Facilitation of persons with cognitive disabilities was done by the Capitol People's First Group of Sacramento, California. Their experience with facilitation was critical to the success of the groups. It should be understood that the participation of persons with disabilities in the groups was not uncommonly antagonistic and contradictory to the views expressed by professionals. Admittedly the professionals were under some additional pressure to acquiesce to the views of persons with disabilities; indeed they had been openly instructed 'not to talk so much and to listen to the persons with disabilities and their parents.' But none of this questions the very serious exchange that took place during this retreat, and the importance of the input of persons with cognitive disability in that exchange. Often their comments would stop the professionals in their tracks. In the group on aging, after a rather long and idealistic conversation about the rights of mentally retarded persons to the same retirement options as nondisabled individuals, one of the persons with cognitive disabilities said, "But most of my friends don't work, and the ones that do hate their work and would leave tommorow if they could." Her remarks quickly shifted the

conversation to a more realistic and relevant level.

[6]These principles bear some discussion and explanation that can not be provided in the current context of writing. What is important to note about these is that they do represent a consensus set of statements. Very few argued with any one of them, although many suggested revisions in language to clarify earlier drafts of the principles. Another thing to consider is how powerful these principles might be if they were actually listened to and acted upon? For example, if we really believed that QOL for persons with disabilities is made up of the same factors and relationships as persons without disabilties, would we have anything like the service system that we have today? Finally, taken as a group, these principles represent a coherent and relevant set of axioms upon which to programmatically build a QOL policy for people with and without disabilities.

[7]In discussing this somewhat controversial recommendation with a Swedish self-advocate in Stockholm, I asked him what he thought about preferential hiring of persons with disabilities to occupy positions of authority in the disability field. He was all for it, citing the fact that "We couldn't screw it up any worse than you have."

[8]These are national accreditation bodies in the United States. The sense of the recommendation is to utilize already existing standards and accreditation processes to promote evaluation of QOL concerns.

[9]For those unfamiliar with the American funding scene, this means that A.D.D. should use QOL as a way to guide their funding in the field.

[10]In my 1990b editorial on QOL measurement, I talked about "a rush to judgment," with many persons around the world developing measurement scales and protocols. There is a clear marketplace for such devices as agencies, both private and governmental, want to use them in order to evaluate the efficacy of their efforts. Their commitment to the phrase QOL as a shibboleth to rename their old concern for accountability in funding and resources should not be mistaken with the meaning of QOL as it has been articulated in this writing. In my experience providing lectures on the topic of QOL, agencies rarely know what they mean when they use this term and what the concept commits one to as a matter of values and principles. In any case, at the time, it was surely the case that the production of some scale would not have advanced these values and principles.

# References

Goode, D.A., 1988a. *The principles and recommendations of the quality of life project.* The Mental Retardation Institute, Valhalla, New York.

_____, 1988b. *Quality of life: A review and synthesis of the literature.* The Mental Retardation Institute, Valhalla, New York.

_____, 1988c. *Discussing quality of life: Framework and findings of the work group on quality of life.* The Mental Retardation Institute, Valhalla, New York.

_____, 1988d. *The proceedings of the national conference on quality of life.* The Mental Retardation Institute, Valhalla, New York.

_____, 1990a. Thinking and discussing quality of life, in R. Schalock (Ed.) *Quality of Life.* American Association on Mental Retardation Monograph Series, Washington, D.C.

_____, 1990b. Measuring quality of life. *News And Notes.* American Association on Mental Retardation.

# 10• The California Quality of Life Project: A Project Summary

Patrick Connally
World Institute on Disabilities

"Our work proceeds from a basic belief that persons with disabilities have the same desires and needs as anyone else. The quality of my life is related to how free I am to make my own choice."
Ed Roberts

Quality of Life has become a popular phrase in current society. What is our level of satisfaction with our daily lives, work, relationships, our living situations? Our quality of life is tied to the freedom to choose our own lifestyle. Granted, research on quality of life has shown that what determines quality of life is complex, subjective, and may be somewhat restricted by economic and social parameters. But if most of us were asked whether we chose the place we live in, the job we go to each day, the people we spend our social time with, we would answer "yes," at least for the most part. If asked whether we were basically happy with our quality of life, we would say, on the whole, "yes." Unfortunately, people with developmental disabilities would be less likely to answer "yes."

Reflecting a growing interest in the subject of Quality of Life in the field of developmental disabilities, the Administration on Developmental Disabilities (ADD) provided a grant to the World Institute on Disability to coordinate the California Quality of Life (QOL) Project. Funding for this and similar projects recognizes the importance of having people with disabilities directly involved in the service delivery and decision-making processes which affect their lives. The purpose of the QOL Project was to speak directly with persons with developmental disabilities (consumers of services) and ask them to define for themselves the issues that are significant in their daily lives. This was accomplished by hosting a series of conferences throughout the state of California in 1989.

Coincident with the California QOL Project, similar projects were being conducted in New York and in Finland. All three projects built upon the findings of the National Quality of Life Project conducted by the Mental Retardation Institute in Valhalla, New York, and were funded by the Administration on Developmental Disabilities, Office of Human Development Services, Washington, D.C.

## Theoretical Background

"Help is most beneficial when I ask for it, not when others feel I need it."
   –Participant, Quality of Life
Conference

The national project on the subject of QOL as it relates to persons with developmental disabilities began with a study of the research literature on QOL. This resulted in a framework for discussion of QOL issues which was piloted by a work group consisting of professionals, advocates and self advocates. The purpose of the work group was to discuss and define QOL issues and to validate the framework as a way to generate guidelines in specific settings and age groups (Goode, 1988). Goode's framework was guided by these four important principles:

1. QOL for persons with disabilities consists of the same factors and relationships that are important to persons without disabilities.

2. The QOL of an individual is intrinsically related to the QOL of other persons in his or her environment.

3. QOL is experienced when a person's basic needs are met and when he or she has the opportunity to pursue and achieve goals in major life settings.

4. QOL should be defined by the consumer and not by professionals. It is how the individual views his or her situation that determines the QOL he or she experiences.

In April, 1988 a National Conference on Quality of Life for Persons with Disabilities was also held in New York State. Approximately one quarter of the participants were persons with disabilities and members of their families. Areas of discussion at this conference were family

life, residential life, community participation, education, and work.

The culmination of the National Quality of Life Project was a final paper entitled *Principles and Recommendations of the Quality of Life Project*. (Goode, 1988) The paper focuses on consumer related, provider/professional and system-wide recommendations on QOL issues based upon the project's activities.

The California QOL Project based its principles and practices on the model described above. However, because all participants attending the California conferences were persons with developmental disabilities, the process for discussion was modified in order to maximize the participation of the participants.

## History of the California Quality of Life Project

"Disabled people can learn to live independently from the experiences of other disabled people."
-Participant, QOL Conference

### Initial Planning

The first activity of the California QOL Project was to convene a statewide advisory committee meeting in April of 1989. Approximately one half of the members attending this meeting were persons with developmental disabilities. Representation included the Center for Independent Living (Berkeley), Capitol People First, as well as area boards, Protection and Advocacy Inc., and the California Developmental Disabilities Council (parts of the Developmental Disabilities service system). David Goode attended as a consultant to the project.

Four members of the committee were

persons with cognitive disabilities and attended the meeting with "facilitators" (in this case the "facilitators" were advisors to People First). The role of the facilitator was to assist the individual with a developmental disability to communicate his/her ideas to the group and to help interpret written and orally presented information which may be difficult to understand.

### Project Goals

A one page project overview was developed which listed the following primary goals of the California QOL Project:

1. To enable consumers to identify for themselves the issues that are significant in their daily lives.

2. To create a data base on Quality of Life issues as defined by primary and secondary consumers.

3. To use this data base to impact social policy, legislation, research, training and the provision of community services in the area of disability.

4. To enhance consumer self-advocacy through participation in the conference process.

5. To establish a statewide network of primary consumers that can influence social policy on decisions which affect their lives.

6. To produce a final report which will express consumers' views on: "What Makes for Quality of Life."

### Participants

The average participant was a single thirty-three year-old, who received special education, now lives in a group home or with parents, and participates in sheltered employment. The majority of individuals rely on public transportation or rides from parents or other family members. A small but noteworthy number of participants were parents. Also noteworthy is that the San Diego and San Jose conferences had the largest number of participants living independently, and by observation, the liveliest discussions.

Although it was not appropriate to ask the nature of the participants' disabilities, our overall impression was that substantial numbers of participants were cognitively disabled, with physically disabled individuals representing about one third of the total. Persons with hearing or visual disabilities were present, but in much fewer numbers.

An average of forty to fifty persons with disabilities participated in each local conference. Each conference participant had the opportunity to attend two of the four workshop sessions offered (Living, Loving, Working, and Playing).

## Summary of Data From Regional Conferences

The following are summary data from the six regional QOL conferences. They can not represent the individual flavor and character of these conferences. However, sufficient overlap of issues existed to allow us to reach the following general conclusions from these six events. In order to preserve some of the atmosphere of these workshops, illustrative quotations from participants are provided throughout the text. In addition, the reader will find an Appendix that includes several speeches by persons with developmental disabilities given at regional workshops or presented to project staff afterward. The data are grouped into four major categories: Working, Living, Loving and Relationships, and Playing and Recreating.

## Working

### Issues Related to Working

1. *Salary*: Wages need to be increased so that people can earn enough money to support themselves. Wages are low and people are limited in the amount of hours they can work to earn more money. Down time periods when there is no work to be done contribute to low earnings by employees paid on a piece-work basis.

2. *Sheltered Employment*: Sheltered employment segregates people with disabilities from the community. Job tasks are often boring and repetitive. Jobs at the workshops were described by some as dead end jobs with no opportunity for advancement.

3. *Public Benefits*: There is a lack of understanding regarding benefits such as SSI, SSA, IHSS, and self- support plans. Consumers feel they will be penalized by a loss of benefits f they earn more money. There is a desire to learn more about these programs and how they can improve an individuals QOL.

4. *Training*: Training is needed in all areas of pre-employment including: job search, such as writing a resume, filling out job applications, job interviews etc. Consumers desire training in knowing their rights and responsibilities as workers and in improving communication skills in order to better relationships with employers and co-workers.

5. *Technology*: Technology, in particular computers and specialized adaptive equipment, needs to be designed and made available to persons with disabilities. The use of technology to adapt job tasks to a person's abilities will broaden the opportunities for persons with disabilities in the area of employment.

6. *Attitudes*: Attitudes towards persons with disabilities have a negative effect on self-image. Persons with developmental disabilities are often treated as children by parents, employers and service providers and are not encouraged to take the necessary risks needed to improve the quality of their lives.

7. *Freedom of Choice*: Freedom to choose a job that a person feels they would enjoy is seen as a essential to job satisfaction. Consumers expressed interest in jobs where they could provide services to other people, particularly people with disabilities. This broad area of job development needs to be given attention by policy makers in the field of employment and disability.

"People get in the way of our decision making by making decisions for us instead of letting us speak for ourselves."

"I would like . . . a job in broadcasting,

disability politics, child care, acting, to work in the family business, with disabled children, in a hospital, with people with disabilities, to be a chef, an electronics engineer, to manage a store, run my own business, take child development classes.

8. *Accessibility*: Accessible transportation is seen as essential to the successful employment of people with disabilities. Some of the major problems mentioned were: inaccessible buses, lack of public transportation to and from the work site, infrequent bus service in certain areas, the high cost of paratransit, and the rules requiring rides to be scheduled far in advance. Consumers also expressed the need for training on how to use public transportation, learning bus routes, applying for discount transit cards, education on disability for transit workers.

9. *Environment*: A pleasant working environment is very important to job satisfaction. Excessive noise, lack of privacy, arguments with coworkers, and lack of friends on the job were stated as some of the major problem areas related to work environments.

## Recommendations Related to Working

1. *Support Self-advocacy*: The system needs to give more support to self-advocacy groups where consumers can learn their civil rights and how to improve their communication skills. Self-advocacy groups should be a priority when it comes to funding and policy decisions. Care providers should be encouraged

and supported by employers to facilitate consumers in the process of starting and maintaining self-advocacy groups. The responsibility for leadership of these groups should be placed in the hands of consumers.

2. *Public Education*: Widespread education programs are needed to teach employers, providers and the greater community "to see the abilities not the disabilities" of consumers. Lack of information leads to stereotyping and labelling and creates barriers to consumers participating fully in the job market and in the community.

3. *Supported Employment*: Consumers need to advocate for supported employment which expands the availability of job opportunities, offers comprehensive training on all aspects of obtaining and maintaining employment, and addresses the need for social support systems in integrated work settings.

4. *Political Action*: Consumers need to vote and lobby local, state and national leaders on issues which affect the integration and full participation of persons with disabilities into society. The issue of transportation was frequently mentioned as an issue where local political action can be effective. According to consumers, writing letters, making phone calls and attending local meetings has already proven successful in making transportation systems more accessible in some areas.

"Basically we want the same things you want from a job: happiness, more mon-

ey, doing what we enjoy, working where we want, regular hours, and privacy."
"For most people, workshops lead nowhere. Workshops should be closed. We want the money to go to supported employment."
"Workshops have the same work that has to be done over and over again."

5) *Work Relations*: Consumers need to arrange meetings with their co-workers to discuss problems at work. Some people suggested organizing a union so that employee's rights can be represented.

## Living

### *QOL Issues Related to Living/ Residences*

1. *Freedom of Choice*: Choosing one's own lifestyle is the first and most important step in determining the quality of a person's life. Options included: living alone, with a roommate or partner, with family or in a small group home. Emphasis was placed on living in a manner as independent and as integrated into the community as possible:

   "I would like to live with my boyfriend."
   "People that live in group homes should speak out"
   "When I was sixteen my mother put me in Agnews, I don't know why."

2. *Decision Making*: Independent decision making should be encouraged and supported by parents, care providers and social workers. Overprotection and lack of communication are seen as major obstacles to achieving goals. For exam-

ple, consumers want a better understanding of their Individual Program Plans (IPPs) so they can have more control over the decision making process which affects the services they receive:

"We are not given any credit for being able to take care of ourselves."
"At twenty three I can make my own decisions. You have to go for it when you know what you want."

3. *Rights and Responsibilities*: The right to privacy, to come and go without restriction (includes moving to a new residence), and to have input into house rules are of utmost importance to consumers in their living situations. Being able to get along with the people they live with and participating in household responsibilities are also seen as important to successful living situations:

"We should be able to come and go freely and spend the night away from the group home. We should not have to ask permission for these things."
"We should have input into any program that is paid to help us. We need to have more control."

4. *Training*: Independent living skills training should be available to all persons with disabilities regardless of their current living situations. Consumers stated a need for training in the following areas: money management, cooking, housekeeping, mobility, communication skills, tenants' rights (including the process of filing a writ to leave the

Development Centers), self-advocacy, hiring attendants, medical management, and the use and availability of adaptive equipment "that could make life easier," such as computers and calculators:

"We need to speak up more for ourselves. Self-advocacy groups help us do this but some consumers can't go to self-advocacy groups because their care provider will not take them or let them go. Self- advocacy needs to be the first priority of the Regional Center. We need funding for self-advocacy, especially transportation, so that all consumers can go to self-advocacy groups."

5.  *Safety*: The importance of safety out in the community and at home was a repeated theme at the conferences. Issues discussed were protecting yourself when you're out in the community, prevention of sexual abuse, hiring the right attendants and procedures to follow at home in case of an emergency. These issues were discussed across the disability groups, however some concerns pertained more to one disability group than another:

"I live alone, I need an emergency device to call for help if I fall out of my wheelchair but my social worker won't pay for it."
"Staff at board and care homes should be screened more carefully before they are hired."

6.  *Accessibility*: There is a need for more affordable and accessible housing. Inaccessibility of friends' and families' homes are obstacles to social integra-

tion and support. This is also true of inaccessible community facilities, services and programs.

7.  *Community Support Services*: Services which support the integration and full participation of persons with disabilities in their communities need increased government funding. Services mentioned were attendant care, ILS, transportation, advocacy and counseling programs.

8.  *Family Support*: The respect, trust and understanding of family and friends contributes to a positive self-image. Consumers feel they are not treated as adults and afforded the same opportunities for challenge as their non-disabled peers.

"There is a double standard for myself and for my brothers and sisters."

### Recommendations Related to Living/Residences

1.  The system needs to provide increased funding for independent living skills training thereby making it available to all consumers regardless of the nature of their disability or where they live. Consumers need to write letters and make calls to federal, state, and local officials to lobby for increased funding of ILS and other community support services.

2.  Peer counselling programs should be made available to primary and secondary consumers receiving services through the system. The provision of positive role models is necessary for empowerment.

3. Widespread training programs are needed to educate parents, care providers, social workers and the general public on the capabilities and aspirations of persons with developmental disabilities. The goal of these programs is to facilitate the process of community integration.

4. Social workers need to offer consumers greater input in the decision-making process which affects their lives. Making Individual Program Plans more understandable, basing IPPs on goals that consumers have defined for themselves and supporting consumer participation in self-advocacy groups were some suggestions towards this objective.

5. Consumers need to learn the process of becoming independent by taking small steps such as asking for support from friends, family and social workers, starting self-advocacy groups, talking to parents honestly, setting up meetings at home to discuss house rules, saving money to move out and calling independent living programs to find out how to hire an attendant.

## Loving and Relationships

### Issues Related to Loving and Relationships

1. *Self-Esteem*: Loving yourself, accepting other people as they are, trust, being able to take criticism, having faith, being able to ask for help, being able to talk with friends about your feelings and being respected and understood by others were said to contribute positive-

ly to a person's self-image. Issues of concern raised were jealousy, fear of intimacy, and recovering from the loss of relationships:

"We need to feel good about ourselves, that's very important."

2. *Attitudes*: Persons with developmental disabilities are frequently treated as children not adults. Some parents and professionals think that people with disabilities should not have sexual relationships, get married, or have children. These messages are frequently given indirectly by placing restrictions on privacy and dating:

"I am not allowed to have sex with my boyfriend in my bedroom, so where am I supposed to go."
"It's like a prison."

3. *Privacy*: Lack of privacy in residential settings was discussed at each of the six workshops. Consumers want be able to have partners in their rooms, spend the night away, come and go without permission, have privacy while using the phone and be able to do what they want in their bedrooms without asking permission.

4. *Relationships*: There is a need to have more relationships of all kinds. Supportive family relationships are seen as very important. For people with disabilities this means being treated equally — not as "different" — by family members. Parents' fears of their children being taken advantage of often interferes with their becoming more

self reliant and independent. More op-portunities to socialize and meet pro-spective friends and partners are need-ed. A major obstacle to this is lack of accessible transportation which makes people with disabilities more depen-dent on parents for rides and less inde-pendent:

"We want the same things as you want: marriage, children, meet new friends, live with boyfriend or girlfriend, a honeymoon, adopting children if we can't have our own, to have someone to cook for and take care of, and travel to see family members."

5. *Parenting:* There exists the need to pro-vide consumers with information on pregnancy, adoption and child rearing so that they can make informed choices regarding parenting. Related to this is the need for parenting classes, for atten-dant care services to assist parents with disabilities in caring for their children, and for legal protection to insure that children will not be taken from parents solely on the basis of disability:

"When my son was two-days-old he was taken from me; I felt sad."

### *Recommendations Related to Loving and Relationships*
1. Support and information-sharing groups are needed for parents of dis-abled children and adults. Such groups, would assist in dispelling myths about disability and provide ongoing support for families with the purpose of encour-aging the independence and integra-tion of the disabled family member.

2. Social workers need to provide con-sumers with information and services related to sexuality and they should also work with residential providers on issues of privacy and the rights of their clients.

3. Services which provide information and counselling on issues related to relation-ships need to be accessible to persons with disabilities both in terms of pro-grammatic and physical access. Issues raised by consumers were sexuality, AIDS, sexual abuse, parenting and adoption.

"I would like to... go out with just one friend, visit a friend, go out on a date on Saturday night, dancing at the Oktoberfest, go out on the bus by myself, go to the beach, opera, ballet, theater, museum, go whale watching, horseback riding, swimming, skiing, take a trip to Hawaii, Catalina, Australia, England, Alaska, Jamaica, play tennis, ride on an airplane, learn to sew, oper-ate a computer. Relax."

## Playing and Recreating

### *Issues Related to Playing/ Recreating*
1. *Decision-Making and Information:* Peo-ple want to make their own decisions on how and with whom to spend their leisure time. Inflexible schedules at res-idential facilities and needing to ask permission from parents and providers to go out are two barriers to the enjoy-ment of leisure time.

2. *Information and Networking:* There is a need to learn what social activities exist

in the community and how to meet people with similar interests.

3. *Accessibility*: Public places and programs need to be made fully accessible in order for people with disabilities to integrate socially in the community: examples of this are closed captions on films and adaptive sporting equipment.

4. *Integration*: Lack of accessible transportation on evenings and weekends is a barrier to enjoying a satisfying social life. There is a desire to participate in integrated social activities; some examples of these are attending community dances, church services and recreational facilities.

### Recommendations Regarding Playing/Recreating

1. ILS training programs need to teach consumers how to find out what activities are available, where they are happening and how to get there. The following were recommended areas for training: saving money, looking up information and scheduling transportation.

2. Mobility training needs to be funded for leisure purposes as well as for work.

3. Funding needs to be made available to pay attendants to assist people with disabilities in their participation in social activities.

4. Consumers need to set up a system in their place of residence to go out in smaller groups and with people they choose.

5. Transportation needs to be available which does not limit the number of rides a person can take. Also consumers need to get involved (attend meetings, serve on boards) with their local transit commissions and inform them of their needs.

## Conclusions about Quality of Life

The most basic form of empowerment is to listen to a person and to take what they have to say seriously. The success of this project illustrates the strength of incorporating this empowerment tool in how we relate to persons with developmental disabilities. During the World Institute on Disability's (WID's) Quality of Life Conferences, persons with disabilities were listened to as participants: they were invited to give keynote addresses and they made up the overwhelming majority of participants at each conference. Because of this approach, we are confident of the reliability of the data included in this report.

People with developmental disabilities share a very strong desire to become more involved in their communities at every conceivable level. They want to live more independently, to be perceived and treated as adults, and to have meaningful and well-paying employment. They want to have choices; they want to travel; they want to participate. They want to develop relationships with others and want to establish their own families.

These recommendations and ideals regarding quality of life for persons with developmental disabilities reflect back upon David Goode's four principles (see above). People with disabilities want the same things as everyone else: they want the support of their families and their community in achieving the goals that they have defined for themselves, and they want to assess for themselves what gives quality to their lives.

People with developmental disabilities have had others speak for them, about them, and for their own good for a very long time. When they speak for themselves, their ideas are cogent, understandable, and clear. The challenge is for policy makers and others who influence their lives to listen.

## References

Goode, D. 1988. *Discussing Quality of Life (QOL): Framework and Findings of the Work Group on QOL for Persons with Disabilities.* Mental Retardation Institute: Valhalla, New York.

## Appendix• The WID Quality of Life Book

Larry F. Rice
Oakland Quality of Life Conference, June 7, 1987
(Extracted from Conference Video)

The following are speeches or written statements submitted to the WID QOL conference staff at regional conferences. Many of you may have heard of self-advocacy. Well in 1979 I met Bob, a dear friend of mine who has cerebral palsy, and he taught me about self-advocacy. Bob knew about the problems I was having in my life and he told me I could make something of myself. I was helping myself. This made sense to me and I began to start self-advocacy groups. I learned how to serve on boards and committees and to understand people like myself.

I have some goals for the future. I would like to see a teenagers People First, so that teenagers can choose for themselves the kind of activities they would like to be involved in, the kind of training they would like to have and even the kind of clothes they wear. People First would teach them to speak for themselves instead of having social workers, doctors and teachers speak for them. They could also do things together like calling each other on the phone and going out to movies.

Also, I would like to see more people with disabilities live independently. The centers for independent living can help us do that. Someday, I would like to take a group of people with disabilities and have them come live with me so I could teach them to live independently. We also need to use computers, in the future to help us at work and at home.

Mostly, I would like to see us work together as a family and get away from those old models of the 60's, 70's, and 80's. Now it's the 90's and social workers, doctors, and teachers need to listen to us and to what we want.

### Colleen Bryant, San Jose Quality of Life Conference, September 26, 1989

Hi. My name is Colleen Bryant and . . . . I am here today to talk about my past, present and future about Living, Loving, Working, and Playing.

### My Past

When I lived at home, the thing I thought

was hard was sharing a room. I kept my things organized; my sister did not. There were things that my sisters did that I couldn't do, like going out nights. Most of my friends lived far away because I went to different schools. My sisters could drive and I couldn't. I wanted to hang out with my sisters.

What was easy about living at home was that my sisters were always there to help me. We all help each other, like with hair, makeup, and clothes. Because I was at home a lot, I had a very close relationship with my grandmother. We spent more time together. Living with my family taught me how to be brave and stick up for myself.

In the past I didn't think I would have a relationship with a guy because of my disability.

In the past working at Hope Mountain View my dislikes were making less money, having the supervisor correct my mistakes, and asking to use the restrooms. The only thing I thought was easy was I had a very good friendship with my supervisor.

In my past it was hard to make new friends.

### Present

In my present I lived at Greater Opportunity where having roommates is still not easy.

Moving out of my parents' house was a bit scary at first. I was not sure if they would like me or if I would like them.

What was easy was that I liked being on my own; no one telling me what to do — like ordering what to do; having more responsibilities for myself, like grocery shopping and making my own appointments. Living at Cortez, the thing I disliked was learning to live with roommates — that was hard sometimes. The things I liked were a nicer area, easy to get on buses, and more privacy, having close family and good friends, visiting my grandmother, going to visit my sister in San Diego, and being with my boyfriend. What I dislike about the job is working on weekends, working at Motel 6 cleaning rooms. The thing I like is helping Sheryl my boss with the other clients, and that there is more restaurants and shops.

Loving in a relationship was hard: honesty,

trust, sharing sharing is not always easy. Other hard feelings were being apart, like going on a big vacation, breaking up, like not seeing each other again, arguing, like having miscommunication.

### Future

In conclusion, in the future I hope to be living on my own in my own apartment taking responsibilities for my own life.

Having a stronger relationship, trying other new jobs like working with disability kids or adults, helping them learn how to read and write for a paying job. I want to find more time for playing. To enjoy life.

It would be hard to get places because I don't drive.

My future is going to be like making decisions and commitments for my long range goals. Having the ability and the understanding to do things that some handicapped people are afraid to try.

Thank you and enjoy your day.

## Cheryl Crowe, San Bernardino Quality of Life Conference, October 6, 1989

(This speech was read for Ms. Crowe at the conference. She was unable to deliver it personally due to illness.)

Hi. My name is Cheryl Crowe and I am a clerk assistant at Pomona Valley Workshop. And I would like to talk about three different subjects: Self-confidence, Self-Control and Your rights. I had to learn all three of these things.

When I was younger, I got into alcohol and drugs real bad. I used to blame my Dad because he used to give it to me, and I used to blame my good friends. These friends that I hung around with, used to help me get the alcohol and the drugs. I was really going down-hill. I didn't have no self-confidence, no self-control, and did not care about anyone's rights.

I got into a deep depression. It was like the more I got into alcohol and drugs, the more deeper of a depression I got in. There were a lot of times I came close to death. But my depression got so bad that my Sis took me to the hospital because I got so depressed, I took an overdose of sleeping pills. I was in the hospital for a month. And a person from Regional Center came out and told me that he knew a place in Upland, so he took me to see it, and I told him that I would take it just to get out of hospital.

So I moved. And a couple weeks later, I ran away to Las Vegas still thinking that no one cared. I spent all my money. And finally my friend talked to me about going back home, so I did and boy, my care provider was mad at me. The one time I felt that she cared; She could kick me out because I had no money to pay the rent, but she didn't.

I lived there for seven years. Over the years things changed when new staff people came and I felt no one cared. So I told my social worker I wanted to move, and I did. I found a place where people do care, like my new care providers, Pam and Stan Roberts, and also my newest boyfriend, Eugene Hagendon. They are there when I need to talk, and they listen.

So you can find people that do care. You got to look for them. They all have to give me a little push when I don't feel like I can do it. All three of these people give me the confidence to say, "Yes, you can. You can do it. Just take your time on it." And I do it. Might be slow on it, but you get it done.

When I got this job at Pomona Valley Workshop, I was working on the assembly line, and I worked on the line about two years. And all that time I felt like I wanted more in life than working on assembly line all my life. I talked to my case manager about a different job. It took her a while. I would ask her every day. Then finally my case manager, social worker, and I had a meeting. And I told my social worker that I wanted a different job. She asked me what I wanted to do. I said, "office work." A couple of weeks later, my case manager asked me do I want to work part-time in the Rehab office. I said, "Yes."

So when an opportunity comes along, you take it and prove to yourself and to them that you can do it.

A year ago I had an opportunity to work in the community, a place called "Treats." They made all different kinds of muffins. It was in the mall. I thought: Wow, the mall, more money, shopping, and discounts. The job was fun for a while. I was learning how to cook different kinds of muffins. But things got rough. My co-worker was making me do most of the work. They were saying I was too slow. And I said if I have the help like most do then I wouldn't be slow.

I got sick of it and I quit and came back to Pomona Valley Workshop. But I know I had an opportunity and I took it and gave it a try. And all you have to do is try. If you fall off the horse you get right back on and try again. I like what I'm doing now. I have learned a lot since I been here: self-confidence, responsibilities, and self-control.

Thanks to people like Lou Marchio, Roberta Eisel, Peggy Harrington, Faye Moore, and Peggy Margaret. Now those are the people who care. I've also learned more skills like using a copying machine, answering phones, typing, filing, and using the cash register.

Just say I am human. I can do anything I want if I have self-confidence, self-control, learn about my rights. Just listen to the social worker and do what you can in your IPP. And if you need help, don't be afraid to ask. Just remember three things: self-confidence, self-control, and your rights. And remember there are people that do care.

Thank you.

## Mike Hansen, San Diego Quality of Life Conference, October 14, 1989

I would like to welcome everyone to this Quality of Life Conference sponsored by Area Board Thirteen and the World Institute on Disability. My name is Mike Hansen and I am happy to see so many of you here!

Many of you may be wondering why this conference is important? This conference gives consumers an opportunity to speak out and be heard. Today it is our turn to do the talking and the professionals to do the listening.

Like many of you, I have been involved in self-advocacy over the past two years. I first became interested in self-advocacy when Nancy Ward, a consumer from Nebraska, came to San Diego to talk about getting self-advocacy groups started. We then organized self-advocacy groups and I've been part of a group for the past two years. We also have a regional self-advocacy group called Council People First of San Diego. I am the president for this group. Because of self-advocacy I have learned to speak out for my rights and my wishes. I would like to explain to you what self-advocacy is.

Speaking for ourselves: An example of this is speaking out at your IPP meeting instead of letting the professionals do the talking.

Solving problems and making decisions: An example of this might be deciding to live in a studio apartment rather than share an apartment and deal with roommate problems.

Knowing rights and responsibilities: An example of this is knowing you have a right to live where you want and if you live in a group home you have the right to open your own mail and to receive all calls without restrictions.

Contributing to the community. Examples of this are having a job, volunteering your time to help others, paying taxes and voting.

Although I've learned to speak out for myself, there was a time in my life when professionals made all of my decisions for me. I have lived in a state hospital and several group homes where my wishes were not heard. When I lived at Camarillo I wanted to visit with my Mom and the staff said no. They also said I could not call her. My visitation rights were taken away. Then I was transferred to a group home in LongBeach for People with Prader Willi Syndrome. This was not my problem and I became very ill because they put me on a diet. Finally, I decided to get out of the group home so I left and came to San Diego. Now I live independently and have for seven years. I have been successful because of professionals who were willing to work with me, not for me. They helped me in decision-making money management, health concerns, organizational skills, cooking and housekeeping. In other words, they helped me learn these things — they did not do them for me. I enjoy living independently because I can do what I want as long as I meet my obligations and responsibilities.

One of the most important things professionals have helped me with is work. Work is very important to me. I have held a number of different jobs such as a popcorn popper at a movie theater, a hotel maid, and in an ARC workshop. Now I work as a courtesy clerk at Vons. I have worked at Vons for four months. Because of my hard work and the support of some professionals, I am happy with my job.

I have talked about the past and the present and now I would like to talk about the future.

One thing we should all think about are our goals and dreams for the future. We need goals for ourselves, as well as goals for all persons with developmental disabilities. For myself, I dream of being a supervisor at Vons, owning a condo, having a credit card and traveling. My dream for persons with developmental disabilities is that one day we all will be able to speak for ourselves, be ourselves, live where we want and work in the community.

So please speak out in your small groups today. Think about your dreams for the future. This is your chance to be heard. And let's have a good time in our workshops.

## Notes

[1]The original write-up of this research was done by WID staff Val Vivona and Deborah Kaplan, with the support of Simi Litvak, Ed Roberts and Mary Pugh. Copies of the original write up titled, *Quality of Life: People with Developmental Disabilities Speak Out*, may be obtained from: the World Institute on Disability/ 510 16th Street/ Oakland, CA 94612. Patrick Connally, the editor of this abridged version of that report, may also be contacted at this address, or at the Marin Center for Independent Living/ 710 4th Street/ San Rafael, CA 94901.

# 11• Capitol People First: Self-Advocacy and Quality of Life Issues

by Robert R. Rosenberg, Consultant on Self-Advocacy
Sacramento, California

The general idea the people who are writing the "intellectual" part of this book have about quality of life is that the more a person's life has what that person wants and needs, the *better* the quality of that person's life.

The key to that definition is that a person has to be able to want things, to *know* he or she wants things, and be able to communicate those wants. The main thing about growing up with the label "mental retardation" in the United States is that too many people who are taken care of by the developmental disabilities system never learn that they are allowed to want things like everybody else, or even if they *do* find that out, their wants are not respected.

For people like the active members of Capitol People First in Sacramento, California, the importance of self-advocacy has been the emphasis placed by that group on finding out who you are, what your dreams for yourself are, and letting the world know about them.

A few years ago, California State Senator Dan McCorquodale led a critical review of existing state law relating to developmental disabilities and how it was being implemented. At one of the major hearings, Capitol People First Board members Tom Hopkins, Sandra Jensen, and Connie Martinez testified before his committee. Not far into their testimony, Senator McCorquodale interrupted.

"It's a real revelation to me," he said. "You folks are all very distinct personalities, and you know who you are. When I visit the group facilities in the Developmental Disabilities (DD) system, I get a sense of sameness from people..."

That gave me a chance to break in.

"That's an awfully important insight, Senator," I said. "What you're seeing is the difference between people who are trapped in the retarding environment, and who have been taught how to behave like retarded people are supposed to behave, and guys like these, who've gotten themselves out of those traps, and have shed that learned retarded behavior. With freedom from the retarding environment comes a discovery of your own identity."

It was Capitol People First that coined the phrase "The Retarding Environment" in its landmark 1984 report to the California State Council on Developmental Disabilities, *Surviving in the System: Mental Retardation and the Retarding Environment.* Tom Hopkins, Chairperson of the Board of Capitol People First, expanded on the concept some years later:

"I'd like to speak to you a little today about the Retarding Environment....The retarding environment means that even though we have a mental or cognitive impairment, the thing that sets us apart is the behavior they teach us in segregated places like state hospitals and sheltered workshops and so-called community facilities that are as disabled intensive as any other institution.

The Retarding Environment means having only other disabled people who have learned how to act retarded as your role models. It means having keepers rather than real teachers. It means that professionals who ought to be helping us to grow and develop and learning to solve our own problems are trying instead to manage *us* as if *we* are the problem. It means people having low expectations and training us to live *down* to those low expectations.

It means on the one hand being culturally malnourished, not getting to experience different stimulating environments, and on the other hand being dragged off to the bowling alley in busloads, where we scare the hell out of the real people, who either whisper and point or else pretend we don't exist at all.

It means trained vulnerability, learning that your own judgment is crap, that you've got to do what the authority figure says, because the authority figure is always right, so that when you ask about independent living, somebody on the staff says "Oh, you'll be ready for independent living training in five years" you know it'll be at least five years because the staff is always right.

When I graduated from high school, they put me in a sheltered workshop, and promised they would teach me to be a carpenter. But then I spent four and a half years sitting next to the Coke machine sanding blocks of wood, and learning to rock back and forth, and how, generally, to act retarded like the others. Finally I started *liking* the rocking and the humming of the Coke machine, and I knew I had to get out of there or go over the edge and never be able to come back.

But, you know? To this day, sometimes I slip back into those habits, and find myself rocking or playing around with my cane or shuffling papers mindlessly. It sort of reminds me of a TV program I saw once, where they were talking about the old buffalo hunters. Those hunters would get covered with buffalo blood, and no matter how they tried to wash it off, they couldn't get rid of THE STENCH OF DEATH! And that's what I carry around with me — the Stench of the Retarding Environment, and believe me, it's like the STENCH OF DEATH!"

• • •

Another member of the Capitol People First Board, Beverly Evans, spoke up for herself regarding the impact of professional perceptions and "help" on the quality of her life:

"All my life most people have treated me like I was always sick, even when I wasn't. I do have a lot of health problems, but the quality of my life was never improved by being treated like an invalid. I was put in a state hospital for twelve years, then I spent quite a few years in nursing homes and other places where they "took care of me" and treated me like I was sick all the time.

I have Spina Bifida, I'm legally blind, I've had an ileostomy and I have chronic kidney problems. I have acute ulcerative decubiti. When I was little I had hydrocephalus, which has created some problems for me in processing certain kinds of information quickly. This sounds like a lot of health problems, which I certainly don't deny. But what I want people to understand — and I really want to make myself understood on this — is that all those diagnoses don't mean that I have to spend my life being taken care of like a sick person. Despite all health problems, *I AM ABLE TO BE, I AM INDEPENDENT and IN CHARGE OF MY LIFE IN MY OWN HOME.*

When my life really began to have meaning for me was when I got into an independent living program, and learned to manage my *own* life in my *own* home. I still need a live-in attendant, and *maybe* I always will, but living in an apartment around people who aren't *all* disabled makes me glad to be alive.

The trouble is that the system doesn't really want to let me have the supports I need to be as independent as possible. It's kind of nutty that it doesn't, because the DD system paid for me to get independent living training. So I can't understand why it won't go the rest of the way and help me really be as independent as I can be.

1.  The system doesn't let me have enough attendant service hours.

2.  Transportation is a killer problem.

3.  I can't get a visiting nurse to come in a couple of times a month to help prevent some of my health problems from getting serious, and so I end up in an acute care hospital every so often, sometimes for a long time. And that's when the DAMNED doctors keep trying to send me back to a nursing home.

Learning how to be a self-advocate is one of the major things that has kept me independent for as long as I've held out against the part of the system that keeps trying to take care of me as a sick person all the time. So I've been able to keep up the fight to be independent in spite of a basically lousy support system except for People First. I think this group here today needs to understand what it could be like for people like me if there was a *good* support system. And I mean we need real, effective services as well as supportive people and attitudes.

If I had adaptable housing I could do a lot more things for myself. Right now, it's hard for me even to make a cup of tea for myself, because the stove top is higher than my shoulders, and I keep spilling hot water on myself when I try to pour it.

So, anyway, I fought my way out of the worst parts of the Retarding Environment, and I have to keep fighting to stay out. If you want to know what I want, it's what everybody else wants. I want friends, I want to be able to get to places in the community, I want to learn lots more things to be more normal, and someday I'd like to be able to get a real job. I'd like to be able to travel. I'd like to live in a real house with a real yard so I could have animals and a garden.

I don't want to be so emotionally wasted all the time that I can't reach out to other people with disabilities and help *them* fight for their independence the way disabled people have reached out to *me* when I was in need of friends and moral support and advice...

I know *this* for sure. If I ever had to go back to a segregated place where they treat people with developmental disabilities like they're sick children, and then instead of helping them grow or get over being sick, the keepers really abuse people and let them suffer and teach them to be retarded, I know I'd lose the will to live. Somehow as tough as it is on my own, it isn't as scary or as tough as it is always being taken care of, especially by people who don't think you're much of anything. So lately I've started saying the same thing Patrick Henry said - 'GIVE ME LIBERTY OR GIVE ME DEATH!' And I mean that!"

• • •

Sandra Jensen was President of Capitol People First for a long time before intensifying health problems made her ease up:

"I was born with Down Syndrome, and that gave me heart and lung problems, and speech problems, and mental retardation, and other problems. When the doctor told my parents what I had right after I was born, he told them they should let him put me in the state hospital and just forget about me, because I would never be any smarter than a three-year-old, and I would never be able to take care of myself, and I would probably die when I was a young teenager. I was lucky to have parents that would not believe the misinformation they got, and they didn't let me go to a state hospital. If they had, probably the doctor would have been right —maybe I wouldn't even have learned to walk or talk, because I sure wasn't the million dollar baby when I was little. They measured my IQ and said it was 30. But I

learned to read, I learned how to handle money, I learned how to take the bus, I learned how to live in my own apartment, where I've lived for more than ten years now.

*I* have learned that being retarded just means being slow, but nobody really knows how far you can keep going, even if you go slow. The other kids learned how to read when they were six. I didn't. But if my parents and my teachers had decided that because I didn't learn how to read when I was six I'd *never* learn, I never *would* have learned. But they believed in me, and I learned how to read when I was 12.

It used to really upset me a lot that I have Down Syndrome and all those other disabilities. I remember even when I was learning to take the bus as part of independent living training, I hated to take the bus because I always thought nobody wanted to sit next to me because I looked different. Sometimes I still feel sorry for myself.

But mostly these days when I think about it I am really angry at that doctor and the other professionals who gave out such misinformation. I am *really* angry to think that some professionals are *still* handing out that kind of misinformation like in the Baby Doe case, and hundreds of cases like Baby Doe.

The truth is just having Down Syndrome, or having any kind of mental retardation, doesn't automatically mean you're doomed to a low quality of life. People with mental retardation often do have a poor quality of life, but that's because of the retarding environment where they have to live, the sheltered and segregated places they're sent to spend their days, the false beliefs people have about them, and the lack of help they get to learn how to live a normal life.

Now I lead a pretty normal life, and in a lot of ways a good quality of life. I'm a little sad because my mother and her new husband just moved away from Sacramento. But I have good friends, and we do things together. I LOVE to party. Sometimes my friends say I've got UP SYNDROME."

• • •

When Roberto "Bear" Negrete was born, the doctors didn't expect him to live. They claimed they couldn't pick up brain waves. Later evaluations indicated he had suffered pockets of damage throughout his brain and his IQ was measured below 30. If only the story could be reconstructed of how his mother fought to keep him out of a state hospital and in integrated community settings, and how she designed prosthetic devices to counteract his spasticity, how she taught teachers how to teach him, and how she influenced positively the lives of many other youngsters with cognitive disabilities and their families, it would be a history-making document. We say with both relief and great sadness that it is quite likely that if Bear *had* been subjected to the state of the art services available from the mental retardation system when he was born, he would, if he were still alive under those circumstances, today be in a crib in a state hospital, uncommunicative, immobile, hopeless and helpless. What follows is his account of the daily round of his life as it now *is*:

"I have a very busy life.

I work at the cafeteria at the State Capitol in Sacramento. I make deliveries to the offices of the Governor and the members of the Legislature. I help keep the tables clean and stocked with napkins and salt and pepper and sugar and so on, and I help with the banking. I know all the members of the Legislature and their staffs by their first names, and they know me.

When I graduated from high school, my folks encouraged me to learn to drive. I found a teacher who was willing to take the extra effort to teach me, and then I passed the test. Now I even have my own car, and boy, does it make a difference in my life.

I have busy weekends going to jazz concerts and plays and art shows and sometimes to Reno and San Francisco with my friends. I have a lot of disabled friends, and I have a lot of friends who aren't disabled. I participate in Sierra Club activities.

One of the things my disabled friends make a big deal about, but I don't notice it as much as they do, is that most people treat me like I'm normal".

• • •

Tom Hopkins told about Ruth Shelton, a relatively new member of Capitol People First, in a speech he made in Japan in 1992:

"...let me tell you about Ruth. We met her when we were registering people to vote, at a large nursing home, a few years ago. She was then about 60 years old and had never been told that she had the right to vote. We explained to Ruth that she indeed had the right to vote, but that to do so, she had to be registered first. Ruth has extremely severe cerebral palsy, has to use a wheelchair, and can hardly use her hands. Bob Rosenberg filled out the registration form for her and told her she had to sign it. She tried to grip the pen with her right hand and couldn't. Then she tried her left hand. That didn't work either.

"Now what do we do?" Bob asked. Ruth pointed to her mouth. It took Bob a minute to figure out what she meant. Then he brought the pen up to her mouth. She clamped her teeth on it, bent over the application, and made her mark on the paper. Incidentally, she now paints pictures holding the brush in her teeth." [Since Tom made that speech Ruth has gotten a helmet which holds her brush.]

Ruth spoke to a large conference in 1992. Some of what she said was:

"I'm proud to be here to help you understand how people like me can live independently. I've lived two lives. My first life was a bad dream. My second life is a fairy tale. My first life began at home. My family loved me, but they weren't given the right supports to help me in those days. And so I was kept in institutions, mostly with hundreds of other disabled people, until I was almost 60 years old. Then, even though a lot of the staff at the big nursing home I was being kept at thought I couldn't manage on my own, I got into an independent living program. My dear friend Laura... was being kept at the same nursing home and got in [the IL program] the same time I did. When we graduated, we became roommates in - for the first time in our lives — *our own home*!!!

Laura does a lot of things for me that most people can do for themselves, because I can't use my hands, and I have to use a wheelchair to get around. I also have an attendant who comes in, but not really a lot considering how much help I need sometimes. The thing is, Laura makes me understand that she feels helping me isn't a burden. I know that if it were the other way around I would do the same...

That's part of the reason I said my second life is a fairy tale. I was always fortunate to have friends wherever I was being kept in my first life, but we mostly shared pain and misery. In this life I get to share good experiences and joy with my friends.

And I get to do things I really like. I'm in a program that's helping me to be a pretty good painter. Right now, I have to hold the brush in my teeth, but we're working on getting me a helmet that will hold the brush.

I go to People First meetings every month, and that's a wonderful experience, because there are so many people there who are taking back control of their lives like Laura and I did, and we can really communicate with each other.

But you know, I still feel a great deal of sadness when I think how many people there are like me and like the folks I meet at People First who are still being kept in those bad dream places. There's no excuse for that anymore.

Some of my friends say I'm too kind to the system. I don't feel bitter about all those years in institutions because I believe the folks who run the DD system didn't know any better.

But now they *do* know better. They can look at my second life, and Laura's, and many other people's, and they just can't say anymore that it isn't possible, because *we're doing it*!!!

So if any of you here today still aren't believers, come visit Laura and me. And if any of you who are being kept in a bad dream feel scared even to think about getting out on your own, come and visit us, and come to People First, too. It's alright to be scared, but don't let it keep you from taking back your life.

Because life doesn't have to be a bad dream. Life *can* be a fairy tale.

Thank you."

• • •

The same Senator Dan McCorquodale who noted the uniqueness and individuality of the Capitol People First board members authored very important legislation in 1992. Senate Bill 1383 calls, among other things, for the evaluation of the Developmental Disabilities (DD) system services in California based on outcomes for the consumers of those services. The services must have been based on the *needs* and *wants* of those consumers. The legislation mandates the agencies responsible for service planning and purchase to provide the best available information regarding potential outcomes to consumers in order to maximize *informed choice*.

In 1991, Connie Martinez, the Vice-President of Capitol People First, who had served on the California State Council on Developmental Disabilities and on the Executive Committee of the President's Committee on Employment of People with Disabilities, and has been considered a superstar of the "political" self-advocacy movement, was invited to visit Japan by the newly stirring movement for the rights of Japanese with "intellectual disabilities". Accompanied by Barbara Blease, co-founder and adviser to Capitol People First, Connie made speeches in Osaka and and Tokyo. Eighteen months later, Tom Hopkins and I made a similar visit to Japan.

Whereas Tom rarely talks about himself, preferring to illustrate his understanding of life in and out of the retarding environment with stories of other people (except for the "stench of death" story), Connie's most moving presentations are autobiographical.

She tells about how her parents were told by a priest that Connie was God's punishment to them for a sin they had committed, even if they didn't know what the sin was. She tells about how she wondered every day of her young life what she had done wrong to draw the angry looks from her parents.

She says with exquisite poignancy that her parents had a dream for her brothers and her sister, but "no dream for Connie - pobrecita!" It was up to her to find her own dream.

• • •

A significant outcome of those visits was the impetus they gave the self-advocacy movement in Japan. By the summer of 1993 a group 30 or so self-advocates, accompanied by family members, attendants and social service professionals (primarily those interested in extending independent living services in Japan to people with intellectual disabilities) had attended the international People First conference in Toronto, Canada, and had visited Sacramento and Capitol People First for several days.

A distressing fact of Japanese life, to many, is that the government provides no assistance to persons with psychiatric or intellectual disabilities other than institutional care. As a consequence, there are 350,000 people with such disabilities who reside in large institutions, equivalent to what have been termed "state hospitals" in the United States. [1]

Many of the Japanese visitors to Toronto and Sacramento were residents of these institutions. Some had been placed as children, and, if past history was a guide, could expect to live out their lives as residents. While in Sacramento, all the Japanese guests made several visits to persons with generally severe developmental disabilities who were living in their own homes. They asked a great many questions, and although everyone politely moved on when it was time to do so, I sensed a widespread regret that there was not more time to learn more and to get better acquainted with the people who were able to manage this wondrous control of their own lives.

A few weeks after the Japanese self-advocates and their colleagues arrived home, we began getting the letters. According to one, a young woman with autism, a resident of a large institution who was believed to be unable to speak more than her name, had become absolutely voluble on the trip home.

"I do not want to live at that place any longer," she said, to the amazement of her traveling companions. "I want my own home."

There were other similar pronouncements. Also a few people said they wished to marry also virtually unheard of among Japanese with intellectual disabilities.

Revolution! A byproduct of discovering the right to want.

• • •

A final set of comments from Connie Martinez.

"... the first thing for the professionals and the parents to understand is that we can have a good quality of life if we have control over our own lives, and if we have the help we need to *keep* that control and independence in our own lives.

After I got out of high school — I really shouldn't say "graduated" even though they gave me a piece of paper, all they really taught me was how to be ashamed of myself, and sad, and angry, I sat at home for many years just watching television. Then I got taken to a sheltered workshop, where I learned to sort hangers they hang clothes on.

Finally I got sent to a so-called school for adults where they taught people how to be more retarded, and to stay that way as long as they were in that school. All that ended about twelve years ago. I was fortunate to have been asked to be in the first class at a program in Sacramento that teaches retarded people to take control of their own lives, and live without supervision. At the same time I joined Capitol People First.

Those two experiences changed my life forever. When I stopped being angry and ashamed about *myself*, and turned it into constructive anger directed toward the retarding environment, abilities I never knew I had came out." [Connie, more than 30 years out of school, is learning to read - in 1993!]

"We don't need KEEPERS, we need TEACHERS."

## Notes

[1]It is important to note that the relationship between the Japanese disabilities movement, particularly the movement for better public services for people with intellectual disabilities, and the Japanese women's rights movement is very strong. In fact, there is a distinct crossover in leadership in the two movements. Much of this is explainable by the fact that if a family does not wish to place a disabled son or daughter in an institution, it falls to the mother to provide care for that disabled family member as long as both of them are alive.

Shortly after the dramatic change in the Japanese government in mid-1993, which saw women and persons with disabilities assume key roles in the new governing coalition, our Japanese friends advised us that a Japanese with Disabilities Act, modeled after the Americans with Disabilities Act, was being drafted for introduction into the Diet. Work was also begun on translation of the Lanterman Act, California's monumental developmental disabilities services law, into Japanese.

[This chapter was put together from audio tapes, notes, and simply recollections of about ten years of working as a volunteer advisor to a self-advocacy organization called Capitol People First, based in Sacramento, California. During those ten years, I met almost weekly with the five or six people who constituted the Board of Directors -I also was fortunate enough to be paid by various agencies to work as "facilitator" for four of those Board members, who often served on local, state or federal advisory boards or commissions as it became a good thing to appoint "consumers" to such bodies. I have taken the liberty of trimming and editing, and paraphrasing the thoughts of the people who originated them, to fit as reasonably well as possible the context of this book and so make the text somewhat more readable. Although I have received permission of the people I quote in this lax fashion to do so, I take full responsibility for misstatements and misunderstandings. In order to protect my sources from adverse reaction to what they've said or from what I report, I've blurred some identities, but if any reader has a legitimate reason for communicating or meeting with anyone mentioned in this chapter, I'll do my best to arrange it.]

# 12• Quality of Life in the United States: A Multicultural Context

Mariellen Laucht Kuehn, Waisman Center,
University of Wisconsin, Madison
John W. McClainm Jr., Meyer Rehab. Institute, University of Nebraska

The concept of quality of life (QOL) and strategies for measuring its implications for persons with developmental disabilities are extremely complex and still largely elusive. Researchers and policy makers within the United States and, indeed, throughout the western world have attempted to identify the precise conceptual framework needed to establish a universal understanding of the concept that can be applied by a diverse group of academicians, governmental officials, advocates, and individuals with developmental disabilities themselves. The majority of the authors in this book are in agreement that the concept of quality of life cannot be segregated from a thorough understanding of an individual's environment — the community, culture, and society in which a person lives. The earliest general model of QOL developed by Goode and Powers (Goode, 1988) and the QOL conceptual framework of person-environment fit developed by Kuehn, Goode, and Powers (Goode, 1988) emphasized the relationship between one's perception of his/her environment and the quality of one's life. Today the importance of this relationship is well recognized. As stated in Dr. Goode's chapter in this book:

> "The QOL of an individual is intrinsically related to the QOL of other persons in his or her environment."
> "QOL of a person reflects the cultural heritage of the person and of those who surround him or her."

Within the United States, the concept of cultural heritage and one's social environment is extremely complex. The United States is composed of multiple cultures and multiple social environments. To begin to develop an understanding of the relationship between developmental disabilities and the cultural diversity that exists within the United States, one needs to have some understanding of the history of racial/ethnic minority populations, the present demographics of race and ethnicity in the United States, and the cultural issues related to the development of quality of life programs for people with developmental disabilities. This chapter will cover these areas and also will discuss the implications of cultural diversity in the

United States for future research on QOL.

Throughout this chapter the term racial/ethnic minority groups or populations is used as a generic reference for all of those United States citizens who are not members of the non-Hispanic white majority racial group. There is little consensus on terminology or definitions for people from diverse races, ethnicities, or cultures at this time. Race is generally used to refer to large groups of people with more or less distinctive physical characteristics, such as skin color. Ethnicity is used primarily to refer to groups of people with a similar national or cultural heritage, such as African-Americans or Japanese-Americans. Some of the specific population terms used in this chapter are neither racial nor ethnic descriptors but are categorizations that have been developed by demographers and statisticians. For example, the term Hispanic, which was developed by the United States Bureau of Census, is not an inclusive descriptor for any particular segment of society. It subsumes black people and white people who are part of the Mexican, Cuban, Latin American, Puerto Rican and other ethnic groups in the United States. In this chapter the term minority refers to racial/ethnic groups which, as a whole, hold an unequal and unrepresentative share of the resources in U.S. society. The term minority refers then, strictly to the social standing of a group, not its size (Kuehn and Imm-Thomas 1993).

## Cultural Diversity in the United States: An Historical Perspective

The historical fact of overt and covert racism in all aspects of life in the United States confounds the search for an operational definition of QOL for those citizens who have developmental disabilities and are members of racial/ethnic minority groups. Ironically, the perpetuation of racism and the quest for strategies to eradicate it have nurtured a diversity of value systems across which a credible definition of QOL must straddle. Historical racism, operationalized through legally sanctioned social segregation and economic disenfranchisement, has strengthened the communal bonds among those who share the same racial/ethnic status. Historically, the inability of racial/ethnic minority groups to access the goods, services, and institutions controlled by Euro-Americans led to the establishment of mutual aid and communal organizations that were both formal and informal (Cloward and Piven, 1974). In that environment, though the data is sparse or non-existent, individuals with developmental disabilities presumably found a place where they belonged and shared in the life of the segregated racial/ethnic communities. It was a life of "accidental normalization."

As a consequence of racism, the racial/ethnic communities experienced economic, educational, and social victimization. People with developmental disabilities (physical and/or mental) were doubly victimized because of their primary identity as members of these racial/ethnic minority groups and secondarily because of their disabilities. The people with developmental disabilities who were members of racial/ethnic minority groups derived their strength and identity from their relationship with their families and the community or tribe. These communities nurtured the individual and utilized the skills of the individual (however minimal) for the maintenance and sustenance of the whole. First and foremost, members of racial/ethnic minority groups saw themselves as members of a unit – a unit based on the realities of race, ethnicity, and kinship. To break these bonds with one's community was to break with one's lifeforce. The "good life" was defined in the context of one's relationship with the group as individuals were too vulnerable in the hostile world of the dominant majority, Euro-American, culture that existed outside of that group.

Within the mainstream of United States culture historically, there has been a dearth of economic and educational opportunities for people who were part of racial/ethnic minority groups. This deprivation helped to reduce class distinctions among members of racial/ethnic minority groups. There was a resignation to endure the will of outside forces (both seen and unseen) and to accept one's "fate." In contrast, Euro-Americans (particularly of the male gender) had greater access to and control of economic and educational opportunities. As a result, they were in a strategic position to establish social class distinctions and to fortify a value system based on the achievements of the individual. For most members of racial/ethnic minority groups in the United States, a quality life required the establishment of a distinct set of new values — in part as a reaction to the pervasive reality of racism and subsequent disenfranchisement. These cultural values emphasized the collective needs of the community and group, over the self-actualization of the individual.

Some of the most overt aspects of racism included the genocide of the American Indian and the Jim Crow laws which discriminated against African-Americans and other Black people. When these more violent forms of racism receded and legislation to support civil rights began to emerge, a new more subtle model of racism was formulated and propagated. That model of racism asserted that "success" was the ability of an individual who was part of a racial/ethnic minority group to realize his or her economic and educational destiny through assimilation or acculturation into the mainstream of the Euro-American social environment. Value systems which appeared to be at variance with this view were seen as deviant or defective. Many members of racial/ethnic minority groups became the focus of these assimilation efforts and often found themselves apologetic for their historical estrangement from the belief systems of the dominant, Euro-American, culture. Euro-Americans, who had little knowledge or appreciation of the values nurtured in the invisible worlds and social environments of racial/ethnic minority groups, maintained a network of boarding schools and other institutions which were the structural symbols of these assimilation efforts. For racial/ethnic minority people, what was normal, what was successful, and in fact the "good life" frequently were defined and dictated by others. Those views of community, lifestyle, or happiness which were at variance with Euro-American perceptions of a quality life were either brutally suppressed or ignored.

Today we find ourselves at a social juncture which we must approach with a mixture of exhilaration and caution. The possibility of ensuring a QOL for all people in the United States, with and without disabilities, and regardless of race or ethnicity is exciting. Those people of goodwill who are working with and on behalf of people with developmental disabilities, however, need to move cautiously to ensure that they do not mistakenly create another Euro-American standard to which people from racial/ethnic minority groups are expected to comply.

## Demographics

Today, significant demographic shifts are occurring within the United States as a result of the rapid rate of growth among racial/ethnic minority populations. According to a recent analysis of the 1990 United States census data over the past decade (Braddock 1991), the Asian American population has increased by 107.8 percent; the number of Hispanic people by 53 percent; American Indians by 37.9 percent and Blacks by 13.2 percent. (Note: Black is the term used by the United States Census Bureau to encompass African-Americans, Jamaican-Americans and other Carribean-Americans.) The non-Hispanic white population in the United States increased by only 6 percent. During the past decade, seventeen of the fifty States have experienced significant growth rates among one or more of the four main racial/ethnic minority groups (African-American, American Indian, Asian-American, and Hispanic). Copeland (1988) states that racial/ethnic minority populations within the U.S. will grow seven times faster than the Euro-American population over the next ten years. By the year 2000 it is anticipated that one-third of the population in the United States will be other than non-Hispanic white and, in many States, the majority of the population will be members of racial/ethnic minority groups.

The number of people in the United States who have a developmental disability is not known. It is generally estimated that 5 percent of the United States population have a developmental disability. However, the incidence and prevalence of developmental disabilities is estimated to be higher among some racial/ethnic minority populations for several reasons. First, there is often a higher incidence and prevalence of infant mortality and morbidity among racial/ethnic minority groups. For example, the incidence rate of children born with a low birth weight is 12.9 percent among Blacks as compared to the United States national average of 6.9 percent (U.S. Department of Health & Human Services, 1991). This would suggest a higher prevalence rate of developmental disabilities among children who are Black. Second, economic poverty is correlated with developmental disabilities. Within the United States, economic poverty is higher among the racial/ethnic minority groups than it is among the non-Hispanic White population. For example, the Indian Health Service (1989) has reported that about 28.2 percent of Native American Indians live below the poverty level as compared with 12.4 percent for all other races. Third, there appears to be a higher incidence of destructive social behaviors among some racial/ethnic minority groups. While all racial/ethnic minority groups are heterogeneous in their behavioral characteristics certain destructive social behaviors, having a high correlation to developmental disabilities, appear to be more prevalent among certain racial/ethnic minority groups. Examples of these behaviors would include the use of drugs and violent behaviors related to the use of guns and other weapons (Jaynes and Williams, 1989).

## Cultural Issues Related to QOL

Despite the fact that the number of people from racial/ethnic minority groups is rapidly growing in the United States and the fact that the percentage of people with developmental disabilities is higher among many of those groups than it is in the overall United States population, there is little information available about the effectiveness of service delivery to people who are members of a racial/ethnic minority group. There is no information available about the quality of life for people with developmental disabilities who are members of racial/ethnic minority populations in the United States.

The concept of the "good life" or a "quality life" as defined by Euro-Americans may well be beyond the reach of many members of racial and ethnic minority groups. For example, the health, education, employment, and social service systems in the United States are designed to meet the needs of all people with developmental disabilities, regardless of ethnic background, however, people do not share equally in the benefits these systems offer. While the number of people with developmental disabilities is higher among racial/ethnic minority groups, the availability and utilization of health services is considerably lower for those groups than it is for Euro-Americans (Hickey and Solis, 1990; McClain, 1990). Of the 13.3 million Americans with a disability, 33.6 percent are in the labor force (Krauss and Stoddard, 1989). Among that cohort of individuals, Euro-Americans are 1-1/2 times more likely to be participating in the labor force (full or part-time)

than African-Americans or Americans of Hispanic/Latino descent. If an individual is an African-American male *without* a disability, he has half the chance of securing a full-time job than does a Euro-American male *with* a disability. Such realities as:

- the high cost of health care (even when subsidies are available),
- the physical inaccessibility of many health care facilities due to location and the lack of affordable transportation, and
- the real or perceived barriers based on provider attitudes in conflict with personal belief systems have historically created a chasm between the services needed and the services received.

The lack of economic opportunities, in an era of steadily decreasing resources, most negatively impacts upon those who have never gained a firm footing in the economic marketplace. These inequalities intensify the separation of racial/ethnic minority groups from the institutional support structures established by the dominant majority culture and promote the development of alternative formal and informal support systems. The legacy of racism has affected many members of racial/ethnic minority groups. To a great extent, it has perpetuated an "equality of deprivation" among the able-bodied and those with chronic disabilities who are members of the same racial/ ethnic minority group.

As one surveys the QOL literature, key phrases such as "personal power", "control of one's life", "the individuality of each person", and "individual decision-making authority" are frequently offered as conceptual building blocks for a universal theory of QOL. The use of these concepts, signify a subtle but profound challenge for the growing number of scholars and activists who are committed to the exploration of the equally elusive concept of cultural diversity. For example, decision-making is a key concept among some racial/ethnic groups. American Indians value self-determination, but most American Indian communities in the United States expect to be an active participant in the development and implementation of services for individuals with developmental disabilities and for the community (National Indian Council on Aging, 1981). In fact, this value was included in the 1975 Indian Self-Determination and Education Act (P.L. 93-638) which mandates that the staff of the Indian Health Service involve communities in the administration and operation of programs. Among Asians the needs of the family and the opinions of certain family members are important components of the decision-making process (United States Department of Health & Human Services, 1990). The inclusion of the family in the decision-making process is important also for Hispanic elders. The family is a source of support which can greatly influence the delivery of services as it acts on behalf of the family members with developmental disabilities (COSSMHO, 1988).

As Goode and others have suggested, most individuals grow up learning about themselves and their social environment through a particular set of cultural, personal, and linguistic experiences. These experiences become part of an individual's conscious and unconscious framework for reacting to the world. Scholars such as Goode (1993, this book) assert that QOL policy, assessments, and programs need to reflect cultural differences and promote cultural identity. However, the life experiences of many members of racial/ethnic minority groups and the values which fuel those life experiences may be at variance with the increasingly accepted conceptual foundation associated with the emerging theory of the basis for developing and maintaining a QOL for people with developmental disabilities.

The cultural values of individualism and self-actualization are most associated with United States citizens of European descent. Given that the Euro-American view of the relationship between the individual and his or her environment has historically dominated United States thought and policy actions (Ballard, 1973; Wilson, 1986), it is not surprising that the concept of QOL reflects this ethnocentric view of the needs or rights of all United States citizens.

The conceptual threat of the "tyranny of the normal" as presented by Holm, Holst and Perlt and by Goode in this book is a critical issue that needs to be further explored. However, for people with disabilities who are members of racial/ethnic minority groups in the United States, the state-of-the-art view of QOL poses a far more subtle threat that could result in yet another destructive form of racist annihilation. This threat is based upon the subtle supposition that persons with developmental disabilities are members of a monolithic culture, bound by the realities of a chronic disability. While there is a rhetoric in the United States among people working with individuals with developmental disabilities which recognizes the rights of individuals, the individual's cultural heritage and belief systems seem to be substantially ignored or subordinated because they are in conflict with emerging paradigms. We must recognize that many members of racial/ethnic minority groups in the United States view their racial or ethnic identity as the primary essence of their life. The reality of a chronic disability, while a legitimate descriptor, is subordinate to the greater reality of their racial or ethnic status. It is generally the cultural values emanating from their richly diverse life experiences that define them most profoundly. Given that the primary identity of people with developmental disabilities is often with a particular racial/ethnic minority group, scholars must systematically cultivate a broader understanding of those cultural values. The failure of scholars and support providers to fully comprehend, appreciate, and investigate the bond between racial/ethnic identity and one's perceptions of a quality life will inevitably result in a tyranny of the normal. It will also be a lost opportunity to reach an intellectual plateau that will be critical to a universal understanding of QOL in the United States and, indeed, in the world in the Twenty-first century.

## Research Implications

Too often researchers appear to conduct studies based upon the assumption that people with developmental disabilities constitute a homogeneous minority culture. However, studies among older adults with developmental disabilities have shown that this is not a valid assumption (Pederson, Chaikin, Koehler, Campbell and Arcand, 1993). The challenge is to develop an awareness and knowledge of the diverse cultural beliefs and behaviors related to assisting and supporting people with developmental disabilities and to develop an understanding of the "good life" as perceived by different racial/ethnic minority groups. Without such knowledge, any quantitative or qualitative analyses of QOL will be imprecise and will limit the ability of researchers to develop a universal theory of QOL for the purpose of research or program planning.

Attention needs to be given to the validity of current constructs and instruments for diverse cultures. Vega (1992) in a discussion of cultural diversity and community research makes the point that one's reasoning can be "murky because of a lack of orienting theory to distinguish psychological processes from social ones" (p. 380). He provides as an example a study by Topol and Reznikoff (1982) which correlates external locus of control to suicide attempts among adolescents. Vega indicates that Hispanics, who are noted for externalizing control have lower suicide rates than adolescents in other cultures which internalize control. He concludes: "Perhaps it is more precise to declare constructs to be culture specific or, at least, to have culture specific expressions, since they involve belief systems, culturally sanctioned behaviors, and culturally conditioned cognitive processes." (p. 380). The QOL constructs that particularly need to be studied from a cultural perspective are those related to decision-making, individualism, and employment.

In addition to conceptual issues, there are several pragmatic problems related to conducting cross-cultural research such as the lack of adequate samples and linguistic problems. The biggest problem, however, may be the reluctance of people from racial/ethnic minority groups to participate in research conducted by Euro-Americans.

Such reluctance frequently stems from a lack of trust. Among Asian-Americans, for example, a lack of trust may arise from a fear of jeopardizing their immigration status or because of past discriminatory acts such as the relocation of Japanese-Americans to concentration camps during World War II (Marioka-Douglas and Yeo, 1990). Similarly among African-Americans, there is often an extreme lack of trust toward research, training, or service institutions because of continued racial abuse, discrimination, and segregation. Hence, a person with a disability who is African-American may be more receptive to working and communicating with researchers or support providers who are also African-Americans, despite the fact that the color of one's skin is no guarantee of culturally competent behavior toward one's own or any other race (Cross, 1988).

In order to reduce the estrangement that frequently exists between racial/ethnic minority groups and the worlds of academia and service that are dominated by the Euro-American culture, there is a need to involve people from racial/ethnic minority groups in the QOL research efforts. The involvement of researchers and people with disabilities from racial/ethnic minority groups would help to ensure the accurate interpretation of:

- cultural differences across ethnic groups;
- intergroup cultural differences; and
- class versus ethnic differences.

The involvement of people from racial/ethnic minority groups, with and without disabilities, requires a commitment to the full inclusion of people from diverse cultures in all aspects of QOL research

design, implementation, analyses, and dissemination. Such a commitment would go a long way toward achieving the goal of a more comprehensive and valid approach to QOL research.

There is also a need to develop a cadre of researchers who are culturally competent and capable of doing cross-cultural research related to QOL. Cultural competence is defined as the awareness, knowledge, understanding, acceptance and valuing of diverse racial/ethnic groups (Kuehn and Imm-Thomas, 1993). The development of cultural competence begins with an awareness that not all people are the same. Values, religious beliefs, assumptions about the causality of disease and attitudes about the use of medical technology and prescription medicines, definitions of "the good life" or a "quality life", the value of research, and related issues can vary greatly amongst different racial/ethnic minority populations. These differences will influence the manner in which different groups engage in research and program planning related to QOL.

Finally, there is a need to recruit young people from racial/ethnic minority groups into the university programs that train people to work as support providers and to conduct QOL research. Given the personnel shortages that presently exist within the health, allied health, social and education systems, the recruitment and retention of people from racial/ethnic minority groups into these professions is a matter of survival. Without them, it is be increasingly difficult to provide support or a "quality life" for people of any ethnicity (Hickey and Solis, 1990).

In summary, culture and ethnicity define QOL. It cannot be ignored or avoided in the design and delivery of services or supports. Nor can culture be ignored in the development of research constructs and measurement instruments. The participation of people with developmental disabilities, family members, researchers, and professionals from racial/ethnic minority groups is critical to the study of QOL. With assistance from these individuals, we can systematically test the validity of current QOL constructs to see if they are culturally specific or generalizable to all United States citizens regardless of race or ethnicity. We may also identify new concepts and approaches to QOL that will enable us to provide culturally competent support services.

## References

Ballard, A.B. (1973). *The education of black folk: The Afro-American struggle for knowledge in white America.* NY: Harper and Row.

Braddock, D. (1991). *Technical note to census data.* Chicago: Illinois University Affiliated Program.

Cloward, R.A. & Piven, F.F. (1974). *The politics of turmoil: Essays on poverty, race and the urban crisis,* 195-196. NY: Vintage Books.

Copeland, L. (1988). Valuing workplace diversity. *Personnel Administrator,* November, 38-40.

COSSMHO-The National Coalition of Hispanic Health and Human Services Organizations. (1988). *Delivering preventive health care to Hispanics: A manual for providers.* Washington,DC: Author.

Cross, T.L. (1988). Services to minority populations: Cultural competence continuum. *Focal Point, 3,* 1-4.

Goode, D.A. (1988). *Quality of life for persons with disabilities: A review and synthesis of the literature,* 7-8. Vahalla,NY: Mental Retardation Institute.

Hickey, C.A. & Solis, D. (1990). *The recruitment and retention of minority trainees in University Affiliated Programs - Hispanics.* Madison,WI: University of Wisconsin, Waisman Center University Affiliated Program.

Indian Health Service. (1989). *Trends in Indian health.* Washington,DC: United States Department of Health and Human Services, Division of Program Statistics, Indian Health Services.

Jaynes, G.D. & Williams, R.M., Jr. (1989). *A common destiny: Blacks and American society.* Washington,DC: Committee on the Status of Black Americans, Commission on Behavioral and Social Sciences and Education, National Research Council.

Kuehn, M.L. & Imm-Thomas, P. (1993). A multicultural context. In E. Sutton, A.R. Factor, B.A. Hawkins, T. Heller & G.B. Seltzer (Eds.), *Older adults with developmental disabilities: Optimizing choice and change,* 327-343. Baltimore: Paul H. Brookes Publishing Co.

Krauss, A. & Stoddard, L. (1989). *Chartbook on disability.* Washington,DC: National Institute on Disability Rehabilitation Research.

McClain, J.W. (1990). *The recruitment and retention of minority trainees in University Affiliated Programs - African Americans.* Madison,WI: University of Wisconsin, Waisman Center University Affiliated Program.

Morioka-Douglas, N. & Yeo, G. (1990). *Aging and health: Asian/Pacific Island American elders.* Stanford,CA: Stanford Geriatric Education Center.

National Indian Council on Aging. (1981). *American Indian elderly: A national profile.* Alburquerque,NM: Author.

Pederson, E.L., Chaikin, M. Koehler, D., Campbell, A. & Arcand, M. (1993). Strategies that close the gap between research, planning, and self-advocacy. In E. Sutton, A.R. Factor, B.A. Hawkins, T. Heller & G.B. Seltzer (Eds.), *Older adults with developmen-*

*tal disabilities: Optimizing choice and change,* 277-325. Baltimore: Paul H. Brookes Publishing Co.

Topol, P. & Reznikoff, M. (1982). Perceived peer and family relationships, hopelessness and locus of control as factors in adolescent suicide attempts. *Suicide & Life Threatening Behavior,* 12, 141-150.

United States Department of Health and Human Services. (1991). *Health status of minorities and low-income groups (3rd ed.).* Health Resources and Services Administration, Public Health Service, Bureau of Health Professions, Division of Disadvantaged Assistance. DHHS Publication No. 017-000-00257-1. Washington, DC: United States Government Printing Office.

United States Department of Health and Human Services. (1990). *Minority aging: Essential curricula content for selected health and allied health professions.* Health Resources and Services Administration, Public Health Service. DHHS Publication No. HRS (P-DV-90-4) Washington, DC: United States Government Printing Office.

Vega, W.A. (1992). Theoretical and pragmatic implications of cultural diversity for community research. *American Journal of Community Psychology,* Vol. 20, No. 3, 375-391.

Wilson, M.D. (1986). Sociocultural aspects of disability in rehabilitation. In S. Walker, F.Z. Belgrave, A.M. Banner & R.W. Nicholls (Eds.), *Equal to the challenge: Perspectives, problems, and strategies in the rehabilitation of the nonwhite disabled.* Washington, DC: Howard University, Bureau of Educational Research, School of Education.

# •Part II•
# Quality of Life Issues: Context, Conditions, Questions, Ages

# 13 • Towards an Understanding of Holistic Quality of Life in People with Profound Intellectual and Multiple Disabilities

David Goode, College of Staten Island/CUNY, and James Hogg, White Top Research Unit & Centre, University of Dundee, Scotland

Increased interest in the relevance of the concept of quality of life (QOL) to the lives of people with developmental disabilities has led to a growing awareness of the tensions that exist between the subjective experience of QOL, i.e. the personal expression of an individual's judgment of that experience, and the administrative or "objective" assessment of QOL. A further dimension is introduced by the extreme difficulty of assessing subjective experience in people with significant communication difficulties. At the outset of this paper we briefly state a general position with respect to subjective and objective assessment of QOL before addressing the specific implications for persons with profound and multiple disabilities.

## Developing concepts of quality of life

### Subjective QOL

Schalock (nd) has identified three basic concepts that appear in definitions of QOL in relation to people with developmental disabilities. They are: general feelings of well being, opportunities to fulfil one's

potential and feelings of positive social involvement. All, it should be noted, are clearly definitions of QOL from the individual's perspective. Such a view is consistent with a variety of recently proposed definitions, e.g.:

> "The timbre of life as experienced subjectively; one's feelings about/evaluations of one's own life...." (NIDRR, n.d., p.4)

> "QOL is experienced when a person's basic needs are met and when he or she has the opportunity to pursue and achieve goals in major life settings." (Goode, 1988a)

> "QOL is defined as the degree to which one enjoys the possibilities of his/her life." (Centre for Health Promotion, 1991, p.9).

In the context of such a perspective, use of the term "QOL policy" refers to the use of subjective assessment of QOL (emphasis on promoting general feelings of well-being, opportunities to fulfil potentials and feelings of positive social involvement) as a guide, common denominator or core principle with respect to decision-making in services and/or supports for persons with developmental disabilities.

Because of this subjectivity, Stensman (1985) acknowledged the "delicacy" of the QOL concept for scientific analysis, but nonetheless concluded that it could only be evaluated from the individual's perspective. Stensman, reflecting problems that have been observed in other areas of research with persons with developmental disabilities, also noted the following concerns regarding the subjective assessment of QOL: differing expectation levels (people with limited experience and low expectations can produce spuriously high QOL ratings); temporary mood influences; interviewer effect (for example, the propensity to acquiescence and agreement noted in studies of interviews with this population); and, conscious manipulation of answers for various purposes.

### Objective QOL

While no one argues that the individual experience of QOL is not subjective as described above, several initiatives stress that QOL has subjective, objective and "relational" components that also need to be assessed holistically with multiple methodologies (Centre for Health Promotion, 1991; Cummins, n.d.; Dossa, 1989; Goode, 1988a; Schalock, n.d., 1992). This perspective is primarily grounded in the research literature and is, in terms of that literature, an empirically valid and methodologically sound approach to assessment of QOL. This view of QOL would seem to contradict that expressed by the "subjectivists". Indeed, the relation between these two ap-

proaches poses one of the basic policy issues in the planning and evaluation of services using the QOL concept.

An administrative expression of this view of QOL assessment is expressed by the Centre for Health Promotion (1991; p.18) that assigns ultimate determination of QOL to a committee structure that will employ a variety of information to make the ultimate determination. This arrangement is somewhat similar to that employed in a typical interdisciplinary team.

### Holistic assessment of QOL

Both of these approaches to QOL, the subjective and objective,[1] have a place in the field of developmental disabilities, though extreme care must be exercised in determining exactly what place each will occupy. Being clear about the role of subjective and objective QOL assessment may not be such an easy matter. For example, in Schalock's recent excellent description of the use of QOL in program evaluation, he makes a clear commitment to a quality assurance and program evaluation approach "based on a number of person-referenced critical quality indicators (CQI) that reflect a person's perceived quality of life" (n.d., p.7). Yet the basic methodology proposed to assess QOL is holistic, employing methods that are objective and reputational (surrogate respondents are used [see below]) that, given research findings, may produce results "highly uncorrelated" with subjective data.

### Policy Perspectives on QOL

While a holistic approach to the assessment of QOL may be judged a legitimate and perhaps long term goal, in its use with regard to people with developmental disabilities they themselves should be formally acknowledged as the primary assessing agents. Service, regulatory and funding agencies should play the role of supporting their aspirations and help them to ask the QOL questions they want. Such a view is consistent with the development of social policy in both the US and Great Britain. In both countries there is a commitment to putting people who are the focus of community care provision in charge of their own lives to the maximum degree possible, including governing their own services and supports. This perspective was adopted in Goode's (1988b, see chapter 9) national project on QOL that involved many people with developmental disabilities, parents and advocates. Several of the recommendations concerned the power of service users to control their own lives, and the importance of involving people with disabilities in the formulation of policy and practice relevant to them.

Thus, QOL policy commits us to the participation of the user-citizen in governance of services because the social forces of history require a redress in the balance of power for persons with developmental disabilities, and for other citizens in receipt of community care services. QOL policy represents one way that this balance can be changed. How this is to be achieved is one of the critical QOL policy issues confronting us today. To find some sort of balanced solution will require that two very important questions be answered in service programs. They are as Kahn (1979) described:

What is the boundary among administrator, professional and consumer prerogative in agency governance and administration?

How should those who are legally responsible resolve competing claims of citizens to represent communities served by agencies? (pp. 186-187).

What balance between bureaucracy and individual control seems to be the key question for persons with developmental disabilities and the agencies serving them. The strategy may be to incorporate the participation of people with developmental disabilities, their views and value choices, individually and collectively, in ways that do not discourage and inhibit development of knowledge and technique, that can help in habilitation and rehabilitation (see Kahn, 1979: pp. 187-188), and that do not prevent administrators from overseeing efficiency and efficacy of services.

## Profound Disability & the Assessment of QOL

People with profound intellectual disability, and particularly those with additional physical and sensory impairments, constitute a major challenge when viewed in the context of the above policy and QOL framework. We are confronted not only with the significant practical and conceptual problems of determining subjective responses to the elements that constitute this aspect of QOL (i.e. general feelings of wellbeing, opportunities to fulfil one's potential, and feelings of positive social involvement), but also of evaluating the quality of a range of objectively definable service elements related to quality of health care, educational effectiveness, and socially defined objectives. These concerns are unified in the common conceptual challenge of how "subjective" and "objective" perspectives are to be integrated in a genuinely holistic fashion.

### Subjective QOL and profound disability

If QOL is to be assessed subjectively at the individual level, and if persons with disability are to participate in the assessment process and implementation of agency policy, then it is no accident that QOL projects all over the world are wrestling with how to achieve these ends with persons who have profound communication and/or cognitive disabilities. The problem is mostly a technical one with persons who are cognitively intact but have problems expressing their understanding (e.g. persons who are paralyzed or who otherwise cannot speak but who do not have intellectual disability). What is usually required in such cases is some form of technology. When dealing with persons who have profound intellectual disability, however, the problems of achieving a subjective understanding of QOL and of involving the individual in the conduct of QOL assessment becomes more complex, especially if the individual in question does not participate in formal language systems.

### Observation and subjective QOL

The range of communicative abilities in people with profound intellectual disability and with additional physical and/or sensory impairments has to be acknowledged as wide. At one extreme we will find the adult characterized as having profound intellectual disability who "has (a) speaking vocabulary of over 300 to 400 words and uses grammatically correct sentences. If nonverbal, may use many gestures for communication. Understands simple verbal communication. Understands simple verbal communications, including directives and questions....Relates experiences in sim-

ple language" (Grossman 1983,p.205). In contrast, such individuals may lack any formal symbolic vocal or gestural language. Communication may be pre-symbolic or action-based (see Goode, 1994), idiosyncratic, and from the perspective of carers entirely absent (see Hogg & Lambe 1988). Paralleling this extreme range in communicative ability is the diversity of such persons' cognitive development (see Hogg & Sebba 1986). This state of affairs will clearly influence the nature and complexity of understanding that, regardless of communicative development, will affect the person's experience of what determines her or his quality of life.

It is perhaps to state the obvious that the approach to subjective quality of life adopted within this communicative-cognitive state will depend upon the individual's experience and competencies.[2] Experience is important because implicit in the concept of subjective quality of life is not only the contemporary experience of personal status but its implications for future selection from options, i.e., choice. Choice has become a central tenet of policy in both the US and Great Britain and is as relevant for the person with profound disabilities as is the case for any user of a human service.

Choice and experience are, however, inextricably bound up. Bannerman, Sheldon, Sherman & Harchik (1990) have emphasized that the ability to make choices is dependent upon experience of choice and that learning choice-making should be part of the wider curriculum. This is important because such a view treats choice not as an absolute but as an inherent part of the person's history. It implies a time course in coming to the state of being able to make informed choices that are responsible and within the person's competencies. If we assume the possibility of choice-making when the person has limited experiences or has even been subjected to highly insulting and hurtful life events, with the attendant difficulty of understanding and codifying experiences of life, then any assessment of QOL is further complicated (see Coulter, 1990). Acknowledgement of this state of affairs minimizes the danger to the person with profound disabilities that <u>any</u> behavior they display is taken at face value as being a choice. The dubious claim that someone should be allowed to continue in self-injurious behavior, "because they are choosing to do so" is thereby invalidated. (While this may be a choice existentially speaking, it is so constrained by lack of experience and/or pathological experience that it may be more of a compulsion than real selection among options). Clearly there are dangers here. We are as yet poor judges of what might constitute informed or uninformed choice, or even choice behavior from communicative expressions *not* explicitly indicative of choice.

Nevertheless, choice is not expressed in a vacuum. It will be related to available options (at least two) and will be expressed vocally, gesturally, motorically, or through some affective expression, conventional or idiosyncratic. It is the understanding of both the environment, that offers options, and its relation to the mode of expression, that is critical to an appreciation of subjective quality of life in people with profound intellectual disabilities.

Several projects directed to this issue are at present being undertaken, e.g. Chauvie, Iribagiza & Musitelli, (1992) in Switzerland, Hogg (1992a) in Great Britain. In the latter work, research is being undertaken which begins with carers and staff defining for the research team behaviors that, from their perspective, are indicative of the way in which a person with profound disability expresses preference and engages sensorily with the environment. The profile for an individual is then validated through direct observation by both researchers and service providers and will, in due course, be used to evaluate subjective response to various elements of service provision and community experience. Other approaches involving observation or videotaping are suggested in Goode, 1980; LEV. 1991; Taylor & Bogdan, 1990; Taylor, this volume.

### Surrogate approaches to subjective QOL

Related to these direct observational approaches has been the use of a surrogate or surrogates to complete standardized assessment instruments (Goode & Gaddy, 1976; Woodill et al.; Holm et al.; Schalock, this volume). Such approaches are practical and efficient, but present very basic methodological and epistemological problems. Simply put, people are so surprising and complex that as well as we might know one another, it is always possible to profoundly misread the other's thoughts and feelings. All of us have probably had this experience with close relatives and friends. And this situation is only compounded when one can not question the other, or obtain direct verbal indications of his or her feelings. Thus, while surrogate-based questionnaires for determining subjective QOL of people with severe intellectual disabilities may be the only practical option in many agencies, they pose the risk of creating a "tyranny of quality," as described by Goode in a presentation to the Danish QOL Project in 1991.

While discussing surrogate or committee determination of QOL for people with disabilities, Goode and the Danish authors in this volume discussed the possibility of QOL assessment becoming something that does *not* reflect the viewpoint or perspective of the individual being assessed. In the same way that normalization, albeit highly misinterpreted, became the basis for a kind of "tyranny of the normal," a standard to which people were held independent of whether they agreed with the elements of PASSING, so, too, could QOL end up being a criteria or standard to which people could be held responsible whether or not they agreed with that standard. This is true for any QOL assessment, but especially those that involve surrogate or objective indicators of QOL. The danger of the "tyranny of quality" exists whether or not the individual we are speaking about is profoundly retarded or not. It is especially dangerous when we are talking about persons with highly unusual countenance and experience, and with whom formal communication may be impossible. This is not to deny the importance or desirability of objective and reputational QOL data, but rather to point to an inherent problem in their use.

Related to surrogate QOL assessment is the concept of life sharing that has been advocated by Goode and others (for example, by John O'Neill and Connie Lyle of Responsive Systems Associates in Georgia) in approaching the QOL orientation with service agencies. A life sharing approach involves the intentional sharing of life histories (biographies and autobiographies) of persons involved in agency life (both "clients" and staff), e.g., the writing of a biography of a person with profound intel-

lectual disability by a staff member that would be published in the agency newsletter, or helping a citizen-user who has marginal language skills to write his or her autobiography. While life sharing does not precisely meet the definition of QOL oriented policy as presented at the start of this paper, it nonetheless creates an atmosphere in agencies that enhances information about and understanding of the lives of people with severe disabilities.

### Objective Quality of Life and profound disability.

There are a variety of reasons why, even within the adult population of people with profound disability, it would not be justifiable to develop a service exclusively within the context of only subjective QOL indices, even if they prove to be sensitive and discriminating with respect to both environmental variation and the subtlety of subjective response. Among those with profound and multiple disabilities, development is inherently slow and the presence of additional medical conditions prevalent. From the perspective of those providing services, and indeed from that of the wider society, a failure to intervene would, and should, be regarded as culpable. Educational and medical intervention is called for to enhance physical and social interactions to extend options for choice, but also to maintain and/or improve functioning and reduce physical distress.

In Great Britain considerable attention has been focused upon the way in which high quality educational services are to be developed for adults with profound disabilities, drawing in part on the sophisticated progress made in the school provision following the incorporation of children with profound and multiple disabilities within the educational system in 1971. "Continuing (post-school) education should aim to meet these needs by offering an individually tailored education program within a properly constructed curriculum framework which uses age-appropriate activities, language, materials and teaching strategies....Such a programme will stretch and challenge the learner within a supportive setting" (Further Education Unit 1991).

Clearly, however, engagement in such a curriculum, or parts of it, might be regarded by the adult with profound disabilities as *not* enhancing her or his subjective QOL. How long do we persist with such educational intervention? To what extent are the subjective indices noted above to be taken as rejection of what is on offer, even when progress is being made with respect to cognitive, communicative, social, and adaptive skills? If we are to admit the holistic view of QOL described above, then the decision for an individual rejecting exposure to adult education might be to continue with such intervention but in a way that continually explores options that may bring subjective and objective indicators into harmony. (Here we are dealing with a clinical question that may require excercise of clinical judgment). In the present absence of any carefully evaluated attempts to explore the interaction of subjective and objective indicators of QOL, it is premature to attempt an a priori, and possibly hypothetical, resolution of this conflict.

Are the same issues raised in relation to the assessment of health-related quality of life with respect to clinical decision making regarding people with profound disabilities? Professional staff will typically wish to ensure that practices are followed that main-

tain good health or deal with evidence of illness or conditions such as epilepsy. For most people with profound and multiple disabilities, informed consent for serious medical interventions, (e.g. surgical procedures) will not be possible. It would be ingenuous, however, to assume that all medical interventions are benign or incontrovertibly for the best. This point can be illustrated with respect to the prevalence of hysterectomies in women in this group (e.g. Kaunitz, Thompson & Kaunitz 1986), the removal of all teeth to prevent self mutilation (e.g., Watts, et al., 1974) or excessive polypharmacy (Hogg 1992b). While pointers to the subjective response to treatment would remain central to any holistic approach to medical treatment, the role of an independent and informed advocate operating within the existing legal framework will be central to much of the decision making in this area. While such a view is threatening to the medical profession, calling into question their clinical judgment, there is sufficient controversy regarding medical treatment of this group, and its adverse impact on QOL, to indicate the importance of an independent advocate.

In the foregoing we have concentrated on two critical areas of service provision in the lives of both children and adults with profound disabilities, i.e. education and health care. It is clear from Goode's (1988a; b) own study of QOL in people with developmental disabilities, however, that the domains that require consideration, from both subjective and objective perspectives, are far more extensive than these areas. He notes, inter alia, housing, with its close links to social life (including family relationships, neighborhood involvement and natural environment features), mobility, friendship, leisure, religion, work etc. In principle, the same general challenges and arguments relating to subjective and objective quality of life apply in these domains. The critical issues remain the manner in which we assess the former and then harmonize this information with the assessment of housing and social work department staff supported by whatever specialized assessments are deemed necessary to determine needs. It might be added that in the context of community care policy in Great Britain, this process of joint assessment now underpins the development of the care management process through which a total program package is implemented (Department of Health Social Service Inspectorate & Scottish Office Social Work Services Group 1991).

### Assessing and Measuring QOL in Persons with Profound Disabilities

There is, and has been for several years now, considerable interest in (as well as pressure upon) the research community in the field of disability to develop measures of QOL to help evaluate and plan services. While the reasons for this are complex, the result has been the production of a wide range of instruments and approaches. Again, without questioning the utility of developing such measures, the speed with which some have been produced is a matter for concern. It is clear that detailed work is needed at several levels, initially on discrete areas of both subjective and objective QOL, and through careful empirical work, on the integration of different measures within a holistic framework. Such an agenda might well best be pursued in the context of unitary integrated services, and is indeed part of the primary focus of the recently

established White Top Centre (for adults with profound and multiple handicapping conditions established in Dundee, Scotland, and directed by the second author). We have already noted ongoing experimental work on assessing subjective QOL. In due course, parallel studies of quality of educational intervention will be pursued, while preliminary work is being undertaken within the framework of health-related QOL described in the wider literature by Patrick and Erickson (1993). The information produced from these studies will become critical components in future attempts at assessing QOL for this population.

## Conclusion

There are many reasons why a holistic approach to the assessment of QOL of people with profound intellectual disabilities may be an important development in their future welfare. We believe that such an assessment will be developed, but that because of the complexity of the issues involved this may take a long time to do correctly. We argued in the beginning of the chapter that this development will take place within the context of social policy in human services more generally: Just as those questions have not been easily or simply answered, we suspect that many of the issues we have raised will also not be quickly resolved.

We also suggested that subjective QOL data (the opinions and perspectives of the person in question) or reputational QOL data (the opinions of others, or surrogates, about the viewpoint of the person in question) *and* objective QOL data (clinical and behavioral data about the persons and environments in question) have their place in assessing their QOL. Admittedly, harmonizing this data may not be easy to do, but we think that the knowledge gained from the experimental and exploratory research in Scotland, Switzerland and other countries represented in this book is important for the development of QOL assessment for this population. We need to develop more systematic ways of recognizing the prelinguistic ways persons without formal language communicate their preferences, ideas, reactions and feelings. The knowledge gained in such studies will be tremendously useful in QOL assessment.

But we also suspect that QOL assessment of people with profound intellectual disability will never be entirely data-based and probably never qualify as a hard science. More likely the scientific knowledge we will gain in the study of QOL for these individuals will always be employed in ways similar to the way knowledge is employed in an art or a craft. Due to the complexity of QOL, and especially due to the differences in countenance and experience between the assessors and those being assessed, determining the QOL for people with profound cognitive disability will probably always rely on very fine judgments and forms of empathy, which are not easily operationalized and put to paper. But also like artists and craftspeople, those in charge of the QOL assessment will probably develop a facility in doing it over time.

This is not to argue that a serious attempt should not be made to try to scientifically understand QOL for this population. There are many dangers involved (see especially Wolfensberger this volume), and there are also many potential benefits, especially if the process can safeguard against the "tyranny of quality." We believe this can be achieved only if subjective data (or reputational approximations of them) are seriously incorporated into the process, and if harmonizing of these different forms of QOL data respects first and foremost the viewpoint of the individual in question. Without glorifying subjectivity, ignoring the problems and limitations inherent in subjective QOL data as discussed above, or suggesting that clinical and other objective data are not relevant to the assessment process, this respect for the individual's viewpoint is the necessary condition for QOL assessment of any person, dictated by the essential subjectivity of QOL as described in the research literature. It is also the only way to guard against the potential for QOL to be misused in the tyrannical way normalization was.

## Notes

[1] Goode has also argued for the existence of "relational" QOL factors. By these are intended QOL components that are not reducible to either subjective or objective factors, particularly social arrangements and relationships. Such social ecological dimensions to QOL have been acknowledged by many in the literature, but relatively little has been done to operationalize and measure these. It is for this reason only that they are not included in this discussion.

[2] We also wish to acknowledge, and will do so in several places in the text, that QOL assessment also depends on the experiences and perceptions of the person(s) designing and performing the

assessment. One of the major problems with this population is that the assessors (scientists and human service professionals) and those being assessed (people with profound intellectual and related disabilities) may not share experiences and even a body that are similar enough to assume a "reciprocity of perspectives." Thus we do not wish to give the impression in this discussion that the only relevant factors in understanding how a person with such profound intellectual disability perceives his or her own QOL are his or her experiences and countenance. What "we" find out in our inquiries is also clearly a reflection of our own experiences and ways of being in the world. This is not to say that scientists/professionals and people with profound intellectual handicaps do not share a great deal, because they do. But, there are also very real, sometimes even insurmountable, differences- for example, being a symbolic language user versus not.

# References

Bannerman, D., Sheldon, J.B., Sherman, J.A. & Harchik, A.E. (1990). Balancing the right to habilitation with the right to personal liberties: The rights of people with developmental disabilities to eat too many doughnuts and take a nap. *Journal of Applied Behavior Analysis, 23,*79-89.

Centre for Health Promotion (1991). Quality of Life project: Phase 1 (October 4.). Unpublished paper University of Toronto. Toronto: Canada.

Chauvie, J-M., Iribagiza, R. & Musitelli, T. (1992). Contribution du groupe Romand sur le polyhandicap profond. Seminaire d'Octobre 1992 du Reseau Europeen d'Echanges sur le Polyhandicap, Consacre au Theme de La Communication.

Coulter, D. (1990). Home is the Place: Quality of Life for Young Children with Developmental Disabilities. In R. Schalock (ed.), *Quality of life: Issues and perspectives.* Washington, DC: American Association on Mental Retardation.

Cummins, R.A. (no date). The comprehensive QOL scale-intellectual disability: An instrument under development. Unpublished paper, Victoria College, Malvern, Victoria, Australia.

Department of Health Social Service Inspectorate & Scottish Office Social Work Services Group (1991). *Care Management and Assessment: Managers' guide,* HMSO, London.

Dossa, P.A. (1989). Quality of life: Individualism or Holism? A critical review of the literature. *International Journal of Rehabilitation Research, 12 (2), 121-136.*

Further Education Unit (1991). *Adult Status for All? Continuing education for people with profound and multiple disabilities. A discussion paper.* Further Education Unit, London.

Goode, D.A. (1994). *A world without words: The social construction of children born deaf-blind.* Philadelphia: Temple University Press.

Goode, D.A. (1980). The world of deaf-blind, in J. Jacobs (Ed.) *Phenomenological approaches to mental retardation.* New York: Charles C. Thomas.

Goode, D.A. (1988a). *Quality of life for persons with disabilities: A review and synthesis of the literature.* Valhalla, New York: The Mental Retardation Institute/UAP.

Goode, D.A. (1988b). *The principles and recommendation of the quality of life project.* Valhalla, New York: The Mental Retardation Institute/UAP.

Goode, D.A. & Gaddy, M.P. (1976). Ascertaining client choice with alingual, deaf and retarded children. *Mental Retardation,* December: 10-12.

Grossman, H.J. (1983). *Classification in Mental Retardation,* American Association on Mental Retardation, Washington, DC.

Hogg, J. (1992a). Behavioural state and affective communication in people with profound intellectual and multiple disabilities as indicators of their response to service provision: Grant application submitted to the Scottish Office Home and Health Department, White Top Research Unit, The University, Dundee.

Hogg, J. (1992b). The administration of psychotropic and anticonvulsant drugs to children and adults with profound intellectual disability and multiple impairments. *Journal of Intellectual Disability Research*, 36, 472-488.

Hogg, J. & Lambe, L.J. (1988). *Sons and Daughters with Profound Retardation and Multiple Handicaps Attending Schools and Schools and Social Education Centres: Final report.* Royal Society of Mentally Handicapped Children and Adults, London.

Hogg, J. & Sebba, J. (1986). *Profound Retardation and Multiple Impairment: Volume 1: Development and Training.* Croom Helm, London.

Kahn, A. (1979). *Social Policy and Social Services.* New York: Random House.

Kaunitz, A.M. Thompson, R.J. and Kaunitz, K.K. (1986). Mental retardation: A controversial indication for hysterectomy. *Obstet. Gynecol.*, 68, 436.

Landsforeningen Evnesvages Vel (LEV) (1990). Quality of life for mentally retarded: Quality of life for all. Unpublished paper, Copenhagen: LEV.

National Institute of Disability and Rehabilitation Research (n.d.). Quality-of-life research in rehabilitation. *Rehab Brief* XI (No.1).

Patrick, D.L. & Erickson, P. (1993). Assessing health-related quality of life for clinical decision-making, in R.M. Rosser & S.W. Walker (eds.) *Quality of Life: Key issues in the 1990s,* Kluver Academic, London, pp. 11-63.

Schalock, R.L. (n.d.). The quality revolution and its impact on quality assurance and program evaluation. Unpublished paper.

Stensman, R. (1985). Severely mobility-disabled people assess the quality of their lives. *Scandinavian Journal of Rehabilitation Medicine*, 17, (2).

Taylor, S.J. & Bogdan, R. (1990). Quality of life and the individual's perspective. In R. Schalock (ed.) *Quality of Life: Perspectives and Issues.* American Association on Mental Retardation Monograph Series. Washington, DC.

Watts, R.W.E., McKeran, R.O., Brown, E., Andrews, T.M., Griffiths, M. (1974). Clinical and biomedical studies on treatment of Lesch-Nyhan syndrome, *Archives of Disease in Childhood*, 49, 693.

# 14 •Quality of Life for persons with challenging behaviors: Intervention goal, contradiction in terms, or both?

Daniel B. Crimmins,
Westchester Institute for Human Development
and New York Medical College

As a colleague of David Goode during the period encompassing both planning and carrying out the National Quality of Life Project (discussed in Chapter 9 of this volume), I feel like I participated in a three-year seminar on the topic. The only gap in my memory is when I try to recall exactly how it was that I signed up for it. I was fortunate to have participated in both a weekend retreat and a national conference that brought together individuals with disabilities, families, advocates and professionals — roles that were not mutually exclusive — to discuss quality of life. Over this period, I had many extended conversations with David about quality of life, its measurement and definition, the role of subjectivity, and the need for articulating a framework for further discussion. These talks returned again and again to the potential usefulness of using quality of life as an organizing construct for evaluating service outcomes for persons with developmental disabilities, which was personally compelling in that it provided a means of unifying my broader training in psychology with my focussed activities in the field of disability.

My professional work centers on ensuring that positive strategies are utilized in service delivery for persons who exhibit challenging behaviors, a role carried out through training and consultation to families and program staff. The outcome of these activities is the development of an individualized behavioral support plan, which examines why behaviors persist, specifies necessary changes in the environment, and describes methods of teaching alternatives to "problem" behaviors. In developing these plans, I almost inevitably find that the individual with challenging behaviors is presented with a very restricted range of meaningful choices, has little formal control over the environments in which he or she spends time, and lives in highly restrictive settings — a situation in which anyone might be expected to exhibit challenging behaviors. Ironically, these conditions are presented as being a response to the individual's behaviors and designed to meet his or her needs; this is, however, not necessarily so. Over the past several years, my colleagues and I have assisted in the development of behavioral support plans based on choice, increased consumer control, access to the community, and learning critical skills, which have had a positive impact on literally hundreds of people.

In this reaction paper, I would like to provide a profile of one man named "Ivan" — a person with mental retardation who also had challenging behaviors. The process of planning and providing support to Ivan illustrates critical issues in the service delivery process in accomplishing the outcome of enhanced quality of life.

## Ivan

Ivan is a man in his thirties who has spent most of his life in large institutional settings in the state of New York. A number of years ago, as part of the de-institutionalization movement, Ivan moved to a community-based residential program serving fifteen people. During the day he attends a day treatment program serving more than 100 people and receives services in an instructional group of ten people. In the service climate of the mid-1980's, this was viewed as highly appropriate for Ivan. He did not have many options for living in a smaller residence or receiving work-related supports because of his extensive needs for support and his long history of challenging behaviors.

Ivan's behavioral concerns continued even after he moved into his new residential program; foremost among them was his severe aggression and property destruction. These occurred most often when he was denied requested items, usually coffee, leading to several incidents each day. This pattern had persisted for several years despite a number of efforts at amelioration. His residential and day program staff joined together in a team effort at comprehensive behavioral support planning during a re-

cently completed training project (Crimmins, 1993).

In planning for Ivan, the team faced constraints that derived from staff training and attitudes, history, and program models. These constraints had shaped the services that Ivan was receiving; unfortunately, no one was happy. Staff members had lost time due to work-related injuries resulting from his aggression, and many expressed fear of him. Because Ivan was considered dangerous to himself and others, he received high levels of staff supervision, which he did not particularly enjoy. Ivan did not use a formal communication system, although he could make some needs known. Even this was problematic, in that he often wanted items (e.g., coffee, food) or activities (e.g., going for a walk) that were not readily available or were felt to be inappropriate for the time he requested them. This set up the conflict of whether to give him what he wanted despite the inconvenience or refuse him at the risk of his aggression occurring. The former course of action was viewed by many of the staff as favoritism and essentially giving in to a form of extortion. In addition, Ivan did not appear to be interested in participating in many of the activities of either the residential or day program.

The training project activities followed a number of steps in developing and carrying out an individualized behavioral support plan. First, the team conducted a functional analysis, which assisted in determining the maintaining variables related to the behaviors of concern. The second step was to assess Ivan's preferences. Third, the team developed an initial behavioral support plan that emphasized his participation in meaningful activities. The final aspect was to set up an instructional plan for the acquisition of alternative, adaptive behaviors. These steps were intended to maximize the likelihood of increased independence, productivity, and integration into the community, as well as improved quality of life for Ivan.

Ivan's service plan at the start of the training project "allowed" him to earn up to four cups per day of decaffeinated coffee as a reward for intervals of appropriate behavior. It became clear that this posed a difficulty for Ivan. Not only did he "prefer" more ready access to coffee, but also the frequent denial of his requests set the stage for conflict. The team discussions on this point were led by a team member who was a self-described "coffee addict" and who staunchly advocated for increased availability of coffee. He made it clear that any one who stood between him and his coffee was at risk of experiencing his "challenging behaviors." While this perspective was shared, for the most part, in fun and with little argument from the rest of the team, it became symbolic of how Ivan had less control over his life than the team members would want for themselves. It also compelled the team to ensure that, as part of the behavioral support plan, decaffeinated coffee would be made available throughout the day upon Ivan's request.

Ivan's behavioral support plan was developed over the course of two months and carried out with periodic modifications for a year. Initial efforts centered on functional analysis and testing the effects of different environmental changes (e.g., increased access to coffee), which then lead to changes in his daily routine to center around the activity of coffee drinking. For example, a formal means of requesting coffee was developed through the use of a tangible cue

system. Later in the year, Ivan was responsible for making his own instant coffee at his residence and assisting in brewing coffee at the day program. By the end of the year, Ivan also assisted staff members in making fresh coffee during the day for others' consumption. The rationale for these changes was to increase the number of social interactions related to activities that appeared to be meaningful to Ivan. In this way, Ivan's behavioral support plan lead to developing competencies in communication, self-help and working with others. Other changes for Ivan were an increase in the number of opportunities he had during the day to choose activities; for example, going for walks was made available as a choice several times a day. The staff also continued to survey new activities that Ivan might enjoy.

There were a number of positive outcomes attributed to the behavioral support plan. Incidents of aggression and property destruction decreased from an average of more than five times a day to less than one every other day. When incidents did occur, they were viewed as less intense or of shorter duration. Ivan was reported to get along better with both staff and the people with whom he lives, and a broader range of staff members felt comfortable spending time with him. He began to request coffee and walks using a communication system. While Ivan's coffee consumption did increase to about six cups per day, this was not viewed as problematic. As Ivan became responsible for the routines of making coffee, he came to tolerate the necessary delay in getting his coffee. A final outcome was that there were increased efforts at involving him in community activities because of the reduced threat of behavioral outbursts.

The team working with Ivan, which included direct care providers, clinical staff and administrators, has to be commended. The administrative staff provided time for team discussions and staff training; the clinical staff involved were philosophically committed to implementing positive strategies for change; and the direct care providers played a central role in working with other staff members to implement preference-based activities at his day and residential programs. While the team members were clearly open to change, it became evident that plans developed during training sessions were not necessarily embraced by their co-workers. Initially, there was considerable resistance on the part of the staff to "just giving him anything he wants when he wants it" despite the history of severe aggression. There was a great deal of effort, for example, in working with the overnight staff to ensure access to coffee late at night; they felt strongly that Ivan was "supposed to be" sleeping, regardless of whether or not he wished to be. The full participation of the direct care providers in the planning process appeared to be instrumental in accomplishing changes in the day-to-day routines. They served as a model for other staff and provided a rationale for the plan that was accepted by others.

### What can we learn from Ivan?

*Challenging behaviors often serve a function for the individual.* That is, they in some way gain a desired outcome for that person (Carr, 1977), such as social attention, escape from unpleasant circumstances, tangible items, and sensory consequences (Durand & Crimmins, 1988, 1992). Determining the function of a challenging behavior assists in identifying an alternative, more appropriate, behavior that achieves the same outcome for the individual (Carr, Robinson, & Palumbo, 1990; Durand & Crimmins, 1991). This approach logically links the results of the functional analysis with critical components of the support plan (Carr, 1988; Dunlap, Johnson, & Robbins, 1990; Horner & Billingsley, 1988).

Ivan's aggression was functional in that it served to obtain coffee, a walk, and other events, which were not readily available under other circumstances. Ivan had in essence learned to "bully" others into giving him what he wanted; the staff who worked with Ivan had learned that denying him what he wanted came at a significant cost. In a learning paradigm, Ivan's aggression was positively reinforced by the tangible items he received; the staff members' behavior (e.g., sometimes giving him these items) was negatively reinforced by the reduced likelihood of aggression. This reciprocal process had continued for several years until a different way of interacting with Ivan was developed.

*While institutions may not be inherently evil, they are inherently unresponsive to individual needs.* The limitations inherent in large institutional settings are certainly familiar to anyone likely to pick up this book. Organizational barriers make it virtually impossible for truly individualized services to be provided on a large scale, creating a competition for social interaction and overwhelming difficulty in providing meaningful activities. Special requests, even for items as mundane as coffee or a preferred food, are often routinely and categorically denied because of concern about the impossibility of "doing this for everybody." Refusal occurs regardless of whether the requests are justified by quality of life (e.g., they would make this person happy) or clinical concerns (e.g., they are part of an overall behavioral support plan), which raises two concerns. First, despite the movement toward institutional closure and innovations in individualized residential options, many people will continue to live in relatively large congregate care settings. By virtue of the size of these settings, a group rather than an individualized perspective will likely prevail with many of the features associated with larger settings. Second, there are many people who spent extended periods of time in large scale settings; if their behaviors are viewed as somehow functional within these settings, this will influence how we address planning for behaviors in the future.

*People with challenging behaviors often have little choice over where and with whom they live.* Service programs, in general, are reluctant to accept planning responsibility for a person with challenging behaviors. This seems to be due to concerns about both the anticipated high costs of supervision/management *and* the perception that it requires highly-specific expertise. Programs that do accept planning responsibility often operate with a philosophical orientation that I term a "Marine mentality." This suggests that, with the right drive and confidence, a clear mission, and enough muscle, an individual can be "brought around" to live in a particular home. Unfortunately, this seems to be accomplished (at the risk of using a second military metaphor) by establishing a perpetual "boot camp," which operates with the goals of immediate compliance to requests without regard to their relevance and an acceptance of an externally-generated schedule of activities. This approach is obviously at odds

with accomplishing quality of life outcomes.

Fortunately, there is increasing utilization of person-centered planning approaches (Mount, 1989) that has resulted in identifying the supports needed for independent living, even for individuals with challenging behaviors (e.g., Allen, Banks, & Staite, 1991). This, in turn, has demonstrated that *individualized* supports are critical and can be provided in a range of settings (e.g., Berkman & Meyer, 1988). Ivan, for example, lives in a relatively large-scale congregate care setting; it is important that we remind ourselves periodically that this is where he happens to live, rather than where he must live. Despite the organizational commitment to Ivan, the setting where he lived clearly contributed to some of the difficulties he experienced.

*People with challenging behaviors are often asked to do things that are uninteresting, are not encouraged to choose, nor are they allowed to say "no."* These are common observations, particularly for persons with more severe disabilities, seeming to result both from ignorance of what is possible and from prevailing models of intervention that place value on external control. The increasing awareness of functional analysis to examine individuals' behaviors in the context of their lives and the subsequent use of individualized planning has ameliorated this somewhat, but these approaches are considered "state-of-the-art" rather than routinely available. Fortunately, a literature is emerging that describes the outcomes associated with providing more interesting activities over which the individual has control. Changes such as these have resulted in increased engagement (Wacker, Wiggins, Fowler, & Berg, 1988), reductions in challenging behaviors (Dyer, Dunlap, & Winterling, 1990), and improved task involvement (Dunlap, Kern-Dunlap, Clarke, & Robbins, 1991). One obstacle to effective choice making has been that many people, especially those with severe disabilities, have limited experiences or opportunities to assert themselves (Shevin & Klein, 1984; Williams, 1991). As this has come to be recognized in the field, strategies for teaching choice-making in a variety of situations have begun to be described (e.g., Gothelf, Crimmins, Mercer, & Finocchiaro, in press; Kennedy & Haring, 1993; Wacker et al., 1988). A final concern is that refusal to participate in an activity reflects a deficiency on the part of the individual rather than the activity itself. There have been significant efforts over the past decade in examining "escape from demands" as a motivation for challenging behaviors (Carr, 1977; Durand & Crimmins, 1992). These efforts have revealed that challenging behaviors may serve as an efficient means of saying "no." An approach to intervention called functional communication training (Durand, 1990) has proven highly effective for a range of individuals with escape-motivated behaviors in providing them with a means of refusal, requesting a break, or seeking assistance, which, in turn, has produced dramatic reductions in the occurrence of challenging behaviors.

In developing a plan for Ivan, a major obstacle was the concern, "What if he just wants to sit and drink coffee all day?" While this concern is a common one, it has not been validated in actual practice. Rather, as in the example of Ivan, requests for items may become self-limiting as the individual both learns that the item *is* available on request and becomes sated as it is requested. When this is paired with the development of more elaborate routines, such as making one's own coffee, there are a number of potential collateral benefits. Ivan was viewed as more social and tolerant of delay as he became engaged in a personally meaningful activity of his own choice that came to occupy a greater portion of his day.

*Individualized behavioral support planning is critical for persons with challenging behaviors.* This generally consists of several activities — functional analysis; assessment of preferences, strengths and abilities; adaptations in environments and instructional methods; and teaching alternative behaviors (Meyer & Evans, 1989). The importance of functional analysis, which assists in determining the maintaining variables related to the behaviors of concern, has lead to the development of standardized approaches to assist in carrying out this activity (Durand & Crimmins, 1990; Meyer & Evans, 1989; O'Neill, Horner, Albin, Storey, & Sprague, 1990). One component of these approaches is the consideration that medical and/or physiological factors may contribute to challenging behaviors. Assessing this component early in planning allows staff to treat it or rule it out, and then focus on other components.

Assessing the preferences, strengths and abilities of the individual is a critical step in formulating any individualized plan of supports (Turnbull & Turnbull, 1990). When challenging behaviors are a consideration, ethics demand the maximum participation of the individual in planning interventions, with the ideal being the full and informed consent of the person who is the focus of the intervention. Many individuals who engage in challenging behaviors, however, are unable to give informed consent and their parents or surrogates may feel pressured by circumstances and obligated to grant consent. This issue is most critical when an intervention plan calls for restrictions to which the individual or the family might not readily agree. Historically when families of persons with challenging behaviors were asked to consent to a plan using aversive procedures, they were confronted with a description of a range of less restrictive measures that had been used without success with their son or daughter. Even when the family was reluctant to agree, there was an implicit message that the program would not be able to serve the individual unless consent was given. On a number of levels (e.g., legal, ethical, good professional practice), it has become clear that efforts should be made to avoid any appearance of coercion in this decision process by presenting individuals and their families with real choices. Developing support plans based on providing increased access to preferred activities, which also reflect the capabilities of the individual, assists in accomplishing the goal of intervention without any appearance of coercion. A number of methods of gathering this type of information have been developed in the last several years (e.g., Turnbull, Turnbull, Bronicki, Summers, & Roeder-Gordon, 1989).

Based on the results of the functional analysis and preference assessments, the behavioral support plan identifies changes in instructional methods and environmental conditions that might minimize the occurrence of the behavior. This is done for two reasons — short-term strategies which help to decrease the frequency of the behavior thereby allowing the individual to be instructed in alternative behaviors, and long-term changes provide a better match between the strengths of the individual and the demands of a given environment.

The final component of behavioral support planning is instruction in alternative, adaptive behaviors to serve as replacements for the behaviors of concern. There are a number of alternative, adaptive behaviors that have proven instrumental in replacing challenging behaviors, including, as examples, communication (Durand, 1990), social skills (Haring, Roger, Lee, Breen, & Gaylord-Ross, 1986), conversation skills (Bradlyn, Hamadi, Crimmins, Christoff, Graves, & Kelly, 1983), play skills (Santarcangelo, Dyer, & Luce, 1987), appropriate use of leisure time (Schleien & Werder, 1985), and anger control training (Goldstein, 1988).

*Behavior support planning should result in meaningful outcomes.* In developing state-of-the art supports for persons with challenging behaviors, there is a need to ensure that the individual receives those supports in a manner that maximizes the likelihood of increased independence, productivity, and integration into the community. Effectiveness of behavioral support plans needs to be defined in terms of movement into less restrictive environments, increases in skills, maintenance of treatment results over time, and other collateral effects (e.g., reduced medications or crises) (Meyer & Evans, 1989). Procedures for designing programs to impact lifestyle change, allowing for increased access to activities, places, people and events, should be utilized (Horner, 1991). Additionally, issues of social validity (Kazdin, 1980; Wolf, 1978) must be addressed to ensure acceptability of behavior change goals, procedures and intended outcomes.

*Enhanced quality of life is the ultimate measurement of successful planning.* The logic in using quality of life as an organizing construct for outcome evaluation is straightforward. The reason an individual or family member requests services and supports is, presumably, because things are not going as well he or she would like. While this may be substantiated by a formal evaluation process, the initial request is determined by the subjective experience of that individual or family member. The ultimate judge of whether a person comes to experience a life of quality is the individual, and, at times, those people who know that person well. To some degree this is independent of the actual services that are provided and may be only loosely correlated with independent assessments of the value of that service. One method of evaluating the effectiveness of these services is through an overall assessment of whether people feel that their lives have been enhanced through the services or supports they have received.

## Summary

People with challenging behaviors often experience lives with limited choices, restricted access to their local community, and few meaningful social interactions. While it cannot be determined whether this is a cause or effect of their behaviors, it is clear that reversing these conditions can contribute to significant decreases in the occurrence of their challenging behaviors and improvements in a range of quality of life measures. The service/support systems, unfortunately, still require a great deal of reshaping to respond to challenging behaviors in this way. Interestingly, I have found that in initial planning for people with challenging behaviors, incorporating components such as increased choice, access to the community and skill development is judged as highly unlikely, even inappropriate. As the support planning and delivery process progresses, however, they come to be viewed as the only solution to intractable problems. We need, therefore, to continue to work for reform in the service systems so that no service or support can be judged as successful unless there are clear improvements in quality of life.

## Notes

1Thanks are extended to Sara B. Woolf and Alison Bottini, project staff for Positive Strategies to Support Behavior Change: A Community-Based Training Initiative, and the team from Community Resource Center of Sullivan County, New York, who provided services for the individual described in this chapter. Preparation of this chapter was supported in part by grants from the Administration on Developmental Disabilities, Administration for Children and Families (90DD0311) and the Maternal and Child Health Bureau (MCJ36029). The opinions expressed in this paper are solely those of the author; no official endorsement by the U.S. Department of Health and Human Services should be inferred.

## References

Allen, D., Banks, R., & Staite, S. (1991). *Meeting the Challenge: Some UK perspectives on community services for people with learning difficulties and challenging behaviour*. London: King's Fund Centre.

Bradlyn, A.S., Hamadi, W.G., Crimmins, D.B., Christoff, K.A., Graves, K.G. & Kelly, J.A. (1983). Conversational skills training for retarded adolescents. *Behavior Therapy, 14,* 314-325.

Berkman, K.A., & Meyer, L.H. (1988). Alternative strategies and multiple outcomes in the remediation of severe self-injury: Going "all out" nonaversively. *Journal of the Association for Persons with Severe Handicaps, 13,* 76-86.

Crimmins, D. B. (1993). *Positive strategies to support behavior change: A community-based training initiative, Final Report.* Valhalla, NY: Westchester Institute for Human Development.

Carr, E.G. (1977). The motivation of self-injurious behavior: A review of some hypotheses. *Psychological Bulletin, 84,* 800-816.

Carr, E.G. (1988). Functional equivalence as a mechanism of response generalization. In R. Horner, R.L. Koegel, & G. Dunlap (Eds.), *Generalization and maintenance: Life-style changes in applied settings.* Baltimore: Paul H. Brookes.

Carr, E.G., Robinson, S. & Palumbo, L.W. (1990). The wrong issue: Aversive versus nonaversive treatment. The right issue: Functional versus nonfunctional treatment. In A.C. Repp & N.H. Singh (Eds.), *Perspectives on the use of nonaversive and aversive interventions for persons with developmental disabilities.* Sycamore, IL: Sycamore Publishing Co.

Dunlap, G., Johnson, L.F., & Robbins, F.R. (1990). Preventing serious behavior problems through skill development and early intervention. In A.C. Repp & N.H. Singh (Eds.), *Perspectives on the use of non-aversive and aversive interventions for persons with developmental disabilities.* Sycamore, IL: Sycamore Publishing Co.

Dunlap, G., Kern-Dunlap, L., Clarke, S., & Robbins, F.R. (1991). Functional assessment, curriculum revision, and severe behavior problems. *Journal of Applied Behavior Analysis, 24,* 387-397.

Durand, V.M. (1990). *Severe behavior problems: A functional communication training approach.* New York: Guilford Press.

Durand, V.M. & Crimmins, D.B. (1988). Identifying the variables maintaining self-injurious behavior. *Journal of Autism and Developmental Disorders, 18,* 99-117.

Durand, V.M., & Crimmins, D.B. (1990). Assessment. In V.M. Durand, *Severe behavior problems: A functional communication training approach.* New York: Guilford Press.

Durand, V.M. & Crimmins, D.B. (1991). Teaching functionally equivalent responses as an intervention for challenging behavior. In R. Remington (Ed.), *The challenge of severe mental handicap: An applied behaviour analytic approach.* London: John Wiley & Sons.

Durand, V.M. & Crimmins, D.B. (1992). *The Motivation Assessment Scale (MAS) Administration Guide.* Topeka, KS: Monaco & Associates.

Dyer, K., Dunlap, G., & Winterling, V. (1990). Effects of choice making on the serious problem behaviors of students with severe handicaps. *Journal of Applied Behavior Analysis, 23,* 515-524.

Goldstein, A. (1988). *The Prepare Curriculum.* Champaign, IL: Research Press.

Gothelf, C.R., Crimmins, D.B., Mercer, C.A., & Finocchiaro, P.A. (in press). Teaching choice making skills to students with dual sensory impairments. *Teaching Exceptional Children.*

Haring, T., Roger, B., Lee, M., Breen, C., & Gaylord-Ross, R. (1986). Teaching social language to moderately handicapped students. *Journal of Applied Behavior Analysis, 19,* 159-171.

Horner, R.H. (1991). The future of applied behavior analysis for people with severe disabilities: Commentary I. In L.H. Meyer, C.A. Peck, & L. Brown (Eds.), *Critical issues in the lives of people with severe disabilities.* Baltimore: Paul H. Brookes.

Horner, R.H. & Billingsley, F.F. (1988). The effect of competing behavior on the generalization and maintenance of adaptive behavior in applied settings. In R.H. Horner, G. Dunlap, & R.L. Koegel (Eds.), *Generalization and maintenance* (pp. 197-220). Baltimore: Paul H. Brookes.

Kazdin, A.E. (1980). Acceptability of alternative treatments for deviant child behavior. *Journal of Applied Behavior Analysis, 13,* 259-273.

Kennedy, C.H., & Haring, T.G. (1993). Teaching choice making during social interactions to students with profound multiple disabilities. *Journal of Applied Behavior Analysis, 26*, 63-76.

Meyer, L.H. & Evans, I.M. (1989). *Nonaversive intervention for behavior problems: A manual for home and community.* Baltimore, MD: Paul H. Brookes.

Mount, B. (1989). *Person-centered development.* Manchester, CT: Communitas, Inc.

O'Neill, R.E., Horner, R.H., Albin, R.W., Storey, K. & Sprague, J.R. (1990). *Functional analysis of problem behavior: A practical assessment guide.* Sycamore, IL: Sycamore Publishing.

Santarcangelo, S., Dyer, K., & Luce, S.C. (1987). Generalized reduction of disruptive behavior in unsupervised settings through specific toy training. *Journal of The Association for Persons with Severe Handicaps, 12*, 38-44.

Schleien, S.J. & Werder, J. (1985). Perceived responsibilities of special recreation services in Minnesota. *Therapeutic Recreation Journal, 19*, 51-62.

Shevin, M., & Klein, N. (1984). The importance of choice-making skills for students with severe disabilities. *Journal of the Association for Persons with Severe Handicaps, 9*, 159-166.

Turnbull, A.P., & Turnbull, H.R. (1990). A tale about lifestyle changes: comments on "Toward a technology of nonaversive behavioral support." *Journal of the Association for Persons with Severe Handicaps, 15*(3), 142-144.

# 15• Quality of Life and Aging

Steven Moss, PhD
Hester Adrian Research Center,
The University of Manchester, United Kingdom

Research and discussion of the issues relating to the characteristics, needs and quality of support received by older persons with mental retardation burgeoned in the late 70s and 80s, followed in the USA by a massive rise in the number of residential and day programs making specific provision for these individuals. Writing this chapter has had to be an extremely selective task because a potentially vast range of influences can, and probably does, have an impact on QOL. Amongst these aspects are issues of relocation (Heller, 1985), Down syndrome and Alzheimer's disease (Zigman et al, 1990) and behavioral and psychotherapeutic interventions (Hogg, Moss & Cooke, 1988). Their omission is not to be taken as an indication that they are not considered important, but rather that lack of space prevents my doing justice to these themes. Instead I have chosen to focus on what I believe to be the central issue here — what are the QOL issues and factors which relate *particularly* to older persons with mental retardation, and how do they differ from those pertaining to the wider elderly population or younger persons with retardation?

I have set the discussion within a broad ecological model for considering the factors contributing to a good QOL, in line with numerous studies in the mental retardation field. Such studies have made reference to the importance of examining the overall ecology in understanding the nature of the complex interaction between individual persons and their service and informal support contexts. This seemed an appropriate framework with which to view the complex array of physical, social and psychological factors affecting the lives of older persons with mental retardation throughout the world.

## Who are we talking about?

That older people, both with and without mental retardation, are treated differently in different countries may be due partly to a piecemeal development of funding and legislation which has taken place. More fundamentally, however, these differences relate to society's norms and expectations about the place of elderly people and of people with disabilities. As a result, it is often difficult to look outside one's own frame of reference when considering what can and should be done to improve people's quality of life. Discussions are often pursued within a national framework which already dictates that only certain individuals are eligible for services, and that these services are dependent upon certain conditions being met. Thus in the French service context, one cannot be "old" before the age of 65, and cannot be "mentally retarded" after 65 (Breitenbach, 1991). In the USA, the social welfare net is generally less comprehensive than in Europe. In Europe, unemployment or lack of adequate income is sufficient grounds for receiving welfare support, often for an unlimited period of time. Many people with mild retardation, particularly in a time of economic recession, are likely to be unemployed because they tend to have fewer skills to offer in a competitive market. In general they do not need the interventions provided by specialist mental retardation services, and hence remain supported by the state but unknown to mental retardation agencies. In the US, being classified as "mentally retarded" is one way of receiving welfare support, and it is probably for this reason that there are many more people with mild retardation administratively defined as retarded in the US than in the United Kingdom.

The main point I want to make here is that, from a service provision perspective, the "population of older persons with mental retardation" differs in age structure from country to country, for reasons of service eligibility and social expectations about how older persons should be provided for. If QOL issues relate specifically to a person's age and level of retardation, then different conclusions will be reached in different countries. This is probably the reason why research on the characteristics of older persons with mental retardation, particularly in relation to medical status, has come to different conclusions in the US and the UK (Moss, Goldberg, Patel, & Wilkin, 1993) – the service population has a different ability structure. Before considering this further, let us look briefly, in an international context, at some of the factors influencing the lives of these individuals.

In a recent monograph (Moss, 1993), I had the opportunity to bring together the experience of nine countries in respect of their service provision to older persons with mental retardation. In the nine countries represented there were three philosophies of service welfare which predominated. These I referred to as the Oriental, Western European and North American models.

In the far eastern countries, i.e., Indonesia, Japan, Singapore and Hong Kong, there has been a long history and tradition of family care through the extended family. Generally speaking, these countries have not had a history of large institutions, and hence show no major drive to deinstitutionalization. Younger couples have been expected to look after their aging relatives, whether mentally retarded or not, and social welfare provision has been geared to supporting families to do this. As a result, a much greater proportion of people have been invisible to services, an extreme example of this being Hong Kong who reported having 90 per cent of its older mentally retarded persons invisible to service providers.

The "Western European" model of care, represented for instance by the Netherlands and Germany, has had, and continues to have, a strong accent on institutional care. While there is certainly evidence of the development of community services in these countries, institutional care remains an important option, although these institutions are becoming increasingly involved in the community. In some cases, reference was made to clusters of houses within the community, linked to a central institution. This model of care focuses primarily on what is believed to be the needs of the *individual*; the primary aim is to provide for the individual's needs by whichever method is most appropriate.

The "North American" model also included Australia and the United Kingdom. These countries are clearly linked by a strong philosophy of normalization and deinstitutionalization, the philosophy adopted by these countries being rooted in a belief that institutional care is fundamentally inappropriate for most people with developmental disabilities. From the viewpoint of the individual client, it is considered that a more fulfilled life will result from a non-institutional pattern of care. At the same time, the philosophy, certainly in the UK, is also making a more general statement about the ways in which the *rest of society* should view its mentally retarded members — i.e. the society at large should be seen publicly to accept and value these people.

With such widely differing philosophies and expectations, it is inevitable that the issues regarded as fundamental to improving QOL will vary. For a country like Hong Kong where so many of this population are living with their families, it is likely that the issues of community integration are very different from a country where institutionalisation has had a long history. Indeed they may well be able to teach us a lot about integration. In the UK, a good QOL is inextricably bound up with *not*

being in an institution, while this concern may be less emphasized in a country like the Netherlands, where they take pride in the quality of their institutional provision.

## Are they a population with special characteristics?

When research on the aging of this population started to gain momentum in the mid 1970s the literature abounded with assertions that this was a population with "special needs" — the "double jeopardy" of being both elderly and mentally retarded (Sweeney & Wilson, 1979). Since that time, some countries seem to have moved to the position that, rather than being a group with special needs, these individuals' need are fundamentally the same as other elderly people, and that strenuous efforts should be made to integrate them into main stream services. What is the reality?

Our research at the Hester Adrian Research Centre has, over a number of years, demonstrated that a population over 50 years of age, with at least a moderate level of retardation, does indeed show special characteristics. But these characteristics do not give the picture one might expect. Rather than being a population with failing health and increasing support needs, most individuals are in basically good health and with good functional skills (Moss, 1991; Moss, Hogg & Horne, 1992; Moss, Goldberg, Patel & Wilkin, 1993). The reason for this is that *differential mortality*, i.e. the tendency for the frailer members of a population to die earlier, operates very strongly in this population, and increasingly strongly the more severe the level of retardation. Thus, we found in a major UK mental retardation register (Moss, 1991) a constantly reducing proportion of people with severe epilepsy over the lifespan, the presence of epilepsy being an indicator of neurological impairment which is associated with early mortality. The reduction over the adult lifespan was caused by the differential mortality of these at-risk individuals, most of whom were severely or profoundly retarded. Overall, there is a relation between level of retardation and life expectancy, which means that older cohorts tend to be more able than younger ones. The population over 50 shows an *increasing* level of adaptive skills from age 25 right up to 70 years of age, and a reducing frequency of problem behaviors. Beyond this age, adaptive abilities tend, as in the general population, to reduce. Such reductions are related to an increasing frequency of age-related medical conditions, mobility problems and sensory impairments.

From the above it can be concluded that, from a *strategic* point of view, the outlook from a service provider's perspective is good. Most of the survivors are likely to be high functioning and in basically good health. In saying this, however, it is important to distinguish between this strategic planning which needs to be made for the population as a whole, and the need to respond flexibly to the changing needs of *individual* members of that population.

In the general population, most people expect to live a normal lifespan, the majority of individuals only needing statutory support services in their later years, if at all. In the mentally retarded population the proportion of people dying in the middle years is much greater. This effect, as already mentioned, is selective and thus leads to a surviving population of greater ability. It means, however, that service providers have

to cope with the needs of a large proportion of people in their last years of life. Thus, while the selective mortality raises the average functional ability of the population, those individuals who do die young are likely to be major consumers of service resources, needing physical and emotional support for increasing infirmity and eventual death. Our research has also shown that the need for such services, rather than being spread among the population members, is more likely to be focused on a smaller proportion of high-risk individuals (Moss, Goldberg, Patel & Wilkin, 1993). This applied particularly to those people identified as suffering from dementia. Investigations of dementia (Moss & Patel, 1992) showed 11.4 per cent to have clear evidence of cognitive decline, with a particularly high risk for people with Down syndrome. They had much poorer physical health than the group average, health index measures indicating poorer scores for both chronic and acute physical disorders, particularly those involving the central nervous system and gastrointestinal functioning. Many of the individuals with a firm diagnosis of dementia showed deterioration in a wide variety of self-care and community skill domains. This, coupled with their generally poor health, suggests that the level of these people's needs represents a major use of social service resources.

Members of our study sample with Down syndrome showed the expectedly high prevalence of dementia for this at-risk group (Wisniewski et al., 1985), 44 per cent showing definite cognitive decline and associated clinical features over a three year period. However, in absolute numbers, there were more *non*-Down than Down syndrome individuals with dementia. This serves to illustrate that, in the continuing attention payed to the link between Down syndrome and Alzheimer's disease, sight should not be lost of the large number of other dementia sufferers in an average service population.

Mental health apart from dementia also needs to be considered as one of the factors having a major impact on QOL for older people, both retarded and non-retarded. Good mental health is essential if people's ability to live independently is to be maximised. Conversely, psychiatric disorder can be a major contributory factor in the decision to hospitalise an elderly person. Gianturko and Busse (1978) show, for instance, that 50 per cent of US hospital and nursing home beds are occupied by psychiatrically ill elderly people. Our studies (Patel et al., 1993) have shown a high level of unrecognised mental illness in a community population of people with mental retardation over 50. Using advanced diagnosis techniques for this population, developed within the Hester Adrian Research Centre (Moss et al., 1993) we found 11.4 per cent of the sample to be suffering from a diagnosable psychiatric disorder (apart from dementia). Only one third of these cases had been identified and treated by psychiatric services.

Two related factors are likely to have been particularly important in producing this relatively high proportion of untreated cases. First, most of the disorders detected in this older population were neither psychotic, nor within the range of conditions where odd behavior patterns are liable to draw attention to the individual. Rather, the majority of cases were of depression and anxiety, conditions which are also underdetected in the general elderly population (Goldberg & Huxley, 1980). Second, the

probability of a person with mental retardation being referred to the family doctor for psychiatric problems is lower than for a non-retarded person. For a non-retarded person, onset of a mental illness is often heralded by being unable to hold down a job effectively, or being unable to fulfill roles which had previously been carried out successfully, e g., parent, spouse, friend. In comparison, people with mental retardation tend to have lower role expectations, so the impact of mental illness on everyday life is less clear-cut. Without specialist knowledge it may be assumed that the symptoms are an aspect of retardation; thus, referral to a doctor for further psychiatric evaluation may not be made.

Overall, it is clear from the above that health needs are a major issue which needs to be considered in the QOL of this population. However, the spread of illness and fitness is likely to be very wide, with many individuals suffering a wide range of age-related problems at an earlier age than in the general population.

Having introduced the population, we now consider an ecological framework within which the various factors contributing to QOL of elderly persons with mental retardation may be discussed.

## An ecological framework for QOL and the aging process

Bronfenbrenner (1979) coined the term "The Ecology of Human Development" to describe the way in which a person develops in interaction with the various settings (e.g. home, neighborhood and so on) he or she encounters. He proposed a model in which a person is seen as living in a social system comprising four layers of interaction, which can be thought of as ever widening circles around the individual. These layers encompass the immediate physical and social environment, right up to the political and economic structures whose influence, although applying in a less direct way, nevertheless have a major influence on life.

While I would not wish to attempt to apply Bronfenbrenner's model in a formal sense of definable social layers, his perspective stresses the importance of considering the person within the complete social context. Within this framework, Lawton and Nahemow (1973) note that the aging process can be seen as one of continual adaptation both to the environment and to changes in internal capabilities and functioning that occur during the span of life. From their point of view the ecology of aging is defined as a system of continual adaptations in which both the person and the environment change in a non-random way over time. A change in the state of either person or environment can initiate a cycle of action in which adaptive responses are demanded.

At a more concrete level, Headey and Wearing, (1989) have provided a dynamic equilibrium model of the ecology in which each person is regarded as having "normal" equilibrium levels of life events and subjective well-being, predictable on the basis of age and personality. Only when events deviate from their equilibrium levels is there a change in subjective well-being. Murrell and Norris (1983) suggested a related model based on Cassel's (1975) discussion of the role of psychosocial factors in the genesis of disease, which I would suggest is very appropriate for the consideration of QOL in this population. They suggest two factors: the agents or causes of stress on the person, and the processes that protect, buffer or cushion against the stressors. Stressors would include such events as divorce, retirement and illness (Dohrenwend & Dohrenwend, 1974), and stressful life processes such as poverty, single parent families, noise and substandard housing (Gersten, Langner, Eisenberg, & Simcha-Fagan, 1977). In persons with mental retardation, particular stressors would include inadequate support from friends, social stigmatization, domination by other clients at the workplace or residence, and conflict between the client and service providers. In one of our studies of older persons (Moss et al., 1991) we found that one of the most commonly given reasons for dissatisfaction was conflict with the person in charge of the individual's residence.

Resources include opportunities, protection and sustenance that are available from the environment to assist in the growth and development, and to act as a buffer against the environmental stressors. Murrell & Norris (1983) suggest that these resources could take many forms, e.g. material, cultural, physical, social, and interpersonal. Specialist retardation services would, themselves, constitute an important potential resource. QOL is regarded, in this model, as depending on the degree to which resources available can meet or surmount stressors. The stronger the resource relative to the stressors, the higher is the quality of life; if stressors dominate resources, however, the degree of unmet needs would be high, and the resulting QOL would be low.

While a considerable literature demonstrates the clear relation between stressful events and low QOL, it is also clear that an environment which demands too little from the individual can also diminish QOL

(McGrath, 1970; Levi, 1974). Wildman & Johnson (1977), for instance, found that well-being was lower for persons who had experienced very few life events than for persons who had experienced a moderate number of these events. Clearly, a model representing the balance between person and environment is the appropriate one.

## Aging, mental retardation and QOL

Within the model outlined above, we can begin to talk about the two major factors with which this chapter is concerned, i.e. mental retardation and aging, and how they affect the balance between stressors and buffers. A person with mental retardation, by definition, has fewer personal resources to act as buffers against the demands of life. This indeed is the *raison d'etre* for having mental retardation services — to support the individual to be able to live more profitably and more independently, and to act as a buffer against the otherwise over-demanding environment. Since this whole book is devoted to the broad topic of disability, I will pursue this topic no further here, except in relation to the combined effects of disability and aging.

As a person ages, they have the potential of becoming more vulnerable, and hence increasingly in need of support. Increasing vulnerability is, however, of widely varying level and manifestation. Many people stay fit and active throughout their lives. Indeed, my discussion of demographic factors above demonstrates that many older people with mental retardation remain in good health. Nevertheless, the QOL of older people is closely bound up with health concerns, although there are other factors, both objective and subjective, which also need to be taken into consideration. Even fit older people are not the same as younger people. Their needs and expectations are psychologically different, although these differences may be subtle rather than gross. In order to explore these age related differences, a discussion of the objective and subjective elements of QOL is a good starting point, since both these elements change markedly with age.

## Objective and subjective factors in QOL

Zautra & Goodhart (1979) perceive quality of life (QOL) as relating essentially to the "goodness" of life. They see "goodness" as residing in the quality of the life experience, *both* subjectively evaluated and objectively determined.

Much of the research which has been conducted on the quality of life of persons with mental retardation has concentrated on the objective indicators of quality of life — such aspects as housing, education, work and leisure opportunities, social engagement, interaction with the community at large, etc. Seeing the progress made over the past 25 years in the material, social and cultural circumstances of persons with mental retardation, it is clear that this focus has been entirely appropriate. With respect to older persons with mental retardation, there is indeed progress still to be made. Barbero (1989), for instance, states that 75 per cent of the aging population with mental retardation still lack adequate mainstreaming services that could enhance their quality of life and prevent premature long-term institutionalization.

Alongside these objective evaluations,

mental retardation research has placed a growing emphasis on direct assessment of the quality of life by reference to the personal perceptions of persons with mental retardation (Andrews, 1974). Thus, Seltzer (1981) noted the importance to community adjustment of the person's own perceptions about the environment and her/his sense of psychological well-being or discomfort derived from the living environment. Such subjective measures of quality of life ensure that the domains under consideration (e.g. feelings about use of leisure time, quality of housing etc) are relevant, and not incidental to, the person being consulted.

Subjective measures of QOL make the distinction between assessment of *satisfaction* and assessment of *happiness*. This distinction is particularly important in the present context, because older and younger populations report markedly different levels of well-being on these two dimensions.

### Satisfaction and happiness

Measures of satisfaction and happiness can be taken to indicate the extent to which the person has positive attitudes and feelings about various aspects of life. Happiness is thought to differ from satisfaction by describing a shorter term emotional state, whereas satisfaction pertains to a cognitive process in which the current situation is evaluated by contrasting it with an external standard of comparison. In other words, the personal evaluation of satisfaction entails a cognitive judgment in which aspiration is compared to current circumstances. It is thus possible for people in relatively disadvantaged circumstances, because of their lower aspirations, to report higher than average levels of satisfaction, and vice versa. Happiness, on the other

hand, refers to an immediate feeling state that is not anchored, or not tied to the same extent, to cognitive frames of reference (McKennel & Andrews, 1983).

Overall, it appears that happiness tends to diminish with age (Bradburn, 1969; Campbell et al., 1976), while satisfaction increases steadily. Zautra & Goodhart (1979) clarify these findings in the following way. Given that happiness may be a shorter term emotional state, younger people may be happier because they are more excited and involved in life's immediate concerns. They may experience more dissatisfaction, however, when they compare their current life situation with their idealised hopes and aspirations for the future. In contrast, while the present circumstances of older persons may be less favorable, possibly accounting for their diminished happiness, satisfaction statements rise because aspirations and expectations have been progressively trimmed to fit the realities of the situation. From this perspective, statements of satisfaction may in fact be statements of resignation, throwing us back once again on our philosophical concept of what constitutes a "good" life. The position with regard to aged retarded persons is even less clear, since the relation between cognitive and affective components has not been fully explored.

While discussing the distinction between happiness and satisfaction it is pertinent to mention the important distinction between satisfaction and level of activity. The gerontological literature has too often adopted an over-simplified "activity" model of QOL. This perspective focuses on the element of intentioned activity and its achievement, activity in gerontological terms being associated with well-being, relationships with significant others and positive affect (Kelly et al., 1986). Over-simplification of this model has resulted in counting frequency or number of activities as a measure of QOL, rather than seeing activity as a resource for coping with change.

## The major QOL concerns of older persons

Although the potential number of objective indicators is high, most lists have some items in common, implying there may be only a limited number of human problems which all people share (Kulckholm & Strodtbeck, 1961). The Office of Management and Budget (1973) listed 8 major social concerns to guide its first statistical publication on social indicators, including: health, social welfare, education, public safety, leisure, housing and the environment, and population. There is an extensive literature on factor studies of QOL. Using the Quality of Life Index, Ferans and Powers (1992) for instance, reported a factor study indicating four dimensions: health and functioning, socioeconomic, psychological/spiritual, and family.

Certainly, the two issues which clearly stand out as major QOL priorities for older persons are health (George & Bearon, 1980), and social support (Antonucci, 1985). Health is indeed a major component of QOL for all ages. However, its perceived significance changes differs from different age perspectives. Younger and middle aged individuals are reported as seeing material well-being as more important than health, while health is more salient for older persons (Bearon, 1989). Generally speaking, younger people are more bound up with the notion of aspiration and progress, older people with

maintaining the status quo and preventing their worst fears being realised. Overall, the notion of "peace of mind" about health issues (Nystrom, Andersson & Segesten, 1990) is more relevant for older people than health definitions stressing physical, mental, and social perfection.

Social networks are a central part of human life, the quality of social interaction being positively associated with psychological well-being in all age groups (Baker, Jodrey & Intagliata, 1992). Regardless of differential opportunities and constraints in interaction with family members and friends, adults benefit from close personal friendships (Ishii-Kunst, 1990). A strong social network can not only act as a buffer against stressful life events, but is also shown to have a positive effect on perceived QOL, independent of major life events (Mor-Barak, Miller & Syme, 1991). For elderly persons, both these aspects are even more crucial than in the general population (Nagpal & Chadha, 1991), social activity being an important factor in the maintenance of adaptive functioning (Haga et al., 1991). Elderly people's abilities to cope with the pressures of life, with or without major life events, tend to diminish, so they have increasing need to rely for practical assistance on their social network (Bowling & Browne, 1991). Also, older people's choice of pleasurable activity tends to focus less on high energy pursuits, and increasingly on family and friends – on the fostering of intimacy through shared tasks (Kelly, 1983).

### Specific QOL issues for older persons with mental retardation

Common sense suggests that all people share certain common experiences as they age. With regard to people with mental retardation, however, the issue of service provision has obviously been central to the issue of QOL in this particular population, since so many persons with mental retardation receive support of services of some kind. Thus, studies of residential provision have reported low levels of engagement relative to facilities for younger persons, producing a situation which tends to generate high dependency (Baker, Seltzer & Seltzer, 1977; Willer & Intagliata, 1984). Both studies demonstrated that the lack of engagement of older people with mental retardation in Health Care Facilities (HCFs) and Private Proprietary Homes for Adults (PPHAs) cannot be attributed to age per se.

Concerning the social network, Seltzer (1985) has made the point that few older people with mental retardation will have their own children to give them support in later life, a situation with the potential for isolation and other debilitating consequences. Where families are offering primary care, Grant (1989) has demonstrated the highly circumscribed role that they permit friends and neighbors to play. In the absence of family members, however, Edgerton (1967) has shown how friends and neighbors can facilitate survival in the community. Flynn (1988) also shows how the nature of a neighborhood will itself influence the extent and quality of informal support from neighbors.

Our own studies in the UK (Moss, Hogg & Horne, 1992) have shown that, irrespective of the level of adaptive skills, older persons were more likely to live in congregate care settings, and were less likely to be resettled to independent locations than younger persons. For virtually all leisure activities investigated (e.g., use of bars, movie theaters, spectator sports etc),

older people were significantly more likely "never" to participate. Older people also tended to go on vacation less. Persons with a higher degree of competence were (a) more likely to be resettled in independent community settings, (b) receive more educational programs, and (c) receive a greater amount and variety of leisure activities.

Not surprisingly, the relative difficulty of obtaining reliable and valid estimates of subjective satisfaction and perceived QOL has meant that most of the earlier studies of QOL of persons with mental retardation concentrated on objective measures. In recent years, however, increasing emphasis has been placed on the soliciting of consumer views, studies which sometimes paint a picture of relative dissatisfaction. Thus Sands et. al., (1991) interviewed 240 Colorado consumers with mental retardation to measure their satisfaction with services and to investigate quality of life issues. Many respondents receiving day services from community centered programs expressed dissatisfaction with information and referral services, and were unhappy with the quality of education and personal dignity afforded to them. The limited opportunities available to these people in choosing where they lived, who they lived with, and how they spent their money constrained the level of independence that they obtained in adulthood. Integration occurred much less frequently than the respondents desired. Elsewhere, Cattermole (1990) reports that choice, privacy, social life, and relationships with their parents and staff emerged as important factors in participants' perception of their quality of life. Disabled people moving to community residences have aspirations that encompass far more than a wish to adapt to life in the community, their relationships with family and staff being central to the achievement of such aspirations.

From the specific perspective of older persons with mental retardation, a recent Australian study (Suttie *et. al.*, 1993) has shown that members of this population experience isolation, concern for their future, depression, a range of medical conditions, and diminishing mobility. These concerns are much as one would expect to hear if asking any group of older people.

## Practical steps: valuing as the same or valuing as different?

The research on needs and characteristics of older persons with mental retardation has gone, essentially, full circle, starting with the contention that this was a population deserving special consideration, having the "double jeopardy" of being both elderly and retarded (Sweeny & Wilson, 1979), and ending with the view that most older persons with retardation experience the same rate of physical and medical problems as other seniors (LePore & Janicki, 1990, p 6).

In the US the stimulus of research and discussion has led to a huge rise in the number of residential and day programs making specific or exclusive provision for older persons with mental retardation (Baker, Seltzer & Seltzer, 1977). This rise in provision can, I believe, be seen in terms of two broad aims: To make services more accountable to the needs of elderly clients, and to integrate clients in the mental retardation network into mainstream aging services. The first of these arose directly from the research of the 1980s, showing that older persons were getting a generally poor-

er service than younger individuals in terms of residential placement, community involvement and options and choices within the service system. In addition, it was becoming clear that one of the primary aims of US mental retardation services — raising the level of independence through day programming, was less appropriate for many older persons. The strong emphasis of industrial-type work meant that a retirement option, with a focus on activities more appropriate to later life, needed to be made available.

These changes in provision, made in response to evaluative studies, clearly indicated the need for change to improve service delivery to older clients. The other major movement, integration into mainstream services, has a more ideological basis. True, integration has resulted in increased availability of certain funding strands, both State and Federal, but this has not been the main impetus. Rather, this movement has arisen from the view that older persons with mental retardation have the same rights to mainstream aging services as the general population, and the beliefs that (a) the needs of persons with and without mental retardation become closer in old age, (b) recipients of older persons' services, both retarded and non-retarded, can benefit from appropriate integration. The pioneering work of Janicki and his coworkers (LePore & Janicki, 1990; Janicki, 1991) has made the USA the undisputed leader in the field of service integration.

I used the term "ideological" because these service developments have not arisen directly from research findings. It is possible, for instance, that a wide variety of population groups could benefit from interaction with one another, but that administrative reasons or attitudinal barriers prevent it being tried out. Service development often proceeds on a partially serendipitous basis. In this case the mainstream aging services were available, their use for persons with mental retardation fitted with the ethos of a community care policy, and most importantly, they were considered to offer *worthwhile additions* to the range of services and experiences currently being received. It is not necessarily the case, however, that the same conclusions would be reached in other service settings. If we compare the experience of North America with that of Britain it becomes apparent how difficult it is to reach a consensus about the direction services should follow in order to improve the QOL of this population. In the UK, the service delivery system is inherently more flexible than in the US, having fewer and less stringent rules governing entitlement. In addition, some people working in mental retardation services are of the opinion that the aging network in the UK offers a poorer service, particularly in terms of community involvement, than specialist services. Indeed as mentioned above, our own research (Moss, Hogg & Horne, 1992) supported this view. These two factors have led to a situation in which service delivery to older persons with mental retardation has developed very differently from in the US.

Community care in Britain is broadly the responsibility of two agencies, Health and Social Services. Health Authorities have been largely responsible for the running of long-stay institutions, and for the provision of a wide range of medical and paramedical services. Social Services, the responsibility of the Local Authorities (local government), have been responsible for residential and day services within the community. These two systems have been largely independent, a situation which has led to a considerable amount of overlap in the services they have provided. This has in the past led to poor coordination and duplication of services, and gaps in provision. Recently, however, a major piece of new legislation has come into force, one of the main aims being to bring together of Health and Social Service Agencies to agree (a) strategic plans for community care, and (b) plans for individual service users.

To achieve these changes, Local Authorities have become the *sole agents* responsible for overall care management. In fulfilling this role they should produce comprehensive care plans, and arrange for independent inspection and quality-checking of services. They are responsible, in collaboration with medical, nursing and other caring agencies, for carrying out an appropriate assessment of the individual's need for social care before deciding what services should be provided. This assessment procedure should lead to the tailoring of a package of services designed to meet the assessed needs of individuals and their carers. The new act recommends that a "case manager" be nominated for each service user, to take responsibility for ensuring that individuals' needs are regularly reviewed, resources are managed effectively and that each service user has a *single point of contact* for service delivery.

The Government's new policy directives on day services emphasize the use of ordinary facilities where possible. In relation to work, for instance, there is an increasing stress on the use of supported employment for those people who are able to work in a normal work environment with additional help. At the present time, however, there are few people with mental retardation in open employment or sheltered work placement. The majority attend day centers called Adult Training Centers (ATCs). In the past, some of these have focused on industrial-type work, now the emphasis is more on social and educational programs. Programs are usually designed to give opportunities for clients of all ages and abilities, including profoundly retarded, multiply handicapped and aging people.

In Britain, people tend to remain at the ATC as long as they wish, often spending a reduced length of time per week at the institution as they age. Adult Training Centre managers generally feel able to offer sufficiently flexible programmes of activities for clients, irrespective of age.

The flexibility inherent within the British model has led to the development of a system where it has not been a priority to develop specific services for older clients. Indeed, there is currently little evidence of specific services in the UK. On the contrary, there is evidence that service providers are tending to *remove* reference to client age as a category for receiving services. This, indeed, is fully within the spirit of the Community Care Act — the objective of assessment being to determine the best available way to help the individual in a way which is flexible and non-bureaucratic. Within this needs-based framework, Local Authorities have generally adopted the view that aging in itself does not constitute a need. Thus, Wiltshire Social Services list of client types includes mental retardation, elderly mentally dependent and elderly physically infirm. The London Borough of Barnet does not use the age category at all on their initial assessment form. Rather,

the kinds of conditions which may result *from* aging appear on the form, ie: sight, hearing, mobility, incontinence etc. Mental retardation is of course a category, but not one which mentions the age criterion at all.

From an ideological perspective British service planners and providers appear uncertain whether a normalized life for elderly persons with mental retardation is best achieved by integration with generic elderly services, or by keeping them with their non-elderly peers — i.e., valuing them by assuming they are the same as everyone else, or valuing them as being special and hence needing special provision. Generally, the view which seems to have been adopted in the UK is away from integration with mainstream services, and away from the provision of age-specific mental retardation programs. Some years ago (Hogg, Moss & Cooke, 1988) we found a few examples of specific provision including pre-retirement courses, age-specific day provision and age-specific residences. Since that time at least one of these day-services has been closed down as being "ageist."

## Conclusions

The many studies which have been carried out on older persons with mental retardation, their characteristics, formal and informal support, have provided a wealth of information from which we can work to further improve their QOL. However, the complex interaction of medical, social and psychological factors, in relation to the presence of mental retardation, will need multidimensional modelling if we are to learn how these individuals perceive aging and illness, how we can better support them to deal with age-related changes in functional ability (Hickey & Stilwell, 1992), and maximise their potential for living a satisfying life.

Within this modelling process, the particular problem in furthering our understanding is, I believe, in the *psychological* sphere. I have already implied that I think it is the more subtle, psychological changes associated with aging which still present the biggest challenge both to service providers and researchers in this field. What is it in this respect that older persons wish to have available from support services? I would suggest that there are two fundamental domains to which we must attend — the need to maintain a continuing autonomy and potential to make choices, and the increasing importance of close personal relationships for support and the pursuit of leisure.

The element of personal choice is enshrined in the service philosophies of many countries, yet true personal choice necessitates a degree of autonomy which many people with mental retardation can only achieve with a great deal of support. As a person ages, this autonomy may become even more difficult to achieve. With increasing age may come an increasing sense of vulnerability as one's physical and economic resources diminish. For people with mental retardation, this vulnerability may already be present to a considerable degree. The problem for service providers is to support the individual to an increasing extent as they age, yet not make the client feel that they have no autonomy. Helping an older person with mental retardation to remain autonomous both in action and personal choice may thus be one of the challenges we have yet fully to meet.

I should like to end by once again drawing attention to the importance of social interaction as a fundamental component of later-life activity. As people age, formal work tends to play a less significant role, while leisure and the independent use of time becomes more prominent. Leisure has a dynamic and multidimensional role which is not fixed at some point in time, but has a place in the development of the individual and in coping with the changes required by external events. Kelly (1983) proposed a sociological model of the involvement of leisure across the life-span. The "core and balance" model draws attention to the fact that adults have a set of central activities, usually centred in or around the home, which persist throughout life. Such activities include interaction with other household members, reading and watching television, walking and play. Distinct from this "core" is a balancing set of more specialized activities which tend to shift and change throughout life, as roles, self-images and opportunities change. As people age, their core of activities can be seen to demonstrate considerable continuity over the lifespan in terms of the pursuit of leisure. However, they also show a consistent shift toward social integration as being the most important factor for the over 65s, and the availability of family for the over 75s (Kelly et al., 1986).

If we assume, as seems likely, that the psychological experience of aging is the same for both retarded and non-retarded persons (Brown, 1989), Kelly's model provides us with an important message for maintaining and improving the QOL of this population. Older people need, first and foremost, a sense of *continuity* in their lives — the maintenance of their "core." Secondly, they need to have available the best possible opportunities for developing close friendships in the context of mutually chosen and shared activity. If we can achieve this goal through good service provision for seniors with and without mental retardation, I am sure that the whole of society can benefit from the increased contribution of *all* its older citizens.

# References

Andrews, F.M. (1974). Social indicators of perceived life quality. *Social Indicators Research, 1*, 279-299.

Antonuccci, T.C. (1985). Personal characteristics, social support and social behavior. In R.H. Binstock & E.Shanas (Eds.) *Handbook of aging and the social science, 2nd. edition.* New York: Van Nostrand

Barbero, S.L. (1989). Community-based, day treatment for mentally retarded adults. *Social Work, 34,* 545-548.

Baker, F., Jodrey, D., & Intagliata, J. (1992). Social support and quality of life of community support clients. *Community Mental Health Journal, 28,* 397-411.

Baker, B, Seltzer, G.B., & Seltzer, M.M. (1977). *As close as possible: Community residences for retarded adults.*: Boston, Mass: Little, Brown, and Co.

Bearon, L.B. (1989). No great expectations: The underpinnings of life satisfaction for older women. *Gerontologist, 29,* 772-778.

Bowling, A., & Browne, P.D. (1991). Social networks, health, and emotional well-being among the oldest old in London. *Journals of Gerontology, 46,* S20-S32.

Bradburn, H.M. (1969). *The Structure of Psychological Well-being.* Chicago: Aldine.

Breitenbach, N. (1991). Personal commmunication

Bronfenbrenner, U. (1979). *The ecology of human development.* London: Harvard University Press.

Brown, R.I. (1989). Aging, disability and quality of life: A challenge for society. *Canadian Psychology/Psychologie Canadienne, 30,* 551-559.

Campbell, A., Converse, P.E. & Rodgers, W.L. (1976). *The Quality of American Life.* New York: Russell Sage Foundation.

Cassel, J. (1975). Social science in epidemiology: Psycho-social processes and stress: Theoretical formulation. In E.G. Struening & M. Guttentag (Eds.) *Handbook of evaluation research, 1.* Beverly Hills, Calif: Sage Publications.

Cattermole, M., Jahoda, A., & Markova, I. (1990). Quality of life for people with learning difficulties moving to community homes. *Disability, Handicap and Society, 5,* 137-152.

Dohrenwend, B.S. & Dohrenwend, B.P. (1974). *Stressful life events: Their nature and effects.* New York: John Wiley & Sons.

Edgerton, R.B. (1967). *The cloak of competence: Stigma in the lives of the mentally retarded.* Berkeley, CA: University of California Press.

Ferrans, C.E., & Powers, M.J. (1992). Psychometric assessment of the Quality of Life Index. *Research in Nursing and Health, 15,* 29-38.

Flynn, M. (1988). The social environment of adults living in their own homes. In M. Flynn (Ed.) *A Place of My Own: Independent living for adults who are mentally handicapped.* London: Cassell.

George, L., & Bearon, L. (1980). *Quality of life in older persons: Meaning and measurement.* New York: Human Sciences Press.

Gersten, J., Langner, T., Eisenberg, J. & Simcha-Fagan, O. (1977). An evaluation of the etiologic role of stressful life-change events in psychological disorders. *Journal of Health and Social Behavior, 18,* 228-244.

Gianturko, D.T., & Busse, E.W. (1978). Psychiatric problems encountered during a long-term study of normal ageing volunteers. In A.D. Isaacs (Ed.) *Studies in geriatric psychiatry* (ed. A.D. Issacs). Chichester: Wiley.

Goldberg, D., & Huxley, P. (1980). *Mental illness in the community*. London: Tavistock Publications.

Grant, G. (1989). Letting go: Decision-making among family carers of people with a mental handicap. *Australian and New Zealnad Journal of Developmental Disabilities 15*, 189-200.

Haga, H., Shibata, H., Ueno, M., & Nagai, H. (1991). Factors contributing to longitudinal changes in activities of daily living (ADL): The Koganei study. *Journal of Cross Cultural Gerontology, 6*, 91-99.

Headey, B., & Wearing, A. (1989). Personality, life events, and subjective well-being: Toward a dynamic equilibrium model. *Journal of Personality and Social Psychology, 57*, 731-739.

Heller, T. (1985). Residential relocation and reactions of elderly mentally retarded persons. In M.P. Janicki & H.M. Wisniewski (Eds.) *Aging and developmental disabilities: Issues and approaches*. Baltimore: Brookes

Hickey, T Stilwell, D.L. (1992). Chronic illness and aging: A personal-contextual model of age-related changes in health status. Special Issue: Gerontology education, research, and policy. *Educational Gerontology, 18*, 1-15.

Hogg, J., Moss, S., & Cooke, D. (1988). *Ageing and Mental Handicap*. London: Chapman and Hall.

Ishii-Kuntz, M. (1990). Social interaction and psychological well-being: Comparison across stages of adulthood. *International Journal of Aging and Human Development, 30*, 15-36.

Janicki, M.P. (1991). *Building the future: Planning and community development in aging and developmental disabilities*. Albany, NY: New York State Office for the Aging.

Kelly, J.R. (1983). *Leisure identities and interactions*. London: Allen and Unwin.

Kelly, J.R., Steinkamp, M.W., & Kelly, J.R. (1986). Later life leisure: How they play in Peoria. *The Gerontologist 26*, 531-537.

Kulckholm, F.R. & Strodtbeck, F.L. (1961). *Variations in value orientations*. Evanston, Illinois: Row, Peterson & Co.

Lawton, M.P., & Nahemow, L. (1973). Ecology and the aging process. In C. Eisdorfer & M.P. Lawton (Eds.) *Psychology of adult development and aging* (pp 619-674). Washington DC: American Psychological Association.

LePore, P., & Janicki, M.P. (1990). *The wit to win: How to integrate older persons with dveleopmental disabilites into community aging programs*. Albany, NY: New York State Office for the Aging.

Levi, L. (1974). Psychosocial stress and disease: A conceptual model. In E.K.E. Gunderson & R.H. Rahe (Eds.) *Life Stress and Illness*. Springfield, Ill: Charles C Thomas.

McGrath, J.E. (Ed.) (1970). *Social and Psychological Factors in Stress*. New York: Holt, Rinehart & Winston.

McKennel, A.C., & Andrews, F.M. (1983). Components of perceived life quality. *Journal of Community Psychology, 11*, 98-110

Mor-Barak, M.E, Miller, L.S., & Syme, L.S. (1991). Social networks, life events, and health of the poor, frail elderly: A longitudinal study of the buffering versus the direct effect. *Family and Community Health, 14*, 1-13.

Moss, S. C. (1991). Age and functional abilities of people with a mental handicap: evidence from the Wessex mental handicap register. *Journal of Mental Deficiency Research 35*,

Moss, S.C. (Ed.) (1993). *Aging and developmental disabilites: Perspectives from nine countries*. International Exchange of Experts and Information in Rehabilitation: Durham, New Hampshire.

Moss, S., Goldberg, D. & Patel, P. (1991). *Psychiatric and physical morbidity in older people with severe mental handicap*. H.A.R.C. University of Manchester: Manchester.

Moss, S.C., Patel, P., Prosser, H., Goldberg, D.P., Simpson, N., Rowe, S., & Lucchino, R., (1993). Psychiatric morbidity in older people with moderate and severe learning disability (mental retardation). Part I: Development and reliability of the patient interview (the PAS-ADD). *British Journal of Psychiatry, 163,* 471-480

Moss, S., Goldberg, D., Patel, P. & Wilkin, D. (1993). Physical morbidity in older people with moderate, severe and profound mental handicap, and its relation to psychiatric morbidity. *Social Psychiatry and Psychiatric Epidemiology, 28,* 32-39.

Moss, S.C., Hogg, J., & Horne, M. (1992). Demographic characteristics of a population of people with moderate severe and profound intellectual disability (mental handicap) over 50 years of age: age structure, IQ and adaptive skills. *Journal of Intellectual Disability Research, 36,* 387-401.

Moss, S.C., Patel, P., Prosser, H., Goldberg, D.P., Simpson, N., Rowe, S., & Lucchino, R., (1993). Psychiatric morbidity in older people with moderate and severe learning disability (mental retardation). Part I: Development and reliability of the patient interview (the PAS-ADD). *British Journal of Psychiatry, 163,* 471-480

Murrell, S.A. & Norris, F.H. (1983). Quality of life as the criterion for need assessment and community psychology. *Journal of Community Psychology 11,* 88-97.

Nagpal, N., & Chadha, N.K. (1991). Social support and life satisfaction among aged. *Indian Journal of Psychometry and Education, 22,* 91-100.

Newman, E.S., Sherman, S.R. & Frenkel, E.R. (1985). Foster family care: A residential alternative for mentally retarded older persons. In M.P. Janicki & H.M. Wisniewski (Eds.) *Aging and Developmental Disabilities:Issues and approaches,* pp 367-377. Baltimore, MD: Paul Brookes.

Nystrom., A., & Andersson-Segesten, K. (1990). Peace of mind as an important aspect of old people's health. *Scandinavian Journal of Caring Sciences, 4,* 55-62.

Patel, P., Goldberg, D.P., & Moss, S.C. (1993). Psychiatric morbidity in older people with moderate and severe learning disability (mental retardation). Part II: The prevalence study. *British Journal of Psychiatry, 163,* 481-491

Sands, D.J. Kozleski, E.B, & Goodwin, L.D. (1991). Whose needs are we meeting? Results of a consumer satisfaction survey of persons with developmental disabilities in Colorado. *Research in Developmental Disabilities,* 1991 Vol 12(3) 297-314.

Seltzer, G.B. (1981). Community residential adjustment: The relationship among environment, performance and satisfaction. *American Journal of Mental Deficiency, 85,* 624-630.

Seltzer, M.M. (1985). Informal support for aging mentally retarded persons. *American Journal of Mental Deficiency 90,* 259-265.

Suttie, J, Ashman, A.F, & Bramley, J. (1993). Problems undertaking surveys of older people with a disability in Australia. Special Issue: Psychological aspects of aging: Well-being and vulnerability. *Irish Journal of Psychology, 14,* 5-24.

Wildman, R.C. & Johnson, D.R. (1977). Life change and Langner's 22-item mental health index: A study of partial replication. *Journal of Health and Social Behavior 18,* 179-188.

Willer, B., & Intagliata, J. (1984). Residential care settings for the elderly. In B. Willer and J. Intagliata (Eds.) *Promises and realities for mentally retarded citizens: Life in the community.* Baltimore, MD: University Park Press.

Wisniewski, K.E., Wisniewski, H.M., & Wen, G.Y. (1985). Occurrence of neuropatho-logical changes and dementia of Alzheimer's disease in Down syndrome. *Annals of Neurology, 17,* 278-282.

Zautra, A. & Goodhart, D. (1979). Quality of life indicators: A review of the literature. *Community Mental Health Review 4,* 1-10.

Zigman, W.B., Seltzer, G.B., Adlin, M., & Silverman, W.P. (1990). Physical, behavioral, and mental health changes associated with aging. In M.P. Janicki & M.M Seltzer (Eds) *Aging and developmental disabilities: Challenges for the 1990s.* Special Interest Group on Aging, Washington DC: American Association on Mental Retardation.

# 16. Helping to Assure a "Quality of Life" for Infants, Preschoolers and their Families

Michael E. Reif,
Rochester Early Childhood
Direction Center, New York

The principles identified by the National Quality of Life Project (NQOLP) conducted by David Goode, et al (1988), serve as the major philosophic underpinnings to this discussion of Quality of Life (QOL). These principles, garnered from numerous consumers, policy makers, professionals, and advocates will be discussed and exemplified by using actual consumer examples to illustrate the individuality, complexity and magnitude of the issues involved when discussing QOL relative to this age group. Most revealing from the national study (NQOLP), and as we look at the literature, is that the truth in defining QOL comes from primary and secondary consumer stories and perspectives.

Helping to assure an optimal QOL for all citizens of the United States is a basic philosophic premise, inherent in our constitution and many of our laws. In 1986, Congress passed Public Law 99-457, the Infant, Toddler and Preschool amendments to the Education of All Handicapped Children's Act of 1975 (now known as the Individuals with Disabilities Education Act (IDEA)) providing U.S. citizens the opportunity to create the assurance of an optimal QOL for our youngest children at risk for developmental delays or with disabilities and their families.

Numerous ethical, public policy, and economic issues surround attempts to define, quantify and evaluate QOL, particularly for young children with disabilities and their families. One argument among our contemporaries is the right to life vs death of newborns with severe disabilities. This issue will not be debated within the scope of this chapter. Suffice it say, it is this author's philosophy, and the law, that *all* newborns are entitled to their constitutional civil rights and assurance to receive care and treatment regardless of the severity of their disabilities. Decision making regarding the viability of life should rest with the family, family physician and local infant review committees, while adhering to our laws and numerous relevant court decisions. For me, it is equally as important to insure the right and assurance that adequate ongoing support will continue for both the child and family throughout the lifetime of the individual. I believe it is our society's moral and ethical responsibility to do so.

The principles and factors affecting the "QOL" of persons with disabilities have gained increased recognition, study and definition by federal and state governments and researchers in just the past few years. In virtually every part of this country, our systems are in varying stages of implementation of PL 99-457. Significant systemic changes are being attempted in our quest to alter the paradigm of service delivery to our most vulnerable citizens. As a nation, we are attempting to assure that we provide family centered care, appropriate early intervention supports and resources from the time of birth; even before birth if possible. Embedded within these issues are efforts desiring to assure QOL in its broadest context and definition.

The effectiveness of our services will only be measurable over the next few years. Indeed, largely because of the law, we have the potential to do better than we've ever done before. The legal basis, the philosophy, and the hope are there. But will it work? Do we as a society have sufficient resources, knowledge, understanding, fiscal, and moral commitment to make it work? Only time will tell.

Two key QOL principles from the national study that most particularly affect young children and their families include:

QOL factors are subject oriented and are represented by unique interactions of child, family and the community over time. We strive for equality of sufficiency for people with disabilities as we do for people without disabilities. We operate on the premise that caring and providing for the needs of exceptional children are built on the same child development foundations and opportunities as those for non-exceptional children.

The "unit" of reference for those from conception to age five must be viewed and treated as the child and family joined as one, very directly interacting with one another.

The significance of these principles can best be illustrated by the story of Julie Moran,[1] a two year old born with significant developmental disabilities. At the time of her birth (their second child), Julie's parents, were young, well educated, and lived near a major northeast city. Both parents were professionally employed; Mary as an educator and Greg as an engineer. Life as they knew it changed dramatically the day Julie was born. Born with significant medical complications, hanging to life by a thread, Julie's developmental problems catapulted the Morans into a situation that one cannot be adequately physically, emotionally, or intellectually prepared for, even if given notice. The "family unit" was called upon to unite all of its resources, to rally support for one another, to confront the difficult decisions, to console one another and to cope with the situation. The "unit" had to function as one, to its maximum potential. Direct support to and from each "unit" member became increasing dependent on one another. Julie was totally dependent on her parents' and physicians' decisions to decide the extent of life support measures. Greg and Mary were dependent on each other, their bond as loving parents and the bond and support from immediate family members. Fortunately for the Morans, the level of support that surrounded them was quite high and included a solid family, competent and sensitive professionals, many friends and most of all, each other. This quality of support helped them to endure daily uncertainty.

---

[1]  Names have been changed to ensure confidentiality.

The "family unit" was dramatically affected by all that was taking place. Their decision making, communications and support for each other were tested to the maximum under these extremely stressful circumstances. Over time the quality of each individual's life was directly affected and linked closely as a result of the unique interactions created by Julie's condition, and its connection to the family, the community and medical support systems.

Following the many tumultuous and intense medical decisions and efforts to save little Julie's life (too many to elaborate) in the months following her birth, the "family unit" encountered numerous QOL decisions. What was their definition of QOL under various circumstances? The primary concern was of course, will she live? And, if she lives, what factors will determine her quality of life? Will she be comfortable or in constant pain? What would the immediate future bring...the distant future? All of these surfaced for the young couple. They knew that many members of our populace go through these struggles and pains. Unfortunately, most experience the shattered dreams described by Moses and others. For those who haven't personally experienced such pain, however, it seems overwhelming to contemplate a newborn's survival of these realities. Their future survival, and our methodology for helping others in similar situations should become a part of current QOL discussions. How will we assure the supports will be there for future family units? How will we address the QOL for all individuals and communities in the face of inadequate levels of support?

Although it is often taken for granted, one of the most rudimentary components in defining QOL relates to the level of physical comfort experienced by the individual with a disability. Level of comfort can best be defined by examining the circumstances of the individual. According to Julie's parents, physical comfort, a lack of pain, is one of their most important and constant considerations. In fact, this single issue serves as a guiding principle and guides almost all of their decisions and activities. Julie's comfort is their number one priority. If Julie is in pain, everything is affected.

Julie's level of physical comfort directly and significantly affects the QOL of the rest of the family unit. Mary and Greg's personal QOL are greatly influenced by Julie's day to day status. Mary does not hesitate to say that she has discovered that it takes a great deal more physical and emotional energy to maintain a functioning family unit and peace of mind while parenting a child with significant medical and developmental needs. A high energy level is essential for Mary to provide consistent love, nurturance and support to each member of her family. Rejuvenation is important, particularly as she becomes physically fatigued from staying up all night to comfort Julie. She can be "wasted" after a rough night, and everyone's QOL suffers as a result. Help is needed. Regular, periodic and reliable supports or her physical and emotional energy is rapidly depleted. Dependable and competent nursing relief helps with medications, meals and basic care and can go a long way to give her a break, or a chance to relax, take in a movie, or just get away from the same routine. Unfortunately, there frequently isn't enough nursing time or available personnel to fully meet the family's stresses.

"Things are never in a static state," says Mary. "We try to put it all together with a holistic approach, because Julie's quality of life is dependent on stability and predictability." Mary's statement shows us how important the family unit is when it comes to QOL. If it is functioning well, the family maintains the holistic effort. Without this effort, QOL suffers. "Parents are the ones who own and feel the overall responsibility for their child's QOL," she says. "The systems certainly help and are essential but it's as if everyone looks at their little part — the therapy they're responsible for, their particular area of expertise— so the family is left to assimilate the pieces. We're the constant in Julie's life, and we'll always be there. The teachers, doctors, therapists, and advocates usually change from year to year." Clearly, when discussing QOL for young children with disabilities we must include and value the entire family unit. This unity must be served and strengthened.

Striving for "equality of sufficiency" is a QOL concept shared with the national study by Al Healy, M.D., Executive Director of the Iowa University Affiliated Program for Developmental Disabilities (Goode 1988). Healy described the Irish concept of a "colup" of land to illustrate the point. In Ireland, land is not only measured in meters. A family is given a "colup", or, that amount of land that will permit the family to do its work and keep itself going. The "colup" reflected characteristics of the land, the family, and the community. Healy advanced this notion of the colup as a concept that could be applied to families with children with special needs, and that they should be given what they need to survive and fit into their community. In many ways this is the underlying premise and intent behind PL

99-457. Congress has established a basic framework around which each state is establishing their community and statewide systems to meet the developmental needs of young children and their families.

Similar to the "colup" concept, P.L. 99-457's Individualized Family Service Plan (IFSP) process is intended to meet the unique needs of each child and family in a flexible, ongoing manner. Defining and agreeing upon what constitutes that plan, the process and how it will be implemented is the current challenge to the entire nation. Will the IFSP document and the process used to develops it be the means by which we manage and improve the QOL for individuals with disabilities at younger ages and their families? How will "equality of sufficiency" be defined within such documents and do we really believe in "equality of sufficiency"? As determined by whom? Do we have the necessary resources to do all that seems to be suggested? How and who will measure the resulting QOL factors for infants, toddlers, preschoolers and their families? Can we quantify IFSP outcomes? How, and who will quantify them? These are but a few of the questions we must raise in the next few years.

The debates are raging nationwide about health care reform, inclusive services, effectiveness of intervention services and who will pay for all the services and supports our citizens (with and without disabilities) need. This raises another principle of QOL from the national study (NQOLP) that lends itself to support possible solutions to these seemingly overwhelming issues, particularly as it concerns young children and their families. Specifically:

QOL is essentially the same for persons with or without disabilities. Persons with disabilities want the same things for their lives, have the same needs and want to fulfill social responsibilities in the same way other members of society do.

In essence, we must consider utilizing, with some modifications perhaps, the array of current resources and alternatives within our given communities. We are challenged to integrate and include individuals with disabilities in the mainstream of our community life. This may be easiest and most effective with very young children. Delivery of services and supports in "natural environments" whenever possible and feasible is one of the foundations of early intervention philosophy and serves as a clear direction for service delivery in the future. Unfortunately, we have much to do before this becomes a reality. Communities, programs accessed by the general public, and public officials need to be sensitized and knowledgeable about the issues concerning those with disabilities — all to often they are not. During the conduct of many early intervention awareness training sessions with generic child care providers in upstate New York over the past few years, the level of receptivity to more inclusive approaches is as varied as the number of potential sites identified. There are still significant fears of individuals with disabilities. This is in part due to our litigious-thinking society, our high degree of specialization, and perhaps partly due to our often fragmented approaches to funding and organizing community services.

The formative years of early childhood serve as a beginning point for significant impact to be made on our society's value system. We need to have a greater appreciation for the many "abilities" of our fellow citizen. The more we can influence young impressionable minds about these virtues, the more likely it is that our society will be more accepting of individuals with disabilities, including when they outgrow the "cute and cuddly" stages of their lives. These thoughts support reinforcing discussions regarding three additional QOL principles forwarded by the national study.

1. QOL is largely a social phenomenon and primarily a product of interaction with others. This requires a "social ecological" definition of QOL for the individual that incorporates the QOL of significant others in the setting.

2. QOL is the product of individuals with disabilities meeting their basic needs while fulfilling their responsibilities in community settings (family, recreation, school and work). Individuals who are able to meet their basic needs while fulfilling responsibilities in ways that are satisfactory to themselves and to significant others in the setting are more likely to experience a high quality of life and;

3. QOL is a matter of consumer rather than professional definition. QOL issues should be defined by consumers and other citizens rather than by professionals in the field. Ultimately it is how the individual perceives and evaluates his or her own situation, rather than how others perceive it, that determines the QOL he or she experiences.

A dear friend of mine, an adult living independently in New York City, was born with a disability and at the age of three institutionalized at Willowbrook State

School on Staten Island, New York. He spent 18 years of his life in the institution. He sometimes finds it difficult to describe the periods of horrid conditions and the total lack of QOL he experienced while an "inmate" at the state run facility. Sometimes his memories are visibly agonizing. He vividly remembers the pain of being separated from his family (age 3), the most vivid of all his memories. He recalls constant physical pain all over his body, due to chronic illnesses, hypersensitivity to touch — perhaps due to lack of nurturance, cuddling and a sense of personal security. He recalls screaming a lot but doesn't remember much relief. When older he remembers physical abuse and neglect. All of these memories are counter to what he desires and seeks today z — a quality of life as defined by him.

Currently an influential and outspoken advocate, he exemplifies all the positive things that have been said about defining QOL and works toward assuring that citizens with disabilities throughout the country have the opportunities to experience it.

He summarizes the essentials of QOL as: having choices; having things to do that are important to you; supporting oneself if possible; living in a nice environment; having friends and people in the community that provide support and happiness; being able to relax, smile and just have a good time.

Recalling his early years, my friend regrets having missed many of the simple things in life, some of the basics as we attempt to further define QOL for young children and their families. Hugging, individual care, sitting on Mom or Dad's lap, playing, laughing. Simple things, individually and family defined.

These early experiences and the essentials described in the previous paragraph are but a few of the things we must assure for all our citizens with and without disabilities. We must assure basic physical comfort as best we can and we must assure that our family units are viewed holistically. We have before us the opportunity to make QOL an important component in the lives of our youngest citizens. If done well, they will be recipients of a lifelong and valued gift.

## References

Public Law 99-457, Federal Register, October 8, 1986: *Handicapped Infants, Toddlers, and Preschoolers,* Parts H and B, 99th U.S. Congress, Washington, D.C..

20 USC Chapter 33, Public Law 102-119, Federal Register: October, 1992: *Individuals with Disabilities Education Act (IDEA),* 102nd U.S. Congress, Washington, D.C..

Tucker, B., Goldstein, B. (1991). Legal Rights of Persons with Disabilities: An Analysis of Federal Law. *Disabled Newborns.*. Horsham, PA: LRP Publications.

Goode, D. *Discussing Quality of Life: The Process and Findings of the Work Group on Quality of Life for Persons with Disabilities.* Mental Retardation Institute, Valhalla, N.Y., December, 1988.

Moses, K. *Notes on Shattered Dreams and Growth: Loss and the Art of Grief Counselling.* Evanston, IL: Resource Networks Inc.

# 17 • Quality of Life at School

Seamus Hegarty, Deputy Director
National Foundation for Educational Research
in England & Wales, Berkshire, England

Scholarly interest in quality of life (QOL) is a relatively recent phenomenon. A familiar concept in everyday life and in literature, QOL is now being recognized as an important variable in the study of individual well-being and distress. The QOL movement represents a broadening out of the concepts of well-being from an individualistic approach to include a wider range of factors including the properties of neighborhoods and societies.

Following the pioneering work of Lehman (1983) on adults with a history of psychiatric hospitalization, much of the work on QOL has focused on the QOL for people with disabilities or those with long-term needs for rehabilitation or care (Orford, 1992). In particular, quality of life has become an important concept in services for people with disabilities and learning difficulties in recent years. Goode (1992) and others have documented a proliferation of initiatives in the United States and in European countries. These initiatives are almost all concerned with adults, with the virtual exclusion of children and young people.

It is striking how little attention has been paid to quality of life in schools. School climate is regularly cited as an important variable in school improvement studies, but there has been very little empirical investigation of it. Epstein and McPartland (1976) drew attention to this nearly twenty years ago, suggesting that one reason for the neglect was the absence of an appropriate instrument for measuring student perceptions of schooling. Accordingly, they developed a Quality of School Life Scale, defined in terms of three dimensions of student reaction: satisfaction with the school in general, commitment to school work, and attitudes to teachers. Despite the availability of this instrument, which combines face validity with adequate psychometric characteristics, very few studies of quality of school life have been conducted in the intervening period, so far as can be ascertained from bibliographic searches, practically none that bear on the situation of the student with special educational needs.

There seem to be two broad sets of reasons for this state of affairs. The first has to do with the near-universal notion of schooling as primarily a preparation for adult life. This was starkly illustrated by a UNESCO survey of special education policies at the national level conducted in 1986-87. Out of fifty eight countries providing information on the aims of schooling, many stressed the importance of school as a preparation for adult life, but only one — Ireland — had an explicit objective that children with disabilities should 'lead full lives as children' (UNESCO, 1988). If schooling is not perceived as an important time in its own right, then quality of life at school becomes a marginal concept and policy considerations that might flow from it have a low priority.

There is a countervailing consideration, of course. While children and young people are minors in law and considered to be in the anteroom of life, in many countries they are indulged to the extent that would have been unheard of in times past. This holds true of countries like China where the enforcement of one-child per-family policies has, according to some commentators, led to the emergence of a generation of "little emperors," as well as of Western societies where affluent sub-cultures confer high levels of autonomy and near-adult spending power on their (few) offspring. The significant factor, however, is the extent to which these countervailing attitudes transfer to schooling. The evidence is that, by and large, they have not done so. Indeed, the experience of upper secondary schools in countries like France and Japan, where competition for post-school opportunities is unremitting, would point to an intensification of schooling as a preparation for life.

The second set of reasons for the absence of quality of life issues from education debates has to do with the fact that educational reform has been driven by its own distinctive imperatives. Where key stimuli for change in services for adults with disabilities have been matters like consumer dissatisfaction and public reports on the impoverished life situations of individuals, educational reform has been driven more by concerns over school efficiency, student achievement levels and the extent to which schools are preparing young people for adult life. This has meant a focus on system factors such as school organization and management, curriculum reform and staff development. School reform is on the agenda in very many countries now, and schools are subject to a host of policy initiatives designed to improve efficiency. To the extent that these revolve around structural matters, less attention is paid to the individual's experience of schooling, and quality of life issues remain at best a peripheral policy concern.

Here too there are some countervailing considerations. Not all students have a happy time at school. Some are deeply unhappy as the sporadic reports of abuse at residential schools and the rather more regular incidence of bullying at all schools testify. When such reports puncture complacency, various policy options with a QOL dimension are likely even if quality of life is not mentioned explicitly. Examples include setting up early warning systems, refining pastoral care and breaking up big schools into smaller management units.

A further reason why quality of life has received so little attention may relate to the perceived frivolousness associated with it. Once children are past the early years, schools do not set much store by the element of play in learning, any more than they attach great importance to being permeated with a sense of fun. This is in spite of the known efficiency of interactive science museums and exploratoria, the power of satire and comedy generally to generate new insights and communicate them to diverse audiences, and the practice of individual teachers whose lessons are simultaneously fun-filled and effective. Schools celebrate the poets for gathering rosebuds or being transfixed at the sight of daffodils fluttering and dancing in the breeze. They do not encourage students to emulate them. Living in the moment has had a bad press, with far more attention being given to the irresponsibility that may be associated with it than to the intensity of the experience, insight and commitment it can generate.

The fact that educators have not paid explicit attention to quality of life does not necessarily mean they fail to have regard for its intrinsic elements in their practice, or that quality of life issues do not have relevance for schools. Before examining quality of life issues in special education, it is necessary to look at definitions of quality of life and, in particular, investigate to what extent the fundamental concepts may need to be modified when applied to education.

## Key Concepts of QOL

At one level quality of life is a familiar concept. In everyday parlance, having a good quality of life implies certain freedoms plus various more positive characteristics. The freedoms are sometimes articulated in negative terms — freedom from fear of physical suffering, loneliness or substance dependence. What will be uppermost in individuals' minds depends on their life situations: for millions of people freedom from hunger is the essence of a good life. For many others regular eating is so much a norm that hunger and its avoidance barely enter consciousness. Likewise, the positive characteristics seen as important to individuals relate to their situations and, in particular, to their value systems. They are likely to include, in varying orders of priority, good health, satisfying interpersonal relationships, reasonable income, cultural enrichment, learning and intellectual stimulation, personal security, sexual fulfillment, interesting work, leisure time and the resources to occupy it, personal development and the power to make choices.

While quality of life may be a familiar concept, it is clearly far from a simple one. It has many facets, and the relative importance of each varies not merely from one society to another but also from one individual to the next. Where systematic inquiry or policy articulation is concerned, there are major problems of measurement. The different facets do not lend themselves to ready quantification, nor is it clear how to weight them in relation to each other.

The different indicators used to quantify quality of life for research purposes have been grouped into three areas: personal characteristics (e.g., marital status, educational level); objective indicators (e.g., use of health care, employment status, income level); and subjective indicators (e.g., satisfaction with personal safety, health satisfaction). Regression studies of both general population data (Andrews & Withey, 1976; Campbell, Converse & Rodgers, 1976) and data based on adults in receipt of psychiatric care (Lehman, Ward & Linn, 1982) have found that subjective indicators have the strongest association with global well-being and personal characteristics the weakest, with objective indicators occupying an intermediate position.

The literature on quality of life in relation to developmental disabilities has produced numerous definitions. The National Institute for Disability and Rehabilitation Research (NIDRR n.d) identified four types of QOL definitions: implicit definitions (for example, assuming that normalization means better quality of life); operational definitions (based upon research methodology); literary and rational definitions (explicitly based upon values and beliefs); and unintentional definitions (reflecting implicit values and beliefs). Increasingly, it is recognized that the different elements of quality of life are interrelated and that both policy and measurement must take into account the holistic nature of individuals. The various papers in this volume elaborate these definitions in the context of services for adults with disabilities and bring out their complexities in practice.

## Quality of Life In Schooling

A further level of complexity arises when we turn to schooling. Where quality of life is a major objective of services for adults with disabilities, within schooling it can have a low priority or indeed be regarded as marginal. The aims of schooling are generally seen as twofold: to develop children's potential in various domains- academic, moral, physical, social; and to equip them for a productive and fulfilled life as adults. These aims shape the common perception of schools and determine how they are evaluated. By and large, they leave out of consideration the extent to which schooling is an important theme in its own right. To that extent quality of school life is of minor importance. Indeed, it risks being

rejected as irrelevant or a distraction from the school's 'real' tasks of developing potential and preparing young people for adult life.

This is unfortunate on several accounts. The traditional aims of schooling are of course important, but a proper regard for the intrinsic value of school days is also important. This can be viewed from a number of perspectives: schooling occupies a substantial amount of time — ten to fifteen years — and it devalues children and young people if it is not accorded an intrinsic worth: Endorsing the intrinsic value of schooling provides a corrective to the instrumental view of education — currently very widespread — which results from an excessive emphasis on schooling as preparation for adult life. Schools that attend to students' quality of life may well be more effective in achieving the traditional aims of schooling anyway.

Quality of school life takes on a particular resonance in the case of young people who have a limited life expectancy. Few would argue that they should not be educated. It would be crass, however, to see their education primarily in terms of preparation for later life. If the schooling they are offered does not each day enrich their present lives and add to its quality, what purpose does it serve?

If it is accepted that schooling is an important time in its own right, then the concept of quality of children's experience of schooling becomes important. This provides a context for examining quality of life issues in the school context.

How would we characterize a school offering a high quality of life to its students? There can be no hard-and-fast answers to this since quality of life is not an absolute. It depends on opportunities, perceptions and values and, in a school context, must take into account students' ages and stages of development. A key aspect of QOL in an inner-city school might be irrelevant in a rural school, and vice-versa.

It would be a mistake therefore to expect a checklist whereby an external evaluator could come to a school and assign it a score on a rating scale. There are underlying principles, however, that inform the practice of schools offering students a good quality of life. The way in which these principles are realized in practice will vary greatly but that does not negate their significance.

What follows then is a tentative effort to set out these principles. It is proposed that a school offering its students a high quality of life would:

- Ensure that all students experience meaningful challenges across the entire range of the curriculum. This may not be what students would regard as enhancing their quality of life! However, apart from the fact that school is not a holiday camp, children need stimulation and finely graded challenges not only to grow and develop but also to escape the *ennui* which is so inimical to the enjoyment of life. Gauging the challenges to students is a significant task for schools: students must be sufficiently stimulated to be engaged by them but should not suffer undue pressure or inhibiting anxiety. This is probably more important for students with learning difficulties than for others, however much more difficult it may be to do so.

- Create an environment where students have fun and enjoy school. This is not in opposition to the preceding requirement or subsequent ones where the work ethic looms large. Schools do not have to offer a laugh a minute but serious endeavor is not synonymous with dullness. If schooling really is viewed as an important time in its own right, students must feel personally engaged in what they do and derive enjoyment from it.

- Ensure that all students, regardless of their levels of ability, experience positive achievements. The demotivating effects of repeated failure have been regularly documented. It behooves schools to construct individual students' learning programs around success rather than failure. Some failure is inevitable of course and it is important that young people learn to cope with the experience of failure and can move forward from it.

- Ensure that all students maintain and enhance their curiosity and sense of wonder about the world. Children do not start off cynical or apathetic — their exuberant enthusiasm is one of the joys of being with small children — yet both qualities are all too characteristic of adults. Clearly, something happens along the way. Schooling is not the only factor but it is a major one. Schools are a major influence on children in their formative years and can be decisive in determining whether or not young people develop questioning, outgoing attitudes to life.

- Provide as much autonomy as possible for all students. This is not to advocate a free-for-all but to reject needless restrictions and to create space for students to exercise responsible choices. This entails risks of freedom but is not possible otherwise. In the case of students with severe learning difficulties there is a difficult balance to be found between facilitating them in real choices and making the choices for them.

- Ensure that every student experience a growing sense of self-worth. For schools driven by competitive ideologies this is a particular challenge. If they are not to espouse a weakest-to-the-wall philosophy, they must respond creatively to this challenge and find ways of celebrating achievements by every student.

- Provide a framework where constructive personal relationships — student to student and student to adult — are the norm and friendships blossom.

- Provide an environment where students are free from physical and moral danger. Sadly, not all schools are safe places and some find the greatest difficulty in discharging their duty of protection. The negatives are all too familiar, physical and emotional bullying, being made objects of ridicule by teachers, physical and sexual abuse, being drawn into drug use and other substance dependence. The presence of any of these is not consonant with having a good quality of life, and schools must take all possible means to eliminate them.

When students with disabilities attend regular schools, all of the above apply to them just as much as to other students, and constitute a stringent test of how well the school is including students with disabilities in its activities. Implementing these principles may be more difficult in their case but that does not remove the responsibility. Just as schools have to take particular steps to ensure that students with disabilities have full curricular access, special measures may be required to ensure that they enjoy as good a quality of life at school as their peers.

There are other considerations specific to students with disabilities. These are generally implicit in the broader criteria applying to all students but there is advantage in setting them out explicitly. Thus, a school concerned to provide a good quality of life for all students would:

- Ensure adequate mobility and daily living arrangements for students with disabilities. For wheelchair users this can mean providing ramps, widening doorways, adapting toilets and reorganizing classroom furniture. For students with visual impairments it can mean clarifying routeways through the school, eliminating unnecessary movement and arranging for the transport of heavy items of equipment. For many students it can mean rethinking the pattern of student movement around the school; the hurly-burly of thronged corridors is a strain for some students and measures taken to reduce needless movement between lessons can improve quality of life.

- Facilitate communication by students with disabilities and maximize their access to the common curriculum. For students with a hearing impairment this can mean installing an induction loop in classrooms and providing signing interpreters. For students with motor control problems it can mean providing adapted keyboards linked to appropriate computer facilities. For many students it can mean adapting curriculum materials (and teaching approach) so that the mode of communication does not inhibit access to the curriculum.

- Ensure that students with disabilities are neither singled out unduly nor disregarded. Students with disabilities create particular challenges for schools; it is important that these challenges are recognized and responded to. Inevitably, this means some special treatment but it should be no more than necessary and not extend to all areas of experience at school. Likewise, facilities and procedures available to the main student body should be accessible in real terms to them also.

The principles set out here are germane to the aims of schooling more generally, although the interplay between the two domains is complex. In the case of some, the relationship is straightforward, with any differences simply reflecting differences in perspectives. Take for instance the effort to provide meaningful curriculum challenges. As well as being conducive to quality of life at school, it is also likely to develop students' individual potential and help prepare them for adult life. In other cases, there can be a tension between the two sets of aims. For example, it could be argued that young people need experience of neg-ative situations, both external danger and personal failures and disappointments, in the supportive frameworks of childhood and schooling in order to equip them for the big wide world. Such considerations moderate the imperatives of the quality of life approach — the traditional aims of schooling are important — but they do not negate them. While such tensions arise in practice, the need is to work out a synthesis that is informed by the relevant underlying principles but rooted in the practical case.

## Putting QOL on the School Agenda

The absence of an explicit literature on quality of life in schools should not be taken to mean the schools have had no concern with it or that no progress has been made. Some of the features set out above as characteristic of schools offering a good quality of life have been the subject of research investigation and policy. For example, a good deal is known about curriculum differentiation and how to match learning experiences to the learning situation of individual students. Likewise, the importance of ensuring that all students experience success is well recognized and some sound educational practice has been built on this recognition. Similar observations could be made about several of the other features.

However, practices do not always match up to the ideal. Many students struggle with inappropriate learning tasks and experience all-too-regular failure. This is probably related to matters such as teacher competence and attitudes, and to structural features such as class size and school organization, rather than to the limitations in our understanding of how these core central school processes work.

Different considerations are raised by other areas such as bullying. This too has been the subject of research investigations and numerous policy initiatives, with the result that we know a certain amount about it and schools have access to a repertoire of approaches to tackling the problem. All the same, there are gaps in our understanding of bullying and why it occurs, and the incidence of bullying in schools remains at distressingly high levels.

A third type of consideration is forced by other areas where our present understanding is limited and the prime need is to build up this understanding so that practical initiatives are well founded. Examples here include finding authentic ways of celebrating achievements by every student in a competitive environment, facilitating real autonomy for students with limited powers of understanding and communication, and integrating students with extreme and marked disabilities into the social fabric of the school.

The upshot of all this is that action has to be taken at different levels in order to put quality of life on the school agenda. There must be a commitment to doing so and a conviction that schools have a legitimate concern with the present moment as well as the responsibility to prepare students for later life. Given that, the requisite action falls under three broad headings:

1.  Where there is a body of relevant knowledge, apply it. This may well be easier to say than to do, as in the examples above. It may be necessary to bring about structural reform in school systems or to change teachers' attitudes

and enhance their professional skills. Effecting such changes can be difficult and can require a prolonged time scale but, conceptually at least, the task requirement is clear: establish what is known about achieving the different elements that make up quality of life in schools and devise implementation strategies accordingly.

2.  Where there is partial knowledge about an area relevant to quality of life, build up this knowledge and test it out in different situations. As in the case of bullying cited above, this calls for a mixture of research investigation to deepen our understanding of the phenomenon and initiatives in schools which are evaluated in order to assess their relevance to practice.

3.  Where knowledge of a relevant area is scanty or non-existent, investigate the area so as to build up an adequate understanding. This will facilitate the planning of practical initiatives to ensure they are well founded.

## Conclusion

Quality of life has received little explicit attention in schools. This is true both of students with disabilities and other students. Quality of school life, however, has many facets, and some of these have been the subject of research investigation and policy concern in other contexts. This points the way ahead as a mixture of capitalizing on existing knowledge and experience and initiating new inquiries as necessary.

The benefits of importing an explicit consideration of quality of school life in this way are considerable. Apart from helping to humanize schools and acting as a corrective to the prevailing instrumentalism in education, it could re-focus the school effectiveness debate, sharpen research questions on student perceptions of schooling and generate additional ways of evaluating school performance. So far as students with disabilities and special needs are concerned, it would bring an additional perspective to research on matters as diverse as relationships between pupils with severe communication problems with their peers, and the development of autonomy by students with severe learning and communication difficulties. Above all, it would extend the notion of inclusive schooling to the whole-school reform that has to underpin it by adding a further layer of planning, program implementation and evaluation that would have a particular resonance for students with special educational needs.

## References

Andrews, F. & Withey, S. (1976). *Social Indicators of Well-Being*. New York: Plenum Press.

Campbell, A., Converse, P., & Rodgers, W. (1976). *The Quality of American Life: Perceptions, Evaluations, and Satisfactions*. New York: Russell Sage Foundation.

Epstein, J. & McPartland, J. (1976). The concept and measurement of the quality of school life. *American Educational Research Journal* 13 (1), 15-30.

Goode, D. (1992, n.p.) *Quality of life policy: some issues and implications of a generic social policy concept for people with developmental disabilities*. Paper presented at the American Association on Mental Retardation national meetings, May, 1992, Washington, D.C.

Lehman, A. (1983). *The well-being of chronic mental patients: assessing their quality of life*. Archive of General Psychiatry 40, 369-373.

National Institute on Disability and Rehabilitation Research (n.d.) *Quality of Life Research in Rehabilitation*, Rehabilitation Brief XI (No.1).

Orford, J. (1992). *Community Psychology: Theory and Practice*, Chichester: Wiley.

UNESCO (1988). *Review of the Present Situation in Special Education*. Paris, UNESCO.

# 18• Training Staff on Quality of Life Issues

Philip H. Levy, Joel M. Levy,
and Perry Samowitz,Young Adult Institute, N.Y.C.

This chapter reflects how a large private, non-profit agency has attempted to improve the quality of life (QOL) for people with developmental disabilities through a concerted and coordinated effort, which includes staff training and development. While this article focuses on staff development and training, the motivating tenets and principles of any organization usually begin with its philosophy and mission and how the upper management team enables both staff and people with developmental disabilities to fully participate in the decision- making process facilitating a sense of empowerment and ownership. Thus, while staff training will be reviewed at length, it is important to note that the guiding principles of an organization must be the foundation for and also support what is being trained.

At the Young Adult Institute (YAI), we strongly believe that the quality of life for people with developmental disabilities is our number one priority. The lifestyle of the individuals we serve and our commitment to the actualizing their human potential are our primary focus and the mission of the organization. How this mission is

translated into concrete actions by the staff will be discussed, but without a clear and concise mission statement to create a framework for our initiatives, there could not be properly trained staff.

This chapter discusses YAI's approach to staff training and development. Before reviewing the training designs, we first provide an historical context for the organization. The Young Adult Institute was started in 1957 by a group of concerned parents whose young adults and children were mentally retarded/developmentally disabled. The parents, with a few professionals, helped to find a venue for their children where they could better develop their abilities in a supportive community based environment. The primary issue for these young adults was isolation. Most reported feeling isolated in their communities and desired to meet people with whom they could better relate, socialize, make friends and for some, marry. In addition, they wanted to experience a sense of productivity. It is interesting to note that in 1957, when the agency was started, the families felt that their children would have difficulties in forming friendships with so-called "normal" young adults. The parents attempted to deal with their children's isolation through contacts among people with similar disabilities. This is not to say that people with developmental disabilities cannot form loving and caring relationships with people who are of normal intelligence, but if an individual truly has a choice of the type of people they want to associate with, this should always be respected.

YAI continued as a very small organization, basically providing a social network for people with developmental disabilities. By 1970, however, the families were aging and the former young adults were now entering their 30's. The families feared that their now-adult children would not have an appropriate home to live in nor the requisite supports if they should die. In 1970, in New York state, there were no community residences, only large institutions, which were definitely not an acceptable alternative for these families. In 1971, YAI opened one of the first group homes in New York state for 13 individuals with developmental disabilities. This was a unique opportunity for these individuals to begin the adult transition of "breaking away" (separation) from their families of origin and commencing more independent life as participants in the "real world." It also, obviously, gave great peace of mind to their families regarding their futures.

Soon after, the Willowbrook scandal surfaced and the Willowbrook consent decree was issued, mandating that citizens of New York State who were wrongly institutionalized and isolated from their communities, be offered housing in their communities of origin. In response to the requests of government and individual families,

YAI proceeded to open numerous group homes in varied socio-economic and cultural communities in New York City and the suburbs of Westchester County & Long Island. Other services were offered including numerous community and family services, day treatment, employment programs, and pre-school and early intervention services. Today, YAI services are based upon the principles of normalization and the least restrictive environment, focused on the goals of independence, individualization, integration and productivity. YAI is now considered one of the leaders in the field of developmental and learning disabilities, providing services daily for over 3,000 people with disabilities in 80 award-winning community-based programs through a staff of approximately 1,500 professionals.

As stated earlier, the mission of the organization is to treat people with disabilities as a person first, always respecting their right to choose and to make decisions that have impact on their lives. This organizational credo, however, would just be words if staff were not properly trained how to implement the mission. In addition to the "people first" concept, discussed elsewhere in this volume, the agency also strongly adheres to the principles of full participation for all citizens and viewing each person as one with abilities as well as special needs, rather than focussing primarily on disabilities. These tenets are reitrated as the basis for the training discussed in this chapter.

Before elaborating on how we train our staff, it is important to note who the people are that we serve. We are now serving people of all ages. We operate early intervention and infant stimulation programs, preschools, in-home respite services for parents, camping programs which are mainstreamed with other children, a full array of adult services (e.g., residential, clinical, vocational training, job placement, recreation, etc.), and programs for our senior citizens. We provide services for people of all different functioning levels, many of whom are multiply disabled. The issue of quality of life for people who have profound mental retardation is very interesting and we have taken great strides toward training our staff in how to help provide a higher quality of life for these individuals, having an appropriate quality of life means being able to participate in decisions that influence one's life and to be empowered to make choices, as we discuss later.

The selection of staff is as important as the training of staff and definitely needs to be reviewed. At YAI, we have a very structured process for hiring staff. Trained personnel specialists meet with prospective employees in small groups, first looking for the qualities of the individual that would seemingly best suit the needs and desires of the people for whom we provide services. If the above stated principles relating to quality of life are to be adhered to, the program participants should have input to the selection process as they will be spending a great deal of time with the staff member. The prospective candidates who are selected from the small groups are asked to visit a YAI program where they will meet the participants and other staff. These persons are encouraged to provide reactions to the applicant. Participants able to verbally provide feedback become part of the decision-making process in selecting staff. If the participants are nonverbal, the staff solicits their reactions through other means of

communication, and if they're not able to clearly give a choice, the staff looks for participants to enjoy the company of the prospective employees. This process is critical.

The selection process usually requires a number of visits before staff are hired. Due to this rather extensive selection process, the staff at YAI tend to be, as a group, dedicated, caring people. They also have very varied educational skills and more importantly, have varied backgrounds in the field of Mental retardation and developmental disabilities (MR/DD). We assume that all staff need to be thoroughly trained, regardless of their educational or work experiences, because we want them to adhere to our service principles.

Perhaps the most difficult dilemma in training staff presents itself initially when staff are hired. It is one of the most difficult issues to change throughout the careers of our staff. There tends to be an US vs. THEM syndrome, a carryover from the environment and social mores of our culture. No matter how much we, in the field, proselytize about people with MR/DD being the same as us, society does not view their sameness, but rather focuses on their differences. Even the name disabled, has a negative connotation, meaning people who cannot do for themselves. We've often thought that terminology such as people who are differently abled, which focuses more on abilities rather than disabilities, would be much preferred. The labeling is just a way of communicating what is really felt by people in the so-called normal population towards the so-called disabled population. And all of us, including our staff, are products of that environment and culture. Consequently, perhaps the most important training need is to continually focus on how these perceived differences affect the lives of the people with whom we work. These are matters of values, personal convictions and beliefs, and are not easily changed, but must be a focus.

At YAI, newly hired staff are required to attend an orientation. This orientation begins with the philosophy of the organization, which begins with the importance of treating people with disabilities as people first, recognizing their unique abilities and needs. Our new staff, (including all levels of managers, direct care staff, clinicians, etc.) attend these sessions together and are challenged to understand that while this philosophy makes sense, it might be very challenging for them to actualize on the job. Examples are offered detailing how we subtly treat people with disabilities in a way that we would not want to be treated. An example used in orientation, which is seen continuously throughout the agency, is when staff might be busy writing a report and a program participant walks in and requires some form of interaction. We have observed that staff will wave them away, saying "not now", even saying, "please don't interrupt me." When we challenge staff to see how they would feel if someone treated them that way, they said that they would find it rude, yet it would seem to be "acceptable" to treat people with disabilities that way. Even the person playing the staff (we use role playing in our training sessions) was asked if they noticed that the person playing the participant felt "put-down." Often the staff did not notice, just saying that the person appeared interested in what they were saying. It's these types of everyday interactions that often have great impact on the self-image and concept of the individuals with whom we work. We tell staff a quote from an old Woody Guthrie verse, that "there are those people that brings you up and those people that brings you down" and part of our responsibility in this field is to support and encourage the individuals whom we serve, and not to "bring them down" through demeaning interactions with them.

Another training example of how we teach quality of life is given in our YAI unit titled "Interacting with People who have Severe/Moderate Mental Retardation." Often our staff need to accompany participants to a doctor.

Traditionally, the doctor will ask pointed questions of the staff, totally ignoring the individual who requires the doctor's service. In role plays, we ask the staff how they felt portraying the individual who's being ignored and again the issue of "feeling put-down" is discussed. We discuss strategies for inclusion, based on the ability level of the individual. How could the staff best ensure that the doctor will speak with the participant; It was suggested that the staff who accompany the participant stand or sit behind the individual so that the doctor has to look at that person (the patient) and direct questions towards him/her. The staff can then serve as a facilitator, helping the person in his/her interaction with the doctor.

An example of how this training affects the lives of the individuals was observed at one of our programs when a staff member was finishing a report. A participant walked in. After saying hello, he began to try to say a few words about what he wanted, even though he had limited verbal skills. Overheard in the background was whispering from a staff person who was out of sight, supporting the individual, helping the individual to better communicate. The individual, through some prompting, was able to ask for the recycling box and was then complimented on his noble efforts to save the environment. The participant then smiled because he was now a productive member of society, and to the best of his ability, was able to participate.

In a subsequent section of the training unit on interactions, we carefully delineate the role of the staff and how this role and its responsibilities impact on the quality of life for the individuals whom we serve. We specifically emphasize that in all the various roles that are assumed by our staff, we recommend that the roles are assumed from an adult to adult position rather than from a parent to child position. Unfortunately, all too often, adults who have developmental disabilities are viewed as perpetual children and staff, by their actions, inadvertently reinforce that role. We have staff examine the roles they tend to play in the lives of the people whom they serve including helping to advocate, negotiate, protect and limit set, teach, be a role model, be a counselor, and just be a fellow human being. We have the staff role play various scenarios in each of the above roles, first showing the non-recommended or "parent to child" way of assuming these roles and then having the staff model the more "adult to adult" style of relating. An example might be two roommates having an argument with the staff helping to mediate. The staff's role is not to totally take charge of the situation and to assume a parental posture. Rather, the desired role is to enable the individuals concerned to listen better to each other and to work on the problem for mutual benefit and need. Often, our partic-

ipants do not have the skill of negotiating. This skill can be taught and enhanced rather than having the staff assume the role of negotiator and hence, keeping the participant in a dependent mode. Another example might be where a few staff and program participants are sitting together on a couch relaxing. Often, the staff will ask the participant numerous questions about their day but might not share their own stories and various scenarios from their life. It is important to recognize that we're all people and that a normal interaction means a give and take from both sides.

The next area of training relates to the very sensitive topic of human rights. All too often, in the name of effective programming or effective treatment, the rights of people with mental retardation and other developmental disabilities are violated, usually in subtle ways. At YAI, we have developed a video training program teaching our staff how to assess 'rights' situations and how to better understand what issues must be examined when dealing with 'rights' situations. For example, a very typical situation occurs when a participant's room is in a so-called messy state. Various staff, who have their own inherent values about cleanliness, as well as the responsibility to ensure a clean, well organized environment, might choose to discuss or not discuss the issue of the messy room with the participant. The participant often gets confused from mixed messages. In response, staff sometimes get punitive. Yet, if someone walked into our room and demanded that we clean it, as adults, we would probably react in a rather defensive manner, and we would probably stand up for ourselves. We suggest to our staff that this is this person's room and that, while no one wants to see the person live in a messy or even filthy condition, to automatically step in and demand that someone clean the room is not treating someone with the respect and dignity that we all demand for ourselves. Rather, we suggest that staff empower the individual by asking that person what they consider to be messy and what they consider to be neat and have them show us examples of both. At that point we can take a picture of their "neat" room and their "messy" room. If we are concerned that the room is getting a little messy and we want to discuss it with the individual, we could ask the person to look at the pictures they agreed upon and ask them to see if the room is what they want according to what they considered to be appropriate or inappropriate for themselves. This enables the person to have much more impact and power on the decisions that affect their lives while also achieving our goal and satisfying our responsibilities as a staff member.

Another example concerns working with someone who has profound mental retardation. Often staff would automatically stop a person who has a profound functioning level from eating more food. The staff member might say the person may be getting overweight, that the food is not healthy for them, etc. This creates a dilemma because most of us would take strong exception to having anybody take our food away from us if we want seconds, even if we're a little overweight, as is most of the population. Obviously, if a participant is under doctor's orders and is very obese, and especially if he/she can not understand the issues, then staff might have to intervene. This intervention however should be done in a more dignified way, which might mean either not having extra portions in front of that individual or having less caloric foods which can be eaten for seconds. Disrespect for the individual, while it seems so obvious, is not always obvious to staff, It has been our experience that staff often revert back to the US vs. THEM syndrome. This causes basic inalienable rights to be violated all too frequently.

One particularly controversial topic regarding the rights of individuals is the issue of sexuality for people who are mentally retarded and developmentally disabled. The United States in general, is rather schizophrenic regarding the subject of sexuality. On the one hand our Puritan forefathers gave us the "Thou Shalt Not" message, which is still prevalent today. On the other hand, there are consistent messages not to follow this creed shown by "an almost anything goes" policy on T.V., newspapers, etc. It seems, however, that people who are mentally retarded/developmentally disabled tend to bear the brunt of this rather schizophrenic view of sexuality. All too often, they are held to standards they cannot meet and therefore are unfairly restricted from enjoying their own sexuality. At YAI, we feel strongly that sexuality is an integral part of the human being. We train our staff to view sexuality (not to be confused with sexual activity) as an inalienable right of the participants. We also strongly believe and train our staff that all people must be protected from harm, *abuse, and exploitation and must act responsibly according* to time and place. All sexual contact must be consensual, meaning that both parties agree to the act, and that either party can stop the act should they so desire. We do not believe that it is important for a person to understand every possible ramification or consequence of their action regarding sexuality, rather that they are adequately protected from harm, abuse, and exploitation. We run intensive staff training on sexuality and often staff will relate issues that concern them, and we often refer them to the agency policy. For example, we had a male participant who enjoyed dressing in female clothing. The staff were concerned and felt that the person's behavior was "wrong." We related to staff that this person has the right to their own sexual expression, but we do have obviously, a responsibility to best ensure that this person does not get harmed, abused, or exploited. The staff learned that their role was to educate as to the ramifications of his dress, stressing that people in his community might make fun of him and could possibly cause him physical harm. This person was of a high enough functioning level that, when he heard this information he used his own judgment of when he would choose to wear the female clothes (which were in his room). His rights were protected, while he was able to make a decision of what would be in his best interest.

In many of the chapters of this book, there is mention of issues of quality of life pertaining to the self-image of the individual. Many of the chapters talk about helping individuals with their emotional needs, because a more emotionally secure person will tend to have a higher quality of life. Due to numerous negative messages about being mentally retarded/developmentally disabled, many of our participants often have experienced much prejudice and antagonism either in school from other children, from the looks and comments of others in their community and by hearing words such as mentally retarded used as a slang for stupid or incapable. These emo-

tional bombardments have had impact on many of the people whom we serve. Therefore, at YAI, much staff training is geared toward counseling people. This cannot be overstated in terms of quality of life issues because when people are anxious or depressed, their quality of life suffers greatly.

We have developed two training modules for YAI staff, one on Individual Counseling, and the other on Group Counseling. We provide intensive staff training on individual counseling, particularly emphasizing the *reflect, probe, support, and advise* model. We have noticed that often our staff, when dealing with an emotional issue of a participant, will start offering advice very quickly and freely, not really listening to what the person needs or wants. For example, a participant might say that she was upset because someone made fun of her at the supermarket checkout line because she didn't have enough money to purchase the items she needed. Often the staff begins the counseling process by reminding her to take the right amount of money. The impact on the person with a developmental disability is to feel put-down and it reinforces the image of viewing her as a person who cannot think.

We teach the staff to first reflect back on the words of the person, saying "Oh, people laughed at you" and then asking, "what happened?" and gaining more of an understanding of what the person experienced. Next, a supportive statement is given, such as "Gee, I really feel bad *that happened to you* and made you feel bad. I'm sorry those people were insensitive. They should not have said those things to you." Then if needed or requested, advice can be given. When most of us are upset, the last thing we need is someone's advice. What we need more is listening and support from someone who cares about our problems. Our staff go through an intensive training program on individual counseling, which also includes how to deal with the cognitive limitations of the people they are working with by being as concrete as needed in the sessions and most importantly, enabling the person to make his/her own decision.

YAI also emphasizes the peer support counseling groups, based upon the work of Dr. Dan Tomasulo, who is a true pioneer in the field of group counseling for people with mental retardation and other developmental disabilities. By documenting the work of Dr. Tomasulo, we have developed a video training program for our staff. In the groups, the participants are taught how to support one another's emotional needs. An example of an issue that arose in a counseling group was a woman who was having problems with her balance and kept falling in her work site. She recently had stitches due to a rather severe fall. She related to the group that she was very frightened. Initially, the members of the group said "You should be more careful", probably repeating parental messages that they had heard before in their past which are relatively ineffective and even antagonistic. The issue is not her being more careful because she was careful, the issue was her being frightened over losing control of her body. Through the peer support model, the other participants are taught to double behind the person and talk about what the person is feeling, standing behind him/her with their hands on the shoulder of the person who is experiencing the problem. They then say, "I am feeling" and try to identify the feeling that the other person is experiencing at that moment, and

then asking the person if that's true. One of the participants stood behind the woman, put his arms on her and said, "I'm very frightened. Is that true"? She said "Yes" and started crying and then he said, "I am also very sad." And she started nodding her head. Another participant then sat in front of her and held her hand and said, "I'm sorry that you are feeling this way". She also responded by shaking her head up and down in a positive way. There was nothing that we could do to solve her problem at that moment other than maybe have her work in a less cluttered environment. However, the most important issue in addition to her safety, was her emotional well-being, which was secured by her receiving support not only from staff, but from her peer group. This is an important quality of life issue because the participants are learning how to nurture and give to others rather than always being a recipient.

The use of leisure time is a important part of our lives especially when our life tends to be unbalanced (i.e., we work too much and enjoy life too little). The people we work with are now entering the employment market and have busy days. But their leisure moments are also critical in terms of their quality of life. We are training staff to educate our participants about their leisure opportunities and allowing them to choose, based on a broader spectrum of activities, what they desire. For example, there was a time when all the participants went to camps, even when they were adults. In the United States, sleep away camps are typically for children and not for adults. At YAI, we started a Leisure Trax program which offers stimulating and often mainstreamed trips to various sites of interest around the country. The staff are taught how to provide real choice by presenting various places of interest in a way that can be best understood by the people we serve.

Staff are continuously trained that their role is to enable people with mental retardation/developmental disabilities to better enjoy themselves in new settings. Often, people with mental retardation/developmental disabilities do not seem to notice many subtle pleasures of life and do need staff to help bring the world a little closer to them. For instance, they may be out for a walk in the community. The staffperson might see an interesting store and ask participants what they see. The participants might then start mentioning what they see in the window of the store they would not have previously noticed. If a person is profoundly or severely retarded and cannot speak, they could point to different objects in the store and then go in and look, touch, and feel the objects to begin to appreciate the world around them. Usually, one can see that the participants are more enthusiastic, and are noticeably smiling on the trips when the staff are more interactive. Staff are trained to do as little as possible for the people in these stores in the community. For example, we train the staff that if someone is profoundly mentally retarded and does not understand the concept of money, that does not mean they have to stand there and rock back and forth while the staff pay for an item. Rather, the staff can hand the participant the money and that person can hand the money to the store clerk and even receive the change. Usually, what we notice is that they stop rocking when they are involved in an activity. We see huge smiles across their faces because they are now involved and feel they have value through their actions. The impor-

tance of training staff to notice these smiles is critical since they are signals these persons with whom they are interacting are enjoying the quality of these moments in their lives.

Another area of training is in the employment sector. YAI operates numerous employment training and placement programs and we spend much time training our staff on how to best help a trainee assimilate into the world of work. We train staff to enable the trainees to do as much as possible to secure their own job, including reviewing want ads, teaching them how to go on interviews and in general, respecting the self-esteem of the person while helping them to find a job. The staff are taught not to be judgmental regarding a person's initial outcome on a job, since they sometimes feel pressured to produce a high level of employment retention for their participants. Through our training, we constantly remind staff that often many of us did not have a positive experience on our first job and still became successful. Our participants have a right to change their minds about a job, to even fail on a job, to succeed the next time around, and to have a choice whether they want to continue working or not in that particular setting. It's often difficult for staff to accept, that the participant may not like their new work setting after the hard work in finding a job. An example which arose in a staff training session was that of an 18-year-old woman with a developmental disability who lived in the inner city and had found a job. The staff felt very proud and fulfilled but the woman called one day to say she was going to quit because she wanted to have a baby. The staff was devastated and felt that she was making the wrong decision. Through staff training, however, the staff realized that this woman had made a decision which she felt was in her best interest and made sense to her. Our job is to expose this woman to various options, and let her make a decision. We cannot assume that we always have the best answers for others. It is difficult at times to find the perfect job that our people want, but that is the reality for many people in the current work environment and it is important to share the frustrations as well as the successes. We have ongoing staff training where these very important issues are reviewed and when staff gain greater insights into what their role truly is, which is to help a person attain a higher quality of life, but not to take over a person's life!

A related but critical issue to those described above is the quality of work life for staff. YAI has a comprehensive personnel development program and a participatory management system which are designed to enhance a high quality of work life. Without these strategies, it would be unrealistic, or even impossible, for staff to promote quality of life among program participants. After all, how can unhappy workers help enhance the quality of life of those they serve? Thus, a paramount objective of YAI is to create an excellent environment for our staff where they are appreciated, valued, and nurtured and where the actual-ization of their potential is given priority.

In summary, at YAI the issue of quality of life is comprehensibly reviewed and emphasized. Quality of life includes enabling people to maintain as much control over their life as possible, helping them to meet their emotional needs, supporting them in times of need as well as at all other times of interactions, allowing people to be self-advocates, and teaching people to have control over their lives. It is a constant training need because often, as so-called "smarter" people, staff sometimes forget what the mission truly is and can revert back to that US vs. THEM syndrome. It is the job of any organization to constantly train staff and remind staff that we are all the same in many, many ways, and we are all looking for a higher quality of life whether we have a disability or not. Ultimately, we believe at YAI, that through this intensive staff training program, our participants have greatly benefitted and truly have a much more fulfilled life. It is not to say that our diligence should ever end because it cannot if we are to continue to achieve our objectives, but we feel we are moving in the right direction through the implementation of the principles stated here. Perhaps some day, people in general will look at a better quality of life for all the citizens of this country as the ultimate goal and we will not have to emphasize it so much with our staff.

## Notes

YAI: Building brighter futures for People with Disabilities through dignity, independence, individualization, inclusion, and productivity.

# 19• In Support of Research on Quality of Life, But Against QOL[1]

Steven J. Taylor
Professor of Special Education and
Director of the Center on Human Policy, Syracuse University

The first time I ever thought much about the concept of quality of life was during my first visits to a back ward at a large state institution for people with mental retardation in the early 1970s. It was difficult to put into words exactly what was so terribly wrong about the ward. Programming was substandard or non-existent, and residents had few opportunities to improve their skills. People lacked privacy, possessions, and personal amenities. Harsh treatment or even abuse were not uncommon. The environment and rhythms and routines of life were decidedly non-normalized. All of these things — and more — were wrong with the ward. The concept of quality of life seemed to capture what was missing there and highlighted the dismal existence of people living on the ward.

The increasing attention devoted to quality of life internationally, evidenced by the contributions in this volume, should be taken as a positive sign. The concept of quality of life provides a counter-balance to a narrow emphasis on behavioral outcomes, regulatory compliance, environmental design, and other features of programs and settings serving people with disabilities and restores the individual's subjective experience to the center of efforts to study or evaluate disability services. Yet, quality of life is not immune from the pitfalls characterizing other concepts applied to people with disabilities generally, and, specifically, those labelled mentally retarded.

This commentary takes the position that inquiries into quality of life should be encouraged, but that efforts to precisely define and measure the concept should be avoided.[2] In short, I argue in favor of research on quality of life, but against QOL.

*Quality of life is a useful sensitizing concept; QOL is a reification.* While there are many definitions of quality of life, the concept generally refers to a person's subjective experience of his or her life (Schalock, 1990, p.1). The concept is important precisely because it focuses attention on how the individual experiences the world. As applied to people with disabilities, the concept forces us to understand and respect what they feel about their lives. Since the perspectives and feelings of people with disabilities have often been ignored or dismissed, the importance of the concept of quality of life should be self-evident.

Quality of life is most meaningful as a sensitizing concept. Blumer (1969) made the distinction between sensitizing concepts and definitive concepts:

I think that thoughtful study shows conclusively that the concepts of our discipline are fundamentally sensitizing instruments. Hence, I call them "sensitizing concepts" and put them in contrast with definitive concepts.... A definitive concept refers precisely to what is common in a class of objects, by the aid of a clear definition in terms of attributes or fixed bench marks. This definition, or the bench marks, serve as a means of clearly identifying the individual instance of the class and the make-up of that instance that is covered by the concept. A sensitizing concept lacks the specification of attributes or bench marks and consequently it does not enable the user to move directly to the instance and its relevant content. Instead, it gives the user a general sense of reference and guidance in approaching empirical instances. Whereas definitive concepts provide prescriptions of what to see, sensitizing concepts merely suggest directions along which to look.

As a sensitizing concept, quality of life suggests a clear direction along which to look: the subjective experiences of people with disabilities.

In contrast to quality of life as a sensitizing concept, QOL is a definitive concept. Most researchers are not satisfied with merely "directions along which to look," a "general sense of reference," or "guidance in approaching empirical instances." Sensitizing concepts are a bit too mushy to be subjected to the rigorous instruments of science. So quality of life is operationally defined as QOL, complete with a set of precise and measurable indicators.

Since notions like the "good life" and "feelings of well being" do not lend themselves to precise measurement, they are replaced by variables that can be counted with precision and reliability. In the process, however, QOL becomes farther and farther removed from the concept it is intended to stand for.

There is nothing inherently wrong with operational definitions. Operational definitions enable us to pursue certain areas of inquiry that would otherwise be closed off to study. The problem arises when the operational definition is reified and the researcher confuses the social construct with the thing it is designed to represent. IQ is simply one way to define and measure intelligence; it is not the same as intelligence itself. Anyone trained in research should know this, but many researchers forget this simple fact when they make sweeping statements about people based on their test scores.

Goode (1992) warns against the "tyranny of quality" — the imposition of standards for people with disabilities that would be unacceptable for non-disabled persons. This danger is real, but only if the concept is defined in precise and measurable terms. When treated as a sensitizing concept or general sense of reference, it is difficult to imagine how quality of life could result in any form of tyranny. The tyranny of quality would be better described as the tyranny of QOL.

*Quality of life means something; QOL seems to mean everything.* The concept of quality of life has a clear, if imprecise meaning: feelings of well-being or "one's satisfaction with one's lot in life" and "inner sense of contentment or fulfillment with one's experience in the world" (Taylor & Bogdan, 1990, p. 34). Goode (1992) quotes a definition from the National Institute on Disability and Rehabilitation Research that provides a flavor of the concept: "the timbre of life as experienced subjectively; one's feelings about/evaluations of one's own life..." ( p.3). According to Goode (1992), Schalock identified three basic concepts underlying definitions of quality of life in the disability field: general feelings of well-being, opportunities to fulfill one's potential, and feelings of positive social involvement. Each of these definitions have face validity and popular appeal. Who could argue against any of these definitions?

In contrast to crisp and meaningful definitions of quality of life as a concept, operational definitions of QOL tend to be all-encompassing. A cursory review of the literature yields the following factors associated with QOL:

*Normalization or Social Role Valorization*
- Choice, personal control, empowerment, and self-advocacy
- Least restrictive environment
- Safety and security
- Social involvement, feelings of belonging, relationships with others, friendship networks
- Mental and physical health
- Integration and mainstreaming
- Income and financial security
- Skill attainment
- Family stability
- Contribution to others
- Acceptance by others
- Personal growth
- Basic human rights and freedoms

- Recreation
- Sexuality
- Environmental comfort and convenience
- Self-esteem

Anything that anyone has ever experienced as good seems to become part of the QOL equation. It's a bit like making soup with every possible food ingredient in order to accommodate everyones tastes and serving an inedible concoction. If QOL refers to everything, it refers to nothing.

Some commentators have argued that quality of life should replace normalization and related concepts as the standard for evaluating services in the 1990s. Perhaps the time will come when normalization will have outlived its usefulness (Bogdan & Taylor, 1987). But the contribution of normalization reflects the fact that it stands for something specific.[3] One can accept it or reject it or consider it along with competing values and principles. This is not the case with QOL. As Edgerton (1990) writes:

If individual choice is replaced by a "Quality of Life Quotient," the result will not only be absurd, it may be tragic as well. To declare that all people should enjoy a quality of life that includes safety, love, friendship, sexual expression, religious belief, personal growth, self-esteem, recreational options, or whatever else is thought to be desirable, may only represent a harmless, if rather vacuous, expression of values; but if taken as a template for action, such statements may create frustratingly unattainable expectations. (p. 150)

*Quality of life is lived and experienced; QOL*

*is superimposed on that experience.* Quality of life has no meaning apart from a person's subjective experience. It would be absurd to treat a concept having to do with the "good life" and "feelings of well being" as something objective and external to the individual. The person him- or herself is the one and only judge of his or her quality of life. Virtually every definition of quality of life recognizes the subjective nature of the concept, and most place primary emphasis on subjective feelings and experience (Goode, 1990; Schalock, 1990).

As an operational definition, QOL is designed to provide an objective measure of the subjective experience of quality of life. At its best, QOL is the researcher's rough approximation of the feelings and sentiments of other people. As various commentators (Goode, 1992; Taylor & Bogdan, 1990) have argued, the study of the subjective experience of quality of life poses a methodological challenge for many reasons: ordinary people do not usually think in terms of their quality of life and may have difficulty talking about it; different people have different expectations in evaluating their lives; people do not always give truthful answers to interview questions; and some people with mental retardation are unable to communicate through language. Of course, any research on people's internal thoughts and feelings poses similar problems, and a rough approximation is better than none at all, as long as it is acknowledged as such and not presented as a scientific measurement.

At its worst, QOL confuses people's subjective experience with the factors that influence that experience. Most QOL frameworks contain a mixture of subjective and objective indicators. For example, normal-ization is commonly cited as an objective quality of life indicator. One might justify normalization as a value position or argue that normalization is associated with quality of life. The former is a moral and philosophical question, and the latter is an empirical one; neither question can be resolved by definitional fiat. To operationally define QOL in terms of normalization not only begs the question of what settings and situations are conducive to quality of life, but distorts the nature of human experience. People can view and experience the same objective conditions of existence differently.

## Conclusion

While the quality of life of people with disabilities is a worthy area of inquiry, this must be pursued with common sense, modesty, an appreciation of the limitations of the scientific method, and a respect for how people themselves define their lives and situations. And it must be recognized that quality of life cannot be the final word on what constitutes a meaningful human existence.

The concept of quality of life has roots in the Western cultural emphasis on individualism. In Western cultures, the "good life" is thought of in terms of the individual's feelings about his or her life and circumstances. Other cultures might define the "good life" quite differently. For example, in some cultures, the idea of the "good life" could not be separated from members' moral responsibility to the society as a whole.

Even within Western cultures, the concept of quality of life is emphasized more for certain categories of people than for others. We usually examine people's quality of life when we suspect that it is lacking. As long as we have categories like disability and mental retardation and treat people differentially based on these categories, it is probably necessary to have concepts like normalization and quality of life. But few of us would want our obituaries to read that we had experienced normalization and a high quality of life during our time here.

We need more reflection on the philosophical implications of quality of life and less emphasis on how to measure it. How is the concept of quality of life related to our conceptions of disability? How does quality of life fit with concepts like morality, duty, and social responsibility. Should the lives of people with disabilities be judged not only by quality of life, but by civic virtue (O'Brien & Lyle O'Brien, 1993).

We should continue to discuss and debate the meaning of the "good life" for people with disabilities as with other members of our society. But the good life should not be reduced to the good life scale. Quality of life should not be reduced to QOL.

## Notes

[1] Preparation of this chapter was supported in part by the National Institute on Disability and Rehabilitation Research for the Research and Training Center on Community Integration through Cooperative Agreement No. H133B00003-90 awarded to the Center on Human Policy, Syracuse University. The opinions expressed herein are solely those of the author and no official endorsement by the U.S. Department of Education should be inferred.

[2] I am grateful to John O'Brien and Connie Lyle O'Brien (1993) for reminding me of the value of a polemic, a commentary intended to stimulate controversy. As O'Brien and Lyle O'Brien (1993) point out, "While this style has an honorable tradition in politics and philosophy, it is little used in the world of human services, where inquiry is mostly shaped by middle-of-the-road academic social science with its conventions of detached objectivity and quantification" (p. 3). This commentary is written as a polemic in order to draw attention to the dangers and pitfalls of many of the current efforts to study quality of life of people with disabilities. I contrast the concepts of quality of life and QOL as a vehicle for accomplishing this purpose. I do not believe that all of the current research and writing in this area succumbs to these dangers and pitfalls, but take the position that these pitfalls are real and should be acknowledged by those researching quality of life.

[3] I find normalization useful as a sensitizing concept. It can be argued that some formulations of normalization are all-encompassing and include factors that have little relevance to the concept itself. Like other concepts, normalization can be reified. To the extent that operational definitions of normalization reify the concept, the criticisms of QOL in this commentary apply.

# References

Blumer, H. (1969). *Symbolic interactionism: Perspective and method*. Englewood Cliffs, NJ: Prentice-Hall.

Bogdan, R., & Taylor, S. J. (1987). The next wave. In S. J. Taylor, D. Biklen, & J. Knoll (Eds.), *Community integration for people with severe disabilities* (pp. 209-213). New York: Teachers College Press.

Edgerton, R. B. (1990). Quality of life from a longitudinal research perspective. In R. L. Schalock (Ed.), *Quality of life: Perspectives and issues* (pp. 149-160). Washington, DC: American Association on Mental Retardation.

Goode, D. A. (1992). Quality of life policy: Some issues and implications of a generic social policy concept for people with developmental disabilities. Paper presented at the Annual Meeting of the American Association on Mental Retardation, New Orleans, May.

Goode, D. A. (1990). Thinking about and discussing quality of life. In R. L. Schalock (Ed.), *Quality of life: Perspectives and issues* (pp. 41-57). Washington, DC: American Association on Mental Retardation

O'Brien, J., & Lyle O'Brien, C. (1993). Assistance with integrity: The search for accountability and the lives of people with developmental disabilities. Lithonia, GA: Responsive Systems Associates.

Schalock, R. L. (Ed.). (1990). *Quality of life: Perspectives and issues*. Washington, DC: American Association on Mental Retardation.

Taylor, S. J., & Bogdan. R. (1990). *Quality of life and the individual's perspective*. In R. L. Schalock (Ed.), *Quality of life: Perspectives and issues* (pp. 27-40). Washington, DC: American Association on Mental Retardation.

# 20 • The Concept of Quality of Life and Its Current Applications In the Field of Mental Retardation/Developmental Disabilities

Robert L. Schalock, Ph.D.
Hasting College and Mid-Nebraska Individual Services

The concept of Quality of Life (QOL) is currently a significant issue in the field of human services, including mental retardation and developmental disabilities. Its importance stems from a number of phenomena including the *quality revolution*, with its emphasis on quality services, quality management, and continuous quality improvement; the current *paradigm shift*, with its emphasis on inclusion, equity, empowerment and natural supports; and the demonstrable results from successful *habilitation strategies* that include skill training, prosthetics, and natural supports. However defined, quality of life generally connotes a general feeling of well-being, opportunities to fulfill one's potential, and feelings of positive social involvement (Schalock, 1990b).

The concept of QOL is not new, as one can find reference to "a life of quality" in the writings from antiquity. What is new, however, is the belief in the 1990's that a person's perception of his/her quality of life is an integral part of service delivery and the evaluation of habilitation outcomes. Thus, we are seeing throughout human services frequent use of the QOL concept in mission statements, program descriptions, quality assurance plans, and program (outcome) evaluations.

Quality of life is not a neutral term. Generally, the concept connotes positive factors such as independence/interdependence, productivity, community integration, and satisfaction. Unfortunately, however, its unbridled use can result in a "tyranny of quality" (Goode, 1991), improper political purposes (Parmenter, 1992), or as a definition of personhood (Luckasson, 1990). Thus, there is a need to look at the concept of QOL from a positive, holistic perspective wherein it is viewed as a guiding principle for enhancing a person's development and evaluating the results of intervention/support efforts. Such is the purpose of this article.

The article reviews current work in the area of QOL, focusing primarily on those factors summarized in Figure 20-1 including:

• quality of life indicators;
• the measurement of QOL; and,
• the application of QOL data/principles to the areas of research, quality enhancement, quality assurance, and policy formulation.

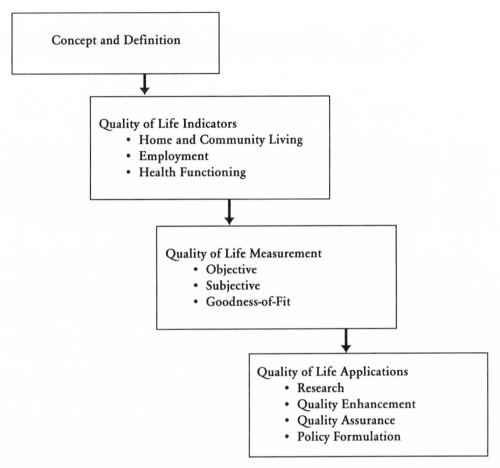

**Figure 20-1. An Overview of Current Work In the Area of QOL.**

Throughout the article, quality of life is defined as "a concept that reflects a person's desired conditions of living" (Schalock, in press).

QOL is a subjective phenomenon; based on a person's perception of various aspects of life experiences including personal characteristics, objective life conditions, and the perception of significant others (Schalock, Keith & Hoffman, 1990). Thus, the central issue confronting the examination of a person's perceived QOL involves understanding the relationship between objective and subjective phenomena. This concept is shown in

Figure 20-2 that depicts the relationship between a person's perceived quality of life and his/her experiences with the three basic life domains of home and community living, employment, and health functioning. Using this model as a basis, Table 20-1 summarizes a number of QOL indicators one finds commonly in literature.

As seen in Table 20-l, some of the critical indicators are objective (such as ownership of home, activities of daily living, compensation, health status, social involvement), some are subjective (such as choices, autonomy, relationships), and some

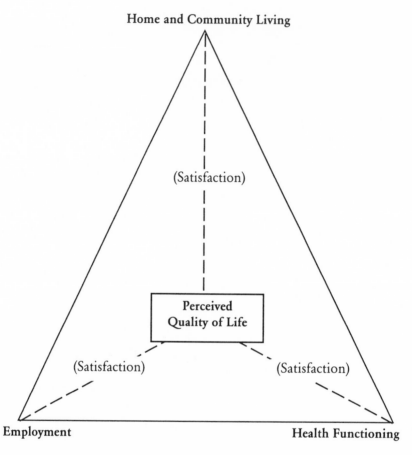

Figure 20-2. Quality of Life Model (Schalock, 1990).

are interactional (such as social support and the fit between the person and his/her environment's demands). These three categories (objective, subjective and interactional) support the notion that quality of life does not lend itself to only subjective and objective dichotomous approaches, but calls for a holistic approach (Dossa, 1989; Zautra & Goodhart, 1979).

## QOL Measurement

Interest in measuring peoples' QOL goes back to the pioneering work of Thorndike in the 1930's (Thorndike, 1939). Since that time, social scientists have developed both objective and subjective QOL indicators (Andrews & Whithey, 1976; Campbell, Converse & Rogers, 1976; Flanagan, 1982). Technical advances in measurement have also made it possible to study the quality of life of individuals, communities, and cultures (Campbell et al., 1976; Donegan & Potts, 1989; Murrell & Norris, 1983; Parameter, 1988); and Zautra & Goodhard, 1979).

There are a number of methodological concerns about measuring the quality of

## Table 20-1. Critical Quality of Life Indicators [a]

| Domain | Quality of life Indicators | |
|---|---|---|
| **Home and Community Living** | Activities and Instrumental Activities of Daily Living | Ownership of Home |
| | | Private Telephone/Number/ Mail Box |
| | Choices | Safety and Security |
| | Possessions | Adaptive Devices |
| | Recreation/Leisure Activities | Enviromental Modifications /Accomodations |
| | Volunteer Activities | Social Interaction |
| | Use of Generic Services | Social Supports |
| **Employment** | Adequate Salary | Job Support (If Needed) |
| | Employment Benefits | Advancement Opportunities |
| | Safe and Health Work Environment | Job Accommodations (If Needed) |
| | Feedback (Performance Evaluation) | Due Process |
| | | Social Interaction |
| **Health Functioning** | Nutritional Status | Health Care Access |
| | Health Status | Health Care Coverage |
| | Mobility | Exercise Opportunities |
| | Medication Level | |

[a] Adapted from Borthwick-Duffy (1991); Brown (1992); Brown, Bayer & MacFarlane (1989); Goode (1991); Halpern, Nave, Close & Nelson (1986); Jenkins, Jono, Stanton & Stroup-Benham (1990); Knoll (1990); Larson & Lakin (1992) (1992); Parmenter (1988; 1992); Schalock et al (1990): Walton (1975); Winlow (1992).

life of persons with disabilities. Chief among these include using relative measures that require a comparison of current with past or future QOL, the use of proxies, the basis for the list of specific life circumstances to be evaluated, the risk of acquiescence, the tendency towards socially desirable responding, and the lack of effective communication systems (Goode, 1991; Heal & Sigelman, 1990; Parmenter, 1992). Despite these potential problems, significant progress has been made in recent years in measuring the QOL of persons with disabilities (Schalock, 1990a). The progress is due primarily to three factors. First, we have a better conceptualization of the significant correlates of a life of quality for persons with disabilities, as reflected in the critical indicators summarized in Table 20-l. Second, we have begun to develop the techniques for direct client interviews (Neal & Sigelman, 1990). And finally, we have seen recently the development of a number of QOL models that suggest critical factors that either influence or reflect a person's perceived quality of life. Examples of these models are those that stress process (Goode, 1991), community adjustment (Halpern et al., 1986), programmatic intervention (Brown et al.,1989), person-environmental interactions (Parmenter, 1988; 1992), and program improvement/outcome evaluation (Schalock et al. 1990).

Based largely on the above models, numerous QOL assessment instruments have been developed recently (Allen, Shea & Associates, 1992). Table 20-2 summarizes a number of these instruments that have published psychometric properties.

A simple frequency count of the "QOL Factors Assessed" summarized in Table 20-2 results in a potentially significant finding: The most common factors assessed by current QOL instruments include:

- Home and Community Living
- Financial (Employment; Possessions)
- Social Integration (Family, Friends, Natural Supports) Health Status/Safety
- Personal Control/Choices/Decision Making

### QOL Application

The application of QOL data and principles is based largely on how the investigator defines quality of life. For example, if one defines QOL as "the worthiness the person experiences in his/her specific situation" (Drugge, 1990), one will stress satisfaction and the changes in the person's perceived worthiness resulting from specific situations. In contrast, if the definition focuses on the "discrepancy between a person's achieved and unmet needs and desires" (Brown et al., 1989), the focus then is on evaluating subjective perceptions as a func-

tion of habilitation-oriented interventions. To quote Brown (1992):

> Quality of life needs to involve assessment of subjective perceptions of individuals and, in our view, these should be viewed as critical to the core or the basis of further interventions (p.6).

If however, quality of life is defined (as in this article) as a concept reflecting a person's desired conditions of living, then one's primary focus is on the person's perception of those conditions and the use of quality enhancement techniques to enhance conditions of living.

The author's reading of the literature to date suggests four areas where the majority of QOL data and principles have been applied. These four include research, quality enhancement, quality assurance, and policy formulation. Each is discussed on subsequent pages.

### Research

The author has a bias: the application of QOL principles should be based on sound research. Otherwise, there is no way to prevent the potentially negative aspects of QOL (such as the previously discussed "tyranny of quality" and using QOL to define personhood discussed previously) from occurring. In discussing the research in this area, five current lines of work will be reviewed briefly including: (1) factors indicative of QOL'; (2) correlates of perceived QOL; (3) predictors of perceived QOL; (4) impact studies; and (5) cross-cultural comparisons of assessed QOL factors and concepts.

## Table 20-2. Current Quality of Life Assessment Instruments for Persons with Disabilities

| Author (Instrument) | QOL Factors Assessed | |
| --- | --- | --- |
| **Brown, Bayer and MacFarlane (1989)** (QOL Questionnaire: Sponsor Questionnaire) | Objective Factors: Income Environment Health Growth & Mastery Skills | Subjective Factors: Life Satisfaction Psychological Well-Being Perceptions of Skills & Needs |
| **Cummins (1992)** (Comprehensive QOL Scale-Intellectual Disability) | Material Things Productivity Safety Emotional Well-Being | Health Intimacy Place in Society |
| **Evans, Burns, Robinson and Garrett (1985)** (QOL Questionnaire) | Occupational/Material Well-Being Social Well-Being Family Well-Being Personal Well-Being Physical Well-Being | Health Care Access Health Care Coverage Exercise Opportunities |
| **Halpern, Nave, Close and Nelson (1986)** (Test Battery) | Client Satisfaction Occupation Residential Environment Social Support/Safety | |
| **Harner & Heal (1992)** Multifaceted Lifestyle Satisfaction Scale) | Home and Community Friends Leisure Activities Self Control Employment | |
| **Keith and Schalock (1992)** (Quality of Student Life Questionnaire) | Satisfaction Well-Being | Social Belonging Empowerment/Control |
| **Larson and Lankin (1992)** (Inventory for Client and Agency Planning) | Social Integration Community Integration | Recreation Integration Domestic Integration |
| **Schalock, Keith and Hoffman (1990)** (QOL Questionnaire) | Independence/Decision Making Productivity Community Integration Satisfaction | |
| **Wrentham State School (1982)** (Quality of Life Index) | Personalization Health/Well-Being Material Resources Privacy Affiliation | Self-Esteem Environmental Comfort Environmental Health/Safety Self-Determination |

1. *Factors indicative of QOL.* This area of research has been the most active and visible thus far, primarily because we are still trying to understand fully what QOL is and how it can best be assessed. The reader is referred to Tables 1 and 2 for a listing of those critical indicators (Table 20-1) and assessed QOL factors (Table 20-2).

2. *Significant correlates of perceived QOL.* Work in two countries has assisted in our understanding of the major QOL correlates. In one study (Schalock, Conroy, Feinstein & Lemanowicz, 1992) the following tested variables were significantly related to assessed QOL for 1600 persons with mental retardation/ developmental disabilities:

   • Personal characteristics including age, adaptive behavior, challenging behavior, health status, need for medication, cognitive level, and number of disabilities.
   • Objective life conditions including income, integrated activities, physical environment, residential size, social presence. goodness-of-fit between the person and his/her environment, and employment.
   • Perceptions of significant others including perceived client progress, environmental control by the person, staff attitudes regarding their jobs, and family involvement.

   Similarly Mattika (1991) in Finland has reported that on a sample of 822 adults with mental retardation, the significant predictors of assessed "happiness" were objective self and self-image. On the same sample, significant predictors for assessed "positiveness of life" were sense of influence, objective self, self-respect and self-image. (See chapter 2, this volume.)

3. *Predictors of perceived QOL.* Recently we (Schalock, et al., 1992) reported data based on a sample of 1600 persons with mental retardation or developmental disabilities involved in the Pennhurst (Penn.) deinstitutionalization process. Nineteen predictor variables, representing personal characteristics, objective life conditions, and the perceptions of significant others, were regressed against the four factors of the QOL Questionnaire (Schalock, et al., 1990). The significant predictors of each of the four factors are summarized in Table 20-3.

4. *Impact Studies.* One of the increasing uses of QOL data is to evaluate the impact on QOL scores of habilitation services or health-related interventions. For example, the Administration on Developmental Disabilities (ADD) has initiated a Quality Enhancement System whereby University Affiliated Programs (UAPs) are to encompass both process (formative) and outcome or impact (summative) evaluation of the impact of federally supported services in promoting the independence, productivity and community integration of program recipients (Davidson & Fifield, 1992).

   Two studies that used QOL concepts discussed previously reflect this type of research. In the first, Brown et al., (1989) investigated changes in QOL

## Table 20-3. Variables that Predict Quality of Life Scores

| Quality of Life Factor Score | Variables that Predict Quality of Life Score | Quality of Life Factor Score | Variables that Predict Quality of Life Score |
|---|---|---|---|
| Satisfaction | Staff Attitude: Working with Person<br>Community Living Status<br>Challenging Behavior Index<br>Adaptive Behavior Index<br>Social Presence<br>Gender<br>Staff Attitude: Job Satisfaction<br>Health Index<br>Residential Supervision | Independence | Integrated Activities<br>Adaptive Behavior Index<br>Challenging Behavior Index<br>Setting Size<br>Social Presence<br>Age<br>Income |
| Productivity | Adaptive Behavior Index<br>Income<br>Community Living Status<br>Age<br>Challenging Behavior Index<br>Employment vs. Day Program<br>Staff Attitude: Job Satisfaction<br>Staff Attitude: Working with Person | Integration | Adaptive Behavior Index<br>Integrated Activities<br>Challenging Behavior Index<br>Staff Attitude: Working with Person<br>Social Presence |

scores for a sample of 240 persons with mental retardation across five agencies in western Canada. Over a three year period, repeated measures were taken on a number of objective and subjective measures. On all measures, QOL scores did not show many significant gains over the three years. Objectively, there was improvement in work skills, but little progress in social education skills or movement into community-based work or living situations. Subjectively, about 50 percent of the clients reported that they enjoyed living where they were, and a majority stated they had friends, most of whom were selected from school, agency, or work. Analyses of changes in the persons' perceptions over the study period showed that for males, significant improvements were reported in the three categories of being happier now, having improved work skills, and having better co-worker relations. For females, significant improvements were in the areas of reading, laundry, getting along with others, leisure time activities, making decisions, being happy, work skills and co-worker relations.

Similarly, Schalock (unpublished data) found that for the 325 adults in the Mid-Nebraska Individual Services program, changes from 1990 to 1991 in the four QOL factor scores (see Table 20-2) were quite variable. Averaging across persons, there was a 3 % gain in scores from 1990 to 1991 in Independence/ Decision Making, and a 1 % increase in Community Integration, but a 4% decrease in assessed scores from 1990 to 1991 in Productivity and a 1 % decrease in assessed Satisfaction.

5. *Cross-cultural comparisons.* One is also beginning to see an increased Interest in cross-cultural and cross-national work on QOL. Although the work in this area is just beginning, two studies reflect potential productive research areas. In one study (Schalock, Bartnik, Wu, Kong, Lee & Reiter, 1990), a consistent trend was found across five countries (Australia, Germany, Israel, The Republic of China, and the United States) in assessed QOL factor scores: higher scores were associated with persons living and working in more normalized environments.

The second study (Heal, Schalock & Keith, 1992) investigated the meaning attributed to common QOL concepts that have evolved during the last decade. These concepts included rights, relationships, satisfaction, environment, economic security and well being, social inclusion, individual control, privacy, health, and growth and development. The approach used was to have mental retardation professionals from six countries (Australia, Finland, Germany, Japan, Republic of China, and the United States) rate the meaning of the ten concepts using nine semantic differential items, three from each of the three dimensions of value, potency, and activity. A number of aspects of the

analyses stood out. First, all concepts were rated above neutral (4.0) on all three dimensions of meaning. Second, raters were most willing to rate value above neutral and least willing to rate activity above neutral. Third, the profiles of concepts was rather flat for every meaning dimension. Fourth, while all concepts were valued, rights, relationships, inclusion, health and development were especially valued, and environment (including adaptations), security, and control were less valued. And finally, the profiles from the countries were quite similar, with respondents rating all concepts high in value and potency, and average in activity.

In summary, although formal QOL research is just beginning, the above summary indicates that we understand better some of the more important QOL indicators and conditions of living that influence one's perceived quality of life. With this information in mind, the concept of quality enhancement techniques emerges as a second QOL application area.

### Quality Enhancement

Once the critical factors associated with quality of life are understood, then the next logical step is to enhance a person's perceived quality of life through the application of one or more quality enhancement techniques. Currently, there are two general approaches to this process. One approach focuses on "quality enhancement techniques" and/or strategies that are implemented vis à vis the person or habilitation program. This quality enhancement strategy is influenced significantly by the current paradigm that emphases inclusion in natural integrated environments, equity among persons, empowerment in regard to personal choices and decisions, and the use of natural supports. The second approach focuses on "quality management techniques" and the need for change-supported management and continuous quality enhancement. Each of these two approaches is discussed in some detail on subsequent pages.

1.  *Quality enhancement techniques.* Again, a number of approaches are being used to enhance the quality of life experiences of persons with mental retardation/developmental disabilities. (Goode, 1990; Bailey, Buysee, Smith & Elam, 1992). Goode's method, as one example, is based on group discussion including persons with disabilities, parents, and staff members. During the discussion, topics are explored commencing with the question, "what is a good life?" Other discussion sessions center on topics such as important needs and ways to fulfill them in different settings. The results of the sessions can be analyzed using a number of need/goal matrices consisting of dimensions such as work, housing and leisure time (dimension 1), individual needs such as friendship, self-image, and security (dimension 2), and different types of integration (dimension 3). The goal of this approach to quality enhancement is to test the capacity of the service system to satisfy the expressed needs of its clients.

A second quality enhancement technique focuses more on what program personnel and program services can do to enhance the person's perceived quality of life. For example, Table 20-4 summarizes a number of quality enhancement techniques that are related to the three critical quality factors discussed earlier in reference to Table 20-1 and Figure 20-2, including home and community living, employment, and health functioning. The goal of this second approach is to encourage habilitation programs to implement those techniques that are under the control of habilitation programs and personnel and that can have a significant impact on the person's perceived quality of life.

2.  *Quality management techniques.* It should not be a surprise that quality management and continuous quality improvement have impacted services for persons with disabilities. Indeed, public and private enterprise is currently experiencing a quality revolution as reflected in recent works dealing with total quality (Linkow, 1989), quality leadership (Scholtes, 1988), total quality control (Mizuno, 1988), total quality management (Coate, 1990), and managing for quality (Juran, 1989).

In a recent excellent book summarizing this quality revolution in management, Albin (1991) discusses five basic principles that summarize how human service management can best respond to the QOL movement and provide the management/programmatic structure to effect significantly the objective life conditions of persons with disabilities and thereby enhance their perceived quality of life. These five basic principles included:

## Table 20-4. Quality Enhancement Techniques

| QOL Factor[a] | Exemplary Enhancement Techniques |
|---|---|
| Home and Community Living | -Allow for choices, decision making, and environmental control.<br>-Interface with person's social support systems.<br>-Maximize use of natural supports such as family, friends, and neighbors.<br>-Stress normalized and integrated environments, social interactions, and community activities.<br>-Emphasize family-professional partnerships.<br>-Promote positive role functions and life styles. |
| Employment | -Facilitate employment, work status, avocational activities, and non-employment volunteerism.<br>-Foster co-worker, as natural supports.<br>-Promote stable, safe environments that lessen stress and increases predictability and positive behaviors. |
| Health Functioning | -Promote wellness by emphasizing physical fitness, nutrition, healthy life styles, and stress management.<br>-Maximize health care coverage and access.<br>-Maximize use of prosthetics that facilitate mobility, communication, and self help.<br>-Maintain as low a psychotropic medication level as possible. |

[a] Factors based on the QOL Model shown in Figure 2.

- Establish a mission to lead quality improvement.
- Develop an obsession with quality.
- Create a unity of purpose.
- Empower employees to work to achieve the mission.
- Use a systematic approach to find opportunities and to improve performance.

### Quality Assurance

The quality revolution and quality of life movement discussed in the preceding sections are having a significant impact on the quality assurance (QA) process (Bradley & Bersani, 1990; Holburn, 1992, a, b; Jaskulski, 1992). What the final impact will be is still uncertain. However, at the onset, it is important to stress that QA is essential because an effective QA system through its standards, monitoring and response processes communicates high expectations for a service delivery system that bases its services on state of the art techniques and values, provides feedback regarding quality and cost-effectiveness, maintains a high quality service through periodic reviews, reflects what the person can expect from the services provided or contracted for, and assists in the protection of persons who are potentially vulnerable or at risk (Bradley & Bersani, 1990).

Defining what is quality is an ongoing process. For example, Knoll (1990) suggests that we have recently experienced three eras in defining what is quality in reference to services for persons with disabilities.

The first era (1967-1975), referred to as the "era of institutional reform", focused on protecting persons from harm and developing standards of care through judicially and federally imposed standards such as the ICF/MR regulations. The second era, which Knoll describes as the era of deinstitutionalization (1976-1986), involved developing community standards and defining the characteristics of quality programs. It was during this era that ACDD and CARF expanded their quality assurance and accreditation efforts, focusing on services driven by the individual habilitation planning process.

The third era is still emerging. It is best described as the "era of community membership" in which people are striving for full community integration and an enhanced quality of life, development of individualized support systems, definition of relevant processes and outcomes to include in quality assurance, and outcomes to include in quality assurance (Schalock & Kiernan, 1990).

The prevailing framework for quality assurance practice in human services, as outlined by Donabedian (1966), proposed that a comprehensive assessment of program quality should address three dimensions including program structure, program process, and program outcomes. A model that shows how this proposed assessment interfaces with the concepts presented thus far in this article is presented in Figure 20-3 and described more fully below.

1. *Program structure*. The focus here is on the program's mission statement and conversion activities. In reference to the need for a strong mission statement, Albin (1992) states:

*Whatever your business happens to be, your mission must be able to lead quality improvement efforts. Establishing such a mission provides the context to support efforts toward quality [and] must guide continuous improvement of the quality of services. To do that, an organization's mission must be defined in a way that will assist its members in recognizing quality, in determining how well the organization is achieving that quality, and in taking any steps needed to improve its performance. (p. 14)*

Currently, we are seeing tremendous efforts towards program conversion, stressing the positive relationship between habilitation programs being related to a better quality of life of these persons. Critical components of this process include moving towards supported living, supported employment, and recreation and leisure from a wellness perspective (Schalock & Kiernan, 1990).

2. *Program process*. The focus of looking at (and evaluating) program process is to continue emphasizing the critical nature of the quality enhancement and quality management techniques dis-

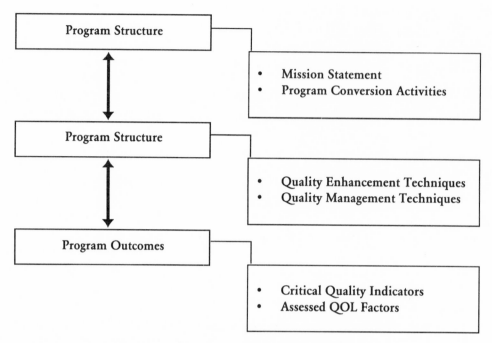

Figure 20-3. A Comprehensive Framework for Quality Assurance.

cussed in the previous section. Focusing on program process is also integrally related to quality assurance.

3. *Program outcomes.* Although each of the quality enhancement and quality management techniques referenced above uses different words, the net result should be enhanced quality outcomes. How these outcomes are monitored and assessed varies, but more frequently will involve the monitoring/evaluating of the critical quality indicators listed in Table 20-1 or one or more of the QOL indices as measured by the QOL assessment instruments summarized in Table 20-2.

However, regardless of how the program outcomes are conceptualized and

measured the author feels that three critical points need to be made. First, one should use a multidimensional approach to QOL outcome assessment that reflects the multifaceted nature of quality of life. As stated by McGrew and Bruininks (1991):

The search to describe the many and varied aspects of community participation and adaptation is beginning to identify important components that describe quality of life for citizens with disabilities in our communities. Early findings strongly suggest that adaptation and quality of life are comprised of many broad areas, including personal satisfaction, employment and economic integration, employment stability, community assimilation and acceptance, need for social support services, recreation leisure Integration, social network integration, and residential integration. (p.21)

The second critical point is that Quality Assurance can be considered a type of internal program evaluation that uses a decision-making model and focuses on self- monitoring and self- evaluation (Mathison, 1991). The attraction of the internal evaluation model is that it is consistent with bureaucratically structured organizations and our culture's predisposition to value business and industry. In today's world of tight budgets, few programs can afford external evaluators (and by inference, fewer external surveyors), and thus we will undoubtedly see an increased need for (and emphasis on) internal surveying and evaluation mechanisms. To quote Clifford and Sherman (1983):

*...internal evaluation is a tool of management science as much as or more than it is either a product or tool of social science. The internal evaluator has a long-term commitment to change through enhancement of the quality of decision making in the organization (p.23).*

With the anticipated increased interest and use of internal evaluation, it is important to consider the strengths of an internal decision-making approach to evaluating or assuring the quality of services to persons with disabilities. Some of the more important strengths of internal evaluation include (Torres, 1992):

- It is part of the organization's information processing system and thus does not require duplicative evaluation/monitoring efforts and data.
- The decision-making model draws heavily from the systems perspective, which is consistent with the need to relate a program's mission statement to habilitation processes and quality outcomes.
- It focuses on self-monitoring and self-improvement.
- It attempts to be comprehensive, correct, complete and credible to partisans on all sides.
- It allows for a better understanding of the contextual variables of the organization and the perspectives of the various stockholders.

The third critical point regarding Quality Assurance is that it should be a shared process between internal and external bodies that collectively complete a formative (internal, self-monitoring, decision-making focus) and summative (comparisons across programs) program evaluation. As stated well by Cronbach (1983), "The logic of science must come to terms with the logic of politics" (p.5).

A model summarizing a shared process is presented in Figure 20-4. Note in Figure 20-4 that the focus of internal evaluation is on formative evaluation, with the "formal" component of that process involving evaluating the agency's program structure, process, and program outcomes, and the "informal" component involving Individual Program Plan review and revision, opportunity development, and feedback from consumers. Note also that the focus of external evaluation is on summative activ-

|  | Internal Evaluation | External Evaluation |
|---|---|---|
| **FORMAL** | Formative Evaluation<br><br>• Agency's Program Structure<br>• Agency's Process<br>• Agency's Program Outcome | Summative Evaluation<br><br>• Legislative Mandated Standards<br>• Accreditation/Certification Standards |
| **INFORMAL** | Individual Program Plan Review/Revision<br><br>• Opportunity Development<br>• Feedback from Person Regarding Their Quality of Life | Shared Problem Solving<br><br>• Opportunity Development<br>• Revenue Enhancement |

**Figure 20-4. Model Depicting Shared Quality Assurance and Program Evaluation.**

ities involving standards (legislative and accreditation/certification) with the informal component of that process focusing on shared problem solving, opportunity development, and revenue enhancement.

### *Policy Formulation.*

The fourth and final QOL application area concerns disability policy issues and formulations as they relate to an enhanced quality of life for persons with disabilities. Currently, there are a number of significant forces impacting this process. Four of these forces include:

- The current consumer-referenced paradigm shift towards inclusion, empowerment, and natural supports (McFadden & Burke, 1992).
- Shrinking resources and increased demands for services with the accompa-

nying demands for program accountability and benefit/cost analyses (Schalock & Thornton, 1988).

- A change in organization control systems that are designed around values, informed norms of behavior, and interpersonal communication rather than formal rules and documentation of the machine organizations (Gardner, 1992).
- A movement towards local, independent systems that are characterized by democratic decision making, consensus building, and cooperative learning (Holburn, 1992a).

These forces are impacting us at not just the policy formulation level, but as discussed above, at the policy implementation and evaluation levels as well. In reference to policy formulation, the future is critical for the various stakeholders in the quality of life movement. As stated in the introductory comments, quality of life is not a neutral term, and while the major emphasis and use has thus far been directed at the positive meaning of the term, one must not forget the potential for the unbridled use resulting in a "tyranny of quality," improper political purposes, or as a definition of personhood. If, however, QOL policy formulation is based on those critical quality indicators summarized in Tables 1 and 2 of this article, then we have reasonable assurance that habilitation programs and services for persons with disabilities in the future will be based on sound quality of life outcomes related to home and community living, financial equity and stability, social integration, health status and safety, and personal control and empowerment.

In conclusion, conceptualizing and writing this article has been both challenging and rewarding. After working in the area of quality of life for a decade, it is becoming increasingly clear to me that the QOL concept will not go away, and that for the foreseeable future it will be the over-riding concept in the field of mental retardation / developmental disabilities. How this concept unfolds — and the use that we make of it — is both challenging and frightening. Challenging because it can result in significantly enhanced conditions of living for persons with disabilities; but at the same time frightening because we can let the concept be diluted and/or bastardized. The QOL concept thus represents potentially either our best or our worst. Hopefully, this article has contributed to our best.

# References

Albin, J.M. (1992). *Quality improvement in employment and other human services: Management for quality through change.* Baltimore: Paul H.Brookes Publishing Co.

Allen, Shea & Associates (1992). Explorations: Selected excerpts from a survey of quality-of-life measurements for the state of Colorado. Author: 1040 Main Street, Suite 200B, Napa, California 94559.

Andrews, F. R.& Whithey, S.B. (1976) *Social indicators of well-being. Americans' perceptions of life quality.* New York: Plenum Press.

Bailey, D. B., Buysse, V., Smith, T.V. & Elam, J. (1992). The effects and perceptions of family involvement in program decisions about family-centered practices. *Evaluation and Program Planning, 15,* 23-32.

Borthwick-Duffy, S.A.(1991). Quality of life and quality of care in mental retardation. In L. Rowitz (Eds.), *Mental retardation in the year 2000.* New York: Springer-Verlag.

Bradley, V.J. & Bersani, H.A. (Eds.) *Quality assurance for individuals with developmental disabilities: it's everybody's business.* Baltimore: Paul H. Brookes.

Brown, R.I. (1992) Quality of life and mental handicap: Consideration for the future-theory, research and practice. Paper presented at the 9th World congress, International Association for the Scientific Study of Mental Deficiency, Brisbane, Australia.

Brown, R.I., Bayer, M., & McFarlane, C. *Rehabilitation programmes: Performance and Quality of Life of adults with developmental handicaps.* Toronto: Lugus Production

Campbell, A. Converse, P.E.,& Rodgers, W.L. (1970).*The Quality of American life.* Beverly Hills California: Sage Publications.

Cliford, D. L. & Sherman, P. (1983). Internal evaluation: Integrating program evaluation and management. In A. J. Love (Ed.), *Developing effective internal evaluation: New direc-*

*tions for program evaluation.* (No. 20). San Francisco: Jossey-Bass.

Coate, L. E. (1990) *Implementing total quality management in a university setting.* Corvallis: Oregon State University.

Cronbach, L. J. (1983). *Designing evaluations of educational and social programs.* San Francisco: Jossey-Bass.

Cummins, R. A.(1992). Comprehensive quality of life scale-intellectual disability (ComQOL - ID; 3rd edition). Malvern, Victoria, Australia: Deakin University- Toorak.

Davidson, P. W. & Fifield, M.G. (1992). Quality and impact measurement of University Affiliated Programs. *Mental Retardation, 30*(4), 205-213.

Donabedian, A. (1966) Evaluating the quality of medical care. *Milbank Memorial Fund Quarterly, 44*, 166-206.

Donegan, C. & Potts, M. (1988). People with mental handicap living alone in the community: A pilot study of their quality of life. *The British Journal of Mental Subnormality, 34* (66), 10-21.

Dossa, P.A.(1989). Quality of life: Individualism or holism? A critical review of the literature. *International Journal of Rehabilitation Research, 12*(2), 121-136.

Drugge, C. (1990). *Using the opinion of people with mental retardation to measure quality of services.* Vasteras, Sweden: County Council Vastmanland, Social Welfare for People with Mental Retardation.

Evans, D. R., Burns, J.E., Robinson, W. E., & Garrett, O.J. (1985). The quality of life questionnaire: A multidimensional measure. *American Journal of Community Psychology, 13* 305-322.

Flanagan, J.C. (1982). Measurement of quality of life: Current state of the art. *Archives of Physical Medicine and Rehabilitation, 63*, 56-59.

Gardner, J. F. (1992). Quality, organization design, and standards. *Mental Retardation, 30* (3),173-177.

Goode, D.A.(1990). Measuring the quality of life of persons with disabilities: Some issues

and suggestions. *AAMR News and Notes, 3* (2), 6-7.

——(1991). *Quality of life research: A change agent for persons with disabilities.* Paper presented to the 1991 American Association on Mental Retardation. Washington, D.C.

Halpern, A.S., Nave, G., Close, D.W., Nelson, D.J.(1986). An empirical analysis of the dimensions of community adjustment for adults with mental retardation. *Australia and New Zealand Journal of Developmental Disabilities, 12*, 147-157.

Harner, C. & Heal, L. W. (1992). The multifaceted Lifestyle satisfaction Scale (MLSS): An interview schedule for assessing personal satisfaction of adults with limited intelligence to communicate their satisfaction with their living arrangement and community, their personal relationships, their recreation and leisure, their employment, their degree of self direction. Paper presented at the 1992 Pacific Rim conference, Honolulu, HI.

Heal, L.W., & Sigelman, C.K. (1990). Methodological issues in measuring the quality of life of individuals with mental retardation. In R.L. Schalock (Ed.), *Quality of life: Perspectives and issues* (pp.176). Washington, DC: American Association on Mental Retardation.

Heal, L. W., Schalock, R.L. and Keith, K.D. (1992). Cross-cultural attributions of meaning to quality of life concepts made by mental retardation professionals.Paper presented at the 9th World Congress, International Association for the Scientific Study of Mental Deficiency, Brisbane, Australia.

Holburn, C.S. (1992a). Rhetoric and realities in today's ICF/MR: Control out of control. *Mental Retardation,*(3), 133-141.

Holburn, C.S. (1992b). Symposium overview: Are we making the same mistake twice? *Mental Retardation,*(3), 129-131.

Holmes, C. A. (1989). Health care and the quality of life: A review. *Journal of Advanced Nursing,* 833-839.

Jaskulski, T. M.(1992). Building effective quality systems. Paper presented at the 116th Annual Meeting of the American Association on Mental Retardation. New Orleans.

Jenkins, C.D., Jono, R.T., Stanton, B.A. & Stroup-Benham, (1990). The measurement of health-related quality of life: Major dimensions identified by factor analysis. *Social Science Medicine,(31),*8 925-931.

Juran, J. M. (1989). *Juran on leadership for quality.* New York: The Free Press.

Keith, K.D. & Schalock, R.L. (1992). *Quality of student life questionaire: 1992 version.* Lincoln, Nebraska: Nebraska Wesleyan University, Department of Psychology.

Knoll, J.A. (1990). Defining quality in residential services. In V.J. Bradley and H.A. Bersani (Eds.), *Quality assurance for individuals with developmental disabilities: it's everybody's business* (pp. 235-262). Baltimore: Paul H. Brookes.

Linkow, P. (1989). Is your culture ready for total quality: *Quality Progress,* 22 (11), 69-71.

Luckasson, R. (1990) A lawyer's perspective on quality of life. In R.L. Schalock (Ed.) *Quality of life: Perspectives and Issues* (pp. 211-214). Washington, DC: American Association on Mental Retardation.

McFadden, D. L. & Burke, E. P. (1991) Developmental disabilties and the new paradigm: Direction for the 1990s. *Mental Retardation.* 29 (1), ii-vi.

McGrew, K. S. & Bruininks, R.H. (1992). A multidimensional approach to the measurement of community adjustment. In M. Hayden and B. Avery (Eds.), *Community living for persons with mental retardation andrelated conditions..* Baltimore: Paul H. Brookes.

Mathison, S. (1991). What do we know about internal evaluation: *Evaluation and Program Planning.,* 14 159-165.

Matikka, L. (1992). The quality of life for mentally retarded adults in Finland. Paper presented at the 9th World Congress, international Association for the Study of Mental Deficiency. Brisbane, Australia.

Murrell, S. A. & Norris, F. H. (1983). Quality of life as the criterion for need assessment and community psychology. *Journal of Community Psychology, 11* 88-97.

Parmenter, T.R. (1988). An analysis of the dimensions of quality of life for people with physical disabilities. In R. Brown (Ed.), *Quality of life for handicapped people.* London: Croom Helm.

Parmenter, T.R. (1992). Quality of life of people with developmental disabilities. in N. W. Bray (Ed.), *International review of research in mental retardation. (vol 18)* New York: Academic Press.

Schalock, R.L. (in press). The quality revolution and its impact on quality of life research, quality assurance and program evaluation. *Evaluation and Program Planning.*

Schalock, R.L. (1990a). Attempts to conceptualize and measure quality of life. In R.L. Schalock (Ed.), *Quality of life: Perspectives and issues.* (pp. 141-148). Washington, DC: American Association on Mental Retardation.

Schalock, R.L. (Ed.) (1990b). *Quality of life: Perspectives and issues.* Washington, DC: American Association on Mental Retardation.

Schalock, R.L., Bartnik, E., Wu, F., Konig, A., Lee, C.S., & Reiter, S. (1990). An international perspective on quality of life: Measurement and Use. Paper presented at the 114th Annual Meeting of the American Association on Mental Retardation, Atlanta, GA.

Schalock, R.L., Conroy, J. W., Feinstein, C.S., & Lemanowicz, J.A. (1992). *An investigative study of the correlates of quality of life.* Unpublished manuscript. Hastings, NE: Mid-Nebraska Individual Services.

Schalock, R.L., Keith, K.D., & Hoffman, K. (1990). *1990 Quality of life questionaire: Standardization Manual.* Hastings,NE:Mid-Nebraska Mental Retardation Services.

Schalock, R.L., Keith, K.D., Hoffman, K. & Karan O.C. (1989). Quality of life: Its measurement and use. *Mental Retardation,* 27 (1), 25-31.

Schalock, R.L. & Kiernan, W.E. (1990). *Habilitation planning for adults with disabilities.* New York: Springer-VerIag.

Schalock, R.L. & Thornton, C.V.D. (1988). *Program evaluation: A field guide for administators.* New York: PIenum.

Scholtes, P. R. (1988). *The team handbook: How to use teams to improve quality.* Madison WI: Joiner Associates, Inc.

Thorndike, E.L. (1939). *Your city.* New York: Harcourt, Brace and Company.

Torres, R. T. (1991).Improving the quality of internal evaluation: The evaluator as consultant-mediator. *Evaluation and Program Planning,14,*189-198.

Walton, R.D. (1975) Quality of work life: What is it? *Sloan Management Review,15*(1), 11-21.

Winslow, R. (1992) Questionnaire probes patients' quality of life. *Wall Street Journal.* July 7, B9.

___Wrentham State School (1982). *The quality of life questionaire.* Wrentham, Massachusetts: Author.

Zautra, A.J., & Goodhart, D. (1979). Quality of life indicators: A review of the literature. *Community Mental Health Review,* 4-10.

# 21 • Let's Hang Up "Quality of Life" As a Hopeless Term.

Wolf Wolfensberger, Ph.D.
Training Institute for Human Service Planning, Leadership & Change Agentry,
Syracuse University, Syracuse, New York

The philosophers of science inform us that science should strive for a discourse in which terms meet the two criteria of clarity and utility. Clarity requires that when a party uses a certain term, it defines the term clearly (in science, perhaps even "operationally"), and uses it consistently as defined. If another party uses the same term in a different sense, then this other party needs to make clear how it defines and uses that term.

Discourse degenerates into confusion, or even chaos or unproductive controversy, when two things happen. (a) Different parties use the same term, but one or all parties fail to make clear how they define and use the term. (b) Even though all parties may agree on the same formal definition of a term, at least one of the parties projects meaning into the term that is not part of the term's formal definition. This "unofficial" meaning violates the boundaries of definition, and is called surplus meaning.

Terms virtually drip with surplus meaning when they become out-and-out code words, far removed from the face validity of the term itself. Currently, such code words include "choice," "the right to control one's body," "multicultural," "diversity," etc. For instance, who ever would have thought that the term "self-advocate" would come to mean largely a mentally retarded person, as in the picture caption, "Three self-advocates having lunch," which referred to three mentally retarded persons?

In a sense, clarity can be linked to the construct of reliability in test construction theory. To the degree that clarity is lacking, validity (in this case, of discourse among parties) is constrained, or even impossible to obtain.

It often happens in social discourse that so much confusion, emotion or acrimony gets tied to a term that rational discourse involving that term becomes de facto impossible, at least for a long time. In Christian history, the mere mention of terms such as "salvation by grace," "works," "the pope," "creed," etc., have often been sufficient to disable all further rational discourse, to the point where the parties involved could no longer even agree as to what they would disagree on.

However, the same phenomenon is found in all disciplines and in all walks of life: politics, economics, history, psychology, psychiatry—even medicine and science. For instance, in about the late 1970s, the term "Alzheimer's disease" suddenly lost the dictionary-based clarity it once had possessed, and became a code word for dementia. Similarly, the term "anencephalic" is increasingly being applied to infants who do not at all have anencephaly in the traditional technical sense, but who have a serious brain impairment, and whom others want to make dead.

Semanticists and philosophers of science have made the point (at least I remember that they did — or if they did not, they should have) that when a term acquires too much "baggage" (surplus meaning; emotion; acrimony; multiple, inconsistent or confusing meanings), then rather than trying to constantly reiterate one's own definition of it in one's own discourse, it may be better to abandon it and craft a new term, or even a new construct. A good example has been the term "normalization." Discourse about it was chaotic, and even my clearly distinguishing my use of the term from its uses by scores of others proved futile. Between 1982 and 1983, I not only abandoned the term but also recrafted the underlying construct into Social Role Valorization (e.g., Wolfensberger, 1983, 1992a; Wolfensberger & Tullman, 1982), and this did, indeed, lay to rest more than half of the unproductive discourse that had swirled around "normalization."

It is my contention that the term "quality of life" (henceforth usually abbreviated QOL) is in a similar situation. It has become such a baggage-laden code term that in my opinion, it should be abandoned. Even if a party were to be utterly precise and consistent in its own use of the term, it is too late to achieve a consensus on it, or to

prevent attachment of code meanings to it.

Below, I will review seven problematic uses of the QOL term and/or construct. After that, I will have more to say about issues of language use in order to augment what some critics thought was inadequate address in my preceding remarks.

## Seven Problems in the Use of the "Quality of Life" Construct or Term

It seems to me that there are seven problematic uses of the QOL term or construct. (a) The intrinsic cultural relativity of what is usually meant by QOL. (b) A confusion between population and individual (or "clinical") applications. (c) A contamination of QOL with various similar or overlapping constructs. (d) Confusion between objective and subjective perspectives on QOL. (e) The promotion of subjective reporting by service recipients of their "quality of life" as being preferable to the assessment of the quality of their services. (f) Different fields and different classes of actors have different perspectives on QOL, and craft different formulations. (g) Highly selective invocation of QOL in the presence of deathmaking motives (i.e., of "the killing thought"). Each of these will be elaborated below.

### The Intrinsic Cultural Relativity of What is Usually Meant by "Quality of Life"

One of the biggest problems with most of the likely constructions of QOL is that they are bound to be relative to the experiences, expectations and aspirations of the surrounding culture and its historical realities. Thus, such concepts will differ widely among cultures, and over time even within the same culture. For instance, today, poor people in an affluent Western society have a higher standard of living than did even rulers of the Middle Ages. Indeed, even a homeless person in an American city today is apt to have a healthier diet than a medieval potentate.

As a general principle, members of a society will be judged to have a lower QOL when they embody the opposite of what the culture values. For instance, in a society that highly values physical beauty, ugly people will automatically be defined as leading lives of lower quality. In an affluent hedonistic culture, it may take vastly more for life to be judged to have high quality than in a culture in which people normatively live on the edge of existence. All this was exemplified by a 1985 newspaper article (Lepach, 1985) in a German-American weekly that claimed that travel for pleasure (as to exotic vacation places) was one of the prerequisites to an acceptable "quality of life."

Yet interestingly, under calamitous conditions, such as warfare or natural disaster, almost everybody may cling to life under conditions they might otherwise have judged to be not worth living, either for themselves or for others. Suddenly, an entire population (as exemplified by 1992 events in Yugoslavia and Somalia) may be experiencing conditions of life that in other contexts would have been deemed to constitute a QOL so low or nonexistent as to warrant the merciful killing of such unfortunate creatures.

The intrinsic relativity of QOL norms can be linkened to the "adaptation level" in human adaptation (especially perception), identified by the renowned American psychologist, Harry Helson, and sometimes also known as the Helson-Judd effect. The range of human judgments of what constitutes a neutral point along a continuum of judgments of perceptual or hedonic continuities (brightness, noise level, room temperature, etc.) can shift dramatically toward one extreme or the other, depending on — to put it in simplified language — what a person has been used to. Also, the neutral point is rarely at the center of such a continuum.

One can easily see that the relativity of a QOL judgment is bound to be attended by all sorts of derivative problems and outright absurdities. Then what does it mean when we perform statistical operations on QOL indices, and relate these operationally to all sorts of other variables and indices?

The cultural relativity of QOL constructs is underlined if one considers that some culture or subculture might choose to define QOL by criteria of moral goodness: the degree to which a person possesses, and practices, the virtues of goodness, compassion, gentleness, generosity, truthfulness, self-denial, etc. A person who scores high on such criteria might be interpreted to have a high quality of life despite poverty, persecution, homelessness, sickness, etc.

### The Confusion Between Population and Individual Applications of a "Quality of Life" Construct

While ideas of QOL have a long history, the term itself made its first appearance *on any significant scale in North America* in the 1960s, and first distinctly in regard to populations rather than individuals. The term QOL was injected in a highly visible way into the national debate at that time on national goals and policies, and *population indices* of welfare, such as quality of air, water, population health, social welfare, etc.

Some people thought that economic growth would be virtually unlimited, while others predicted that some tough priority decisions lay ahead. Publications that were pessimistic about the long-term prospects included *Limits to Growth* (Meadows, Meadows, Randers & Behrens, 1972, revised 1974), *Toward Global Equilibrium* (Meadows & Meadows, 1973), and *Dynamics of Growth in a Finite World* (Meadows et al., 1974). Other publications of the same genre included various reports to the Club of Rome (several edited by Laszlo in the mid-1970s), and *Search for Alternatives* (Tugwell, 1973).

Related discussion had to do with whether economic growth which the US had been experiencing was actually resulting in a better and happier life for people, or whether it produced as many or more problems than it solved. There was an entire series of publications that was part of this debate – and that, I believe, was a major trigger for people beginning to use the term QOL in a facile way, but initially in relation to population welfare. An early document in this series was *Goals for Americans* (Commission on National Goals, 1960). A great deal of consciousness was generated within circles of government and leadership about developing so-called "social indicators," in order to identify and monitor population welfare. A number of publications came out with statistics on such presumed social indicators, and the term was given particular prominence in a 1969 government publication (US Department of Health, Education and Welfare, 1969) called *Toward a Social Report*.

In contrast to the pessimism of the Club of Rome and other parties, some people held the attitude that anything was possible, and that no serious conflict would develop between quantity and quality – at least for the US, which was even expressed in the title of a 1970 report of the US National Goals Research Staff, namely, *Toward Balanced Growth: Quantity With Quality* (see especially p. 30).

In 1974, United States Senator Philip A. Harter had entered into the *Congressional Record* a speech he had given, and a manuscript by Prof. Robert C. Juvinall of the University of Michigan, both under the title "Life Quality Index" (Hart, 1974). These related to what Hart called "the need for a yardstick to measure progress toward achieving an environment that promotes `mental, emotional and spiritual health' as well as material security" – obviously all dealing with population indices. Presumably, a better "yardstick" would reveal more clearly which way things were going on a population level.

A major 1970 article in *Science* (Coale, 1970) spoke specifically of "the quality of American life," still referencing it to environmental health factors (air, water, waster disposal, etc.), availability of resources, population density, and similar indices. Between 1971 and 1982, a series of other publications included references to "the quality of American life" in their titles. Also, for a time, there was a Panel on the Quality of American Life, functioning under the President's Commission for a National Agenda for the Eighties (President's Commission for A National Agenda for the Eighties, 1980, 1982). Its name was probably inspired by the theme of Coale's article.

The series of studies on "quality of American life," some co-authored by Campbell between 1971-1980 (see Campbell,

1971; Campbell & Converse, 1980; Campbell, Converse & Rogers, 1976), have even been called the "Quality of American Life Studies." This series already evidenced a subtle shift from population to individual perspectives in that it collected both population indices *and* self-reported satisfaction of citizens with their life experiences.

Such self-reports fall somewhere between a population and an individual use of a QOL construct as long as they are treated as collective data and in reference to collectivities, rather than for clinical (personal) applications.

Another series of studies got almost entirely away from population indices, and *only* focused on self-reported satisfaction with life conditions. This was the Monitoring The Future project launched in 1974 by a White House initiative (see description in Rodgers & Bachman, 1988). Over 17,000 US high school seniors filled out questionnaires, including questions about "satisfaction." Also, for some cohorts of this sample, there were follow-up questionnaires about subsequent experiences.

One can see how the emphasis crept from nothing but objective population indices, to subjective but collectivized self-reports mixed with population indices, to subjective collectivized self-reports more or less stripped of population indices — and then relatively suddenly, the QOL construct got hijacked for individual and clinical application, to characterize the lives of individuals regardless of the quality of population, or even collective, indicators. Thus, a person in a population enjoying very high QOL in a population sense could be said to individually experience a low QOL — or vice-versa. But in fact, no sooner

had QOL been hijacked for individual, clinical and medical ethics use than its population use declined very quickly, and some people are no longer even aware that QOL can have such a meaning, or had this as its major signification in the 1960s and early 1970s.

While I am asserting that there has been a shift in interpreting QOL from a population to an individual perspective, and that this is confused and confusing, I do not mean to imply that the term QOL is never found anymore in connection with population indices of welfare, but only that it is somewhat vestigial. For instance, in 1982, a University of Pennsylvania study by Richard Bates constructed a QOL index that included 44 components, such as natural disasters, race relations, infant mortality rates, political participation, voting equality, status of women, etc. This index was applied to 107 nations, and the resulting scores were then rank-ordered. The US came out 41st — maybe this is one reason population indices fell into disfavor in the US (*Philadelphia Inquirer*, 15 August 1982, p. 25A).

Redefining a term is scientifically permissible, as long as clarity and utility are retained. But confusion sets in when the two uses overlap, or people shift from a population to an individual usage without preserving the necessary precautions. It is a bit like concluding that a specific deaf person must be illiterate because the deaf as a group have a very low reading achievement.

Later, we will have more to say about the fact that the application of a QOL construct to individuals took place in connection with efforts to make dead certain devalued people, and that low *individual*

QOL began to be invoked as a justification for medical deathmaking, especially in hospitals.

When I use the term "deathmaking" in this chapter, I intend to point to the fact that there are many ways of contributing to the spread of death in the world, and overt and direct killing is only one of these ways. The subtleness with which death can be promoted has been so well concealed that the English language has not even had a single term to refer to all its different forms. That is why I had to translate one from other languages (French *faire mourir* and German *totmachen*). By "deathmaking," I mean to refer to any action or pattern of actions which either directly or indirectly bring about, or hasten, the death of a person, group or class. Deathmaking includes actions ranging all the way from explicit, overt, and direct killing of another person, to very concealed and indirect killing that may take a long time to accomplish and may be very difficult to trace; and it can include active participation as well as silent, unobjecting collusion.

### The Contamination of "Quality of Life" Ideas With Related Constructs

A major problem with ideas about QOL is that all sorts of notions that have some kind of relationship to a potential QOL construct get confused with each other. So far, I have identified two clusters of such confusions.

#### "Quality of Life" Gets Problematically Mixed-Up With Notions of The Good Life

A major problem with ideas about QOL is that quite clearly, they get mixed-up with diverse notions about what might otherwise be called "the good life," welfare, happiness — even Social Role Valorization (SRV) (Wolfensberger, 1983; Wolfensberger & Thomas, 1983; Wolfensberger & Tullman, 1982), or its predecessor, normalization. One reason for this confusing contamination is that the term "quality of life" seems to have so much — albeit highly subjectified — "surface meaning" that people will unconsciously attach *their* meaning even to a QOL term that others have defined rigorously and operationally in a different way. This is exactly what happened to the term "normalization," mentioned before, so that discourse even about an objectified *construct* (rather than merely term) of normalization became almost impossible to conduct with and among certain parties. Each party thought it had the "right" idea about what normalization was, and could not relate to any normalization definitions, even if clearly explicated, that differed from its own. No amount of "definition shouting" could overcome the mental blinders and linguistic traps.

One of the cardinal sins in telling and interpreting history is to commit historical anachronisms, such as projecting onto people past concepts or language idioms that developed much later. A good example in regard to QOL is found in the very first sentence of the 1988 book by Rodgers and Bachman in which QOL plays a major role: "An overriding concern in our society since its very inception has been with the quality of life of its citizens" (p.1). Prior to the 1960s, there was sparse use of the term (e.g., would it be found in any pre-1960 dictionary, even specialized ones?). But the problem here is not just that the term "quality of life" was rarely used, and unfamiliar to most people, but that even when different terms are applied to roughly the same entity, they still carry different connotations, and people of an earlier era who used terms such as welfare, prosperity, happiness, etc., may not at all have projected into them the same meanings that people now project into the term QOL.

Of all the things with which QOL is confused or equated, by far the worst is the equation of "quality of life" with the value of a life. Because this confusion and equation has been deliberately fostered by some parties, I will treat it in more detail in the section on "The Promotion of the Quality of Life Construct with Deathmaking Motives."

### Definitions, Components, Determinants and Predictors of "Quality of Life" Get Confused With Each Other

Not only is there confusion between QOL and other broad visions relating to the good life, but there is also confusion at a lower level among definitions of QOL, components thereof, and its determinants or predictors (e.g., Birren, Lubben, Rowe & Deutchman, 1991). This, by itself, would make for considerable chaos.

These days, one can find herbal supplements advertised as "improving the quality of one's life," which is an amusing confusion of components (i.e., subjective feeling of bodily well-being) with a potential larger QOL construct.

### The Confusion Between Objective and Subjective Perspective on "Quality of Life"

Closely related to the above problem is that no matter what people may *say*, in their minds, they tend to equate the QOL construct with the subjective perspective that they themselves, or perhaps even most people, have *on their own lives*. In other words, humans form a subjective perspective on their own lives that one could call "happiness" or "contentment," and equate this with QOL. I will use the term "contentment" because "happiness" is perhaps even more overloaded with meaning than the construct of QOL.

Any equation of (subjective) contentment with an objectified QOL construct is faulty because most people can be quite contented even though they would be said by those who "talk QOL" these days to have very poor QOL. And vice-versa: people who may rate quite high on QOL may be very discontented with their lives — perhaps so much as to commit suicide.

One reason why people may be relatively contented despite "low QOL" could be that they lack an image of how things might be better. For instance, this image may be lacking to societally devalued people who have been made to lead very restricted lives.

However, even people who have broad previous experiences, and who possess sufficient relevant information, may still prefer a lifestyle and life circumstances that would rate low by prevailing concepts of what constitutes QOL. Reasons that are apt to play a big role here are adherence to higher values that call for a different lifestyle, preference for certain cultural styles, positively experienced earlier patterns of living (e.g., in childhood), or a link of a lifestyle at issue to certain social relationships that one values.

I suspect that most people who are heavily "into" QOL would say they agree that (a) QOL and subjective contentment are not the same, even though there is probably a statistically significant correlation between the two across a population, and (b) people should have a right to seek and find contentment in their own way even if they would rate low on QOL criteria. However, that people who rely heavily on QOL talk *do*, in fact, mentally equate QOL and contentment despite the above verbalization comes out over and over, both in their behavior and their language. Two examples should be readily recognizable by experienced observers of the current human service scene.

1.  The discourse on what is the best thing to do about impaired unborn or newly-born children routinely drips with simultaneous messages that such children are better off dead because they would "have" low QOL *and* would be unhappy. If the invokers of QOL *really* decoupled QOL from contentment, then they would not link the two constructs so routinely.

2.  One can observe over and over that people in human services will exert great efforts to push societally devalued clients into life situations that rate higher in QOL — but lower in contentment. A good example are mentally or bodily limited young adults who live with their parents, and are quite contented. Such young adults may be exposed to relentless pressure by the QOL invokers in human services to move out into "independence," which often means into loneliness and/or poverty. In contrast to all this, family members of handicapped persons are much more apt to be concerned with the person's contentment.

We can now also see how the issue of objectivity-subjectivity relates to population and individual QOL constructs. Population QOL can be objectively constructed. After all, there will be very little disagreement on things such as what constitutes a continuum of air or water quality, and that higher readings on any such continuum are more contributive to health. But when individual QOL indices are to be constructed that are unconnected to population QOL indices, then we get into ever more subjectivism, or at least controversy.

Obviously, there is a great urgency to separate any construct or term that smacks of "happiness" from any construct or term that is related to QOL. One could even go further and say that *both* of these should be separated from traditional notions of the good life (e.g., Wolfensberger, 1984), since the good life could conceivably be said to be led by someone who is neither happy nor possesses QOL. In this connection, it is noteworthy that life conditions consistent with the principle of normalization, or even with Social Role Valorization, are often not what can be equated with happiness. What happens when "happiness" is bought at the expense of independence, self-sufficiency, and respect for or from others, or if it creates devaluing attitudes in the public's mind toward people who are different? The importance of "happiness" at the price of social devaluation is especially dubious when one considers how the devaluing attitudes of the public are brutalizing to the public *themselves*, and in a sense make *them* morally self-destructive.

The confusions about subjective and objective QOL perspectives could, in theory, be independent of the confusion between population and individual QOL perspectives, but often, the two confusions interact, especially since a subjective QOL perspective demands an individual perspective as well.

Take, for instance, the extreme emphasis that some parties give to "choice" as a criterion of QOL, i.e., people getting whatever they say they want is said to constitute QOL for them. Such a QOL construct celebrates subjectivism, and means that agreement on a single index can hardly be obtained. I could live with that, but then there is an additional problem that the modernists, with their idolatrous exaltation of individualism, apparently do not know: hell is a place where people get what (they said) they wanted. A good example of this is contemporary China with its one-child family policy. Parents of only children give their little "emperor" children (as they are called) everything they say they want — but these children are growing up a scowling, unpleasant lot, half of whom say they actively dislike their parents.

The confusion of objective and subjective perspectives, and the contamination of ideas about the good life, also reinforce each other in a maladaptive way. For instance, the above confusion can also play itself out in connection with people equating SRV with QOL. (I must say that I feel rather embarrassed by some people's virtually equating normalization with SRV and QOL). SRV posits that people who hold societally devalued social roles will be much more likely (i.e., probabilistically, and across population groups) to be afforded by others the good things in life — but the relationship can only be said to be probabilistic. Thus, holding a valued social role is no absolute guarantee of scoring high on a QOL criteria. Also, in a society in which the

good things in life are not readily available even for people in valued roles (one need only think of the former Yugoslavia in 1993), then even the vast majority of people in valued roles may be said to have a very poor QOL.

However, one can not infrequently observe societally devalued people being pushed toward more valued roles, even when this actually increases the likelihood that the QOL attributed to them will thereby become poorer. For instance, consider once again the many people who get pushed into greater independence, and the role enhancement that this often entails. However, this independence often also entails a very precarious existence: vastly higher risk of becoming a victim of fire, crime, violence and sexual abuse; de facto exclusion from medical care, or from quality medical care; a lack of advocates in one's life; and a very significant lowering of life expectancy.

How the subjective/objective, and individual/collective uses of a QOL construct can interact was also addressed by Rodgers and Bachman (1988). They acknowledge that government agencies try and keep track of "objective" indicators of the quality of life"(p.1), but quickly added that "subjectivity is implicit in the very term "quality": any assessment of quality, whether with respect to beauty or to any other dimension, lies in the eyes of the beholder. It is because of such truisms that increasing emphasis has been placed on the *subjective* quality of life."

One must give Rodgers and Bachman (1988) credit for the fact that their extensive study of QOL was clearly framed (even in the title of their book) as a study of "subjective well-being," operationalized by quantification of self-reports of the subjects.

In the concluding section, I will return to the confusion of subjective and objective QOL formulations, and offer what will probably be an indignantly received solution.

### Subjective "Quality of Life" Reporting by Service Recipients Has Been Promoted as Preferable to Service Quality Assessment

Since roughly the early 1970s (as best as I can remember), three assertions have often been made that bear on how at least some people have invoked QOL.

1.  It has been asserted that the quality of service should be determined by "outcome" rather than "process" measures.

2.  It has been asserted that service recipient satisfaction should be the key measure of service quality. For instance, in 1993, the Accreditation Council on Services for People with Disabilities held two-day conferences all over the United States, entitled "Quality Plus: From Organizational Process to Outcomes for People." This Council rests its accreditation on the evaluation of services by teams of people that it sends out, charged with applying its evaluation instrument.

3.  It has sometimes also been asserted that service recipients' satisfaction *is* an outcome measure, and hence a valid measure of service quality.

Insofar as satisfaction of service recipients is operationalized as a subjective reporting by such recipients on how well they are satisfied with the service they are — or

have been — getting, the QOL term has often been linked in some way or other to the three above propositions. For instance, Ralph and Clary (1993) very explicitly speak of QOL as being an outcome measure of human service quality. Linkage of QOL to the three propositions seems to have been particularly tempting where the service at issue has been a residence, because the quality of one's residence so dominates how one feels about one's life.

Key elements of the above propositions can easily be dismissed after even only the most elementary logical considerations.

1.  Service recipients' feelings of well-being, contentment, etc., are only partially and probabilistically the result of service program structures. Some persons will be unhappy under even optimal conditions, and will quite literally create their own hell. On the other hand, some individuals are very serene under even very adverse conditions. About the only thing that one can say in this regard is that one can construct instruments which measure service conditions that have an impact on how contented service recipients will report themselves to be. Such self-reports by an entire recipient group are likely to have some probabilistic relation to service quality, but one must expect a very large amount of the variance to be accounted for by other factors.

2.  Life conditions that are generally considered valued ones in a society can nonetheless be associated with, even be the causes of, great discomfort and stress. For example, situations that contain what Perske (1972) has called the

"dignity of risk" can be extremely stressful, and even result in death — at which point one can hardly call the situation one of high quality of life. In contrast, service settings that make few demands on recipients, or that even cater to those of their motives or whims that are primitive, hedonistic, and maladaptive (at least in the long run) may produce a clientele that at least for the moment is very contented.

3. That which makes a service recipient satisfied, and which may be expressed as satisfaction with a service, may not at all be the service's doing. It may be the doing of the service recipient him/herself, or of other parties outside the service. For instance, a recipient in a community residence may lead a very socially integrated life due to the aggressive positive ideology of his/her family and other actors or services in his/her life, rather than because of any actions or even encouragement on the part of the service being assessed. Yet this situation may not only yield recipient reports of satisfaction with their life conditions, but even with their residential service itself. Other resident receiving the identical service, but without the same support from family and/or other outside parties, might be miserable and dissatisfied with the residential service. Also, the less a service is a total environment (such as a "total institution"), the less either an "outcome," or recipient reporting of satisfaction, can be attributed compellingly to what the service has been doing. After all, essentially the very same thing has been amply proven in regard to higher education: the universities with the highest reputations are successful much less by what they do to or with students, but by either the selectivity with which they admit students, or the self-selection of the students who choose to go there. In other words, if the very same educational institutions had to admit students comparable to those of mediocre universities, their students would also end up with a mediocre education. A mediocre university with top-notch students would soon become a highly-rated university. Thus, without doing one other thing, any service could improve its "outcome," and then lay claim to higher quality, by merely upgrading its clientele, which often would mean serving those who are less needy in the human identity domain that the service addresses.

4. Yet further, some recipients (and their families) report high satisfaction (perhaps even in glowing terms) with a service simply because they do not know any better or any different. For instance, there have always been people in snakepit institutions who reported high satisfaction, sometimes because their "adaptation level" for quality and life conditions was so low.

Obviously then, the quality of a service must be determined via criteria other than recipient self-report of satisfaction.

The argument that service "outcomes" should be used as criteria of service quality would not be a relevant issue here in this context if some people would not link it explicitly with QOL language or issues.

The people who insist on "outcome

measures" are caught in a semantic trap from which they can actually be easily liberated, if only they would let themselves be liberated, by deconstructing the term "outcome."

First of all, if one only assessed "outcomes," one would only be able to assess what a service did in the past. In the case of some services, it takes years to produce "outcomes." Thus, outcome measurements are totally inappropriate to determine the quality of an ongoing service "at this time." I have been amazed that this self-evident fact seems to have eluded so many learned people.

Secondly, if one applies even only a minimal amount of deconstruction to what constitutes the elements of so-called "outcomes," one is astonished to discover that they consist just about of the same things that would otherwise be called processes. One could say that virtually all so-called outcomes are reducible to (merely hidden and relabeled) processes.

Even such a supposedly "hard" outcome as change in an IQ is really no more than the quantification of two or more interactive *processes* between a person being tested, and an examiner, a set of materials, and certain aspects of the environmental stimulus situation. Much as the measurement of IQ itself is merely the quantification of such an ongoing behavioral process, one could similarly quantify any number of behavior or organizational processes, and derive measures which are no more or less outcomes than a change in IQ is, but which might well be defined by people to be much more one than the other. Thus, more meaningful than speaking in terms of process or outcome assessment would be to speak about *which* process to assess, and to

also distinguish between assessment of processes which are applied to a service recipient (this includes the environment), versus assessments of processes which are emitted by such a person.

Another confusion arises from the fact that for reasons of social, political, or service theories or ideologies, many people refuse to acknowledge that even within their own outcome idiom, certain phenomena qualify as desirable service "outcomes." For instance, to a person oriented to normalization or Social Role Valorization, social integration can be a desired "outcome," and not merely a service process or methodology. Valued appearance and dress, functioning in age-appropriate surroundings, etc., are seen by normalization/SRV as significant measures of habilitation, whereas to other persons with different service "theories," they may merely be half-way processes toward higher functioning.

In other words, process and outcome are not always as distinguishable as may at first appear, especially if one does not share the same theory. For instance, most people in human service adhere to a clinical mind set or model as to what the problem is, what is needed, how it should be pursued, what works, and what success is. This is most evident — to cite an extreme example — in behaviorist contexts, where the answer to a toilet problem of an abandoned, deprived person in a snakepit institution may be a thousand electric shocks, and where the problem is considered solved when the toilet problem then seems to have disappeared during the next weeks or months.

In contrast, in a theory that is as broad and multidimensional as SRV (and to a lesser degree, normalization), social role-valorizing the processes of life is a desirable "outcome" — even if things like toilet problems persist; and the disappearance of the toilet problem only in response to 1,000 electric shocks would be seen as a severe image insult to the client, and a degradation in at least some role elements, not to mention other reasons for objecting to it.

To cite another example: according to a purely clinical outcome way of thinking, nothing has changed when a mentally disordered elderly man who has been devalued, rejected, despised, etc., is now addressed and spoken about with genuine respect because he is just as disordered as he was earlier. Within the normalization/SRV framework, however, a highly desirable objective has, in fact, been reached when people around such a person (including service staff) have been brought to genuinely respectful and status-enhancing ways of speaking to and about him.

Obviously, what people call "outcomes" cannot possibly be the most valid measure of service quality. Also, it should be clear that people with an "outcome" orientation are easy prey to the temptation to justify means by their ends, as the history of human services has amply demonstrated. This is less likely to occur once one perceives just about everything as a process. Then one's mind is much less encumbered in resolving which processes are desirable, or even effective, in bringing about yet other desirable processes that one may label outcomes.

Aside from the semantic and theoretical issues discussed above, outcome assessment tells us little about the forms or nature of service-system strengths or weaknesses; nor is outcome by itself an adequate measure of program quality. Indeed, some specific outcome could be derived via a

number of grossly differing processes — processes which may differ in economy, quality, and perhaps even moral acceptability.

The upshot of all this to QOL issues is that when one uses QOL language in connection with services, one should observe the following rules.

1. One should not equate the reported subjective experience of one service recipient (which may be interpreted as an index of QOL) with that of other recipients, or other potential recipients, even if there exists a significant correlation between such reports.

2. Subjective recipient reports on their feelings about a service or its setting should not be interpreted as tantamount to a valid index of service quality, even though the two are apt to be positively correlated.

3. One should not assume (or use language that leaves the issue ambiguous) that what happens to a recipient after having received a service (and such a person's "quality of life" at that time) is the outcome of the service, even though there is often a significant correlation.

### Formulations or Perspectives on "Quality of Life" Diverge in Different Fields and Among Different Classes of Actors

From Birren, Lubben, Rowe and Deutchman (1991), we learn that not only do formulations of and perspectives on QOL differ among fields (e.g., in aging as distinct from some other field), but even among different classes of actors, such as residents of long-term care facilities, staff, and the families of residents.

Illustrative not only of differences across fields, but also of several other of the above five problems (especially the confusion among definitions, components, determinants and predictors) is brought out by a chapter by Chaffee (1990) who asked, "How does one define a good quality of life for those with developmental disabilities?" And then we are told that "Congress has answered that question in a variety of ways," namely, in 1975 by the passage of PL 94-142, the Education for All Handicapped Children Act; in 1981 with PL 97-35, the Medicaid waiver program in the Omnibus Budget Reconciliation Act; and in 1984 with the passage of PL98-527, amending the Developmental Disabilities Act. In the book in which this passage appeared, it was indexed under "Quality of life –definition of, for developmentally disabled" (p.364).

### The Promotion of the "Quality of Life" Construct with Deathmaking Motives

The six problems reviewed so far could, at least in theory, be handled by application of intellectual and scientific rigor. This is not the case with the seventh problem, because it is primarily one of high-order worldview and morality. The seventh problem is the invocation of either the QOL term or construct — and recently both — in order to morally justify the deathmaking of humans. [How QOL has been invoked in the context of "euthanasia," and what some of the problems with such an invocation are, has been elaborated by Lusthaus (1985)].

The sequence of thinking and argument in invoking QOL on behalf of deathmaking has gone something like this.

1. Right from the first, proponents of a QOL concept in a deathmaking context conveyed the message that the value of living was related to the quality of one's living or life. Even the very grammar of the term "quality of life" facilitated a line of thinking that went via "quality of life" to "quality of living," to the "quality of a life," from there to both "the quality of a person" and the "value of a life."

2. Once people began to equate quality of life with value of life or living, they could easily be recruited into endorsing a belief many people already had been harboring unconsciously anyway, namely, that some people are less valuable than others.

3. In turn, by characterizing different lives, and different phases of single and individual lives, as having more or less quality, the idea was conveyed that the value of lives and of people could and should be judged in a quantitative rather than qualitative fashion, i.e., in terms of continua without clear and unequivocal benchmarks, rather than in terms of qualitative, discrete and indivisible criterion entities. In other words, some lives were to be judged as more valuable than others, and some parts of one's life (e.g., one's youth) were judged as more valuable than other parts (e.g., one's senescence). Thus, the unborn were automatically of little or no value, the newborn and very young were less valuable than adults, and as one progressed from one's mid-years into senescence, one again became less valuable.

4. Once the value of life is defined in terms of its quality, it seems inevitable that people who are judged by society to be valued and productive would also be judged as having more quality of life than others, and would therefore be given preference over societally devalued people in matters such as medical treatment.

While most people are not even aware that they have been led from a qualitative to a quantitative conception of human life and value, those whom I call the dupers who lead the flock astray have been very clear on the issue.

For instance, that miserable German philosopher, Friedrich Nietzsche (1844-1900), (I could never understand why anyone other than people of decadent or confused moral mentality would celebrate and teach him, or consider him an ethical giant) had already promoted a concept related to QOL (although of course not the term, aside from it being in English), together with (a) virulent attacks on the notion of sanctity of life, and (b) notions of getting rid of people who were of low utility to others. He spoke of higher and lower "types of man," and of "ascending" and "descending" ones. He said that the higher type is to be esteemed "higher in value" and "worthier of life" (Schacht, 1983, pp.333-334). One class of humans Nietzsche called the "sick," "botched," "broken," "misbegotten," and "enfeebled" (some translations add "bungled") (Werkmeister, 1961, p.195). To him, *Übermensch* (superhuman, or literally "overhuman," sometimes translated as "superman") was the ideal. All of this Nietzsche subsumed under his call for an *Umwertung aller Werte*, i.e., an inversion of all values, by which he meant specifically Christian values, and their alliance with "everything that is weak, low, botched" (Werkmeister, 1961, p.207). Indeed, the culture of modernism has since become totally inverted, as compared to its Judeo-Christian ancestry, and Amir (1977) called Nietzsche one of the "modern apostles," together with Thomas Hobbes (1588-1679), Herbert Spencer (1820-1903), and various social Darwinists.

Nietzsche was a major source of inspiration to the Nazis, because of his celebration of power, strength and will. His exaltation of will also underlies our own contemporary modernism that more and more focuses on *individual will* over either intellect, rationality, or collective welfare, or even collective will. At any rate, Nietzsche's explicit attack on the notion of the sanctity of human life served both Nazism and modernism well. Nietzsche's assertion that "each individual invent his own virtue" is precisely what modernism asserts: each individual is his/her own god, and not beholden to any values from outside, including any from above. Obedience to higher external principles he called "a sacrifice to the Moloch of abstraction" (Werkmeister, 1961).

And while Nietzsche did not advocate hedonism, he did exalt the human body over the soul, implying that the soul was just a name for a bodily manifestation (Werkmeister, 1961). Not surprisingly, such an interpretation is very consistent with the modernistic body obsession, and is a stepping stone to the materialistic indulgence of the body of which we see so much these days. The very reason Nietzsche rejected hedonism is instructive: in his hatred toward divinity, and Christianity especially, he wanted the human to be full master of the universe, and hedonism would be an obstacle to the disciplined exertion of the human "will to power," as he called it. (A better translation may be "the determination to seek power." We should thus not be surprised about the contemporary "empowerment" crazes.)

Many modernists would recoil at the idea — true as it is — that their ideology has much in common with the ideological sources of Nazism. In fact, they would "will away" in Nietzschean fashion, or "emote away," such a suggestion, rather than study it rationally.

The single most influential book underlying the movement to get rid of dependent people in Germany was the 1920 *Die Freigabe der Vernichtung lebensunwerten Lebens* by Binding and Hoche (1920), freely translated as *The Legitimization to Annihilate Unworthy Life*, but often rendered more literally as *The Release of the Destruction of Life Devoid of Value* (Sassone, 1975). These authors explicitly used the term "value of life," and invoked a construct of QOL, though again, not the term itself. They interpreted the two as continuous rather than discrete variables, and closely intertwined the QOL concept with the value of life. These continua were to be judged by objective, external social criteria of utility, and not by subjective ones, such as whether a person wanted to live. At a certain (low) level of quality, they said such a "ballast existence" should be terminated. We can assume with confidence that if Binding and Hoche had had the term "quality of life" at their disposal, they would have used it with abandon.

As has been amply documented, the orgy of killing of handicapped people in the territories under Nazi control during World War II had its roots in a combination of Nietzschean philosophy, a materialistic worldview, and a materialization of medicine, with medicine ending up playing a major — if not the major — role in the killing and advocacy of it. As has recently been documented, this kind of killing was apparently in the early stages of breaking out in other countries as well, especially in Britain and in the US. It was inhibited from unfolding by what happened under Nazism, and by its linkage with other events, that the world was *more* willing to acknowledge as atrocities than the killing of the handicapped. After the shock of the Nazi era, materialized medicine lay low for a short generation, but then collected itself, and once more sallied forth forcefully, becoming increasingly open about wanting to get rid of people whom it saw as affording little utility to others.

One of the single most influential developments in getting people to shift from a qualitative view of the value of human life to a quantitative one was the effort by leaders of the deathmaking culture to get people to think in terms of "persons" rather than humans. And two events in this effort were particularly impactful.

The first was an incredibly silly set of "indicators of personhood" developed by a supposed "theologian," Joseph Fletcher, and published in a series of elaborations starting in 1972 (e.g., Fletcher, 1972, 1975). He asserted that all of the following "indicators" had to be present in order for someone to qualify as a "person:" (1) minimal intelligence (IQ below 40, "questionably a person"; IQ below 20, "not a person"); (2) self-awareness; (3) self-control; (4) a sense of time; (5) a sense of futurity; (6) a sense of past; (7) capability to relate to others; (8) concern for others; (9) communication; (10) control of one's existence; (11) curiosity; (12) changeability, and not being opposed to change; (13) balance and rationality of feelings; (14) idiosyncrasy; and (15) neo-cortical functioning.

This set of indicators was very swiftly embraced by the deathmaking culture all over the world, and has ever since been ceaselessly cited as an authoritative, almost axiomatic, formulation.

The second development occurred in 1973 when the United States Supreme Court ruled that unborn children were not persons and — with the federal government having no overriding interest in the matter — could be killed on demand by their mothers.

These two developments sketched above convinced many people (a) that the morality of killing someone should be drawn on the issue of personhood, not humanhood, and (b) that personhood was not a qualitative entity but a quantitative continuum, so that the less personhood someone possessed, the more permissible it was to kill him/her/it. In other words, the construct of "quality of life" came to replace the traditional Judeo-Christian belief in the absolute and intrinsic value of the life of each individual, or what one might call the "quality of the value of the human." The concept of "quality of life" also began to be used to characterize the lives of individuals rather than of societies, as mentioned; the three concepts of *quality of life, value of life,* and *value of people* began to merge; and the merits of the lives of certain individuals could now be denied. Some people could be interpreted as having no value whatever.

Because Americans have had a tradition of looking to the law as a major moral authority, the Supreme Court's semantic de-definition of the unborn as persons under the law had not only legal effects, but also helped change the minds of many Americans about (a) the humanness of the unborn, and (b) the morality of killing them. In fact, the pattern of changes in opinion polls before and after the 1973 US Supreme Court decision suggests that about a third of Americans rather quickly changed their minds about the morality of abortion.

Even the leaders of the deathmaking culture agree on the interpretation I am giving to the 1973 US Supreme Court decision, and similar decisions elsewhere. For instance, Peter Singer, one of the leading contemporary philosophers of deathmaking, said, "The ethical outlook that holds human life to be sacrosanct — shall I call it the 'sanctity-of-life-view' — is under attack. The first major blow to the sanctity of life view was the spreading acceptance of abortion throughout the western world" (Singer, 1983).

However, Fletcher's scheme had more impact than the 1973 US Supreme Court decision on how people viewed the newborn, severely retarded, and demented. His scheme thus became a taking-off point, or a launching point, for all sorts of utilitarian arguments in favor of deathmaking. Once Fletcher's "sliding scale" of personhood was more or less accepted, a sliding scale of QOL as a relevant variable in life-and-death decisions could also be easily conceptualized and swallowed.

One thing that all of this illustrates is just how difficult it is to think straight or moralize well once one has abandoned moral absolutes, and perhaps even abandoned thought framed in terms of discrete and qualitative criteria.

It is no coincidence at all that in North America, a major shift of the QOL construct and term from a population use to an individual and clinical one took place shortly after (a) the 1973 US Supreme Court decision that legalized abortion on demand, (b) the appearance and popularization of Fletcher's schema, and (c) the reemergence from the closet of a utilitarian materialized medicine that demanded the right to decide who was unfit to live. This "coming-out" started in connection with medical infanticide. Physicians once more began to call openly for deathmaking of impaired infants, and several prominent medical parties admitted openly for the first time that they had, in fact, been secretly making such infants dead for several years.

Several publications in the early 1970s were landmark "coming out of the closet" cases of medical deathmaking after World War II.

One of these in the US was the highly publicized starvation of a newborn infant with Down's syndrome at Johns Hopkins University Hospital in Baltimore, Maryland. A widely-disseminated and shameless film, "Who Shall Survive?", was even made in 1971 of this shameful episode. Another was a 1973 article by Duff and Campbell (1973) in which they admitted that they had been practicing so-called passive euthanasia on newborn infants at the Yale-New Haven Hospital in Connecticut for several years.

In Britain, John Lorber started coming out with a series of studies (commonly referred to as the Sheffield studies) that increasingly recommended against active treatment of many infants born with spinal anomalies or hydrocephaly. In 1971, he said that at most 7% of the survivors "may

be considered to have a quality of life not inconsistent with self-respect, earning capacity, happiness and even marriage." His overall recommendation was that "only those should be given active treatment who may look forward to a life without grave handicaps." (By the way, the invocation of the word "grave" as an adjective or adverb in life-and-death medical contexts almost invariably reflects a deathmaking mentality, and anticipates the "grave" as a noun). From at least 1971 on, Lorber (1971) used the phrase "quality of life" in a prominent fashion, together with "quality of surviving children" and "quality of survivors," many of whom were said to create an "unbearable situation" for their families. Lorber also contributed to the reemergence of the term "selection" which had been a euphemism for killing people under the Nazis. Until the "coming out" period, people had eschewed that term.

These events opened the floodgates on other kinds of deathmakings, on deathmakings elsewhere, and on other comings-out. [However, a year before the 1973 article by Duff and Campbell, Shaw (1972) had already admitted in a professionally less prominent medium (The *New York Times* magazine of 30 January 1972) that he had withheld medical treatments from impaired infants.]

Shortly thereafter, one of the directions into which deathmaking promotion expanded was toward chronically medically dependent and severely impaired people, and the senile elderly. De facto deathmaking expanded also toward other groups, though this was less likely to be publicly acknowledged, namely the following: street people; mentally impaired people who were not senile, including mentally retarded people, especially when these became hospital patients; and mentally disordered people, as these began to be made dead mostly through excessive long-term dosing with prescriptive psychoactive drugs.

As touched on previously, it was particularly since ca. 1980 that the term and construct of QOL has been seized by parties (including materialized medicine) that promote the deathmaking of members of unwanted classes. These parties have used the QOL term and construct in order to promote their goals, often in ways that sow confusion among more naive people, and thereby recruit them into acquiescence to — or even collaboration with — deathmaking.

Sages throughout the ages have instructed us that violence is *always* attended by deception. Therefore, it is to be inferred that many people who promote medical deathmaking really have no genuine interest in diminishing the moral and mental chaos that surrounds the QOL term and construct that they have found to be so useful in service to deathmaking.

For instance, deathmaking leader Peter Singer (1983) explicitly titled one of his articles, "Sanctity of Life or Quality of Life?" In this article, Singer said that compared to a "severely defective human infant," a healthy dog or pig "will often...have superior capacities...for...anything...that can plausibly be considered morally significant."

Yet more recently, deathmaking promotion has taken the twist of persuading people to commit suicide, or to help others to commit suicide — and QOL talk has played a big role in this. For example, the notorious suicide assistant Dr. Jack Kevorkian claims that he only helps those people to commit suicide (according to

some accounts, he also kills people) whose "life quality has to be nil" (Time, 31 May 1993), but this is either a blatant lie or a gross misinterpretation of "life quality," since some of his victims had very good life conditions, and only poor *long-term* prognosis. Another example is the Columbia Foundation, dedicated to the "quality of life for residents in the Bay Area" (i.e., around San Francisco), awarding a major grant to Hemlock of Northern California, an organization devoted to the promotion of suicide (*International Anti-Euthanasia Task Force Update*, January & February, 1993, p. 5). In other words, dying and helping people to kill themselves, is interpreted as improving their QOL! Is there now even QOL after death? One almost wonders how people ever managed to kill themselves before without access to this term. (For a much more extensive coverage of the contemporary dynamics of deathmaking of devalued people see, Wolfensberger, 1992b).

An example of attributing differential value to the lives of different people, and how this leads to deathmaking, is the use of the word "futile." In just a few years since the late 1980s, there has been an explosion of discourse on "futility," "futile treatment," and "medical futility" in the medical and "bio-ethics" literature. Some writers are building their publishing reputation on this theme. However, "futility" is also quickly going the way of "quality of life" in that the definitions of futility have begun to proliferate.

"Futility" would be a perfectly legitimate and useful term if it were used exclusively to characterize a treatment that does not have efficacy, i.e., that has no positive effects on outcome. But almost normatively now, "futility" is invoked with multiple and mixed meanings, and is almost always linked to discourses on QOL, and often even discourses on how costly modern medicine is, how costs must be contained, how crowded hospitals and nursing homes are, and how expensive aged and dependent people are. Inevitably, the term "futile" gets transferred in a listener's or reader's mind to these other issues, and begins to convey a sense of the futility of the *lives* of debilitated people.

A good example of the above is found in an article in the *Journal of the American Medical Association* (Murphy, 1988). A closely related example occurred in another article in the same key journal (Hackler & Hiller, 1990). For two pages, it compellingly discusses instances in which medical treatment is technically "futile," i.e., brings no benefits, and on top of that is even torturous. Yet following this, the discourse suddenly begins to intertwine QOL with questions of technical efficacy of treatment, although the QOL issue is totally irrelevant to a discussion of how likely it is that a treatment will be efficacious in a technical sense.

All this is a most subtly deceptive way of confusing people, and duping them into agreement to deathmaking. Now readers will end up with the idea that for many debilitated patients, treatment is futile because of their low QOL, rather than because it is ineffective!

One of the profound errors or deceptions that one encounters over and over again in the "futility" literature (e.g., Jecker & Pearlman, 1992) is that QOL is associated with medical treatment rather than the affected person. Whatever QOL is or is not, it refers to the life circumstances of a person and, in the above case, after medicine has

done its thing. To link QOL to the medical measure applied, or not applied, is absurd. A smallpox vaccination has no QOL, but a person who gets one may have something that someone can define as QOL. One cannot even say that it is a medical treatment that determines QOL, except in very constrained ways, e.g., when the treatment itself debilitates someone. Otherwise, treatment can only, and at best, *remove obstacles to QOL*.

Schneiderman, Jecker and Jonsen (1990), and Jecker and Schneiderman (1992) came right out and proposed that the term "futility" be used equally for two very distinct situations: (a) where the likelihood of achieving treatment benefits is exceedingly low, and (b) where even successful treatments leave a patient with "a quality of life well-below a threshold considered minimal." Jecker and Pearlman (1992) then elaborated on the earlier two Jecker and Schneiderman (1992) components by calling them quantitative and qualitative futility, with treatment benefits and the patient's eventual QOL being quite illogically combined under the qualitative component. Jecker and Pearlman (1992) also confusingly juxtaposed "futility" with things such as rationing of health care, health care costs, and aged patients; and the authors were chaotically insistent in violating the very distinction between efficacy of treatment and patient QOL that Jecker and Schneiderman (1992) had distinguished in their earlier article. (By the way, I found it ominous that Jecker and Schneiderman (1992) quite unnecessarily used the term "qualities of persons" in their article.)

"Bioethicist" Daniel Callahan and others are said by Jecker and Schneiderman (1992) to have claimed that "life extending care in old age is futile in a broader sense; death in old age is inevitable...," as if death were not inevitable for everyone.

In May 1993, no less than the editor of the *Journal of the American Medical Association* published an editorial (Lundberg, 1993) calling for 90% of US hospitals to have in place by 1996 what the author called "futile care policies," thereby saving up to scores of billions of dollars. He cited as exemplary the policy of one hospital that included in its definition of "futile care" those treatments that do not have a reasonable possibility of restoring "a quality of life that would be satisfactory to the patient." (Of course, in actual practice, people other than the patient often make the determination of satisfactoriness.) And what about all the lowly afflicted people so familiar to us in our work who never had what modernistic medical people would have considered a satisfactory QOL even prior to any treatment at issue? We can easily see how the earlier linkage of the construct of "futility" to QOL in the same journal was a stalking horse for the ever-expanding juggernaut of deathmaking of medically debilitated people, in part in concert with cost-saving arguments.

We want to impress upon the reader how seriously the publications on "futility" are apt to be taken; they were, for the most part, published in highly prestigious medical journals.

The difference between futility of treatment vs. futility of life (as implied by a judgment that QOL of the patient would be low after treatment) is absolutely crucial, if for no other reason than this: futility of treatment is a relatively objectifiable phenomenon on which the vast majority of technically qualified people can eventually come to an agreement in the vast majority of instances. This can never be the case in regard to QOL—and particularly not if one claims that QOL is subjective! And yet, when it comes to invoking QOL on behalf of deathmaking, the deathmakers act as if QOL were as objective as determining treatment efficacy. What hypocrisy in most cases; and in the others, what stupidity by smart, educated people! In practice, the arguments here become totally circular: if party A decides that it is time for party B to die, then party A invokes poor or "nonexistent" QOL, and/or "futility." Most of the time, this seems to "work."

We also believe that we can discern one of the motives in the linkage of futility, costs and QOL issues. Namely, the new concern with costs is not really a concern with bringing better health to the population, or lightening the public's burden of taxes, health insurance and medical payments. After all, imperial medicine was blissfully driving costs up with abandon, without such concerns, and will continue to strive for an ever larger slice of the gross domestic product (GNP). Instead, imperial cost concerns now are an effort to stave off external controls for awhile by appeasing public discontent by transferring funds from the care of devalued people to the rest of imperial high-technology medicine, so that it can go on its way undisturbed. The yoked invocation of futility and QOL is an expedient way to garner public support for this strategy, even though external control will probably come anyway. If costs were the real issue, there would be other ways to cut them dramatically, but in ways that would be vastly more painful to imperial medicine than making feeble people dead.

Of course, all this discourse deals with

who should be made dead, and when, because of low QOL. *How* people are made dead would presumably be covered by a QOD (quality of death) construct.

Once QOL began to be successfully invoked as a basis for deciding who should be made dead, a British economist named Alan Williams "improved" on this process by inventing the QALY (pronounced qually) construct, i.e., "quality-adjusted life years," which refers to how many years someone is expected to live, and what the presumed QOL of that person would be during those years. Quickly, the QALY construct got enscaled (Gudex, 1987), so that one could establish a quantitative QALY score for each patient. In turn one could decide how much presumed benefit would be obtained from treating one patient rather than another, or what the presumed cost/yield ratio would be for giving a treatment of known cost to different patients. First, the formula establishes the QALY score by inserting an estimate of how long the person is apt to live after a medical procedure, and what the quality of a person's life would be. These two figures are then multiplied by each other. Next they are divided into the cost of the procedure, which yields a cost-per-QALY-point index. Differences in the cost-per-QALY of different treatments, figured on a class or population basis, can be dramatic. For instance, as of 1983, it would have been $1220 for injections for pregnant women so as to prevent Rh disease in their babies; hospital dialysis for kidney disease raked up a score of $54,000 (Torrance & Feeny, 1989). One could thus decide that a certain treatment should be given if it could be expected to yield so many QALY points, which are referred to as QALYs, or cost less than so-

and-so much per QALY. Medical economists waxed ecstatic at this development, but one writer (Ragg, 1993) called QALYs the "rather-be-dead rating."

The deathmaking of societally devalued classes that we now see in progress would have occurred even without the invocation of QOL, but was certainly facilitated by it. One way in which the deathmaking culture did this was by subverting the traditional Judeo-Christian belief that human life was intrinsically sacred, and the following sequence of arguments and developments played a big role in this subversion.

The moment QOL is used in a way that implies something about the value of human life, it becomes part of all sorts of older ideas about the differential value of human lives. For instance, outside the Judeo-Christian value system, it has been widely believed, throughout history, that members of societies other than one's own had less value as human beings — if they could even be considered to be human at all. Social Darwinists used to argue that the less evolved a race was, the less value did the lives of its members have. The lives of Negroes were less valuable simply because they were viewed as closer to dogs and apes than to civilized Europeans (Stein, 1988).

Once we perceive the politics and historicity of the QOL term, then we are no longer surprised to note that it (and related terms, such as value of life) have an extremely high likelihood of being encountered whenever efforts are underfoot to deprive an impaired or sick person of life. Yet the same people from whose lips QOL language oozes with ease where it serves deathmaking purposes will seldom be heard to invoke the term in order to decry the gross injustices that are inflicted on certain groups and classes in society by those who are more advantaged and privileged.

One can turn this discovery around, and assert that when people who virtually never invoke QOL language in pursuit of social justice and in confrontation of systematic societal oppression begin to invoke it in reference to a debilitated or devalued person — and especially in medical contexts — then it is likely that a fundamental commitment (even if still unconscious) to death has already been made. This likelihood is further and dramatically increased if QOL language is emitted contiguous with other deathmaking-related terms, such as "death with dignity," "right to die," "brain death," "persistent vegetative state," etc., or when QOL is discussed in explicit connection with whether a person should live or die.

Once people got the idea that life with low quality was not worth living, then people who had been deprived of the good things of life by others, usually via oppression and devaluation, could be said to be "better off dead." This results in a gruesome vicious circle. On the one hand, people *always* oppress. This is a human universal: all societies sooner or later engage in social stratification and oppression of their lower strata, and often also of populations outside their own. Such oppression is normatively onerous, and produces what could be called low QOL. By the above circular logic, this implies that at a certain point, oppressed people develop something that one can call — and that has occasionally been called — a "need to die." What about people in concentration camps? Should one kill them because of their low quality of life? Or for that matter, when a sick person

is about to be taken to a concentration camp, should one first give them medical care? That the answers given by many people would tilt toward death seems underlined by a survey done in Australia that asked people questions about QOL. Seven percent of the respondents said that being dead was better than "having a disability," which goes beyond even saying that I would rather be dead than "have a disability" (personal communication from Ross Womersley).

This whole vicious circle fulfills Nietzsche's dictum that the one who is about to fall down should be pushed down. Nietzsche also said, "The weak and the failures shall perish: first principle of *our* love of man. And they shall be given every possible assistance." *"Vernichtung des Missrathenen — dazu muss man sich von der bisherigen Moral emancipiren"* ("The annihilation of the misbegotten — for that one must emancipate oneself from the previous morality") (Bernstein, 1987, p.142).

Just how intertwined a QOL construct is in people's minds with life conditions that are the result of being, or not being, devalued and oppressed by others becomes apparent when one examines some proposed QOL indices and operationalizations. For Boone and Stevens (1991), QOL includes socioeconomic status, access to people willing to form and maintain positive relations, and opportunities for personal development, for being productive, and for participating in social, community and civic events. Aside from reeking of Fletcher if such criteria were to be tied to questions of humanhood or personhood, this kind of QOL construct comes close to being an index of participation in the experiences of valued classes. If that is what we want, we should call it that, and make a better index thereof. And if such an index is to play a role, perhaps even a determining one, in deciding whom to kill, then the Jews in Nazi Germany could indeed have been said to be better off dead.

We can cite a specific example of how QOL has gotten to be invoked as a death-making ploy in the service of cultural values. In a major 1990 article (mentioned before) in the *Journal of the American Medical Association*, Hackler and Hiller (1990) argued that the medical profession should ignore, and be legally allowed to ignore, a family's wishes that a patient be treated if the treatment would not sustain "an acceptable quality of life," with quality of life being in effect defined by majority opinion in the culture, namely, when the family's "views about suffering and quality of life differ substantially from those of most reasonable people...then the physicians should not be forced by hospital policy to adhere to family preference" (p.1283).

This position not only reflects the modernistic ideas of QOL reviewed above, but also the arrogance of the medical imperium, and its lack of introspection upon itself, as if this imperium, once granted authority to determine who should live and die, would restrain itself of its own accord. At any rate, what about a patient and family from an ascetic religious subculture, and/or with a belief system that suffering can be redemptive? Are the values of a decadent hedonistic modernism that views suffering the way people once viewed the devil to be allowed to dictate who should receive medical treatment among those minorities who are not of these values and this worldview?

Of course, Hackler & Hiller (1990) are not the first ones to demand that the family be factored out of life-and-death decisions.

See, for instance, Murphy (1988), and to some extent Jecker and Pearlman (1992).

We might also contemplate the curious fact that QOL constructs are often so conceptualized or operationalized as to actually reinforce the values that underlie the construct. In our modernistically materialistic society, the good things in life are considered to include youthfulness, beauty, intelligence, education, competence, material possessions, and hedonistic sensualistic enjoyment thereof. Thus, the ugly, old, retarded, poor, suffering, etc., who lack these qualities, or who embody their opposites, will automatically be seen or defined to "have" low quality of life, and therefore be better off dead.

Furthermore, and quite obviously, it will be inevitable that it will be people who possess the attributes perceived to make for a high quality of life who would *decide* the needs, quality of life, and life itself, of people who are deficient in them. However, the people who lack them commonly have been brainwashed into the same value system, and can often be brought to agree that they would, indeed, be better off dead if they cannot be or have what the privileged sector of society is and has. Thus, the "adaptation level" effect discussed earlier enters in here, and people who live like kings once did may now be deemed to "need" to die for lack of QOL.

Within such a framework, there occurs a radical reduction in any incentive to perceive or comprehend the vicious circle of societal wound-striking, oppression and deathmaking. What is interpreted as low QOL does not get addressed so much by raising consciousness about oppression as by making dead the "incumbents" or "inhabitants" of low QOL — those who are said to "have" it.

That I am not exaggerating can be illustrated by just one example among many — an example useful here because it comes from a source that had received much publicity. In his 1985 book, *Playing God in The Nursery*, Jeff Lyons (1985), a brother (!) of a retarded person, advocated the deathmaking of impaired infants. He came to this conclusion after becoming aware of the miserable conditions of the institution in which his brother had been put. So here is how he fell victim to the above circularity, and then became a true-believer propagator of it: an impaired child is born; society treats this child badly, so that the child grows to live in very bad conditions; these conditions evoke our compassion; blinded to the societal processes of social devaluation, he concludes that the disadvantaged person should have been made dead outright when it was first discovered that the person was likely to become a societal victim. And failure to make the person dead in timely fashion is interpreted as "playing God"!

This whole episode also illustrates another extremely common phenomenon, namely, how people first duped by leaders of deathmaking often end up becoming deathmaker dupers themselves.

Many have argued like Lyons. For instance, the very fact that parents who want to take care of their handicapped infant are apt to receive little support and help from society is often cited as a rationale for making the child dead in order to preserve it (and its family) from a poor QOL. When handicapped children are involved whose parents are not functional or who have abandoned them, the deathmaking arguments intensify. For instance, Lorber (1971) recommended as early as 1971 that among children born with spinal defects, less treatment efforts should be invested if these children had less functional families, even if the clinical conditions were comparable to those of children of functional families.

A parallel to this whole line of moral reasoning can be drawn from what used to be an immensely popular American comic strip called "Li'l Abner." In one of its episodes, someone was putting poison into the canned beans of the people of Dogpatch. Charged with protecting the people, detective Fearless Fosdick would creep around outside people's houses, peek through their windows, and quickly put a bullet through the head of any unsuspecting victim about to eat beans, thereby insuring that the person would not die from poisoning.

Yet another policy very remindful of all this was the one practiced by the US military in Vietnam, namely, "destroying a village in order to save it." This was no idle or humorous figure of speech, because a high military officer who was being interviewed actually agreed that this was the policy — and the correct one.

As part of the assault on the notion of sanctity of life, some people (including highly prominent medical leaders of deathmaking) have argued that whenever one fails to apply so-called extraordinary or "heroic" medical measures, one has made a judgment about QOL, i.e., that support of the particular life at issue is not worth the "cost." However, moral and/or rational allocations of treatment resources *can* be made on the basis of criteria other than perceived value of the patient. A common logical (and potential language) error in such instances is to claim that *any* preferential treatment constitutes a judgment of the value of people and/or their lives.

Just how perverse the use of the QOL term has become, and how it has become mostly a killing phrase springing from a killing thought, is exemplified by the widely-cited proposal by Shaw (1977) for how to decide whether a newborn child should be given life-defending medical treatments. Shaw proposed what he called a "formula," as follows: $QOL = NE \times (H + S)$, where QOL stands for quality of life; NE stands for natural endowment of the child, both physical and intellectual; H stands for the contribution made to the child by the home and family; and S stands for contributions made to the child by society. Thus, one is somehow supposed to calculate how much a child's home and family, and how much society, would give to the child, add these together, multiply them by the child's natural endowments (which one is supposedly able to determine), and this would result in an index of the child's quality of life!

Of course, little of all this can be determined, and least of all at the beginning of a child's life. And further, none of these variables consist of quantities that could be inserted into a mathematical formula. But how undermined people's thinking and morality have become, at least in part through the manipulation of their linguistic systems, is clear from the fact that when Shaw's "formula" is presented, people do not laugh! They are no longer able to recognize its ridiculous and deceptive pretentiousness. By using mathematical symbols and formulas of science, it pretends to be scientific, and therefore respectable. Had people rolled on the floor laughing when it was first presented, that would have been the end of it. Instead, Shaw's "formula" caught on like wildfire, and like Fletcher's "indicators," has frequently since been cited

in the "bioethics" and medical culture as a given — an authoritative and axiomatic beginning in the discussion of which infants to make dead. It was his publication of this formula in 1977 that shot Shaw to prominence, rather than his 1972 article in the *New York Times Magazine.*

How Shaw's formula was soon widely invoked is exemplified (and one could cite many other examples) by a series of major articles (by no less than Jeff Lyons himself) in the *Chicago Tribune* (6,7,8,9,10 & 24 February, & 3 March, 1983) that gave a very prominent role to considerations of "quality of life" and the costs involved in saving damaged newborns.

Why did people fail to realize that Shaw's formula was no more than a killing thought fraudulently expressed in a fashion so as to lend it the cloak of scientific and medical respectability — the aura of objective medical and factual judgment? After all, this use of formulas with abbreviations is the grossest form of deception, because these abbreviations try to convey to observers the idea that the formula is scientific, since science uses such abbreviations in mathematics, physics and chemistry. Yet in this case, the formula neither expresses an exact quantitative mathematical operation, nor was there any compelling reason to use abbreviations for something that could have been said briefly, and much more clearly and forthrightly, in plain prose.

The answer is probably three-fold. (a) People's minds have been crazified by the shift in the culture from a qualitative to a quantitative conception of human life and its value. This makes so many moral decisions relative, slippery and uncertain, and mushes people's moral minds. (b) Shaw's deception "worked": people were prepared by their culture to acknowledge deathmaking as legitimate if it could be shown to be "scientific." That people have had a tendency to do this in many parts of Western culture since the age of the enlightenment has been documented before. (c) In their hearts, many people really want to see certain devalued classes or persons dead. Thus, they do not need much persuasion to let their inner feeling out of the bag, only permission and detoxification (i.e., interpreting something bad in a way that makes it seem good) such as QOL talk provides.

I have tried to raise people's consciousness about the phony scientificness of Shaw's formula by inventing the following *reductio ad absurdum*, namely, a "scientific formula" for determining who should be killed, where and how in Nazi Germany, viz., JG + JR = CC + G, where JG stands for Jewish genes, JR for Jewish religion, CC for concentration camp, and G for poison gas. In other words, according to this "formula," if someone had Jewish ancestors through several generations and was of the Jewish religion, even if only on paper, then the person was to be taken to a concentration camp and gassed to death. This formula is much more quantitative than Shaw's, and we can count our lucky stars that the Nazis did not think it up, else more people — at least, the morally gullible modernistic people of today — might have concurred in the Holocaust.

We should also note that many people become furiously incensed at such analogies, even when made in jest, and yet many of those same people concur in the killing of other "undesirable" people by pseudo-mathematical formulaic medical "prescription."

There have been others who also not only recognized the phoniness of Shaw's "formula," but also deconstructed it satirically. For instance, columnist Edward John Hudak had the insight that Shaw's real formula was HC1 - HC2 = 0, where HC1 is the handicapped child, HC2 human care, and 0 equals death. The funnily sad thing is that Hudak's is probably the most mathematical of all three "formulae"! (This was in one of his late 1985 or 1896 columns; I have the clipping but was unable to trace the date.)

How about this:

QOL - L + QOD = 0; QED.

A participant at one of our workshops on the deathmaking of devalued people gave us a ca. 1985 cartoon by Brian Peterson, showing a cheery physician with a hand-held calculator telling a mother (Mrs.Bifida), "I can appreciate this may be difficult for you to follow, so I will just calculate this out. O.K., QL = NE x (H + S). You see QL is quality of life, NE is natural endowment, H is the expected contribution from home and family, S is the expected contribution from society. Well, let's see, hmmm..big zero on the credit side. We are talking a big deficit here. Too bad these things are not covered on warranty. Well, Mrs. Bifida, no sense being unrealistic, let's just nip this one in the bud. Mrs. Bifida, Mrs. Bifida..." who, by that time has fainted away and is lying prostrate on the floor.

A Canadian whose name we cannot retrieve wrote the following poem about the same time.

*QL = NE x (H + S)*

*or*

*...Death as a Management Option*
*Management by drugs or knife*

*improves the quality of life,*
*but to really take your breath*
*consider management by death...*
*(Management by death, you say?*
*Well, keep your options open, eh?)*
*Until it has passed the "human" test*
*it's just a bunch of cells, at best.*
*If it doesn't get a passing grade*
*a management decision will be made.*
*(Management by death, you say?*
*Well, keep your options open, eh)*
*QL equals NE squared-*
*unless of course the babe's impaired;*
*then we look at H plus S*
*to determine human-ness*
*(Management by death, you say?*
*Keep your options open, eh?)*
*The Executive Level will play God*
*with your tiny baby's bod'.*
*It isn't murder that we're doing,*
*but management options we're pursuing.*
*(Management by death, you say?*
*Ah, keep your options open, eh?)*

An era is ahead of us in which there will be ever greater demand for, and agreement to, the deathmaking of all sorts of limited, impaired and devalued people, where their deathmaking will become ever more legitimized and legalized. Among the most immediate targets will be the impaired newborn, the debilitated elderly, and people in between these ages who are very medically dependent with little likelihood of recovery. The latter includes people with impaired consciousness, paralyzed people when they become ill, and people in the more advanced stages of AIDS. People at the lower end of mental retardation are also very much at risk. Almost literally every day, we learn of yet another attempt to legitimize deathmaking of such people, or

of actual deadmakings. The construct of QOL, or constructs without that name but with pretty much the same content, play a large role in the arguments in support of such deathmaking, and/or the reasoning or sentiments behind it.

The medical deathmaking that is now rampant in the Netherlands, and that is so detoxified by being referred to as "euthanasia," and as "voluntary" at that (which is at least in part a lie), is a striking example of where accepting QOL arguments in regard to life and death can lead. While the exact figures are debated, it is estimated that anywhere from one in every six, to one in every three, deaths in the Netherlands is medically induced, some in response to a desire by the patient to avoid or end suffering, and some to a desire by the physician to end or prevent a patient's misery. Of the eight neonatal centers in the Netherlands, five have been actively killing newborns who have a predicted "poor quality of life," and three have done it to older impaired infants (*National Right to Life News*, 23 February 1993).

Soon we can expect a call to mercifully make dead the babies of cocaine-addicted mothers, buttressed by arguments for how the human service system is ever less able to provide for such babies, and how difficult it is to find wholesome adoptive and foster homes for them.

Exaggeration? Well, consider thisthen: a survey of 247 neonatal specialists revealed that they favored letting babies of women with AIDS die because the babies would have a poor "quality of life," even if the babies themselves were not infected (AP, *Syracuse Herald Journal*, 12 June 1991)! Dear reader, pinch yourself! The neonatalist culture in the United States wants to make dead *healthy* babies whenever it appears that they will have poor QOL due to inadequate parenting! Soon it will become chic to let anybody die whom anybody *else* thinks *might* have a poor quality of life, but even this will not be enough. Deathmaking movements expand until they devour themselves. Thus, one Dutch physician has already voiced the logical extreme of all this. He asserted that it was the duty of the physician to kill as many people as possible in general because life consisted of innumerable and endless sufferings, and killing people would spare them having to endure suffering (Fenigsen, 1990), which is quite true, as far as it goes.

While many afflicted people are getting brainwashed into believing that they ought to be dead, advocates of QOL criteria for deathmaking purposes have commonly not been particularly interested in ascertaining, or acknowledging, what handicapped or otherwise afflicted people themselves think about the value or quality of their lives. Yet every formal (e.g., Diamond, 1977, p.70) or informal inquiry I have heard of has found that the vast majority of handicapped people were glad they were born, wanted to live, and had positive anticipations for the future. (Even some non-handicapped people keep expressing the same sentiments.) That afflicted people are so often not asked these questions should not surprise one, since we noted before that the people perceived to possess QOL will be deciding who does not.

However, even if society did succeed in making the lives of handicapped people so miserable that they say they would rather die or wished that they had never been born, this still could not be used as sufficient moral grounds by others to grant them their wish.

Of all the problems of QOL reviewed in this chapter, the hijacking of QOL in service to deathmaking is by far the worst. After all, the other problems are often associated with worthy motives, whereas the clever systematic, and successful yoking of ever more massive deathmaking to QOL language has something demonic to it.

## A Call to Abandon the "Quality of Life" Phrase, and Improve the Related Constructs

We can now see not only how profoundly problematic the QOL term and construct have become, but also how many of the above problems interact, each time "making chaos worse," if that were possible. For instance, if someone confuses definitions with components, determinants or predictors, and then talks past another party in terms of population or individual application, and in terms of subjective or objective criteria, one might just as well quit communicating — perhaps take early retirement instead.

Thus, I propose that the term "quality of life," and the mental constructs that are widely associated with it, have lost so much utility for interpersonal discourse — especifically supposedly scientific or professional discourse — that instead of trying to rescue them, they ought to be abandoned, hopefully to be replaced by better or clearer concepts, constructs, and terms, or at least less encumbered ones.

In both more remote and recent history, many other constructs related to the human condition or human services enjoyed immense popularity, but eventually proved to be either vastly less helpful than they had been interpreted to be, or to have been built outright on thin air. What are the reasons QOL should be more meritorious than they? Where are the popular "syndromes" or manifestations of yesterday, such as hyperprosexia, intrapsychic ataxia, heboidophrenia, onomatopoiesis, pather-gasia, and thousands more, many vastly more ephemeral than the above? How does QOL compare to other currently immensely popular but scientifically extremely problematic terms and constructs, such as "the self," "learning disability," "autism," "mainstreaming," "persistent vegetative state," "brain death," etc.? Why should one wait for QOL to die some years hence rather than inter it now?

As mentioned before, one might attempt to rescue the term by engaging in "definition shouting," such as there seems to be a good deal of in this book. Technically, that is legitimate: each person carefully defines and announces his/her terms, and uses them consistently as defined. But when too many people shout out different definitions for the same term, things break down. When it comes to QOL, we are past the point where definition shouting will work. In further support of this assertion, one might contemplate how Knoll (1990) — apparently without intended irony — underlined the chaotic state of individual QOL conceptualizations and definitions by inventorizing 96 (!) QOL components in a table, checked off in terms of which of them were included in the various definitions or specifications of 17 authors or state governmental units, an astonishing exemplification of what must surely be futile definition-shouting.

Just how faddish, indiscriminate, and hence meaningless the construct and term "quality of life" became in normative professional discourse is also very strongly

brought out by the chapter titles in a book entitled *Quality of Life in Severely and Profoundly Mentally Retarded People: Research Foundations for Improvement* (Meyers, 1978). Five of the eight titles include "Origins and Control of Stereotyped Movements," "Analysis of Rocking Behavior," "Profound Developmental Retardation: Descriptive and Theoretical Utility of the Bayley Mental Scale," "Maternal Speech to Normal and Down's Syndrome Children Matched for Mean Length of Utterance," and "A Nonvocal System for Teaching Retarded Children to Read and Write." The book was sponsored and published by the American Association on Mental Deficiency (since renamed the American Association on Mental Retardation).

Well, let's face it: if these things are QOL issues, then *everything* is a QOL issue, and one might as well rename all books, and all journals in psychology, sociology, medicine, mental retardation, politics, etc., so as to have the phrase "quality of life" somewhere in their names. How about the American Association on the Quality of Life of People with Mental Retardation? Or the *Journal of the American Medical Association on Quality of Life*?

In what I call shrinkery (in order to avoid legitimizing terms such as mental health), a whole new movement has rallied around the idea that *the* goal of shrink services (my term, of course) should be to improve the clients' QOL (e.g., Ralph & Clary, 1993). Is this now to become the goal for *all* human services, or at least the new formulation of the goal? What is left that can *not* be construed to deal with QOL? "Daddy, may I have an ice cream cone for my quality of life?"

In the lead article for an eight article

symposium of the *American Journal on Mental Retardation*, Zigler, Hodapp and Edison (1990) argued on behalf of large asylums for retarded people as part of efforts to provide them "a better quality of life" (p.7) — indeed, for "large mental institutions", even with "several hundred people in one building." If this is QOL, no wonder so many people prefer QOD (quality of death), especially considering that this is what one of the most frequently cited authors in mental retardation in recent decades understands as QOL.

A common phenomenon in recent years has been for people to try to co-opt a term that becomes associated with something that has become popular, and attach to it something entirely different so as to encapture some positive imagery for the latter. For instance, when "advocacy" became a popular construct in the late 1960s, suddenly all sorts of things that were not advocacy began to be called advocacy, including very ordinary, traditional residential, vocational, educational, etc. services. For instance, ordinary social case work began to be called "casework advocacy," and case management became "case management advocacy." People who thought that "normalization" sounded glamorous began to pirate it for whatever it was they were doing, including building and running institutions.

This is one of the things that has happened to QOL. Once people figured it was a chic, "in," glamorous term, everyone began to use it for everything. For instance, earlier, we mentioned that an herbal supplement might be advertised as improving the quality of one's life. This illustrates not only the confusion of a potential QOL component with a larger QOL notion, but also the craze nature of the QOL term, and how people try to hijack it for their own "thing."

I call this the Kraft cheese phenomenon, in analogy to a long history of Kraft cheese commercials. Kraft cheese is a very bland, cheap and low-level soft cheese. The commercials for it commonly have shown foods that people would ordinarily eat, accompanied by the admonition, "...and simply add Kraft cheese" to it, or melted over the top of it. Ice cream was one of the few foods that was spared from the endless list of foods to which we were simply to "add Kraft cheese." In other words, QOL has become one of the Kraft cheeses of the human service and psycho/socio-pop discourses.

Elsewhere in this book, it is pointed out that many people have argued that "the experience of QOL is essentially subjective and should be assessed subjectively," perhaps by recourse to qualitative research methods. Such a statement does violence to the philosophy of science, and even to linguistics. In science, anything is set equal to whatever we *decide* to call it. If we say, as scientists, that QOL is subjective, then we have defined the term "quality of life" as restricted to subjective experiences. But we do not have to say this. We could say, " 'quality of life' refers to being wealthier than 50% of the rest of the population in one's country", or " 'quality of life' refers to being able to scratch oneself where it itches." These are all equally legitimate "choices" (as they say these days) in terms of clarity, though not necessarily in utility. And if one defined QOL entirely in objective terms, then unlike what some people claim, this is no loss at all, since one can still establish at the same time a definition for something that would not be called QOL that refers to subjective experiences, presumably those of well-being or hedonic tone. In fact, here is the answer everybody needed but apparently did not know: let us henceforth refer to the subjective overall reasonably long — term feeling state as "hedonia."

The futility of definition-shouting is underlined if one imagines a physics with thousands, or even only scores, of definitions of velocity, gravity, grams, lumens, etc.! No wonder we are the laughing stock of "real science."

One could argue that the problems I have described in association with the "quality of life" term and construct are merely normative expressions of the use of language and constructs in science. However, there are two heavy replies to this argument.

1. While I consider the dysfunctionality and limitation of human conceptualization and language to be a universal, not all terms and constructs are equally bad. There exist many huge handbooks in physics, chemistry, engineering, etc., that contains tens of thousands of terms, formulae, equations, etc.,on which everybody in those fields agrees, and often have agreed for hundreds, sometimes even thousands, of years. For instance, we all agree on what pi stands for in geometry. When we speak of meters and liters, we are using terms that are many orders of magnitude superior in terms of clarity and utility to terms such as QOL. When the signification of these terms changes, it changes in terms of minute quantities that are imperceptible to ordinary human phenomenology, as when pi is computed to a million digits, or the

length of a meter undergoes an infinitesimal refinement of standardization.

Even in basic psychology, there is a small dictionary of terms that lend themselves to more consistent, objectified and rational discourse, and hence often also to superior problem-solving.

2. In recent decades, something has happened to language that goes far beyond the normative problems of language use in general, and in science specifically. It is that (a) within the culture of modernism, there has taken place a degradation of language, and (b) code language is exploding where the intended meaning and the face meaning of a word or term have little connection, or are even contradictory. Both (related) phenomena should be vigorously resisted — and I am not singling out QOL here because I am trying to oppose the two above trends in respect to many terms.

One phenomenon that is very relevant to an understanding of the quality of thought and language in the public realm is this: the more closely a discourse deals with human nature and the human condition, and the closer it comes to the human essence, the less rationally and truthfully will educated, intelligent people (including scientists) deal with it. This principle helps us understand why astronomers deal better with their subject matter than medicine, why medicine deals less worse with its subject matter than does psychiatry, why so much anthropology is just plain ideological fantasyland, etc. That the brightest and best-educated people in droves embraced

Fletcher's "indicators of humanhood" and Shaw's phony QOL formula (both mentioned earlier) shows not only how utterly corrupted the scientific and scholarly mind can become on issues of human essence and morals, because that we all know or should have known beforehand, but also how *easily* it can corrupt.

How futile definition-shouting can become is illustrated by what happened to the principle of normalization. I tried to shout my definition of normalization for almost fifteen years, and it did not work. Everybody had their own idea of what it was, and would not only fail to relate to other people's definitions, no matter how loudly they shouted, but even would claim that the definitions that other people shouted were something other than what got shouted. This really did lead to a communication breakdown, confusion, and an incredible waste of effort and publishing. Instead, I reconceptualized, normalization as Social Role Valorization (Wolfensberger & Tullman, 1982; Wolfensberger, 1983, 1992a). This brought great relief because when confronted with an esoteric term that was not widely used by others, people had to begin to deal with the content of this construct in a more disciplined fashion if they chose to invoke it.

I tried something along the lines of devising a construct related to what people might call QOL, but without using "that phrase," namely, in the PASSING instrument (Wolfensberger & Thomas, 1983) for the evaluation of service quality. We chose the term "felicity," which was specifically defined *not* to be equated with "happiness," but to reflect the *probability* that services with a high Felicity subscore would be more likely to make recipients, families, and even

service workers feel better, and recipients therefore more content with the service. For instance, it was posited that the sense of well-being of recipients would be enhanced by aesthetic and comfortable service environments, by service individualization, by easy access to the service, etc. Felicity is thus not an individualized index, but the service equivalent of a population index, i.e., an index of *likely* feeling of well-being by the aggregate of recipients of a particular service.

Elsewhere in this book, it is argued that efforts to establish concise and clear definitions in the social sciences invariably lead to proliferations of definitions. There may be truth in this, but merely doing more of the same does not seem to be an ideal to work toward.

First of all, if it is true that efforts at precision in social science beget chaos, then maybe this bespeaks either the immaturity of the field, or even that there can be no science of the human because the human mind is incapable of dealing with the essence of the human in a purely rational and scientific fashion.

Secondly, just because everyone else in one's field goes crazy or irrational when one tries to uphold conceptual clarity is no reason to join their insanity or to interpret it positively.

Thirdly, I always suspect efforts to cast out the devil through Beelzebul. Where would this lead? A definition of a term that includes all other definitions? "My definition of QOL is the sum total of everybody else's definition of QOL"? Is this the social science equivalent of politically correct celebration of diversity? Will it end in a professional Yugoslavia?

And when we get to the point where

there is a proliferation of classification of definitions of something like QOL, are we not getting to the tail end of utility where a dramatic paring or paradigm shift is called for? At the very least, there should be a fractionating of QOL into more clearcut components with different names.

One possibility would be to work first and foremost toward factoring out some of the elements that have commonly been subsumed under QOL. For instance, one could think in terms of something like "verbalized life satisfaction," and distinguish it from "physical environmental quality" (air, water, weather, etc.), "physical infrastructure quality" (roads, bridges, electric grid, communications facilities), "social harmony" (crime, social integration, tolerance, civility), etc. Even a "lifestyle satisfaction" construct such as "enscaled" in the Lifestyle Satisfaction Scale (Heal, Harner, Amado & Chadsey-Rusch, 1993), might clarify at least one element of what is often subsumed under a broader and confusing QOL construct.

A reviewer (Acton, 1989) of a book on QOL (Brown, 1988) said, "The term 'quality of life' is great in speeches, but when it is given the stature of a research concept, it becomes an uncertain tool unless it is controlled by a precise definition and rigorous discipline in both thought and word." To this I would add that it becomes a deadly term when pressed into service of making life-and-death decisions, and especially so over societally devalued people.

In light of all of the above, one is alarmed (or at least one of us is) at the prospect that "...quality of life may replace deinstitutionalization, normalization and community adjustment as *the* issue of the 1990s" (Schalock, Keith, Hoffman & Karan,

1989). These authors clearly underestimated the craze nature of our culture in general, and human services even more so. Other craze contructs are already nibbling vigorously at the heels of QOL. A good successor candidate is the Kraft cheese term "empowerment." After all, we already have the no longer missing link between it and QOL in the title of an article, "Improving the Quality of Community Living to Empower People with Mental Retardation" (Lakin, 1992). (By the way, I find absolutely hilarious such efforts to combine several Kraft cheese terms into a single conglomerate with one's own "thing" so as to aggrandize its image.)

Soon we can expect books with "empowerment" in their titles dealing with "rocking behavior," maternal speech of children with Down's syndrome, and the utility of the Bayley Mental Scale. *The* issue of the 1990s is most likely to be the same one as in the 1960s, 1970s and 1980s: Kraft cheese!

Even if readers were not convinced of all my other rationales for abandoning QOL talk, I appeal to them to be convinced of it for just one reason: to take QOL talk away from the deathmakers!

As to myself, for some years now, I have scrupulously avoided using the phrase "quality of life" for any purpose whatsoever, and have found that despite the fact that much of my work revolves around service quality, the life conditions of societally devalued persons, the deathmaking scene, and the defense of the lives and welfare of devalued persons, I have managed quite well without invoking QOL. In fact, I wonder how people ever got along before they coined the term QOL, or discovered that there was such a thing, especially on the individual level. How did they describe their lives then? How was the professional and "scientific" human service sector ever able to talk about people's QOL when they did not have the term? Since humans often cannot think about things for which they lack language, did people in the pre-QOL days know whether they, or somebody else, had a high or low quality of life? Obviously, if they did, this is not the language that they used to talk about it. So what language did they use? My memory and guess is that they talked about welfare, about people being free or not being free, prosperous, happy, well-adjusted, miserable, etc., living under favorable or awful conditions, people's well-being, and similar terminology. To go one step further, I can honestly say that my abstinence from the QOL craze has not diminished my own QOL in the least, nor diminished anyone else's — the way our rendering of human services so often does — except perhaps that of otherwise already privileged academicians and researchers. Thus, I hope that this chapter will put the jinx, at the very least, on the *term* QOL, but I doubt it will.

# References

Acton N. (1989) [Review of: Brown, R.I. (Ed.). (1988). Quality of life for handicapped people. London: Croom Helm] *Disability Studies Quarterly*, 9 (2), 19-20.

Amir, A. (1977). Euthanasia in Nazi Germany. *Dissertation Abstracts International*, 38, 4976. (University Microfilms No. CEN 77-32241). (Doctoral Dissertation at SUNY-Albany, 1977).

Bernstein, J.A. (1987). *Nietzsche's moral philosophy*. Cranbury, NJ: Associated University Presses.

Binding, K., & Hoche, A. (1920). *Die Freigabe der Vernichtung lebensunwerten Lebens: Ihr Mass und ihre Form*. Leipzig, Germany: Felix Meiner.

Birren, J.E., Lubben, J.E., Rowe, J.C. & Deutchman, D.E. (Eds.) (1991). *The concept of quality of life in the frail elderly*. San Diego, CA: Academic Press.

Boone, H.A. & Stevens, E. (1991). Towards an enhanced family and child quality of life. In M. Krajicek & R. Tompkins (Eds.), *The medically fragile infant*. Austin, TX: Pro-Ed.

Brown, R.I. (Ed.) (1988). *Quality of Life for Handicapped People*. London: Croom Helm

Campbell, A. (1971). *The Quality of American Life*. Computer tape 3508. Inter-University Consortium for Political & Social Research, Instructional subset.

Campbell, A. & Converse, P.E. (1980). *The quality of American life, 1978*. Inter-University Consortium for Political & Social Research.

Campbell, A., Converse, P.E., & Rodgers, W.L. (1976). *The quality of American life: Perceptions, evaluations and satisfactions*. New York: Russell Sage Foundation.

Chaffee, J.H. (1990). Balancing the quality of care and quality of life. In V.J. Bradley & H.A. Bersani (Eds.) *Quality assurance for individuals with developmental disabilities: It's everybody's business*. (pp.95-101). Baltimore: Paul H. Brookes.

Coale, A.J. (1970). Man and his environment. *Science*, 170, 132-136.

Commission on National Goals. (1960). *Goals for Americans*. Washington, DC: US Government Printing Office.

Diamond, E.F. (1977). *This curette for hire*. Chicago: ACPA Foundation.

Duff, R.S., & Campbell, A.G.M. (1973). Moral and ethical dilemmas in the special-care nursery. *New England Journal Of Medicine, 289,* 890-894.

Fenigsen, R. (1990). A case against Dutch euthanasia. *Ethics & Medicine, 6*(1), 11-18.

Fletcher, J. (1972). Indicators of humanhood:A tentative profile of man. *Hastings Center Report, 2,* 1-4.

Fletcher, J. (1975). The "right" to live and the "right" to die. In M. Kohl (Ed.) *Beneficent euthanasia* (pp.44-53). Buffalo:Prometheus Books.

Gudex, C. (1987, November). QALYS: An explicit outcome measure for todays NHS. *Public Finance and Accountancy,* pp. 13-15.

Hackler, J.C. & Hiller, F.C. (1990). Family consent to orders not to resuscitate: Reconsidering hospital policy.*Journal of the American Medical Association, 264*(10), 1281-1283.

Hart, P.A. (1974, May 29). Life quality index. *US Congressional Record-Senate,* S9168-S9172, Pp. 16664-16666.

Heal, L. W., Harner, C.J., Amado, A.R.N., & Chadsey-Rusch, J. (1993). *Lifestyle satisfaction scale (LSS).* Worthington, OH:IDS Publishing.

Jecker, N.S., & Pearlman, R.A. (1992). Medical futility: Who decides? *Archives of International Medicine, 152,* 1140-1144.

Jecker, N.S. & Schneiderman, L.J. (1992). Futility and rationing. *American Journal of Medicine, 92,* 189-196.

Knoll, J.A. (1990). Defining quality in residential services. In V.J. Bradley & H.A. Bersani (Eds.), *Quality assurance for individuals with developmental disabilities:It's everybody's business* (pp.235-261). Baltimore: Paul H. Brookes.

Lakin, C. (1992). Improving the quality of community living to empower people with mental retardation. *OSERS News In Print, 5*(2), 30-35.

Lepach, P. (1985, January 12). Reisen gehort zur Lebensqualitat. *Amerika Woche.*

Lorber, J. (1971). Results of treatment of myelomeningocele: An analysis of 524 unselected cases, with special reference to possible selection for treatment. *Developmental Medicine & Child Neurology, 13,* 279-303.

Lundberg, G.D. (1993). Editorial: American health care system management objectives: The aura of inevitability becomes incarnate. *Journal of the American Medical Association, 269*(19), 2554-2555.

Lyons, J. (1985) *Playing god in the nursery.* New York: W.W. Norton.

Lusthaus, E. (1985). "Euthanasia" of persons with severe handicaps: Refuting the rationalizations. *Journal of the Association for Persons with Severe Handicaps, 10*(2), 87-94.

Meadows, D.H., Meadows, D.L., Randers, J., & Behrens, W.W. (1974). *Limits to growth:A report for the Club of Rome's Project on the Predicament of Mankind* (rev.ed.) New York: Universe Books.

Meadows, D.L., et.al. (1974). *Dynamics of growth in a finite world.* Cambridge, MA:Wright-Allen Press.

Meadows, D.L., & Meadows, D.H. (Eds). (1973). *Towards global equilibrium.* Cambridge, MA:Wright-Allen Press.

Meyers, C.E. (Ed.) (1978). *Quality of life in severely and profoundly mentally retarded people: Research foundations for improvement.* Washington, DC: American Association on Mental Deficiency (Monograph No.3).

Murphy, D.J. (1988). Do-not-resuscitate orders: Time for reappraisal in long-term care institutions. *Journal of the American Medical Association, 260*(14), 2098-2101.

Perske, R. (1972). The dignity of risk. In W. Wolfensberger, *The principle of normalization in human services* (pp.194-200) Toronto: National Institute on Mental Retardation.

President's Commission for a National Agenda for the Eighties. (1980). *The quality of American life in the eighties: Report of the Panel on the Quality of American Life.* Englewood-Cliffs, NJ: Prentice-Hall.

President's Commission for a National Agenda for the Eighties (1982). *The quality of Ameri-*

*can life in the eighties: Report of the Panel on the Quality of American life*. Englewood-Cliffs, NJ: Prentice-Hall.

Ragg, M. (1993, March). The rather-be-dead rating. *The Bulletin* (Australia), p.33.

Ralph, R.O., & Clary, B.B. (1993). Quality of life:Outcome measures for three case management models:Psychiatric rehabilitation, broker, and traditional. *Disability Studies Quarterly*, 13(2), 38-42.

Rodgers, W.L., & Bachman, J.G. (1988). *The subjective well-being of young adults: Trends and relationships*. Ann Arbor, MI: University of Michigan/Institute for Social Research.

Sassone, R.L. (1975). *The release of the destruction of life devoid of value*. Santa Ana, CA: Life Quality Paperbacks.

Schacht, R. (1983). *Nietzsche*. London:Routledge & Kegan Paul.

Schalock, R.L., Keith, K.D., Hoffman, K., & Karan, O.C. (1989). Quality of life: Its measurement and use. *Mental Retardation*, 27(1), 25-31.

Schneiderman, L.J., Jecker, N.S., & Jonsen, A.R. (1990). Medical futility: Its meaning and ethical implications. *Annals of Internal Medicine*, 112, 949-954.

Shaw, A. (1972, January 30). "Doctor, do we have a choice?" *New York Times Magazine*, pp.44-54.

Shaw, A. (1977). Defining the quality of life. *The Hastings Center Reports*, 7(5), p.11. (First presented at a conference on Decision Making and the Defective Newborn, Skytop PA, May 1975).

Singer, P. (1983). Sanctity of life or quality of life? *Pediatrics*, 72(1), 128-129.

Stein, G.J. (1988). Biological science and the roots of Nazism. *American Scientist*, 76(1). 50-58.

Torrance, G.W., & Feeny, D. (1989). Utilities and quality adjusted life years. *International Journal of Technology Assessment in Health Care*, 5, 559-575.

Tugwell, F. (1973). *Search for alternatives:Public policy and the study of the future*. Cambridge, MA:Winthrop.

US Department of Health, Education and Welfare. (1969). *Toward a social report*. Washington, DC:US Government Printing Office.

US National Goals Research Staff. (1970). *Toward balanced growth: Quantity with quality*. Washington, DCUS Government Printing Office.

Werkmeister, W.K. (1961). *Theories of ethics: A study in moral obligation*. Lincoln, NE:Johnsen Publishing.

Wolfensberger, W. (1983). Social Role Valorization: A proposed new term for the principle of normalization. *Mental Retardation*, 21(6),234-239.

Wolfensberger, W. (1984). The good life for mentally retarded persons. *National Apostolate with Mentally Retarded Persons Quarterly*, 15(3), 18-20.

Wolfesnberger, W. (1992a). *A brief introduction to Social Role Valorization as a high order concept for structuring human services* (2nd revised edition). Syracuse, NY: Training Institute for Human Service Planning, Leadership and Change Agentry (Syracuse University).

Wolfensberger, W. (1992b). *The new genocide of handicapped and afflicted people (rev.ed.)* Syracuse,NY: Training Institute for Human Service Planning, Leadership and Change Agentry (Syracuse University).

Wolfensberger, W., & Thomas, S. (1983). *PASSING (Program Analysis of Service Systems' Implementation of Normalization Goals): Normalization criteria and ratings manual* (2nd edition). Toronto: National Institute on Mental Retardation.

Wolfensberger, W., & Tullman, S. (1982). A brief outline of the principle of normalization. *Rehabilitation Psychology, 27*(3), 131-145.

Zigler, E., Hodapp, R.M., & Edison, M.R. (1990). From theory to practice the in care and education of mentally retarded individuals. *American Journal on Mental Retardation, 95*(1), 1-9.

# Index

# About the Editor

David Goode was born and raised in New York City. He received a B.A. and M.A. in Sociology from Queens College and his Ph.D. in Sociology from the University of California, Los Angeles. He is currently Associate Professor of Sociology at the College of Staten Island of the City University of New York. Dr. Goode is the author of numerous articles about people with disabilities and lectures nationally and internationally on issues related to their quality of life. He has a special interest in persons born deaf and blind and has published a book on this topic with Temple University Press. He lives with his wife Diane, a children's book author and illustrator, son Peter, student/artist, and dog Katie, a Welsh corgi, in Watchung, New Jersey.